de Gruyter Studies in Organization 71

Constituting Management

de Gruyter Studies in Organization

Organizational Theory and Research

This de Gruyter Series aims at publishing theoretical and methodological studies of organizations as well as research findings, which yield insight in and knowledge about organizations. The whole spectrum of perspectives will be considered: organizational analyses rooted in the sociological as well as the economic tradition, from a socio-psychological or a political science angle, mainstream as well as critical or ethnomethodological contributions. Equally, all kinds of organizations are considered: firms, public agencies, non-profit institutions, voluntary associations, inter-organizational networks, supra-national organizations etc.

Emphasis is on publication of *new* contributions, or significant revisions of existing approaches. However, summaries or critical reflections on current thinking and research are also be considered.

This series represents an effort to advance the social scientific study of organizations across national boundaries and academic disciplines. An Advisory Board consisting of representatives of a variety of perspectives and from different cultural areas is responsible for achieving this task.

This series addresses organization researchers within and outside universities, but also practitioners who have an interest in grounding their work on recent social scientific knowledge and insights.

Constituting Management
Markets, Meanings, and Identities

Edited by Gill Palmer and Stewart Clegg

Walter de Gruyter · Berlin · New York 1996

Gill Palmer, Professor and Dean of the Faculty of Commerce,
University of Wollongong, Wollongong, Australia

Stewart Clegg, Foundation Professor of Management,
University of Western Sydney Macarthur, Campbelltown, Australia

With 11 tables, 9 figures, and 15 exhibits

♾ Printed on acid-free paper which falls within the guidelines of the
ANSI to ensure permanence and durability.

Library of Congress Cataloging-in-Publication Data

Constituting management : markets, meanings, and identities /
    edited by Gill Palmer and Stewart Clegg.
        p.   cm. − (De Gruyter studies in organization ; 71)
    Includes bibliographical references.
    ISBN 3-11-014454-9 (alk. paper)
    1. Management.   2. Marketing − Management.   I. Pal-
mer, Gill.   II. Clegg, Stewart.   III. Series
    HD31.C6257   1996
    658.8−dc20   96-14871
                                                                CIP

Die Deutsche Bibliothek − CIP-Einheitsaufnahme

Constituting management : markets, meanings, and identities ;
[with 11 tables] / ed. by Gill Palmer and Stewart Clegg. −
Berlin ; New York : de Gruyter, 1996
    (De Gruyter studies in organization ; 71 : Organizational
    theory and research)
    ISBN 3-11-014454-9
NE: Palmer, Gill [Hrsg.]; GT

Preface

The chapters that constitute this book began their life with a request from the conference organizers that I convene a section on "Organizational/Managerial Ideas and Social Science," at the 11th EGOS Colloquium on "The Production and Diffusion of Managerial and Organizational Knowledge," held in Paris between the 6th and 8th of July, 1993. I wrote a number of letters to people, others initiated responses, and before very long the session was massively over-subscribed. Late in the day, Gill Palmer, a colleague that I knew from Australia, agreed to help me out by co-convening the sessions that I could not be at, a role that my friend, Roberto Venosa, was initially to undertake. However, at the last minute, Roberto was unable to get from Brazil to be in Paris, and so Gill stepped in to save the day. Hence, these papers came initially from the two sessions that we coordinated in Paris. They have undergone, in every case, substantial subsequent revision.

Back in Australia, after the EGOS Colloquium, Gill and I edited the volume, assisted by the unstinting efforts of Constantine Kallas, Leanne Sharp and of the University of Western Sydney Faculty of Business and Technology. It is doubtful that we could have done the editing without the benefit of modern technologies: e-mail, fax and computers that could, allegedly, read "both" Macintosh and DOS discs, proved themselves to be invaluable management aids.

The translation and management of technologies and languages characterized the task to such an extent that we came rapidly to think of managing the product, in all its complexity, as a shorthand form of the issues that we were struggling with. Amongst these were the assembly and management of meanings, over great space and considerable time, at a considerable distance, often in different everyday languages, with occasionally incompatible technologies, displaying moments of management by fiat and imperative exercise of power, as translation was effected and our embryonic enterprise took shape.

Producing this volume has been a venture in international co-operation, and we wish to thank our contributors and the organizing committee for the EGOS Colloquium for making it happen. We would also like to acknowledge the generous support and assistance of The University of Western Sydney, Macarthur, especially that provided by the Dean of The Faculty of Business and Technology, Roger Alexander, as well as the help of the University of Wollongong. The commitment of these institutions, second to none, has been very important for the fruition of this project. Finally, we wish to thank Bianka Ralle and her colleagues at de Gruyter for their commitment to the project and effortless expertise in seeing it through to the form in which you see it today.

June, 1996   Gill Palmer
                                                                          Stewart Clegg

Contents

Contents

Contents

Constituting Management

Stewart Clegg[1]

What Is Management?

What is management? It is whatever it is made to be, according to the different social fabric that it is constructed from, its weft and worp, its embeddedness in various social contexts. What managers do is what managers know what to do. They know in many ways: through example, training, experience, intuition, novels, biographies, education, instinct and more. The sources of knowledge are many and varied. The effects of knowledge are complex, often contradictory but always situated in practice, in what managers do.

This book is about knowledge that enables managers to act, the knowledge that constitutes management in its many facets. It is not intended to be a "how-to-do-it" book. There are plenty of other texts in the market place that offer that advice. Instead, the focus is analytical; resolutely so. Our contributors explore a space created through diverse answers to a series of simple questions:

- What makes management possible?
- How do managers know what to do in different contexts of practice?
- What do managers do when they do management?
- What are the societal contexts that embed their knowledge?

The manufacture of management is not easy, despite what is said by some of the authors who retail those "how-to-do-it" books with all the conviction of an Elmer Gantry. Outside of these rhetorics, management and its effective accomplishment, is less easy. The reasons are simple. Management actions are often contested, sometimes resisted, rarely effortless. They vary historically and comparatively.

For the purposes of this book we suggest that, at present, the salient arenas define themselves principally by struggles over identity, markets and meaning. It is this trinity of concepts that frames our text.

The first part of the book advances the analysis of markets in the context of management. The second part of the book concentrates on the way in which management as work creates a sphere of meaning and significance. Such significance draws not only on global projects, such as the formal curriculum of a management knowledge that is technically disinterested in the specifities of space, place and time, but also on local and specific cultures and struggles to secure specific meanings. Examples of the former are institutional projects, at their most comprehensive in phenomena such as particular concerns and responses to issues such as "corporate governance," an emergent international concern for the 1990s. Of the second, one has to look at the empirical particularities of organizational change, in particular national and firm specific contexts. It is how these local and global meanings become institutionalized that fixes management's meaning and meanings. The third part of the book looks at management in relation to issues of identity, particularly those related to gender.

Finally, having looked at the constitution of management and knowledge about it in the context of the present, the final section of the book turns toward the future. What will the contours of tomorrow's management, of postmodern management, look like? What does it mean to manage as if tomorrow mattered, not as one simply here today, gone tomorrow? How do Organization and Management Studies relate to transformations in modern society?

Markets, Management and Organizations

From the perspective of "planning," whether state or corporate, the notions of market and organization seem antithetical to each other; opposed principles of management. Markets, in theory, are free spheres of invisible harmony. In practice, organization sought to ensure that the order that markets were supposed to produce, through the touch of invisible hands, actually materialized. It mattered little if the fetish of the plan was championed over the fetish of the market by corporate planners, state bureaucrats, or elites committed to "plannification." Organization meant planning, power, control. The market, other than in its fictional form, implied chance, disorder and a lack of control. At least, these were the views that one would encounter not so long ago, in boardrooms, state rooms and elite parlors. Times changed rapidly.

Markets have been the preferred mechanism of political rhetoric everywhere for over a decade. Yet, organizations are an obdurate and brute fact that markets and their protagonists frequently have to confront, rather than ignore.

Once upon a time markets seemed destined to be replaced by hierarchy, with the emergence of large scale modern organizations. To many observers, from Weber onwards it seemed organizations would dominate what had previously been small, scattered and local markets. Of late, such confidence has waned. The transfer of energy from markets to organizations has been reversed. Today, almost everywhere, markets are glorified as the solution to pressing matters for which organizational "hierarchical" solutions are increasingly derided. Managers of organizations have responded to this changed climate by making their organizations function more like markets.

The emergence of new social knowledge and discourses of the market is the focus of Muetzelfeldt's chapter, in which he assesses critically the aptness of the market metaphor for the activities of organization and organizing. Can market-like relations in organizations be insulated from the discontents with, and of, the market that are increasingly apparent in the wider society? This is the critical issue addressed by Muetzelfeldt.

Economic markets are social systems, wherever we study them. They will vary in their institutional specificities as social systems vary. Such social systems may be conceived of, organizationally, as collective games of competition and/ or co-operation, or both simultaneously. Such games are analyzed empirically by Thoenig and Dupuy, with reference to the white goods industry in France, Japan and the USA. They develop a strategic social systems model to do so. The focus of the volume is international, and the next chapter switches to Australia, with Marceau, who examines the language of management in the context of recent Australian public policies. Taking the ways in which the language and rhetoric of "economic rationalism" have been translated into political and bureaucratic or-ganizational and policy choices under the title "managerialism," the chapter sug-gest that the principal use of "economic rationalism" has been as a tool for unify-ing policy decisions across many portfolios. It suggests that, while the techniques associated with the "doctrine" have been only crudely understood by politicians and policy makers, the central concepts have provided a rhetoric that can be used across widely divergent portfolios to measure and trade off policy choices. It pro-vides a means of trading expenditure suggestions in education off against those in defense and in social security or industry departments. It helps constitute manage ment across the policy board. In particular, notions of "cost-benefit" analysis have been used to make decisions when disagreements become too profound. It enables an apparently "neutral" tool to hide political and organizational maneuvers. In or-ganization terms, other tenets such as "efficiency" have been used in a similar way to focus the attention of bureaucratic staff on issues of process rather than policy.

The use of economic rationalism in this way, the chapter suggests, was facil-itated by the alleged fiscal crises of the 1970s in many western countries and in Australia in the early years of the 1980s. These "fiscal crisis" periods became as-sociated with the alleged "excesses" of the welfare state, particularly in expendi-ture, which made it difficult even for social democratic governments such as the one elected to federal power in 1983 in Australia to use the more traditional con-cepts of "social welfare," "equity" and "social justice" as underlying themes.

The chapter takes Australia as an example of this more general phenomenon and uses the case of education to illustrate the theme. Diverging views of the de-sirability of particular relationships between individuals and the state are implicit in much of the language used and this is illustrated by analyzing education policy both in historical and contemporary context.

The contemporary context is one increasingly conceptualized by social scientists in terms of modernity in transition to something beyond: depending on the theory, this will be conceptualized in terms of hypermodernism, postmodernism, late modernism and so on. Without delving deeply into what are substantial debates, we may note the following basic points. Management in its modern forms was irremediably tied into the ascent of mass society. Mass society no longer exists as it did in the age when mass production delivered a relatively small number of undifferentiated products for mass markets. Rather than consumers being free to choose from only a limited number of artefactual commodity forms for the expression of their identity, in postmodern times personal identities become "demassified" and disassociated from mass production relations as mass markets become niched and microtic. These themes frame the chapter by Sturdy and Knights. Increasingly, diffuse consumption patterns, fragmented commodity ownership and complex market segmentation create diverse populations of subjects, segmented in different markets of consumption, with differently managed forms of "governance" associated with them. In particular, this characterizes the production, consumption and marketing of those most immaterial of products, "financial services." Increasingly, it is claimed, modern management practices create the segmented needs that they can then claim to identify, measure and address. Management makes the world as it markets the soul of the consumer whose subjectivity is segmented.

The Mystification of Management

Management is something that has become increasingly mystified. A massive apparatus of the state, through education and policy, is oriented towards it. Business schools proliferate; business commentators saturate the media; management gurus become household names amongst an audience that even the most entrepreneurial business schools rarely touch. Paradoxically, the upshot of this elaborated discourse about management is not to render it more calculable, more transparent, but more opaque, more mystified.

It is not only "expert" talk that occludes. Not all management owes its opacity to its complexity. Some very simple forms of management survive, forms that are extremely transparent in their exploitation while they are almost invisible in their practice. Above all, the survival of forms of management by "putting-out," where the contractor "manages" the labor of others in their own homes, is a case in point: prevalent but practically opaque in terms of both public policy and management knowledge. The incidence of homeworking in Britain in the 19th and early 20th centuries has been consistently underestimated and ignored in academic and public policy debates. In contrast, the current incidence of teleworking, or new technology homework, is greatly exaggerated and widely discussed.

Brocklehurst documents this paradox and explains it in terms of conceptualizations of labor that are related to wider political, economic and patriarchal agendas. Using historical data, he argues that clear conceptual contrasts between work and home developed in the 19th century. Because homeworking challenged the conceptual divide between the public sphere of employment and the private sphere of home, it was ignored.

In contrast the political agendas that support the current British enthusiasm for teleworking are fueled by a number of ideological beliefs. For example that, by reintegrating home and work, teleworking will create solutions to the problems of urban commuting, sectoral unemployment, the dysfunctions of large scale organizations and female demand for paid work. Conceptually, in metaphoric terms, we may say that old wine is being poured once more into new bottles, there to settle and be seen, but through a glass, darkly.

From Britain to Brazil, where Rodrigues uses the case of the Brazilian Telecommunications Company in a study of the relationship between corporate culture and personal identity. Rodrigues describes attempts by management to change the corporate culture in this organization from 1979 to 1991. After the military dictatorship, new, civilian managers attempted to de-institutionalize an older authoritarian, technocratic culture and replace it with concepts of devolved, participatory management. However, they did not succeed in creating a uniform culture of commitment. Instead alienation and lack of commitment developed, especially among the engineers. A counter-culture, fostering derogatory metaphors about politically manipulative management, emerged. Rodrigues concludes that culture, power and identity are closely interrelated. If management degrades values that give identity to a group, they will weaken their legitimacy and power basis. Brazilian Telecoms strategy debased technical rationality and thereby threatened the occupational base of the engineers. This fostered an identity that was insecure and led to detachment and alienation amongst the engineers.

Brazil also furnishes the data for the following chapter, by Machado da Silva and Silva da Fonseca, in a case study of a private company in Southern Brazil, used to explore the way an interpretative approach to organizational change can show how dominant meanings link with institutional demands in creating organizational structure. The formal bureaucratic structure of this family controlled company was reorganized in response to external contingencies which promoted a perceived need to develop new markets, and introduce improved quality control.

Despite the structural changes that were made, the traditional power of the family and its values were maintained. Despite environmental contingencies, the founders of the firm, and one person in particular, still constituted the main source of institutionalization of values in the organization. Where management is "in the family" it is evident that family matters more than management. To outsiders, management seems less opaque than the family. Family governance is a specific form for managing the corporation. Also, it varies comparatively, from type to type, according to the next chapter.

Clarke and Bostock compare and contrast different national approaches to corporate governance. They find significant differences related to three different models. The Anglo-American model, represented by the UK and USA, characterizes a market for corporate control which places emphasis on short term financial returns for shareholders. In contrast both the European model, represented by Germany, and the model represented by Japan, rely on trust, cross-shareholding and a close reliance on bank serviced debt rather than shareholding. These have traditionally encouraged a longer term, wider view of the organization's raison d'être.

All systems of corporate governance are under pressure from the increasing internationalization of financial markets. In the European and Japanese systems there are signs of a more active market for corporate control, whereas in the Anglo-American model past collapses have stimulated attempts to shift corporate power from management to independent Board members.

Identity in Management

Despite the assumptions of an older literature not all managers are men. In the Anglo-American world the social tensions surrounding the movement of women into managerial positions have the potential to influence the analysis of the management process. Three perspectives on management can be used to discuss the ways in which managerial processes can be used to both maintain and challenge gendered stereotypes about management.

Administrative, political and cultural processes have traditionally been used to maintain managerial stereotypes that discriminated against women. However all three processes provide mechanisms that have been used by women (and other disadvantaged groups) to re-define the purpose of management.

A sociology of management that analyses the managerial strategies of disadvantaged social groups focuses attention on the impact of management on wider social structures and cultural meanings. It can challenge the social conservatism and elitism that has been assumed to be an integral component of management education and thought, as Palmer demonstrates in her contribution to the volume.

In the past, the international airline business has been one of the most segregated of labor markets along gender lines. Men in the cockpit, women at the counters and in the cabin, has been a general rule, one reinforced subtly by many aspects of management action. Documentary evidence of these claims is examined by Mills with respect to the organization that assigns itself the "World's favourite airline," British Airways.

British Airways in-house "Newsletter" is ostensibly designed to inform and unite the activities of its staff members. However a detailed analysis of the 'Newsletter', from 1926 to the present, reveals a series of selective, and (changing) images that have served to construct a narrow set of male and female subjectivities.

Mills argues that the Company 'Newsletter' both reflects and produces the organizational culture. It has served to render mundane a series of discriminatory viewpoints and practices and as such plays a vital role in the organizational construction of gender and gendered practices at work. The images projected still do not support a managerial image for women and changes will need to be made if the newsletter is to change its role in the organizational construction of discrimination.

The identity of management is a function of institutionalized meaning. In one time and place they may be regarded as "running dogs of imperialism," to recall a half forgotten Maoist slogan from the 1960s. Today, critical theory is more sophisticated than its erstwhile Maoist manifestation, as Tsivacou shows by using critical systems thinking to analyze the function of meaning in contemporary complex organizations. The chapter links Luhmanns theory on the function of meaning with Cleggs discussion of "postmodernism." It suggests that on the one hand, de-differentiation enriches individual experiences and meaning. On the other hand, the increased opportunities for selecting meanings are reduced in value by the homogenization of selections. The paper concludes that, if there is to be the emancipation of individual consciousness in the postmodern world, then there will be the need to create a play context in order to allow individuals to experiment with, and evaluate different meanings.

Management Today, Management Tomorrow?

Much of what managers do and did as well as much of management knowledge is increasingly irrelevant. We live in an age that is, arguably, postmodern, one where management as an activity premised on the control of a singular conjunction of space and time enveloped in the fabric of the organization is of diminishing relevance. Some indicators are emergent in the literature of what the contours of postmodern management and its knowledge might be, as Clegg elaborates. This chapter explores these, balancing the tension between varieties of postmodernism.

Management is often defined in terms of the attempt to reduce that uncertainty or equivocality that is contingent on processes of organizing. In some old, well established organizations, the absence of internal novelty and external turbulence may aid management in minimizing sources of difference. However, in organizations that are freshly born, with little in the way of precedent or history to guide them, the management of equivocality is far more difficult. Such organizations are to be found, especially, in embryonic industries. Embryonic industries are a future form of enterprise premised on an at present immature or rudimentary stage of development. Embedded in developments that already exist, they are, metaphorically "in embryo." Embryonic industries enable the development of new products, processes, services, and organizational arrangements for their delivery. They

may be premised on incremental innovation, in terms of the progressive modification of products, processes and services or radical innovations (those discontinuous events that drastically change these products, processes or services). Radical innovations are embedded, typically, in one of the "generic" technologies that
have created radical innovation in technology systems, or they may be premised
on cultural innovation. The emergence of embryonic industries signifies the development of new forms of organization, that Clegg earlier termed "postmodern" to signify their radical break with older, "modernist" models of bureaucracy
premised on hierarchical controls. In their place develop new process technologies, premised on "learning organizations" and the centrality of communication
rather than control. This chapter, by Clegg, Dwyer, Gray, Kemp and Marceau, explores these implications, considering what it means to manage as if tomorrow
really matters.

   Fundamental changes in society have significant effects on organizations and
their study. These effects are intermediated by the linkages between changing social theory and changing social reality. These are explored in the changing terrain of organization studies by Paul Jeffcut as a reflection on multicultural human
practices pursued through a human science that is increasingly multi-disciplinary.
Management, rather than becoming the site of a single new knowledge, one that
"science" provides, is, according to this view, the site of a radical degree of dis-
juncture and difference. Management knowledge will seek in vain for its equivalent of a unified field theory.

   The themes of this book may be reflected upon in terms of notions of continuity and discontinuity, of consolidation and fragmentation, of progression and
regression, of questions concerning the future direction of organization studies,
management theory and management practice. Is it clear, any longer, which way
is up? David Boje leaves us in considerable doubt: there is no simple progression
from less to more sophisticated knowledge, from worse to better practice, from
simpler to more complex systems. Living in the postmodern world is to partake
of considerable, and often, doubtful, possibilities, even for those who would manage doubt, uncertainty and ambiguity.

   The contributors to this volume do not categorize management knowledge in
terms of its goodness, its productivity, its value. The aim is more modest, more
analytical. Each contribution highlights some aspects of how the knowledge that
is management is constituted. Each facet is only partial, capturing only some of
the brilliance of the phenomena being refracted and reflected through the prism
of these chapters. That is what management is like, in our account: partial, plural
and sufficiently multi-faceted that one can never see it in its entirety. And, just as
one might think one knows it, one's knowledge can reflexively change that which
is known such that we know it no longer. Finally, this is the fate of management,
constituted on a terrain where esoteric knowledge struggles with prosaic practice,
where each illuminates and changes the other, where the currency of ideas·cre-
ates both an uncertain and dynamic market, one where each participant seeks to

stabilize what they know as what should be done, never to succeed, by definition, in any long term. Management, as knowledge, as multiple and shifting meaning, is nomadic as it wanders in and out of fad and fashion, science and art, war and peace, power and resistance, and all the other great dichotomies of humankind. This volume records some of its traces.

Note

[1] I would like to acknowledge the helpful comments of Constantine Kallas, John Gray and Salvador Porras on earlier drafts of this chapter.

Part I
From Markets to Organizations and Back Again

The Organization and the Market

Michael Muetzelfeldt

Introduction

Market-like principles of decision-making, exchange and consumption are increasingly being advocated as appropriate for organizational design. They are said to be supplementing or replacing the bureaucratic principles that previously structured the relationships that constituted western administrative organizations. This parallels the changes in prevailing broad social discourses and practices during the 1980s and 1990s, when market mechanisms were being increasingly celebrated and practiced in economic activity and public policy (Krieger 1986; Muetzelfeldt 1992a; Pusey 1991; Yeatman 1990: 101). This paper explores the marketization of organizations, and argues that, contrary to the expectations of the advocates of this process, it promotes strong authoritarian leadership, rather than devolved or dispersed decision-making. That is, it encourages the very antithesis of the ideals held up by the advocates of market-like or postmodern organization.

Market principles provide a basis through which actual practices are structured: Gidden's term structuration is appropriate to this. That is, actual organizations are expressions of those principles as these inform and organize practices, and so the practices will generally be partial, incomplete and more or less contingent representations of what market principles ideally represent. Further, I take the implementation of market principles as a project, and a contested one at that, within organizational theory and practice. So market principles are more often advocated and celebrated than actually implemented, and market rhetoric seems to be belied by the continuation of at least some practices that are deeply rooted in the pre-marketized organization.

The notion of "market" itself has many aspects: market culture, marketing as strategy (that is, competition in contested markets), and market tactics (the specific tools and techniques of marketing), to name but a few central features. Also, many organizations are positioned in producer-led markets, despite rhetorically asserting that their market is consumer-led. These distinctions are not taken up here, because they are more relevant to the issue of how and where market principles have been applied, rather than to the issue of the market project and its consequences. The general argument of this paper does not depend on fully elaborating the implementation of market principles. To the extent that any aspects of market principles are being advocated, this paper warns about the consequences of implementing them. To the extent that they have been implemented, they show up in the organizational forms described here and have the consequences that are discussed below.

Market Processes in Organization

Market-like principles are being introduced in a wide range of organizations. This can be seen in the use of "internal franchising" and internal markets in accountancy and management services organizations; in the destruction of internal labor markets and career paths in a range of "downsizing" organizations; and in performance evaluation, contracting out and customer service practices in public sector organizations. More structurally it can also be seen in the emergence of new organizational forms, where franchised or networked organizational clusters are increasingly displacing or replacing conventional organizations and their self-evident boundaries. In this section I describe some examples of market mechanisms in private sector and public sector administrative organizations.

The Private Sector, for example ABC Management Consultants

The local office of ABC, one of the large multinational accountancy firms, has a substantial management consultancy practice, with over 50 consultants and other professional staff. Each consultancy project is based on a contract between ABC and the customer to provide specified services at a set cost. ABC in turn establishes for each project a one-line budget that covers all costs including staff time, and staff are required to complete the project within budget.

The consultants are technically employees of the firm, but in practice operate more as franchised sub-contractors. They, together with all other staff from secretaries and typists to computer people and other professional service staff, charge their time to customer accounts in 6 minute units. The cost of each unit depends on the staff member's remuneration rate. If consultants seek advice, information or practical assistance from others in the organization, those who provide the assistance can charge their time to the account in question. That is, the individual or group responsible for each project can decide to "buy" the services of other staff rather than doing work themselves, in effect sub-contracting part of the project. These decisions are based on assessments of the cost effectiveness of such purchases, considering the variations in skill, knowledge and charging rates of their various colleagues, together with whether the account can afford the costs involved. In short, there is an internal market between staff, who have to make decisions about buying one anothers services.

In general, there is no organizational demarcation between those staff responsible for finding contracts and those responsible for executing them. However partners in the firm normally concentrate on finding and arranging contracts, as do the few business development staff who are employed more for their professional or social contacts than for their professional skill, and who are in effect brokers between consultants and prospective clients. Apart from these exceptions, consultants are required to seek out and negotiate contracts on behalf of ABC, and then to fulfill the contracts that they have negotiated. Their continuing employment depends on being able to find work and win contracts for themselves, and on delivering contracted work on time, in cost and to specified quality. In the interest of presenting a unified corporate face to clients, despite the variations between ABC's consultants with regard to their reputation, negotiating skill and knowledge of the consultancy market, they may not compete with one another for contracts, and disputes between consultants over market territory are resolved internally by negotiation between partners.

As a norm, a consultants employment agreement with ABC is based on around 70% of the working week being "chargeable time," that is, time that can be costed against a specific customer account. For individual consultants this can be negotiated up or down, depending on their charging rate, their perceived medium term value to ABC, and expected fluctuations in work coming in. For example, newly appointed consultants who have not yet built up a client network are "carried" for some months before being expected to reach 70% chargeable time, and established consultants may also be carried at a lower percentage at certain times in order to maintain team and individual expertise in anticipation of future organizational needs. In non-chargeable time, each consultant is required to seek new contracts, maintain their market presence among potential customers, and develop their professional knowledge, skill and networks. In order to complete projects within budget, consultants frequently work after hours, not charging the time against any account. This "free work" appears to be free to the customer, but is in effect free to ABC, because it lets the organization fulfill its contracts within budget.

The relationships between ABC, its employee consultants and the customers are complex. In some senses, these are relationships between ABC as a coherent organization and its customers. Customers, especially new ones, may well contract with ABC because of its reputation as a market leader, or because of what they know about its actual previous performance. So consultants may be seen as merely employees of ABC: they may draw on ABC's standing and may not be assessed in their own right by prospective customers. Equally, ABC internally decides which consultant/consultants may seek out contracts in specific territories, and internally resolves demarcation disputes so as to present a unified corporate face to the client base. This is the conventional organizational model. However customers may also see themselves as dealing with known individual consultants, and may move their business with those consultants if and when they leave ABC. That is, in some cases there are direct relationships between individual consultants and customers, with ABC being seen by both as providing no more than a framework within which these relationships are expressed. This can be called an "internal franchisee" model. Of course and importantly, there is often considerable ambiguity and uncertainty as to whether the organizational or internal franchisee model applies in particular cases. Depending on the circumstances, each party has interests in invoking either one or both types of relationships. In particular, ABC itself does not have a clear-cut interest in invoking or supporting the organizational model: it implemented the internal franchising system in order to maximize profits and market share, even though in the process it relinquished some direct organizational control and authority over its employees and their relationships with its customers. In short, it has been a strategic decision of ABC to make market relationships amongst its employees, and between them and its customers, central to its own organizational form.

ABC is not alone in this. Indeed, systems of chargeable time, internal markets and employee-generated work are widespread in management, consultancy and legal organizations. Legal firms differ somewhat because they are and conventionally have been set up as loose frameworks within which the senior "partners" pursue and carry out their own business. The shift from traditional legal chambers to corporate law firms has seen the introduction of formalized internal time accounting systems, with senior partners preserving much of their traditional authority. By contrast, in accountancy and management organizations the authority of senior executives is less based on traditional authority. I return to this later in the chapter.

The Public Sector, for example Government Business Enterprise (GBE)

GBE provides civil engineering services to design, implement and support/maintain major public sector infrastructure projects. Its charter is to operate within one of the seven jurisdictions established by the Australian federal system, and it has had a monopoly within that jurisdiction. In the late 1980s the government moved to place GBE and other public sector organizations on what was said to be a commercial basis. GBE was corporatized: that is, it was changed from a highly centralized bureaucratic organization, along the lines of a government department, to a somewhat decentralized network of budget centers under strong central executive control, modeled on a private sector corporation. Some projects and sub-projects were contracted out, staff numbers were reduced slightly through not replacing those who left voluntarily (although at that time there were no forced retrenchments or even incentive resignation packages), and a new corporate culture program emphasized customer service, concern for stakeholders, and budgetary efficiency. This was, in the Australia of the late 1980s, a fairly standard example of putting public sector organizations on what was said to be a sound commercial basis. There was at that time no talk by either governments or unions of this being the first step in preparing the agency for possible privatization, this silence was consistent with the anti-privatization policy of the government of the day, and reflected the influence of established unions. However in retrospect this corporatization may be seen as setting the scene for a possible future privatization of either the whole organization or of substantial parts of it.

Contracting out has had a major effect upon the sense of mission within the organization. GBE maintained viable engineering services groups within the organization. Under the new policy of putting projects to tender, the internal engineering group that would in the past have done the project was free to tender for it, and could expect to win the tender if its bid was competitive. However, even in cases when an engineering services group did win projects through the tender process, there was a subtle but important shift from the sense of mission that had applied in that same group when it had done similar projects before the contracting out/ tendering policy was introduced. As with all engineering work, safety is a major consideration, and in the past, fail safe or maximum achievable safety was considered to be a foremost objective in system design and implementation. This does not appear to have been a formal or explicitly stated policy position. Certainly, engineers did not comply with it primarily because it was formal policy. Rather, it was part of the shared tacit value system in GBE, at most alluded to and never blatantly invoked. It was embedded in the culture at a depth that most corporate culture programs can only dream of achieving. Maximum possible safety was an assumed part of the mission in each project, and the cost of achieving this was not questioned.

However when projects were put to tender, safety requirements had to be explicitly specified and benchmarked. This was standard private sector practice, and it was necessary in order to ensure compliance with expected safety levels as described in each contract. It also reflected recognition within GBE that private sector tenders responded to commercial pressures, and did not share the public service ethic implicit in the objective of maximum possible safety. The result was that the design objective shifted from maximum achievable safety to compliance with specified safety requirements.

GBE tenders, seeking to put in commercially competitive bids, designed to the new safety requirements, and those who advocated retaining the prior maximum safety objective lost out in the debates that went on within GBE at the time[1]. A core value within GBEs culture, and one that was a primary expression of the organizations public service ethos, was displaced at the very moment that it was made explicit, and this within months of the introduction of tendering, even and especially in the cases where the work remained in GBE.

Although this old core value was widely recognized as obsolete in terms of the organizations new practices and objectives, it remained a deeply held personal value for many GBE engineers, who saw their work as part of the public sector project of working for the maximum public good. As a result, there was a widespread undertone of personal disquiet and dissatisfaction amongst these staff. This did not stop them from throwing themselves into the new commercialized practices with enthusiasm. They did this for the sake of preserving as much as possible of GBE and what it stood for, and, as part of that, to protect their jobs. But it did leave a discrepancy between their old public service values and their new commercial practices.

The safety issue is but one instance of the changes in ethos that occur as public sector organizations are changed. This ethos is in effect the discursively available constellation of meaning and knowledge about what is happening in the organizational setting. It impacts not only on what is or could be appropriate organizational practices and personal action, but also on appropriate ways of feeling about these things.

The first stage of public sector changes, dating in Australia from the late 1980s, involved establishing organizational divisions and sections as budget centers and sub-budget centers, imposing tight budget restrictions, introducing some contracting out, and reducing middle-level staff (often while increasing the number of senior managers). As a result, planning and day-to-day operations became heavily budget-driven, and organizational practices increasingly fell outside what was understood to be best for the public good. To give a simple and direct example, in the Victorian Police Force budget restrictions have led to some policing practices that fall outside both police and public understandings of policing for the public good. For example, when clearing traffic at the end of a major sporting event at a venue surrounded by residential areas, police say they

just aim to fill up [residential as well as arterial] streets with cars. We fill up one street, then the next one, and just keep going. We've got to get them all out of [the venue] before our overtime budget is used up (30/3/93).

Budget driven public sector management was introduced in Britain and Canada somewhat earlier that in Australia (Metcalfe and Richards 1987: ch.8; Stewart and Walsh 1992; McDavid and Marson 1991), and its adverse impact on ethos was noted in Canada in the mid-1980s. Papers from a 1986 Institute of Public Administration of Canada/University of Victoria conference led to the pessimistic "Fear and Ferment" collection of essays (Langford 1987). In Australia similar effects have occurred, although they are less well documented.

One response has been to adopt a customer service orientation, in which the mission of serving the public interest was replaced by the mission of satisfying clients or customers (e.g. Barton and Marson 1991; Woodhouse et al. 1993). Some public sector managers have adopted this new market-oriented approach with enthusiasm, taking pride in their turning away from public sector values. Writing from Canada, Barton and Marson note the "buoyant" mood of

the entrepreneurial civil servant. Creativity, a willingness to take risks, responsiveness to clients, and a political flexibility were characteristics of this new breed. Such persons would have much in common with their private sector counterparts. Serving something as abstract as the public interest would not be a part of their personal agendas (Barton and Marson 1991: 9).

These authors note that politicians (whom they call "elected clients") do not fit well into their model of "the well-performing government organization," and should not be able to stand in the way of the "emerging cultures of service quality." This overlaying of customer service onto budget driven management can be characterized as a shift from a funding driven mode of organization to customer driven organization: from a partially commercial to a fully commercial organization. It involves abandoning any sense of public interest that can not be measured by customer or client responses. And, completely in character with economic rationalist views of how and why the state should function, it involves discrediting politics in favor of the market as the only legitimate mechanism through which interests can be expressed and articulated (Muetzelfeldt 1992a).

In Australia, the economically rationalist government elected in the State of Victoria in October 1992 is moving strongly in this direction. It is attempting to put all Victorian public sector operations on a commercial basis, using Osborne and Gaebler (1992) as a benchmark text[2]. Drawing on the school coming from Auster and Silver (1979) the new government's agenda-setting Commission of Audit Report takes as a premise that "There is no fundamental difference between the delivery of government services and the running of a private sector company" (Victorian Commission of Audit 1993, Vol. 1: 184), in effect "[rejecting] social goals and social utility as factors in public spending" (Carney 1993). The application of this extends beyond public sector businesses to include core state functions.

For example, in the Victoria Police force,

a six month intensive review of operations has identified a new direction for police which includes contracting out, corporate sponsorship, improved marketing and increased accountability to the community. In the terminology of the review, to be finalized this week, police become 'service providers' and people – criminals, victims and bystanders alike – are 'the market' or 'the customer' (Kermond 1993: 1).

This may in the short term improve the work satisfaction of public sector managers, but it has pernicious social effects. Amongst other things, it changes and potentially diminishes citizenship and other social rights. For example, the Victorian Public Transport Commission has moved to replace heavy rail suburban trains with light rail trams. This might increase customer satisfaction as measured by patronage rates and market research of actual patrons, but it will exclude some categories of physically disabled people from using public transport. Or again, the national government, which is moving more gradually in a market policy direction, has recently offered money in the form of resettlement payments to Cambodian and Vietnamese applicants for refugee status if they agree to be repatriated rather than pursue their claims to refugee status in Australia. However it has told them that if they decide to exercise their legal right to pursue those claims and then are unsuccessful, their resettlement payment will be substantially reduced (Radio 3LO, 26 April 1993, 11.55 p.m.; Gregory 1993). Within public sector organizations, the relationship between work satisfaction (as measured by customer satisfaction) and the sense of having achieved social benefits (as warranted through political processes) is complex and largely unexplored. It is far from clear that in the long run customer service criteria will satisfy and sustain public sector staff.

Knowledge and Power

Organization is an expression of knowledge. It is through a body of knowledge, made available and rendered coherent through discourse, that those who participate in organizing and organizational practices know that they are indeed organizational actors and that the social site of their practices is an organization. It is through discursive knowledge that they know what the organizational mission is, what it is that they (together and individually) should and could do to work towards that mission, and how they might and do feel about that. Thus the culture of an organization, and the culture within which organizing happens, is both much wider and deeper than the "corporate culture" of the managerial project (Pettigrew 1979; Peters and Waterman 1982; Maccoby 1981; Schein 1986).

The changes described in the previous section reflect a shift from an emphasis on bureaucratic culture towards an emphasis on market culture. Bureaucratic culture is based on the legitimacy of procedural rationality. Within organizations it leads to the notion of a career service that links individual and organizational goals, and so binds individuals into the organization. The resulting hierarchical organizational form crystallizes authority in ways that from Thompson on are said by some to disempower staff and inhibit innovation (Thompson 1961; Kriegler et al. 1988-1992). By contrast, market culture is based on the legitimacy of practices that achieve desired results. In organizations, as in other social sites, it emphasizes and enhances individuality and weakens social solidarity. The resulting network organizational form displaces conventional hierarchical authority, and conceals its own power relations so well that some analysts celebrate the empowerment of staff and the innovative and adaptive practices that are said to result in these apparently postmodern organization (Clegg 1992; Mathews 1989: 172).

The Market and its Discontents

Despite the enthusiasm of its advocates, market-based organizational forms have their own shortcomings. Some of these are recognized in the Kochan and Useem (1992) collection, where traditional bureaucratic conceptions of organization are rejected not in favor of a market model, but rather in favor of a conception in which "individual *and collective* voices" are heard within "institutions and practices that sustain trust and install values of community and concern for mutual welfare" (Kochan and Useem 1992: 5; my emphasis). Here I want to focus on two general discontents of the market. These appear throughout market based society in general, but they are important here because in particular they permeate market-based organizations.

First, market rationality can fly in the face of organizational rationality: individual decisions made with market rationality can lead to overall system irrationality, and intended outcomes are put at risk by the drive for outputs. This is in part a result of technical market failure due to externalities, incomplete information, collusive or oligopolistic tendencies, etc., all of which may be important in market-like organizations. But it is also, and importantly, due to the aggregate of individual intentions and decisions being incommensurable with the intentions and decisions of the collective organization. In the short run, systems of self-maximizing individuals are not necessarily most effective at maximizing their collective ends. And in the longer run, they can be unstable, leading to severe gyrations rather than to self-correcting damped oscillations around an optimum state. In the economy, boom-bust cycles, social inequality, and for that matter the existence of macroeconomics as a response to these, speaks to these central problems in the microeconomic model.

In organizational studies, the debate over market-emulating "managerialism" in the Australian public sector highlights these same problems (Considine 1988 and 1990; Patterson 1988; Alford 1993). One of the problems that Considine identifies is the inhibitions on adaptation and organizational learning that come with a managerialist emphasis on the short-run maximization of narrowly defined outputs. This is a clear organizational correlate of the central problems in market-based economic systems, where the focus of decision-making and action is on short-term maximization of narrowly defined outputs.

Stewart and Walsh (1992) identify several inadequacies and limitations in the new patterns of market-oriented public management in Britain, which go beyond the Australian managerialism of the late 1980s. They argue for an appropriate balance between continuity and change, between conventional and market-emulating organizational practices. However, in the absence of evidence as to the outcomes of the new practices (Stewart and Walsh 1992: 510), we have no sense of where that "balance" might be, or even if it could exist. Hence their critique of some excesses in applying the new public management implies an unacknowledged critique of its central planks. For example, they point to limitations in the quasi-markets in areas such as health and education, and argue that these limitations result from these being quasi- or structured markets, rather than free or unstructured ones (Stewart and Walsh 1992: 515-516). However there is and can be no truly free or unstructured market: even the minimum regulation via the law of contracts and credit, without which there would be no market, imposes structure that favors some transactions over others, some market participants over others, some practices over others, and in the end some outcomes over others. In practice all markets, private as well as public, are structured by the state, and in being so structured they position participants in ways that result in them contributing to outcomes not of their own choosing (Muetzelfeldt 1992a: 195-199). These outcomes include effects on others as well as on themselves.

The second discontent of the market has to do with people's self-esteem. The openness of market processes, which is intended to motivate and empower individuals, can lead to them feeling inadequate and insecure. The long term result is to insidiously undermine self-confidence and self-worth without providing (as bureaucracy does) an external object that can be held responsible. That is, market organizations lead to a disenchantment of the self that is as profound as bureaucratic disenchantment, but that is different in that there is no recognized social framework within which that disenchantment can be processed and resolved.

In his innovative and extensive critique of the market experience[3], Lane (1991) argues that markets impact upon human development through, amongst other things, self-attribution: "the belief that a person is effective in influencing his or her fate." This is contributed to by "the market's indifference to the fate of persons [which] requires people to develop what is likely to be called self-reliance" (Lane 1991: 10-11). He celebrates the benefits of self-attribution "it helps people to feel autonomous, resist pressures towards conformity, and lead happier lives, and it is associated with more complex cognition." However it has its costs, namely,

the encouragement it gives to hierarchical views of society, the misleading explanations of events it fosters[4], and a limited ethical perspective favoring only the justice of deserts and leading to a concept of the world as just. Another cost is the painful inferences of self-blame by people who fail in the competitive system (Lane 1991: 180).

Self-attribution can be seen as having both detrimental and advantageous effects. When people are encumbered by what they take to be their responsibility for outcomes that leave them discontented, self-attribution can become a burden. People can respond by evading or renouncing their responsibility, abdicating in favor of charismatic authoritarian leaders (Fromm 1941; Mannheim 1948: 71-75). Lane recognizes this, but sees it as a negative and irrational response to an overload of collective complexity, rather than as an intrinsic aspect of self-attribution (Lane 1991: 146-147).

He prefers to focus on the positive and advantageous responses that behaviorist psychology has documented: "[a sense of] personal control contributes to feelings of well-being under both favorable and unfavorable circumstances," and it is associated with tendencies to resist conformity and resist submission to authority (Lane 1991: 174-175). Lane presumes that these positive responses occur in nearly all situations, because nearly always there is no overloaded of cognitive complexity. That is, these responses occur in the type of situations that people characteristically encounter in market relationships. For him, failure is an intermittent market experience, and in any case it is one that self-attributing people can cope with. Further, the market encourages and cultivates self-attribution, so the whole system works in a positively reinforcing way (Lane 1911: 64-65).

However there is a case to be made against this optimistic scenario. Markets regularly position people as accepting what they consider to be second best outcomes in their transactions. As soon as consumers have more than minimal information about what is on offer in a market place, and as soon as sellers have some knowledge about the prices consumers may be willing to pay, both parties can use that information to extend their expectations about the likely outcome of a prospective transaction. Rarely do people get all that they hope for from a transaction. However high or low their expectations, the market generally has on offer a possibility that is beyond reach and, frustratingly, often just tantalizingly beyond reach. There is a dual mechanism at work here. Markets are organized to provide a never-ending ladder of ever more desirable outcomes, and in this they play on the capacity of our aspirations and expectations to expand to include the possibilities we see around us.

Markets invite us to act as optimisers, and instruct us to expect to be optimisers. But compared to our aspirations and expectations we regularly find ourselves being sub-optimisers or satisfiers. Yet in the moment of frustration when we settle for what we can get rather than what we want, the market also gives us nowhere to lay responsibility except with ourselves. The result is that our self-esteem is routinely eroded.

Lane recognizes this process, but minimizes its importance. In part, and revealingly, he does this rhetorically: the problem arises from the person's "fevered imagination" rather than from the market (Lane 1991: 194), but also he argues that expectations (more than aspirations) are shaped by experience and so are unlikely to be too much higher than what can be realized, that both expectations and aspirations tend to adjust to accommodate actual situations, and that in any case happiness does not depend on income. So,

> if they are frustrated [in their market transactions], people may be temporarily dissatisfied but not permanently unhappy... frustrated expectations may modify the more vulnerable *state* self-esteem but leave untouched the basic *trait* self-esteem (Lane 1991: 195, original emphasis).

> He concludes that it is change in conjunction with the market that 'threaten[s] the kind of certainty that seems to favor self-esteem' (Lane 1991: 195).

There are several points to be made against Lane's claim that market disappointment is not a deep threat to self-esteem. First, markets regularly not only deliver

less than they display and offer, but it is intrinsic to them that they do this while simultaneously holding market participants themselves responsible for getting less
than they hope for. In short, it is intrinsic to markets that they generate the experience of failure while purporting to generate the experience of achievement. There
is an experiential sense in which we can talk of "market failure": that is, a market
induced sense of failure experienced by all market participants. Second, Lane argues that happiness is not primarily dependent on markets, so failure in markets
does not undermine self-esteem: that is, that self-esteem is primarily produced in
non-market experiences. This might arguably apply to life in general. However
it certainly does not apply in the context of market-based organizations. This is
because organizational self-esteem is centrally dependent on organizational practices, and when these practices are market-focused, the market relations and market experiences of organizational life are the central determinants of organizational self-esteem. Third, people engage in different types of transactions, with very
different investments of self. The minor compromises and accommodations of everyday market transactions may arguably have more effect on state self-esteem
than on trait self-esteem, but people also occasionally engage in major transactions in which the personal investment is very high, and in these cases the impact
on self-esteem is liable to be considerable[5]. Such transactions where the personal
stakes are high also occur in organizations. They can occur when strategic decisions are being made, or where there has been a high personal investment of time,
effort, energy and prestige, or where a sense of organizational mission or professional expertise is involved. And they frequently occur when a person's career is
at stake.

Finally, Lane points to change in conjunction with the market, rather than the
market alone, as a threat to self-esteem. However it is a characteristic of the market, indeed one of its supposed virtues, that it induces change. If market dynamics
worked to produce smooth necessary adjustments to optimum conditions, as mi-
croeconomics proposes, then this change could be seen as desirable, necessary and
appropriate. But markets actually produce excessive swings around and past the
conditions that are seen to be optimum. That is, they generate change that is inappropriate, damaging and draining. In organizations, this can be seen first in the
"feeding frenzies" of the mid-1980s boom, when the desire for organizational expansion drove new missions, values, strategies and leadership changes that soon
turned out to be excessive, and following that in the retractions of the subsequent
recession, when organizational consolidation drove different new missions, etc.
that are turning out to be equally inappropriate. The wild gyrations of both these
restructurings, each supported by the managerial fashion of the day, have inflict-
ed enormous change upon and within organizations. This change has had little to
do with organizational adaptation to changing environments, and much to do with
the internal instability of market based systems within organizations and in their
environments. There are of course considerable differences in the extent to which
organizations and their environments are market based, and correspondingly in

the extent to which the boom-bust cycle led to extreme change within organizations. The finance industry and its organizations lived the boom cycle most fully, and felt the bust most acutely. However because of its supposed central position in the modern economy the managerial and organizational styles adopted in that industry have become the fashion leaders for all industries, and have been purveyed throughout a wide range of administrative organizations by management consultants, MBA courses, and practitioner literature. In short, the boom bust economy and the organizations through which it has been enacted have both led and imposed market-induced excessive change in two ways: through the environment in which organizations operate, and through the knowledge which organizations employ in their own practices. Management text books testify to the impact of this rapid change, for example, in their self-marketing opening pages they frequently approach the new reader by recalling the rapid change that envelops organizations (e.g. Ansoff 1987).

Markets do, then, deeply threaten self-esteem, both directly and indirectly. They directly generate experiences that can be understood by the persons involved to be failures precisely because markets themselves hold people to be independent and responsible for the outcomes of their transactions: these experiences vary from the frequent routine and often eroding experiences of everyday transactions to the rare, crucial and at times undermining experiences of special and highly charged transactions. Indirectly, they generate rates of change that most people sooner or later will experience as being beyond their ability to adjust to, while still representing to people that they alone are responsible for their conduct and should be capable of responding to those changes.

Market-based practices in organizations, then, lead to dual discontents. On one hand, they promise a level of instrumental efficacy that they can not deliver. On the other hand, they call on individuals to experience personal satisfactions that are often in small ways, and occasionally in big ways, beyond their reach. To the extent that individuals are incorporated into and hold as their own the organization's projects, they are disenchanted by the failure perhaps, but it is not necessarily seen as their failure to achieve these organizational ends and missions. To the extent that individuals aspire to achieve their own projects through and in the organization, they suffer a loss of self esteem through what they see as their inevitable failure to achieve these personal objectives. These two are often compatible, and the perceived failure of both compounds as an experienced failure of the self. The growing literature and industry built around stress in organizations testifies to this.

Authority and the Market

I have argued that the market experience leads to a sense of market failure, a failure of self and of identity. This provides the conditions for a flight to certainty, to any externalized certainty that removes from the individual the sense of personal responsibility through which they see that through their market failure they have failed themselves, rather than having been failed by an exterior condition. One certainty that can be fled to is fundamentalism, and in secular western society that is more likely to be the secular fundamentalism of pure and unsullied market theory itself. We have seen much of that in politics and public life since the early 1980s.

Another certainty that can be escaped to, and the one that is my prime interest here, is strong authoritarian leadership. Of course current social circumstances are different from those about which Fromm (1941) and Mannheim (1948) wrote. One characteristic of contemporary circumstances is that there are many aspiring authoritarian leaders who subscribe to and express economic fundamentalism.

Consequently these two certainties can be embraced, or, rather, can envelop one simultaneously. It is precisely this double appeal, neither arm of which is explicitly expressed and each of which in its partial presentation provides distracting cover for the other, that energizes and conceals the draw of secular authoritarianism in the west today.

There is a process of mutual encompassing of organization and market. Just as the organization brings the marketing of its corporate image into the organization through its corporate culture program (Muetzelfeldt 1992b: 298), so it makes the external market felt deep within the organization through customer service, contracting out, etc. in public sector cases, and through internal franchising in private sector cases. The result is that the organization positions itself in relationship to its staff as being benign and constructive, while at the same time exposing them to market pressures that require them, in some cases against their own sense of what is best or right, to take responsibility for acting in ways that benefit the organization. Corporate culture and personal identity interact here (Mousli 1987), and in market emulating organizations they do so in ways that lead to a strong need for authoritarian leadership that is simultaneously concealed behind the apparent openness of market processes.

In market emulating organizations there is a need for strong and centralizing authority, expressed through the emphasis on leadership and vision as key organizing factors. At a very general level, there is an indication of this in the changing pattern of jobs. Across the Australian economy, there has been an overall increase in leadership positions, despite a decrease in administrative positions. According to Bureau of Statistics employment figures, in the economically recessed three years to February 1993 the number of clerical workers declined by 4.8%, yet during this time the number of managers increased by 2.8% and professionals increased by 7.9% (Colebatch 1993). These are very broad-brush figures, but their general trend is consistent with the more specific and internally consistent figures for the Victorian public sector: from 1983 to 1990 the number of senior executive service staff-executives and senior managers, more than doubled, and this at a time when managerialism was being vigorously introduced and the over-all growth in public servants was being curtailed (Considine 1992: 196).

Marketization affects inter-firm arrangements so as to generate small firms that are nominally separate from but actually dependent upon large firms. Shutt and Whitington (1986) examine the growth of small firms in Britain, which they at-tribute in part to the fragmentation strategies of large firms. These fragmenting strategies of decentralization, devolvement and disintegration have the effect of shifting responsibility and employment from large to small dependent firms. The effective organization and control of large firms remains, or is even enhanced due to the dispersal and lack of organization of the new small firms, while respon-sibility is dispersed. This is a specific example of the practice of devolutionism, which involves a centralization of strategic control while tactical responsibility is decentralized within a context of management-controlled incentive structures and corporate culture (Muetzelfeldt 1992b).

At the level of specific organizations, authoritarian leadership shows in many ways. In the private and public sector organizations described earlier, leaders eschewed the distance of a multi-layered bureaucracy. Instead, cultivating and claiming charisma, they presented themselves as human, visionary, and con-cerned. But these performances remained superficial. They demanded a loyalty from their immediate subordinates that denied any space for debate or disagree-ment. As well, within the flat structures through which market devolution was im-plemented, they carried a high decision-making load across a very broad brief. The combination of their workload and the complexity and range of the factors that they dealt with effectively distanced them from the life and concerns in the organization. This distancing was as effective as, although less apparent than, the distancing of intermediate layers of bureaucracy.

The mood at an end of financial year party in a finance sector firm was edgy. The computer system had crashed three days before the end of the financial year, and many deals that had to be finalized then to maximize their "taxation efficiency" could not be completed. The system was made operational again, to everyone's relief, on the last day of the year. I asked a partner what would have happened if the system had not been restored in time: "We would have sacked the systems an-alyst." This was hardly a reasoned response: the partner was not computer literate, and was in no position to know if that action would have either visited retribution on the person who was responsible for the failure, or would have been likely to minimize the chance of future failures. Later a consultant pointed out that such talk should not be taken as conclusive evidence as to what would have been done. None the less, it was at the least a claim to having arbitrary and highly personal-ized authority. And in the common situation of staff dismissals, it is widely held by middle level staff that dismissal decisions are likely to be and often appear arbi-trary. Indeed, making them arbitrary is one way in which executives can neutralize themselves from the human consequences of their actions.

In the public sector, the situation is different in its specifics, but basically much the same. The evidence building up about the new market-right Victorian government is that arbitrary and decisive authority is central to its functioning. The Premier is said to demand total acceptance from his ministers and from public sector chief executives. This is completely consistent with the way in which he and his government has exercised public political power. And the system of employment contracts that is being introduced gives chief executives similar power over their staff. Stewart and Walsh (1992) argue that, ironically, contracts for staff make things more rigid, and increase short-term focus. That is, they fail to produce the flexible strategic organizing that is claimed for them, even though they do become vehicles for the centralization of strategic control.

Conclusion

I have argued that the market generates two discontents, because of its problematic instrumental efficacy and its cultivation of perceptions and feelings of personal inadequacy. These establish the circumstances for profound disenchantment among organizational members. They promote a turning to apparently strong and charismatic leadership, in effect authoritarian organizational leadership. This is the very antithesis of the ideal of the market or postmodern organization.

What, then, should we make of the postmodern organization? Less, I suggest, than is fashionable. A central feature of supposedly postmodern organizations is their pattern of differentiation and de-differentiation. Compared to modern organizations, postmodern organizations are said to de-differentiate production and differentiate consumption (Clegg 1990). However, consumption is not becoming as differentiated as at first seems, and nor is production becoming so de-differentiated. The differentiation in consumption is not a functional differentiation, but is rather a superficial set of image-based differences between commodities for the sake of market positioning. Considering the overall functionality of a car compared to any other form of transport, the degree of functional differentiation between the current 100 Toyota models is not significantly greater than between the old six models. On the other hand, the degree of functional differentiation in production (including administrative production) is as great as ever. At the level of the corporation, functional differentiation continues to be a central feature, and the now fashionable multi-functioned executive (typically, one line and one control function) is a technique for increasing coordination between functions, not for de-differentiating them. At the level of the work group or individual worker, the same applies. All the functions are still there and necessary, even though each group or individual is competent at several of them. The apparent de-differentiation is a technique for managing motivation and job satisfaction within a functionally differentiated production process.

The market, of course, lies behind all of this. It conceals its own processes and its power mechanisms, even as it cultivates them and incorporates organizational workers and organizational analysts alike into its projects. Organizational analysts' incorporation is surprising: they should be in a better position to not buy this.

Notes

[1] GBE is probably typical of what happens when public sector organizations are corporatized. A similar shift from maximum safety to specified required safety is reported to have occurred in air safety operations following the commercialization of the Australian Civil Aviation Authority. The head of an inquiry into air safety concluded that as a result "safety has been damaged or weakened" (Middleton 1993: 10). We can reasonably expect that many staff in that organization would feel the disquiet that was widespread in GBE.

[2] This book has been held out by the newly-appointed Head of the Victorian Premier's Department, Ken Baxter, as the agenda-setting text for the changes he was introducing to public administration in Victoria (Royal Australian Institute of Public Administration seminar, Melbourne, December 1992). Copies of it were distributed to commissioners and senior staff of the Victorian Commission of Audit, and "[t]he ideas in this book became the most important map the commission followed in its quest to find a remedy for Victoria's ailing public sector" (Walker 1993: 19).

[3] Lane's critique is innovative because he evaluates markets not in the conventional terms of whether they deliver maximum utility, but rather in terms of whether utility is itself an adequate measure of the well-being and the satisfaction with life-as-a-whole that people seek through market and non-market relationships.

[4] Lane earlier argues that self-attribution reinforces inequality by (i) giving market advantages to those who are already advantaged, and (ii) justifying inequality (1991:175 176). And it fosters misleading explanations by favoring those based on individual action, neglecting structural and circumstantial factors.

[5] An informant described the process of buying his first hi fi system as part of reestablishing himself after his marriage ended. He put aside money freed up through the sale of the matrimonial home, studied the hi fi magazines, discussed it with knowledgeable associates, after some time decided what he thought was appropriate, and started shopping. He found that, even when he went as far above his planned upper price as he could possibly manage, he could just afford a system that was barely suitable (as he had come to understand that term). He said: "It was supposed to be a moment of joy, but I found an enormous chasm [of technical and quality possibilities] opening up in front of me."

References

Alford, John (1993), Towards a New Public Management Model: Beyond Managerialism and its Critics, *Australian Journal of Public Administration*, 52(2), pp. 135-148.

Ansoff, H. Igor (1987), Preface, pp. xi-xiii, in Michel Godet (ed.), *Scenarios and Strategic Management*, Butterworths, London.

Auster, R.D., and M. Silver (1979), *The State as a Firm: Economic Forces in Political Development*, Martin Nijhoff, The Hague.

Barton, Joan A., and D. Brian Marson (1991), *Service Quality: An Introduction*, The Service Quality B.C. Secretariat, Victoria, B.C.

Carney, Shaun (1993), The Great Audit Becomes a Social Study that Leaps the Economic Boundaries, *The Age*, 15 May, p. 19.

Clegg, Stewart (1990), *Modern Organizations: Organization Studies in the Postmodern World*, Sage, London.

Clegg, Stewart (1992), Postmodern Management?, *Journal of Organizational Change Management*, 5(2), pp. 31-49.

Colebatch, Tim (1993), More Bosses Watch over Fewer Workers, *The Age*, 5 April, p. 3.

Considine, Mark (1988), The Corporate Management Framework as Administrative Science: A Critique, *Australian Journal of Public Administration*, 47(1), pp. 4-18.

Considine, Mark (1990), Managerial Strikes Out, *Australian Journal of Public Administration*, 49(2), pp. 166-178.

Considine, Mark (1992), Labours Approach to Policy Making, in Mark Considine and Brian Costar (eds.), *Trials in Power: Cain, Kirner and Victoria 1982-1992*, Melbourne University Press, Melbourne.

Fromm, Erich (1941), *Escape from Freedom*, Rinehart, New York.

Gregory, Peter (1993), Cash to Go, *The Age*, 10, June, p. 1.

Kermond, Clare (1993), Corporate Plans Overhaul Police, *The Melbourne Times,* 26 May, p. 1.

Kochan, Thomas A., and Michael Useem (eds.) (1992), *Transforming Organizations*, Oxford University Press, New York.

Krieger, J. (1986), *Reagan, Thatcher and the Politics of Decline*, Polity Press, Cambridge.

Kriegler, R.P., Dawkins, J. Ryan, and M. Wooden (1988-1992), *Achieving Organizational Effectiveness*, Oxford University Press, Melbourne.

Lane, R.E. (1991), *The Market Experience* Cambridge, Cambridge University Press.

Langford, John W. (ed.) (1987), *Fear and Ferment: Public Sector Management Today*, Institute of Public Administration of Canada and Institute of Public Policy, Ottawa.

Maccoby, Michael (1981), *The Leader: A New Face for American Management*, Simon and Schuster, New York.

Mannheim, Karl (1948), *Man and Society in an Age of Reconstruction*, Harcourt, New York.

Mathews, John (1989), *The Tools of Change: New Technology and the Democratisation of Work*, Pluto Press, Sydney.

McDavid, James C., and D. Brian Marson (eds.) (1991), *The Well-Performing Government Organization*, Institute of Public Administration of Canada, Ottawa.

Metcalfe, Les, and Sue Richards (1987), *Improving Public Management*, Sage, London.

Middleton, Karen (1993), Air Safety Has Been Damaged, Expert Claims, *The Age*, 26 May, p. 10.

Mousli, M. (1987), Corporate Culture and Identity, in M. Godet (ed.), *Scenarios and Strategic Management*, Butterworth, London, pp. 200-203.

Muetzelfeldt, Michael (1992a), Economic Rationalism in its Social Context, in M. Muetzelfeldt (ed.), *Society, State and Politics in Australia*, Pluto, Sydney.

Muetzelfeldt, Michael (1992b), Organizational Restructuring and Devolutionist Doctrine: Organization as Strategic Control, in Jane Marceau (ed.), *Reworking the World: Organizations, Technologies and Cultures in Comparative Perspectives*, de Gruyter, Berlin.

Osborne, David, and Ted Gaebler (1992), *Reinventing Government: How the Entrepreneurial Spirit is Transforming the Public Sector*, Addison-Wesley, Reading, Mass.

Patterson, John (1988), A Managerialist Strikes Back, *Australian Journal of Public Administration*, 47(4), pp. 287-295.

Peters, Thomas J., and Robert H. Waterman (1982), *In Search of Excellence*, Harper and Row, New York.

Pettigrew, Andrew M. (1979), On Studying Organizational Cultures, *Administrative Science Quarterly*, 24, pp. 570-581.

Pusey, Michael (1991), *Economic Rationalism in Canberra: A Nation-Building State Changes its Mind*, Cambridge University Press, Cambridge.

Schein, Edgar H. (1986), *Organizational Culture and Leadership*, Jossey Bass, San Francisco.

Shutt, John, and Robert Whittington (1986), Fragmentation Strategies and the Rise of Small Units: Cases from the North West, *Regional Studies*, 21(1), pp. 13-23.

Stewart, John, and Kieron Walsh (1992), Change in the Management of Public Services, *Public Administration*, 70, pp. 499-518.

Thompson, Victor (1961), *Modern Organizations*, Knopf, New York.

Victorian Commission of Audit (1993), *Report*, Volumes 1 and 2, Government Printing Office, Melbourne.

Walker, J. (1993), Government Course Best Charted from the Bridge, *The Age*, 8 May, p. 19.

Woodhouse, Scott A, Greg J. Conner, and D. Brian Marson (1993), *Listening to Customers: An Introduction*, The Service Quality B.C. Secretariat, Province of British Columbia, Vancouver, BC.

Yeatman, Anna (1990), *Bureaucrats, Technocrats, Femocrats: Essays on the Contemporary Australian State*, Allen and Unwin, Sydney.

The Analysis of Markets: From Transaction to Regulation[1]

Jean-Claude Thoenig and François Dupuy

The Market

Today, nothing seems more straightforward than a market. Everyday language and technical discourse combine to turn it into a banal phenomenon that we think we know well in its components and expressions. Various operators appear in it, transactions form there, and consequences for users and for jobs flow from it.

The market exists, transforms itself, and evolves, because it reflects, besides economic and institutional factors, the result of social action. It is one solution, among others, to a problem that is neither easy to manage nor straightforward to live with, the problem being co-operation between these actors, i.e. the lines of exchange and interdependence linking a multitude of groups and individuals, and hence of constraints and resources. A market is a form of social action, a collective construct. In this sense, there is no market "per se," but as many forms of market as there are different situations, in time and space, and in the social, political and cultural fabric.

Our interest in the market is as sociologists, with our own modes of thought, concepts and tools of observation. The approach may come across as sacrilege. Frequently, the demand is for an attitude of reverence when dealing with phenomena pertaining to the discipline of economics. Its achievements and methods seem not only to prevail but also to make incontrovertible sense on the subject. From this sacred perspective it is simply a question of testing whether there exist similarities and differences between the two types of systems that are organizations and markets. There are heretical alternatives.

We take as our point of departure a banal question. Co-operation between various actors is an essential problem for action, whether it takes place in public administration, between the heads and their subordinates, or in a firm, between the headquarters and the branches, or in the market-place, between producers and distributors. How, in each of these cases, do we deal with the fact that we must simultaneously act together while having particular interests? To act means to act across a network relationships we call a "system." Now, the "relationality," the basis of the social system, is not visible to the naked eye. It is not something that one can see, as a specimen, immovably pinned down on the scientific bench, a pure, lifeless form but something that is, that exists, that is its own practice and accomplishment. In what way is it practiced, through what process, under what conditions, and through what expressions: that is the objective of our analysis. In other words, treat the economic parameters as constraints and resources amongst others, bearing upon the collective game that the actors take part in, alongside factors such as consumers tastes, public regulations and available technologies. The relational, i.e. the regulation of "living together," thus constitutes an object whose components and effects it will be our task to explain.

The relational, we must remember, is not reducible to purely affective, cognitive and cultural variables. In this regard, such and such a market, at such and such a time, in such and such a context, represents a social, global, and thus specific, phenomenon, which defies adequate summary as the aggregate of "micro" factors, nor as the projection, in certain economic conditions, of universally transposable "macro" determinants. Our postulate is a methodological one. Each market is an individual case. If it is useful to draw up typologies of universalist value, and if it is essential to outline laws or "grand theories," one must, before doing so, equip oneself with relevant modes of analysis, as in the best examples of the sociology of organizations.

The problem is both theoretical and methodological in nature. It goes back to our way of thinking and the constitution of a satisfying heuristic tool that would enable us to treat the following question: what are the conditions governing action when a structure of relationships of interdependence and exchange is built between firms and actors otherwise autonomous in relation to one another (Hirsch 1975; Lebledici and Salancik 1982; Burns and Flam 1987; Thompson et al.1991).

From the observation of the relations between industrial producers and commercial distributors in the domain of "white goods" (washing-machines, dishwashers, refrigerators, ovens), and with the help of a comparison between France, Japan and the United States, it is possible to sketch a few characteristics of more general value[2]. Here we will rely on the approach known as sociological strategic and system analysis. If the clarification of the concept of "system" will be subject to developments in the course of our paper, that of "strategy" needs immediate further explanation.

The term "strategy" does not conform to the use usually made of it by specialists in business policy. Our use of the term is different. It defines a structure of real behavior by an actor, this being a response by the actor to the task she/he has set him or her self or to a problem she/he is managing, taking into account the constraints and resources she/he faces. In this sense, any agent pursues a strategy, whether she/he is conscious of it or not, whether their behavior appears erratic or not, imposed or chosen, for any actor adopts a certain behavior in so much as she/he is acting alongside or up against other actors. The strategy is therefore more simply what responses she/he makes in a relational situation. Strategic analysis, as practiced by sociologists, is thus a methodology that consists, on the one hand, of observing the everyday and concrete behaviors of the players in a collective game, and, on the other, that observation being made of identifying the conditions that make it so that each acts in their particular sphere and through the others as she/he does so.

Towards a Systematic Approach

The concept of the market is difficult to delimit. It presents the appearance of an investment heavy with legitimacy respected both by practitioners in it and by the discipline of economics that makes it its conceptual cornerstone. To prefer the concept of organized or quasi-organized system to that of the market is to assume, at the least, that one can justify the superiority of the reasoning used on the basis of a debate on the content: what does an analysis using the tools of systems and strategic reasoning bring that is different and richer?

Economists thinks about the market in terms of flows, costs and transactions. Sociology, and more recently, political science, have turned their attention to collective action and mobilization. The stimulation triggered between sociology and political science has a bearing on the analysis of the firm, on the one hand, and on the modalities of state action, on the other. It therefore privileges the point of view, or perspective, of such-and-such a particular actor. To understand what markets are, when one starts from theoretical or normative reflections rather than from questions of empirical analysis, is to see the market re-situated as a particular mode of co-operation, one considered as more elaborate or artificial, within the hierarchy of authority, political action, bureaucratic action (see Williamson 1975).

It is not easy to find an acceptable definition of the market, except by banal reduction of it to a place where goods and services exchange. On this subject, at least, Williamson's (1975) point of view is worthy of attention. In his eyes, the market is similar to a state of nature, comparable to that imaginative and fictitious condition described by Hobbes.

In order to be efficient as a mechanism of co-operation, such a situation, a market, must satisfy a number of conditions. In particular, it must deal with relatively simple transactions. This is because every transaction entails costs. By transaction cost, Williamson means the price derived from the encounter between two economic actors, individual or collective. Now, as soon as the exchanges leave a state of simple bilateralism and gains in complexity, then the transaction costs increase at an accelerating pace until they rapidly become prohibitive. In this case, complexity results from several factors: uncertainty, the frequency of transactions, and the level of specific investments induced by the same transactions (Williamson and Ouchi 1981; Hegner 1986; Dahl and Lindblom 1963; Moullet 1982; Maitland et al. 1983)[3].

The market remains an appropriate relational situation when transactions are direct, without mediation between participants, and if the terms of exchange are easily specified, and so long as no partial supplementary investment is necessary, unless it involves a simple gathering of information. From this perspective, one can see the market as a slightly more elaborate form of barter.

By giving such a simple view of the market, the analyst must go on to address more complex forms of exchange. This is because, beyond this minimal catalogue of contextual conditions, it is the organization that becomes essential as an alternative that can manage the market's transactions when the conditions conducive to bartering are absent. The organization, in fact, offers the possibility of a better structuring of the confrontation between actors' bounded interests and their rationalities.

In concrete terms, no one behaves like a constantly and absolutely rational decision-maker whose choices might reflect the quest for scientific criteria. In daily life, the agent acts as a decision-maker who seeks to avoid making too many mistakes, and to find solutions that are psychological satisfying. As such, one does one's best one thinks one can at the moment one makes one's decision, taking into account the information at one's disposal, and one's own feelings and intelligence. To integrate with this egoism, as Williamson does with his notion of transaction cost, the contribution of the theory of bounded rationality, allows analysis to make an important step forward. It relativises the profit-motive, this relativization being all the stronger when we think in the long term.

In such a universe, the hierarchy of authority and the explicit division of labor offer alternatives for collective action more favorable than the market. If the market is incapable of operating, taking account of uncertainty and the frequency of transactions, prices become fixed by negotiation. Negotiation is a very costly way of settling the terms of exchange in so much as it opens the door to opportunism. This is why internal organization is preferable, not because it reaches a fairer result, but simply because it is more efficient.

Figure 1: An orthodox approach to markets by economics

The "state of organization," which represents the opposite of the "state of nature" that is the market, is vital for action. Recourse to "trusts," to formal organizational integration, responsible to a single center, constitutes a relevant response to the need to reduce the costs incurred along the chain linking the raw material to the finished product sold to the consumer. Cotta says as much in his study of the mechanism of price-fixing in the field of food-products, even if he does not directly take a side on the issue. After pointing out that "a 'filiere' of social product manifests itself as a succession of three markets," he shows the articulation of relationship between the agents as it is expressed in the issue of mark-ups and margins, which are nothing other than transaction costs, in Williamson's sense. However, unlike Williamson, Cotta accords the market a status of superiority over any hierarchical form of organization, i.e. to use his own expression, over any " 'filiere' of social production" (Cotta 1985).

Comparative Transactions: White Goods in Japan and France

Transaction-cost theory enables us to shed light on a quite glaring contrast between the situations in Japan and France, in the quite unexceptional case of household electrical goods. In Japan, the most powerful manufacturers control the whole "filiere" of distribution right up to the final consumer. If we concede with Cotta that the "public price" is equal to the bill of the internal transformation costs at the various stages (industry, distribution), we understand better how these producers are in a position to dictate to the market high prices while reducing the cost of intermediary transactions. Thus, the Japanese market may, perhaps, be considered as the best organized, in Williamson's sense of internal organization, while at the same time presenting to the external observer a diversified collection of agents belonging to organizations that are independent of one another (producers, distributors, consumers associations, etc.) and that pursue particular, rather than concentrative, interests.

White goods are quite unexceptional, to repeat. With only the slightest variations in design and manufacture, they are cultural universals of developed modernity. Perhaps, then, all that we need to know of their organization is contained in the technologies that determine their form. Williamson makes a radical, albeit implicit critique of research that emphasizes the decisive influence of technology and its evolution on the structure and workings of firms as organizations as Woodward (1958) and Perrow (1967) present them. The case of the white goods industry in Japan seems to support such a skeptical critique.

It is particularly obvious, when studying the Japanese case, that analysis in terms of the influence of technological determinism runs up against a number of difficulties when dealing with the problem of integration, which is the dominant logic of the hegemonic actor around which the other logic's and agents negotiate their divergent interests. On the one hand, in the domain of white goods, the firm does not perform the function of technological integration so much as one of assembly. On the other hand, what is at stake in integration is the control of intermediary costs and, "in fine," the fixing of the final retail price. The latter does not, however, result from the confrontation of interests in the market-place, as Williamson would have us believe, nor from the fairness, in the sense that Ouchi gives to the word, that the market brings to all its agents, but from a veritable unofficial integration, the constitution of a shadow hierarchy, officially unrecognized as such. In some way, what Williamson attributes to the firm as the advantages resulting from the constitution of a hierarchical organization, occurs in the marketplace, i.e. in the relationships between actors in the form of what sociologists call an inter-organizational network (Benson 1975).

The shadow hierarchy, integrated on the Japanese internal market by the nodal firms that are the big national manufacturers, if need be by threat and coercion, places under their power all other actors. These include distributors (wholesalers, retailers) and final consumers. It is this control that gives the Japanese, in return, a considerable game margin on the foreign markets. We are dealing with a system of action composed of power relations, not an internally efficient organization or a perfectly competitive market. We are not dealing with an internal organization, in the sense where a pyramid of command and a formally legitimate division of labor integrate the actors. If we are not dealing with a market, we must point out that neither are we dealing with a plot hatched by a conspiracy of villains co-ordinating the carve-up of their booty, conspiring to trade. Instead, we have before us what we call a system of action.

A system is a collective construct for action that takes the form of an arrangement of games more or less tightly integrated, articulating with one another, and assuming regulation of the whole. The existence of these articulations and of their regulator assumes in turn a concrete system that includes them. The Japanese case shows that in a system of action, opacity, to use Cotta's felicitous expression, is a characteristic essential for the activities of its members and for its maintenance as a collective construct.

If we look at the French market through the same analytical optic, the situation is very different.

In an as yet unstabilised universe, marked by the brutal confrontation of divergent interests through the "meeting of the few," the integrating element that is vital to producers, consumers and other actors such as consumers' associations and public authorities, is the distributor, or rather, to be precise, a particular distributor: the big consumer specialist stores. Transaction costs play a central role, as the capacity that one or the other may have to reduce them to their advantage is the key condition for success.

Large-scale French distribution, the integrating pivot of relational practices, remains all the same a universe still weakly stabilized, or too "young," in Cotta's sense. The discounter has given way to the consumerist specialist distributor but competition remains sufficiently open for redistributions of territory and sweeping revisions of policy to take place. Trade has not yet reached its stage of maximum concentration, even if the constitution of big joint-venture central purchasing offices (*supercentrales d'achat*) marks a big step in this direction. The trade situation resembles more that of a market in Williamson's sense than that of a Japanese-style hierarchy. It remains too unstable for it to be possible to arrive at modes of hegemony and integration over industry and the consumer close to those of the Japanese model of the nodal industry. The game remains open, even if the consumer pays and if the national industrialist remains trapped between the anvil of falling trade and the hammer of rising costs of production.

Intervention by public authorities in France goes against the grain of the forms of organization observable in Japan. To prohibit the discriminating effect of the opacity of negotiations, as trade regulation demands, and to struggle against big central purchasing offices, as the public authorities try to do, amounts to outlawing the successive encounters that make up any competitive life. In other words, by wanting to establish real transparency where there was opacity, under the vague moral pretext that transparency is more virtuous than opacity, or that it benefits the consumers more, you condemn the French market to bearing the cost of all the confrontations that mark it, and to fail before the challenge of integration, or at least that of a partial degree of integration upon which others – the Japanese – draw their essential resources. By integration we mean the capacity and the power to have the different rationalities that make up the system of the market negotiate amongst themselves, without anyone triumphing. The integrating actor is the one around whom the whole strategies arrange themselves, or which is capable of controlling them: this is the case of the Japanese manufacturer, and this is beginning to be the case with the big specialized distributor in France. From the point of view of analysis of the market by way of the firm, this difference is radically important. From the point of view of analysis of the market as a specific human construct, it is a completely different story.

Observation of the facts shows that in France, the big national producers themselves form, at the heart of their own firms, weakly integrated organizations. Taking up again Williamson's analysis, which here becomes more relevant, the transaction cost is no longer simply that of the producer encountering the distributor, but also that which is constituted by phenomena such as intermediary stocks in the factories, quality deficiency, the autonomy of factories in relation to the rest of the organization, and the spiral of sales strategy as criteria of success. The particular interest of the sales force of the firm, in striving to live up to the normalized judgments explicit in the quantitative criteria they must meet, also constitute these transaction costs. The multiplication of encounters right at the heart of the business shows, if demonstration be needed, that transactions do not limit themselves to specific entities legally identified and hierarchically independent of one another. In order to take account of such a reality, the concept itself of the market appears too vague. To the extent that application of the concept of the market describes only an abstraction that enables us to study the exceptions to the rule, we would be better to abandon it in favor of the concept of a system of action, in which we strive to identify the specific regulations that appear at the point of the production and distribution of a good or a service.

In the same order of ideas, the concept of hierarchy, understood not in an organizational but systemic sense, takes into account the actors independently of the structures they belong to. "Hierarchy" then means a particular form of integration of the productive and distributive systems of goods or services.

The work of Ouchi extends and completes, albeit critically, the analysis put forward by Williamson. According to Ouchi, co-operation between actors finds its principle motivating force neither in the will of each of them to arm themselves against the dishonest use of strong hands enjoyed by such and such other actors in the negotiations, nor in the difficulty of reaching an agreement on a fair distribution of the costs and profits of the transaction. It flows rather from the difficulty of measuring the contribution of each party involved in the transaction. Finally, for Ouchi, the problem of efficiency comes down to the achievement of fairness or of the perception of fairness between the contributions of contractual parties. This line of reasoning can be summarized in a syllogism:

The fact that the transaction is made through the intermediary of the market, the bureaucracy or the clan, depends on the mode which proves to be the most efficient, taking account of the nature of the transaction and the degree of trust between the parties.

Efficiency consists of minimizing transaction costs, i.e. any activity which is undertaken in order to assure the parties of fair terms of exchange.

Thus, the means of transaction will vary (market, bureaucracy, etc.) by virtue of the perception of which type best generates a sense of fairness.

The classification of the modes of governance, on the basis of the notion of fairness proposed by Ouchi, is not without interest. Governance by the competitive market assures each party of fair terms of exchange. In a bureaucratic system, the perception of fairness depends on social consensus around the fact that the bureaucratic hierarchy exerts legitimate authority. In the clan, finally, the perception of fairness is the result of the congruence of the objectives of the parties in the exchange.

A paradox emerges from such reasoning applied to household electrical goods. Just as Williamson's analysis helps us to understand better how the Japanese market regulates itself, so Ouchi's approach sheds light on what may be called the American "free market." This corresponds quite well to the competitive market as described by Ouchi. An equilibrium between the parties establishes around accepted values that define better than any regulation what is tolerable and what is not. The problem is not one of transparency or healthy competition, but of responding to the demand for fairness formulated by each party. It is fair trade that the state must guarantee and the question of its capacity to intervene in this domain is clear to see. The USA itself recognizes that the field of concentration extends across the globe and attracts the presence of national, if not continental, champions, unencumbered by any competitive preoccupation other than in terms of international levels.

In Ouchi's terms and from the American perspective, if the conditions are to exist so that American industry performs competitively on the international markets, each party must satisfy the demand for fairness on the national market. This approach to fairness as a weapon of economic warfare throws light on the success enjoyed today by the themes of deregulation of international trade and competition. In Japan, on the other hand, producers ensure organizational integration that allows them to levy from their internal clients the investments they need to take on international competition.

From Transaction to Regulation

To substitute the concept of market for that of system is not a simple exercise in modifying vocabulary. The reasoning itself changes ground, and this grounding concerns the status we give to relational phenomena.

The research we have just surveyed reintroduces decisive contributions that touch upon behavior. This is clearly the case with borrowing from the concept of bounded rationality. That said, a major point of dissatisfaction remains. Just as the approaches we have examined allow us to make sense of transactions, so they do not allow us to get to grips with relational situations other than transactions.

The transaction itself remains trapped in a linear and compartmentalized conception. Each relationship of this type is a process involving two partners. Any analysis of a transaction occurs independently of another. The market unfolds as a succession of bilateral meetings, a discontinuous series of encounters.

Confronted with the reality of the terrain, no matter how seductive linearity may be, and even if they show us some important actors' strategies, these lines of reasoning seem singularly reductive, and the model-making they work towards satisfy more the demands of formal logic than the need to understand complex phenomena. For, as the evolution of organization theory demonstrates, the progress of scientific analysis depends upon the aptitude of one mode of thinking to integrate complexity, the characteristic inherent to all forms of collective action[4]. It is both the whole and the parts that any analytical dissection must try to pass under the microscope.

The Market, Systems and Game Margins

Applying systems thinking to a social and economic construct such as the market, pushes it to its logical endpoint. One is then able to detect the margins of action that come into place inside a field that is structured by the strategies and games of the agents who interact there.

In order to avoid simplistic reification of the system of action that the market forms, the analysis seeks to understand its mode of regulation. Where Williamson, for example, sees a market as seemingly equivalent to a state of nature, there appears instead a group of actors, individual or collective, pursuing private objectives that they attempt to reach by putting into action relational strategies in a universe that offers them resources even as it imposes constraints. These agents do not define themselves in their relationships (and thus in their behavior) by their simply belonging to a legally defined entity (firm, administration, etc.). This notion of organization, close to that of structure, falls to pieces when confronted with the facts. In the French market for household electrical goods, it seems that there is more solidarity, convergence of interests, or integration, between the members of the commercial networks of the manufacturers and the distributors, on the one hand, than there is between these sales forces and their own organization, on the other. One result is the emergence of particularist strategies integrated neither by the different "visible" organizations, nor by administrative, technical, institutional and hierarchical rules and procedures. The actors use these rules and procedures more as resources, constraints, elements of the game, than as statutes defining the game itself.

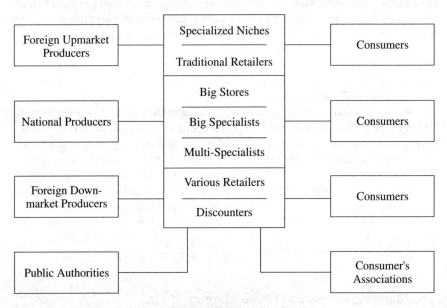

Figure 2:   The French System of Household Electrical Goods

For the succession of encounters, for interactions between two agents around a transaction cost, for the segmented vision of the market, it is therefore preferable to substitute the concept of a system of action. A system of action comes across as an arrangement of strategies played by actors implicated closely or at a distance, implicitly or explicitly, in the management of the same problem: for example, manufacturing and distributing household electrical goods.

The exchanges and interdependencies that mesh around the problem involve the intervention of various actors. Some intervene directly and voluntarily. Others come on the scene implicated in an indirect fashion, to the second degree, through others, and independently of their will. In this common arena, each manages her/his own specific problem, not identical to that managed by the others. In some way, the commercial exchange is no-one's problem in the daily life of a sector like household electrical goods. At the same time, the collective game that the others help, on an individual level, to structure, directly concerns everyone. One acts against but also through the others and the whole that they weave together. This dialectic between the system and the agent is at the heart of the analysis of action.

To each problem its own system. If the deal and the context are dissimilar then identity neither will nor should necessarily inhere in the system. What is more, the capacity of the actors to play strategies does not result mechanically from the examination (*marge d'appréciation*) which is particular to him or her, and which results from the calculation she/he makes. Again we must note that these systems are relatively stable. Thus, concerning the big household electrical goods producers in France, we can note a strong stability of the strategies, which reduces the uncertainty that such behavior may constitute for other actors. There are hardly any "moves" played in the field of technological innovation that the competitor does not know of before the marketing of the product that benefits from them and to which the competitor is able to react swiftly. At the same time, to say that the system structures itself around a problem, amounts to legitimizing the existence of the system as a specific construct, mediating between society as a whole and private individual interests.

To sum up these systems as either the aggregation or the accretion of bilateral adjustments, by referring to a logic of more global micro-phenomena, or to think of them as a kind of reproduction of hard realities better situated on a national or world scale, at political, technological or industrial levels, is quite mistaken.

Very different modes of collective construct emerge by different schemes of reasoning. Some come together around the fact of actors belonging to a common structure or organization. In this case, the analysis covers a field marked with attributes such as the phenomena of common "membership," a hierarchy of authority and a division of tasks, be these attributes more or less formalized. The classic example is that of a firm.

Other constructs mesh around a problem. Here, there is no formal co-ordination, and very little or no process of control through procedures but, instead, phenomena of redundancy, a social control of behavior, and a common system involving other actors whom we cannot escape from if we want to act. An example is the market for household electrical goods.

What can be said about much more complex and secret markets, across which their circulate goods that are both material (a certain quantity of petrol, for example) and immaterial (a cargo that does not yet exist)? Let us consider for one moment the definition often given of the petrol "spot market." Through this definition, we come to realize the exhaustion of classical approaches, and the valuable contribution of strategic systems analysis.

The free market becomes all the more difficult to grasp because, as it takes multiple forms, it is also very secret, seldom transparent, and only obeys unwritten rules, known and respected by the initiates alone. With the exception of the Merc[5], no organization centralizes its transactions, registers its market prices, or settle all its legal disputes. In the case of accidents, and they are more and more frequent at a time of crisis, each sorts out his own business. There is no real bankruptcy, just 'people we no longer deal with,' and who disappear in silence, occasionally to re-emerge after a long eclipse. Their name is hushed up, like the level of losses and profits achieved by the winners (Maurus 1986).

Each sorts out his own business. In fact, through the arrangement, it is the concept of regulation that becomes vital. What constitutes the regulation of a system is the collection of arrangements that the actors of this system reach in order, with time, to render compatible their divergent strategies (Crozier and Thoenig 1976). A postulate underlies such a definition: stability, or at least the survival of the system itself, marks the limit upon the actors' strategies, and thus a kind of minimum common objective often implicitly sought.

Thus, in France, among the three main national producers, the thousands of salesmen and the millions of consumers, no-one wants to see the electronics market brutally disintegrate and become totally dependent on other actors or systems, be it the state, through the authoritarian fixing of prices, qualities and quantities, or abroad, by the "uncontrolled" importation of products lacking any household name recognizable to the consumer.

The modes of regulation constitute a type of meta-rule of the game, one that regulates other rules in the game. They are widely implicit. Their content is constructed in the course of action itself. Their nature is widely social. The player does not simply operate within the parameters of utility, in the narrow and egocentric sense of a game. S/he takes part in a system, a collective whole, and their status as member imposes upon them much wider obligations. The player is in fact an actor, in the sense where the concept of actor evokes more clearly the collective dimension that relational life underpins. The actor perceives, reacts, lends support, and is moved; she/he manages issues, resources and constraints that are financial and commercial, but also cultural, normative, symbolic, convivial and political. Systemic interdependence and exchange constitute an instrument that actors use and fashion in their own way, but they also constitute a norm that they integrate and bow to.

An example taken from a domain other than that of household electrical goods illustrates better the concept of regulation and allows us to show what it offers us in terms of action. It is to do with the system that is being created in France, assimilated to a market, around the public transportation of goods across land (Dupuy and Thoenig 1979).[6] The attention that public authorities, in this case the head of transport in the ministry of that name, pay to transport, follows a line of reasoning that mixes legalism and cynicism. The world of road-haulers in an amoral one in which everyone commits fraud (on the distances covered, on the quantities or qualities carried, on driving time, etc.). This fraud is harmful to the collectivity in so much as it is first and foremost an intolerable disorder (disrespect for the law). More concretely, it translates into a growth in the number of heavy lorries involved in road accidents. From this appreciation of the situation, there result both the solutions proposed by the administration corresponding to increases in regulations and controls, and the vicious circle that these set off: the more controls and regulations there are, the more fraud there is.

The analysis of the "transport system" allows us to discover a reality that is very different and much more complex. The haulers are not the only actors. Also present are loaders, those who have goods to transport, and who decide to do it through a transport company. Why do they not do it themselves? It is precisely because they live with the contradiction between their constraints as producers – to get out a product, then to transport and deliver it – and specific constraints bearing on transport itself: the respect of loads and driving times, etc. In some way, the loader seeks to pass on to others the legal constraints that he does not want to transgress directly. Thus, one may note that it is not surprising that the hauler is not always addressed directly. Generally, one passes through an "auxiliary" (*auxiliaire*), a veritable specialist in bulking, in the search for a good hauler for the right load, an expert in the art of fraud, which is sub-contracted, of course, to the one person in the system who is sufficiently impoverished to accept it: the small hauler, the least powerful actor in the system of actor relations.

In this world, what distinguishes the big from the small is not the abstract economic and statistical criteria of the number of lorries owned, but the capacity to make the weaker carry out "high risk" tasks or potential fraud situations. For the systemic problem is not fraud, but freight. Fraud just represents a means, a solution in a way, of trying to control the real uncertainty, which is loading. From then on, not only does everything regulate itself around fraud, but, moreover, the public authorities, by targeting it, only serve to increase the degree of dependency of those who are already the most dependent: the small haulers. By taking fraud as a problem, and not as a regulation, we prevent ourselves from finding real means of reducing it. Knowledge of the system is the pre-condition for action.

The example is not unique. It recalls a famous case from the annals of organization theory. Crozier shows with great insight that in the workshops he studies (Crozier 1973), the breakdown of machines is not a problem for the actors of the systems, but rather a solution, a regulation enabling us to understand the strategies of different groups. The time for machine repairs thus becomes the result of a negotiation, of an agreement between the parties concerned, much more than a piece of objective technical data.

In the analysis of the French market for household electrical goods, disrespect for the law (refusal to sell [*refus de vente*] on the one hand, dumped prices and sales drift on the other) are so many solutions found by the actors present, in order to manage their obligatory interactions. Even the Japanese market, with its reputation for being so different, seemingly regulated under the auspices of the "Free Trade Committee," knows these type of regulations. One can identify them as the multiplication of false technological innovations, entailing an over-rotation of household equipment.

The problem becomes more interesting, but also more delicate to touch on, when we turn our attention to the cost of these regulations. It is doubtless one of the limits of the sociological analysis of organizations not to have looked at this problem, probably because the regulation's practice is not obvious at first sight.

Let us first of all make a distinction between what we call a regulation cost and what Williamson calls a transaction cost. In the latter case we are dealing with the directly economic stakes of an encounter between two individual or collective actors. The regulation cost represents, however, the imperfection of the agreements at the heart of the system, the fact that the regulations, in so much as they are products of one or several negotiations, cannot be analyzed as perfect solutions, in relation to a theoretical optimum that would be a nil cost, or a maximum gain for each party. On the contrary, we are talking in most cases of half-way solutions, acceptable to everyone, but in reality, satisfying to no-one. In that sense, the analysis abandons any moral or emotional view of things (they're all fraudsters! Nobody works!). In fact, no-one commits fraud, cheats and transgresses the rules and procedures through desire or vice. It is prosaic, but fraud turns out to be the least evil individual adjustment in a system of given constraints.

Regulations and their Cost

It is because they are imperfect solutions, in the sense defined, that regulations have a more or less easily identifiable cost. In the example quoted above of the industrial production workshop, the machine breakdown and the game played out within or around it result in a fall in productivity. In the case of the road transportation of goods, to drive for too long or overloaded significantly increases the risks of accidents. In the same way, the rotation of household electrical goods on the Japanese market entails a high price level for the consumers.

Identifying who bears the cost of regulation is of obvious documentary interest. In fact, the usefulness of the approach goes well beyond the designation of those excluded and those who pay. It performs the function of revealing the workings, and hence, the process of stability-change, of the system.

The actors who bear the brunt of collective adjustments can be internal or external to the system itself. The effects induced by the modes of regulation are sometimes directly financial, most often indirect, and their content brings together factors that are ascriptive, emotional, symbolic, physical, etc. Who are the payers, what do they pay for, and how does the system give rise to particular processes of costs and payers?

Without doubt, the reply is more difficult to find than in Williamson's zero-sum game; or in the distribution of fairness, in the work of Ouchi. We are undoubtedly dealing with the markets "opaque" zone whose legitimacy Cotta champions. By referring to the observation of the different types of collective constructs – bureaucratic organizations, open organizations, systems of action – a more general proposition emerges. The actors of a system have all the more chances of reaching agreements and finding regulations, as they are making other people bear their costs.

Despite its banal appearance, this proposition enables us to make progress in the reading of the regulations of social systems. In the case of the production workshop, the three groups of actors present come to an agreement all the more easily upon the time taken repairing breakdowns as neither productivity nor the cost-price of production are a major problem for them. In the domain of an industrial monopoly (the manufacture of tobacco and matches), they have every latitude for making the customers pay for their arrangements, through, for example, the taxes slapped on the product they manufacture. As for the management of the factories in which these workshops are situated, its "laissez-faire" approach derives neither from laziness nor cowardice. It is the downside that this management agrees to pay in order to see social peace assured directly in the workshop by the dominant group of workers.

In the case of the land transport of goods, the cost of fraud lies in an excess of accidents (i.e. *sur-accident*). Now, the French road system is able to spread across the whole of car drivers this excess cost (i.e. *sur-coût*) by way of having the insurance companies and therefore the private car owners paying for the fraud of the haulers. The universe of freight transport looks after itself even better around fraud as the actors implicated (loaders, auxiliaries, carriers) pass the cost of it onto actors who are not themselves implicated, particularly personal car-owners. It is this mechanism that we call the externalization of costs, and which explain the greater or lesser capacity of the organizations and the systems to resolve the problem of bounded rationalities, finding agreements and regulations that enable us to solve the problem that all sociological writings agree to recognize as at the heart of the problematic of collective action: co-operation.

The externalization of regulation costs is neither a fatality nor a condition for stability, let alone of smooth functioning. When the cost is internalized, i.e. taken charge of by the actors themselves, the organization or the system shows real stability, just as real as in the case of transfer to paying third parties. The difference lies in the fact that in the latter case, the organization or the system must put into place management processes that allow internal payers, those who bear material pressure, social or psychological, to stand up for themselves, to take the shock in the medium term, or else this shock must provoke a transmission of these costs amongst a larger number of persons and groups.

Such is the case in a business that uses industrial managers – factory bosses and production leaders – as the social mechanism called on to arbitrate between the contradictory requirements, demands and pressures of marketing, quality, management control and purchasing. It is up to them to come up with compromise, flexibility and the balancing act between producing both at low cost (and thus obeying effects of scale and apprenticeship) and flexibly (minimal stocks, immediate reaction to the variations in the tastes of the consumers). Their situation is difficult. Many cannot bear the shock, be it physical or psychological. The flip side of this internalization, and which assures the organization of great stability, lies in the setting-up, through career management, of safety-nets for those individuals who snap in the face of so many pressures, whose integration they have to ensure alone, in their own little corners. The safety-nets combine periods of conversion to other functions, periods of retreat, and temporary "retirement," the retirement being managed so that each receives a second chance. This reading grid leads us to a classification or model-making of the organizations and systems that would start with the greater or lesser capacity to externalize the costs of their regulations. First of all, the concept of externalization of costs allows us to record in terms other than strictly economic, the opposition established by the theorists between the public and private sectors, or even the opposition market/hierarchy so dear to Williamson. In fact, the more an organization, a system, or even a subsystem of a vaster whole finds itself in a monopoly situation, the more the actors that make it up have a strong capacity to make their customers, external partners, and more generally their environments, pay for the costs of their own inner adjustments. Conversely, the competitive situation diminishes this capacity and obliges the actors to divide these costs amongst themselves.

The theory of bureaucracy thus takes on a significance completely different from that of exploring it by the culture of peoples or the wickedness of leaders. What the public, for instance, sees in administrative bureaucracy (to use the current sense of the word) as length in procedures, waiting, and complication of dossiers, can be understood as the externalization of the costs of the agreements between the civil servants onto a clientele not simply captive, but under obligation. If the phenomenon does not take on greater scope, it is because the administration, forming a system with its environment, is obliged to find agreements other than those allowing it to live quietly with its hierarchical relationship.

It is thus the distinction between competition and monopoly, much more for example, than that between public and private, which appears to be at work when trying to understand the working of systems. Thinking of an analogy, we can take up for systems what Kornai wrote for bureaucracy, that its nature tempts it to extend its field of intervention with a view to reducing any erratic process imputed to the market or to its own errors (Kornai 1984). Any system, however open it may appear to be, tends to constitute itself as a monopoly, in order to control its environment and thus facilitate the negotiation of agreements, between its members. In this sense, the word market, which ensures the plurality of actors and rationalities, should not leave us under any illusions. Under cover of openness, a market can set itself up as a monopoly, and co-ordinate economic activity that depends on it in a bureaucratic way, i.e. through vertical relationships (between producers and consumers, for example) bringing into existence a hierarchy of functions.

"The acceptance of orders dispensed by the co-ordinator is ensured by a pressure or constraint codified by a piece of legislation recognizing rights and duties" (Rochet 1985: 26).

To this Weberian inspired definition, we will simply oppose the idea that pressure does not take for granted written codes. It may be completely informal and result from a power situation at the heart of a system. This is the case of the Japanese market for household electrical goods, on which the dominant position of the manufacturers allows them to impose a very hierarchized form of co-ordination (producers → distributors → final customers). Integration, or co-ordination among the three parties, translates the capacity of the producers to impose their logic on the distributors, who pass the cost on to the customers.

Thus the learned distinctions between forms of co-ordination no longer appear relevant. Co-operation across the market, bureaucratic co-ordination, be it ethical or aggressive, appropriation by vote, bargaining, the market or the plan appear as models that are too abstract when set alongside what the strategic analysis of markets reveals.

Similarly, this perspective enables us to advance in the analysis of the business. Understand it as a combination of subsystems, which, on their own or with their relevant environment, try to create for themselves monopoly or power situations. The situation can be frequently observed in the purchasing services of the firms, who, playing with the suppliers, and in order to find arrangements with them, externalize the excess cost arising from the accumulation of over-large stocks. The logic of purchasing in great quantities, which constitutes the ground for agreement between the firm's buyer and the supplier, to the detriment of their management logic, generates these stocks.

More generally, the heart of the universes of production, the often insoluble problem posed by the reduction of intermediary stocks is not a technical problem, but a sociological one. The stock does not result solely or mainly from the logic of a given process of production, but is rather an arrangement between the different services making up the productive sector, and managing conflicting constraints. This is why the pressure to reduce stock does not put into play the good will, habits and routines of the different actors, but their deep regulations. By not understanding that, or paying attention to the internal mechanisms of externalization of costs, we end up with the computerized management of phantom stocks, a modernized version of the traditional implicit agreement.

Change and the Systems Analysis Approach

Thinking in terms of actors strategies and systems of action definitely provides us with a method, a concrete tool allowing us to know the workings of human and social universes, which structure themselves around problems demanding co-operation, and thus exchanges and interdependencies.

In a synthetic way, the analytical approach breaks down into a series of steps that aim to identify key points, situations and processes:

- identifying strategies and actors (or coalitions of actors) who control relevant uncertainties to the players, the issues at stake, and constraints and resources;
- the nature of modes of regulation, apprehended through the type of cost derived from relational games;
- the actors, internal or external to the system, bearing the cost of agreements other actors negotiate directly or not to make their strategies compatible inside the system;
- the consequences of these processes for the system under consideration, particularly in terms of change and adaptation to new realities, in the face of other collective constructs and problems.

Applied in the form of a grid to the example of household electrical goods and for each of the three countries considered on the question of this market (France, Japan, United States), this approach translates itself into a graph that summarizes the diagnosis, the strengths and weaknesses, but also the degree of stability of each of the systems or markets under scrutiny.

In the perspective of systems analysis, change takes on an absolutely precise meaning. The term of systemic or organizational change applies to any transformation of the modes of regulation governing the collective construct and its actors. The strategies of change consist of modifying the game, redealing the cards and the rules, for example by structuring new integration's of contradictory rationalities. For that, two conditions are necessary: that one or several actors have an interest in changing and at the same time have the power to change the collective game, or that resources and constraints are reallocated in another way, for example by a modification of the context and by an outside body (the public authorities). The method of change consists, then, of reintroducing the costs of arrangements into the system itself or, on the contrary, to pass on internal costs to the foreign third paying parties, peripheral to the system or the organization.

Systemic analysis, finally, reveals itself to be extremely stimulating when helping to give a less abstract and ideological grounding to the question of action by public authorities. It completely overturns the usual thinking that consists of taking as read, as the point of departure, the existence of a governmental actor, its laws, public agencies, and the rhetoric of its objectives and measures. Systems analysis settles on exactly the opposite, the point of arrival: the detection of a certain number of concrete effects induced in the system, its actors and their regulations, by such an intervention or non-intervention of its agents, but especially by the use of public rules and governmental agencies as resources and constraints that other actors make in regard to third parties and in daily life. The graph thus sketched takes on another dimension. It involves showing the state in practice.

Concretely, it is a sprinkling of direct and indirect effects that emerges from the analysis. The temptation is to conclude from this that major effects are perverse, unexpected or dysfunctional, and that the discourse is thus hollow. From this, to slip into an apology for the absence of the impact of the state upon the markets would be vain, as vain as the simplistic idea that the state wants to or must defend the people against the bosses, the consumers against the monopolists. Such an idea dominates the legitimacy of public action, and founds it on a moral vision, much more than on a concrete perception of reality. In this sense, public policies of intervention in the market remain marked by a lack of realism and bring about a certain number of uncontrolled effects of which the consumer is far from being the first and main beneficiary.

Conclusion

In good methodological fashion, the feeling of mosaic-like dispersal disappears rapidly if the veil of ideological prejudices and iconoclastic critiques lifts through the adoption of reasoning in terms of regulations and arrangement costs. To take the case of France, it is true that the state is at the periphery while it claims to place itself at the heart of things. Should we then throw out the baby with the bath water? To rephrase that, public intervention is not negligible, far from it. Simply, its structuring impact is not found in daily life where measures taken twenty or forty years ago once situated it. A brilliant illustration of this is the case of the outlawing of the refusal to sell decreed (*refus de vente* in France) in 1945 in order to "protect" the consumer against the black market. It is a lever, little spoken of, but whose gradual effects are essential at a collective level. It has considerably helped the great consumerist distributors gain a strong advantage upon national brand manufacturers, by allowing their stores to use brands having a high score of awareness as *produits d'appel*, the attracted end-consumer being offered house-brands and foreign products once in the shop. Is it simply a question of casting aside its existence or, more wisely, of managing more consciously its nature in a complicated world for which no-one is completely responsible, and of which no-one is master? Without doubt, better reasoning means truer debate.

Notes

[1] The authors would like to thank Stewart Clegg for the detailed editorial work that he performed on their text.
[2] The specific comparison about white goods in France, Japan and USA has been analyzed in details by Dupuy and Thoenig (1986).

[3] In Williamson and Ouchi's reference the debate is broad (see Greffe X. 1991). Hegner
     F. makes a distinction between three modes of institutional arrangement structuring
     coordination, the evalation of performance and guidance of actors: solidarity, hierar-
     chy, market exchange. An interesting but sometimes abstract critique of Williamson's
     perspective, has been offered by Moullet.
[4] A good contribution to this debate from the theory of organizations has been made by
     Astley and Van de Ven (1983).
[5] Merc or Nymex: New York Mercantile Exchange. This is a market where future oil
     contracts are made.
[6] The interface between the actors of public authorities and the market as a system of
     action in the field of public transportation has been analyzed in this reference.

References

Astley, G.W., and Van de Ven, A. (1983), Certain Perspectives and Details in Organization
    Theory, in *Administrative Science Quarterly*, 28, pp. 245-273.
Benson, J.K. (1975), The Interorganizational Network as a Political Economy, in *Adminis-
    trative Science Quarterly*, 20, pp. 229-249.
Burns, T., and Flam, H. (1987), *The Shaping of Social Organization*. London, Sage.
Cotta, A. (1985), *Distribution, Concentration et Concurrence*. Paris, Institut de Commerce
    et de la Consommation.
Crozier, M. (1973), *The Bureaucratic Phenomenon*. Chicago, Chicago University Press.
Crozier, M., and Thoeing, J.C. (1976), The Regulation of Complex Organized Systems, in
    Administrative Science Quarterly, 21, pp. 547-570.
Dahl, R., and Lindblom, C. (1963), *Politics, Economics and Welfare*. New York, Harper
    and Row.
Dupuy, F., and Thoenig, J.C. (1979), Public Transportation Policy Making in France, in
    Policy Sciences, 11, pp. 1-18.
Dupuy, F., and Thoenig, J.C. (1986), *La loi du marché*. Paris, L'Harmatton.
Greffe, X. (1981), *L'analyse économique de la transaction*. Paris, Economica.
Hegner, F. (1986), Solidarity and Hierarchy: Institutional Arrangements for the Coordina-
    tion of Actions, in Kaufmann, F.X./Majone, G./Ostrom, V./with assistance of Wirth, W.
    (eds.). *Guidance, Control, and Evaluation in the Public Sector*. Berlin, New York, de
    Gruyter, pp. 407-429.
Hirsch, P. (1975), Organizational Effectiveness and the Institutional Environment, in *Ad-
    ministrative Science Quarterly*, 20, pp. 327-344.
Kornai, J. (1984), *Socialisme et Economie de Pénurie*. Paris, Economica.
Lebledici, H., and Salancik, G.R. (1982), Stability in Interorganizational Changes: Rule-
    making Processes of the Chicago Board of Trade, in *Administrative Science Quarterly*,
    27, pp. 227-242.
Maitland, I., Bryson J., and Van de Ven, A. (1983), Sociologists, Economics and Oppor-
    tunism, in *Academy of Management Review*, 10 (1), pp. 59-65.
Maurus, V. (1986), Un marché sans foi ni loi, in *Le Monde Aujourdhui*, 2-3 February, pp. 3-
    4.

Moullet, M. (1982), Modes d'échange et coûts de transaction: une approche comparative du marché et de la firme, in *Sociologie du Travail*, 4, pp. 484-490.

Perrow, C. (1967), A Framework for a Comparative Analysis of Organizations, in *American Sociological Review*, 32, pp. 194-208.

Rochet, X. (1985), Une bureaucratie peut en cacher une autre, in *Analyses de la S.E.D.E.I.S.*, 48, pp. 25-27.

Thompson, G., Frances J., Levacic R., and Mitchell, J. (eds.) (1991), *Markets, Hierarchies and Systems*. London, Sage.

Williamson, O.E., and Ouchi, W.G. (1981), The Markets and Hierarchies: Program of Research: Origins, Implications, Prospects, in Van de Ven, A., and Joyce, W.F. (eds.), *Perspectives on Design and Behavior*. New York, Wiley, pp. 347-370.

Williamson, O.E. (1975), *Markets and Hierarchies: Analysis and Antitrust Implications*. New York, Free Press.

Woodward, J. (1958), *Management and Technology*. London, HMSO.

Rational Expectations? Education Policy and the Language of Management in Australia

Jane Marceau

Introduction

In recent years a succession of policy decisions in the education field in Australia has created an impression that the language of policy has become subservient to the language of management and "rational expectations" in all spheres. This impression is probably not unique to Australia. In many countries, the last decade has seen a shift in the kinds of policies thought appropriate in different spheres and in the language used to justify policy choices. When decision-makers wish to advocate particular directions for policy change they seem to feel that they must first translate their proposals into a more apparently "neutral" language, a technocratic tongue that appears to take the politics out of policy. Derived from the province of rational economics, the language dominates the policy "implementation" doctrines summarized in the phrase "managerialism."

The Goals of Education

Two elements are central to this chapter. The first is the tensions inherent in the expectations which western societies have developed about the roles the education system is to play. These societies have wanted education to play simultaneously socially unifying and socially sorting roles and to be at once the major vehicles for social continuity and for social transformation. These broadly inconsistent expectations have been incorporated into law in many cases and into the training of the teachers who are charged with translating the goals laid down by government into the every day learning activities of pupils from every social milieu. Thus the controllers of the system frequently hold views about its goals and functioning which are different from those of the systems operators.

The second element is the failure of law makers to recognize the ambiguities in making policy choices. In particular, the language used now, especially at federal government level in Australia, acts to disguise basic differences of objective by seeking to reduce the making of all policy questions to a set of limited common criteria: efficiency and effectiveness. This reduction is achieved by the use of the "language of management" in both the development and the justification of the policy directions selected rather than simply the implementation of choices made.

Failure to come to grips with contradictions in the broad goals vitiates much thought about education. In the past, the lower levels of the system, particularly lower secondary education, were the place where both sorting and equity functions were concentrated. It was there that the problems were most obvious. With the shift to, or at least towards, mass tertiary education, the incompatibilities of goal have become obvious at higher levels. Instead of recognizing these problems openly, however, policy-makers have come increasingly to interfere in the internal workings of the system as though managerial changes would be enough to reconcile major goal differences. The focus is on the running of the system rather than on the goals.

While public interference in education is not a recent phenomenon, in the past it was justified by explicit reference to broad social and political goals: now the justification is couched in the language of business and owes much to the preoccupation with the economy rather than broader social efforts towards social justice or equality. Many shifts in education policy over time derive from the efforts of decision-makers to come to grips with the tensions involved in their arena. The choice of policies swings between emphasizing the instrumental and expressive, between education for what economy and society are thought to "need" and what individuals want and need beyond the demands of the labor market. As educational goals have again swung towards the instrumental so too the language of management has come to dominate discussion. Let me illustrate this with a little educational policy history, but first a potted history of public policy in Australia.

The Rise and Rise of Public Policy

The idea of "public policy" relates intimately to the rise of the state as a central actor in the social and economic affairs of a community. Beginning with external defense and internal security, by the mid-twentieth century the state in western societies had acquired an overwhelming role in regulating almost every sphere of life. Reflecting this process and following the trend in all OECD countries, until 1983 public expenditure in Australia grew to ever higher levels and increased as a proportion of GDP.

If we think of public policy as decisions about directions and actions which are made by public authorities – from the Cabinet of Ministers down to the clerks at the counter in local employment offices – as decisions which involve first the raising and then the allocation of public revenues between competing goals, we have a very general definition. If we think of public policy as a state's attempts first to interpret the world and then to use the interpretations to achieve particular results with specific decisions we are getting closer to an operational definition.

Public policies regulate the activities of citizens as they go about their daily business. That regulation may be "active," where public decision-makers seek to achieve given ends, or it may be "passive" in that the regulatory activity is designed to provide the conditions in which people can take initiatives. In other words, public policy and state intervention may be permissive, imperative or stimulatory. The organizational knowledge or managerial theories which underlie policies selected are not necessarily the same in each case.

Public decisions in any arena may necessitate the creation of new institutions, productive or administrative, or at least the reform of old ones. When this happens state intervention has created new actors in the arena, actors who will develop a new set of interests and to some extent define their own purposes and policy directions, thus influencing policy decisions. In examining public policies and their impact on education we therefore need to consider not just the policies as such, the initial intentions, but also the way in which they are implemented, financed, developed and evaluated as these also influence what is recognized as appropriate "organizational knowledge" and become essential parts of the policy adopted.

Finally here, it is important to remember that policies are usually the result of compromise and conflict rather than fact and consensus. Policy-making in modern societies is highly complex and the influences behind particular policy decisions are related to the positions of the players in the wider social and economic as well as the organizational and properly political environment. Policies are therefore about power relations as well as about particular intentions.

Theories and Models

As Carol Weiss (1977) has taught us to recognize, inside every policy decision is an implicit causal model. Every time policy-makers develop and ultimately choose between alternative courses of policy action they are using a theory. That theory is necessary to interpret the world, to explain why it is operating as it is and to deduce what it is necessary to do to get the world to change in the way desired. The policy-maker choosing a course of action is saying in effect that if we do "x" we will achieve "y." In other words, the decision-maker is using a theory about why the world is as it is, a theory of the past, and also a theory about how the world will be when the intervention has been made, how it can be induced to change permanently and prevented from reverting to the initial position after a short period.

Policy-makers always operate with such theories. Like writers of prose, however, they mostly do it without realizing. The theories they use are mostly based on "ordinary knowledge," pragmatic knowledge based on experience, on social practice, on observed correlation's or half-remembered ideas. But sometimes a discourse structured from particular elements comes to dominate, becoming the widely agreed vehicle for expressing policy ideas. This has recently become the case with the language of management. Part of policy-maker's "ordinary knowledge" is composed of "ideas in good currency." These ideas are derived from research by social scientists and others which is gradually incorporated into the accepted discourse of any policy field. The major constituents of the discourse are the concepts linking broader social theory and the "facts" of the policy situation. They are a filtering device and constitute the building blocks of what Stewart (1982) calls the "policy story," the story which must be constructed so as to make policy alternatives and choices first intelligible and then acceptable as well as effective.

In developing their discourse, in constructing the "stories" which underlie policy advice, decision-makers attempt to convince their audience that their solutions are appropriate to the problem in hand. Since policy problems are socially constructed there is "choice" about the importance to allocate to specific issues or indeed about the recognition of "issues" as amenable to policy action at all. In that construction, the choice of issues and the way they are put together are too often taken for granted and insufficiently examined.

It has become commonplace to say that one cannot have education without a notion of "education" which will vary over time and place. It is still worth understanding, however, that different interpretations will suggest different policy interventions. Since the system (as indeed the concept) of education is a social construction, we need to see who, socially speaking, is determining it at any one time and to what ends. Before the Second World War, for instance, educational ideas were much shaped by notions of "intelligence," devised by psychologists who dominated the debates. In contrast, much post-war research pointed to the predominantly social nature of so many characteristics once thought of as "natural" and therefore not amenable to policy action (Bourdieu and Passeron 1970). In recent years governments obsession with the economy rather than the society they are in charge of has changed operational notions of what education is about and thus the policy interventions deemed appropriate. More important, managerialist language has become so dominant that it defines not only what to do about an issue but also understanding of the issue itself. This has occurred because the language of management has been used in the creation of a new policy paradigm.

Paradigms and Approaches

The concepts and the theory used to create policy build up to form an internally coherent paradigm. Paradigms, according to Kuhn (1962) who popularized the term in his seminal work, "The Structure of Scientific Revolutions" are ill-defined collections of value-orientations, theories, techniques, and criteria for selecting problems and defining acceptable solutions on which scientists more or less tacitly agree. It may be suggested that policy decisions are made within a policy paradigm in the same way that scientific discourse occurs within a scientific paradigm. Like scientific ones, policy paradigms are continually tested in interaction with other elements of the "real world" and, again like scientific ones, policy paradigms occasionally fail. When this happens they have to be replaced and, after a period of what Blume once thought of as "casting about in the broader stream of intellectual debate," a new paradigm emerges. During that period of "casting about" there is considerable discussion about how to explain observed phenomena or, in the case of policies, observed problems and unsolved issues.

Paradigms, then, are essentially a set of lenses for looking at issues, and the theoretical and analytical interconnections which can be perceived within them guide the advice given to policy-makers in any given area of public concern and intervention by the state. At any time one is usually dominant and is used by the controlling areas of government to mold decisions made in the "follower" segments, such as education.

The growth of the state in western nations from the mid-19th century onwards was everywhere accompanied by growth in public interest in the process and content of the education of a nation's young people. The state intervened everywhere extensively in the system of education, determining largely not only what is taught, but also how, where, by whom and at which point in the life cycle. In the 19th century, state education policies aimed at social stability, at "attaching" children to the society being created around them. In the post-1945 period, in the minds of public policy-makers in many western societies education changed its role, becoming in their vision a major agent of social change, charged with "destabilizing" existing relationships so as to create a new society. In a period when the state was much better established and its legitimacy came to depend essentially on successful economic management, education was charged with a further major role in the economy.

While the economy was growing it seemed to public policy-makers that the production and distribution roles and the equality of opportunity roles of education could be relatively easily adopted simultaneously as major policy goals. Three decades ago many students saw university education as a "consumption" good, a vision linked to a general belief in a broad liberal education as the basis of the proper citizen. Recently, however, education has come to be seen again as predominantly a "production" good. The current paradigm sees education as a service activity, as essentially "reactive" to the forces or "needs" of other social areas. Paradoxically education is still given a transformation role but it is one which is essentially linked to fitting individuals into the niches created by the economy. In other words, education is given the role of facilitating "economic" change but not of facilitating overall social transformation.

Education and the State

Formal education, in the sense of classroom learning in special institutions, did, of course, exist before the 19th century in western Europe but only on a very small scale. Schools, like hospitals, developed at the same time as the industrial revolution; as changing technology and markets took production out of the home and into a special building with specialist labor, so too the broader need for the skills of reading, writing and calculation, linked to greater social and professional mobility, brought formal education out of the "nursery" and into the "public" sphere, into special buildings with special labor. Early schools were, of course, wholly privately funded. Following the upheavals of the industrial revolution, however, the state quickly became involved and the existing private schools were soon swamped by establishments of the newly created public system – publicly funded, publicly regulated and publicly accountable.

Why, then, was the state so interested? There were, of course, many reasons, some linked to the growing disaffection with the industrial system of many groups among the working class and the displaced rural proletariat in most European countries. In Australia, as in Europe, the "lenses" or paradigms used by policymakers were focused on the need to attach individual citizens to the state. Periods of political and economic turbulence suggested to dominant social groups the need to find a method of systematically developing a value system which could be the base of a new social consensus. The exact recipe for this varied from country to country but it is striking that countries as geographically, culturally, politically and socially distant as Britain, Germany, France, the USA and Australia, all developed state-dominated public education systems within a very few years of each other and used much the same rationale.

Political concerns were clearly important in late 19th century discussions of the aims of education in Australia. The interests of the state and the cultivation of "good citizenship" were heavily emphasized in the 1890s and directly related to the extension of the vote and responsible government. As the author of a Schools Commission Discussion Paper on "Equality of Educational Opportunity; Diversity and Choice" pointed out in 1980, parliamentarians of the late 19th century were wont to assert that "where universal suffrage is, then universal education must be" while in New South Wales the claim was made that it would be "easier to govern educated people." In Tasmania, one parliamentarian, when asking himself what the state wished to accomplish by undertaking to provide and perpetuate state education, concluded that "they wanted to make all children good and useful citizens, to have them taught to respect and obey the laws of the state and to fill the various positions they were fitted for with profit to themselves and advantage to the state" (quoted, Schools Commission 1980: 14).

During the early decades of the 20th century the political theme was still common. Tate, arguing in 1909 for an extension of the number of years of compulsory education, pointed out that, "It is not possible when dealing with immature minds to build up [quickly] a body of instruction that shall guide men and women in fulfilling their wider duties as citizens" (quoted, Schools Commission 1980: 18). Even as late as 1940, when Charles Fenner, then South Australian Director of Education, explained the reasons for providing a new kind of school, he said that the education provided would ensure that pupils went "back to their homes, their shops and their farms better citizens, with greater... ability to fulfill their place in the world" (quoted, Schools Commission 1980: 18).

In this early period, then, the provision of public education was clearly dominated by directly political issues. The impact on education of one of the principal concerns of public policy in recent western societies, that of ensuring political stability within a democratic framework, was extremely powerful. From the mid-19th to the mid-twentieth century, however, following other social and economic developments, new rationales for public investment in education, new lenses with which to see the role of schools, gradually began to command policy attention. By the late 19th century, industrialists were beginning to complain about the lack of skills of the workforce. In response, institutions of technical education were established in most western countries. Ideas about education's role in training for social and economic development as well as political stability began to influence educational decision-making.

From the end of the Second World War another major shift in policy paradigms took place almost everywhere. The major justification for the increased government intervention and regulation of social activities which has characterized all western societies since 1945 has been government responsibility for the proper management of the economy and, to a lesser extent, for the proper distribution of the "fruits of economic growth" to different sections of the population. That shift in the basis of the public legitimacy of state powers ensured that education policy would come to be dominated by two principal concerns. On the one hand came the "social compassion" concern, which gave to education the enormous task of being the vehicle through which left – leaning governments sought to promote their ideal of social equality which they interpreted as equality of opportunity. Schools were to be the mechanisms for developing the potential of every child so that he or she could rise in the social hierarchy through moving up the occupational ladder. Prolonged secondary education was to be the means of selecting the brightest so that they could continue their training in university or some other tertiary level institution. For the others provision was also to be made to enable them to obtain minimum occupational skills before entering the labor force. In effect, governments were forced into prolonging schooling by a huge increase in national demand as a means of individual betterment through greater educational and hence occupational opportunity: during the 1950s and 1960s members of the public began to keep their children in school well beyond the minimum school leaving age, although less so in Australia than in many other OECD countries.

On the other hand, it was increasingly argued that education should contribute to increased social and economic efficiency and effectiveness. Increased social

demand for education coincided with particular government concern about the
economy – first in the immediate post-war reconstruction period but secondly in
the 1960s when governments were first beginning to grapple with the impact of
new technology, changing markets and balance of payments crises. One "solution," which also owed something to the influence of the education industry itself,
was the expansion of the education system, this time including the universities.
Together often unlikely ideological bedfellows – ideas about social justice, views
which saw education as an investment good, and the interpretation in education
terms of "to each according to his desserts" – provided the rationale for quite radical policy choices such as the massive expansion of the higher education advocated by Robbins in the UK. In the 1960s, policy-makers in many western countries
felt that they could combine private opportunity and public benefits from expanding the education system: not only were young people to be allowed to develop
their potential to a maximum, but the country as a whole was also to benefit from
the education and training of a much larger "pool of talent."

During this period the dominant view among government advisers on education, however, came to be an "instrumental" one: public expenditure on education, they saw, could best be justified in terms of the return on investment seen in
increased productivity. At the same time, however, because the period was also
one of much broader social concerns, a different view of education, that which is
focused on the child and on his or her needs as the central concern of educational
endeavor, was also extremely strong. The second view focuses on the need to devise institutional and curricula arrangements which maximize a child's chances of
developing fully his or her "potential," in an expressive as well as an instrumental
manner. Rather than seeing education as a response to social or economic imperatives, the second view tends to focus on general education, on a child's wishes
as well as on aptitudes and aspirations. In policy terms, this view was translated
first into the extension of the years of common schooling so as to allow the child
to "mature" before making long-term judgments about his or her future. Second it
was translated into the increasing use in policy decisions of "individual demand"
as the parameter for deciding the amount and direction of education spending by
public authorities.

The view of education as a social "liberator" for the brightest of the disadvantaged classes was soon threatened by sociological research that indicated that the
education system in modern western societies functioned largely to sort children
so that once in the labor market they usually obtained posts that in terms of social
prestige and power were close to those of their parents. Far from being a force for
the massive transformation of social chances through providing greater equality
of opportunity, education systems had begun to seem conservative.

The sociological findings which referred to whole societies took public
decision-makers' attention off the functioning of schools and educational output
measured in terms of the particular achievement of individual children (Schools
Commission 1980) and returned to the overall relationship between education, hu-

man capital and social needs. This swing was facilitated by the 1970s recession. Particularly, the high incidence of youth unemployment began to turn policy attention once again to the economy and to an instrumental view of the purposes of education. At this stage there was a renewed focus on what took place inside individual schools. The book by Michael Rutter and his colleagues on what happened during the "15,000 hours" of secondary education suggested strongly that outcomes in terms both of equality of opportunity and intellectual skills were significantly affected by the organization and ethos of particular educational institutions. Thus, while in general, one might agree with Emerson who remarked in 1831 that "things taught in school are not an education," Rutter and his colleagues provided some evidence that inputs to schools are indeed very important in the outcomes. This and similar evidence became a justification for increased intervention in the functioning of the establishments of the education system. If individual children were to be helped as well as possible, government had to intervene.

The political rationale for supporting schools thus gradually shifted to a highly instrumental one. In Australia as elsewhere, recurring economic recession in the late 1980s and early 1990s meant that as part of their efforts to shift the Australian economy forward into an era of low industrial protection and greater exposure to the pressures of world trade, the government began to focus more on "value for money" and efficiency and effectiveness in the education system. Education in the last decade, even under Labor governments, had again become viewed as an adjunct of the economy. What, then, does this schematic history tell us about the impact of public policy on education policy?

The Importance of the Broad Political Agenda

The first lesson of our potted policy history is the importance of broad political concerns in shaping not only the education policy which is adopted but also in keeping certain education issues, even ones of priority to the teaching profession, off the policy agenda. The centrality of politics is particularly clear when major reforms of the system are undertaken or even contemplated. This is true both of reforms which aim to widen equality of opportunity and of reforms aimed at reinforcing the link between education and perceived economic interests. Major reforms depend on values: the impetus for change in a radical direction seldom seems to come from inside the teaching profession or indeed from inside public departments of education. Major reforms are part of a more general political package, as can be seen, for example, in the decision to end the socially divisive selective secondary schools and move to a comprehensive system.

In Australia, the domination of education policy by political concerns at federal level in the 1970s was seen in the period of reforms under the Labor government lead by Gough Whitlam from 1972-1975. In his major policy speech in

1972, the newly elected Prime Minister proclaimed that "the most rapidly growing sector of public spending under a Labor government will be education. Education should be the great instrument for the promotion of equality…" (quoted, Mathews 1983: 149). The creation of the new instruments of the Schools Commission and the Tertiary Education Commission gave the federal role in education an enormous boost. Such change could only have occurred as part of a package of reforms designed to increase the role of the Commonwealth government in areas traditionally not of much federal concern.

The political environment of the current Australian federal government, is, of course, very different. The Labor Party that Bob Hawke lead to electoral victory in 1983 inherited perhaps the high point of the consensual belief that the *raison d'être* of central government is to manage the economy and that only a government strong enough to change the parameters of action by all sectors of the nation can undertake that management successfully. As the economy has floundered in the face of international trends economic restructuring has become the central thrust of most government policy and economic goals have largely replaced social progress as legitimation for policy choices. Education has been bent to the task while at the same time suffering real losses in resources. Economy as well as economics has become the test of legitimate policy. The second thing our potted history tells us, therefore, is the great extent of the dependence of education policy both on the economy and on the controllers of government economic policy.

While both the education system and the economy were growing, the function of education as a redistributor of social chances could be as easily accepted by all decision-makers as the contribution to the economy expected from the system. In contrast, in times of stringency and where pensions, health and, above all, unemployment costs are politically more salient, education policy will be the poor relation. Similarly, in a situation where measured outcomes – whether in terms of increased equality of opportunity or the number of sums right on a given day – are apparently not giving "value for money," education policy must expect to be redirected. If education is seen to be failing on the production count, it would seem to have no chance at all of maintaining a strong position on a redistribution platform since the prevailing belief that redistribution can only occur once the overall size of the pie has been increased, will inevitably mean that attention is focused on productive and employment outcomes rather than social outcomes. In line with many other areas education policy will be scrutinized in terms of outputs rather than inputs. In Australia, the conclusions of the Quality in Education Committee's Report in 1985 was an early sign of this change. The third lesson our history teaches, then, is that the evaluation of the functioning of education is greatly dependent on a state's willingness to incur massive expenditure to achieve change in the social sphere as a whole. The emphasis on efficiency and effectiveness rather than broader goals is fed by concern for public expenditure as a whole.

The days of the paradigm describing education as a leader rather than a follower in social terms would seem to have gone, for the foreseeable future at least.

Very many of the contextual changes mentioned above are the results of deliberate government policy; others are the flow-on results inevitable in the densely-packed policy space of a modern western society. The fourth lesson from our potted history, therefore, is that once education has begun to define itself as essentially reactive to events and trends in other spheres of the society it will be judged by the criteria applying to policies in those other areas. To survive as large scale spender in an era of public sector thrift, the language of education has to emulate those languages which are dominant in other policy fields and shift its policy and evaluation justifications accordingly.

Australia is by no means alone is this. The increasingly politicized nature of the educational debate and to the increasing extent to which interests traditionally external to education are seeking to intervene in education decision-making and control of directions is general throughout the OECD.

It is noticeable, and goes far towards explaining the apparent paucity of achievement by education in its goal of promoting social equality, that education alone as an area of public policy has borne the major share of responsibility for progress towards offstated triple aims of achieving social equality, or at least equal opportunity, and social cohesion while also improving the national supply of productive skills (industry in Australia has been a very poor contributor to the latter task, see Marceau 1989). Each of these is an enormous task; trying to achieve all three in the context of a class divided as well as a multicultural society is probably impossible. Education is bound to be seen as failing on many counts and is therefore highly vulnerable to interference in its operations by a state and other players interested in clearly definable results.

In sum, then, policy cannot be separated from politics, as recognized by the French who use the term "politique" for both. Political decisions, closely related to the balance of social and economic power at any one time, ultimately determine education policy. Decisions in areas outside education shape both processes and outcomes within education and increasingly education's own values, as the system is forced to justify the public expenditure it receives in terms not of its own choosing but emerging from a different policy paradigm.

The Language of Management and Policy in Education

In his recent book on the economist mandarins who dominate public policy-making in Australia's federal capital, Canberra, Pusey (1991) has pointed to the extent to which privileged social background and secondary education have combined with a particular set of policy ideas. Drawn from and transmitted through a specific section of tertiary education these ideas, Pusey suggests, have become a screen for all other areas, the criterion against which all policy proposals are examined. Until now we have seen the rise and rise of public policy; so it seems at first sight paradoxical that it is the language of the market and the economic arena that has come to dominate policy discourse in all fields.

One important reason for the dominance of economic and managerialist ideas, it seems to me, is the need for governments to play both politics and policy and for Ministers representing widely divergent policy areas to win major battles in Cabinet. Political leaders must not only present the case for policy changes, especially for desired initiatives, but they must provide a language in which their proposals can be compared with the propositions of others. In a crowded policy arena and in a context of fiscal restraint proposals for expenditure on defense, social security, the arts and education must vie for space in both discussions and in budgets. To do this they must be seen as occupying a common arena. For the debate to be undertaken at all a common language of evaluation must be provided.

Second, the development of the social sciences and their concern to establish themselves as "scientifically respectable" has led to a focus on quantitative data as the basis of social analysis. The discipline of economics has established itself as an apparently "value-free" tool which permits decision-makers to focus on quantitative data which seem irrefutable to the uninitiated. In addition, the discipline has developed in such a way that it can provide powerful tools for dealing with the enormous complexity of the societies and economies with which ministers and their advisers must come to grips. It does this by simplifying social phenomena so that models can be created and manipulated to indicate the flow-on effects of particular decisions, not only in the immediate future but also in the longer term. In a policy space where no new policy can be brought in without affecting an existing one and in a situation of fiscal constraint when governments are seeking to gain what they see as full value for every dollar spent, such models have an obvious attraction to overworked decision-makers.

To some degree at least the means of arriving at policy goals have begun to subvert the ends because the means can be measured while the ends cannot and require other judgments. The problem with the emphasis on quantitative tools is that more "qualitative" data have been crowded out and broader thinking is discouraged. Indeed, the economic paradigm itself discourages the analyst from looking beyond what the "data" seem at first sight to be saying. This kind of blinkered thinking can be seen in education policy but perhaps the most telling recent example in Australia comes from EPAC and Treasury analysis of the "problem" of the increase in numbers of the aged. Rather than looking broadly at career arrangements which cast the elderly aside while forcing everyone to work full time for most of their lives or at the contribution of the aged to younger members of the society's welfare and good functioning through informal care arrangements, the authors of these documents focus only on long term projections of the cost of the aged to the workforce as though all other socially relevant arrangements could not change (EPAC 1994).

The Policy Process

For elucidation purposes analysts have broken the public policy decision-making process down into a number of stages. These are:

- creation of an agenda (salience of an issue);
- preparation of alternative options for action;
- choice of options and legitimation of the choices made;
- implementation of options;
- monitoring and evaluation;
- feedback, termination or recommencement etc.;
- legitimation of decisions taken.

While this model began as an analytical tool, it has come to have normative overtones as can be seen in the fact that the stages together have become known as the "rational" model of public decision-making. While its limitations are well documented and recognized, the great advantage of this model for people trying to change policy directions is that it can make plausible claims to be the approach "best" suited to analyzing policy options within an area or between and across areas in the current political and economic environment.

Rational economics is a unifying knowledge which fits well with the acceptable forms of legitimation associated with belief in rational decision-making. It further provides the methodologies used to define policy options. Even more important, it seems to be taking the politics out of policy. While policy-makers know from experience that in the real world most policy decisions are political, personal and ultimately chancy, that "muddling through" is usually the name of the game, they also know that in many cases they are supposed to make their recommendations seem apolitical and as the "logical" outcome of rationally developed and considered alternatives. But as long as dominant sources of policy advice, such as Treasury and Finance, use the "rationalist" approach the others are condemned to use it too.

A glance at the model outlined above indicates the division of the policy process into areas of "politics" and areas of "rationality." One can see the place where the quantifying and standardizing approaches of rational economics are indeed appropriate.

Recently, however, this approach has increasingly been used to take over the additional stages where the politics of the issue involving recognition of important social and cultural values have normally been the criteria used for the choices. The stages of the policy process which currently seem to be most subject to "rationalist" takeover and removal from the overt political arena are those of agenda creation and the justification of options selected. The criteria associated with "rationality" are now applied both to selecting and legitimating the choice of the items to put in central place on the political agenda (among the many that call for attention and scarce political time) and to justifying the options selected.

A further inroad is also being made. After policy options have been selected, during the stages of implementation and evaluation, the same criteria are applied again. It is here that the other language of the 1980s, that of "managerialism," takes over and corrodes the evaluation process. Managerialism is the organizational equivalent of economic rationalism and seeks to apply the same rather limited notions of allocative efficiency and policy effectiveness. It stresses the need for transparent budgeting and "getting value for money." While the first is unexceptionable the second raises major issues of value, timing and the interests of the clients of the policies concerned. More particularly, it tends to lead both to over-rapid evaluation and policy termination because the real rate of social change that is possible through most policy decisions is much slower than is imagined by observers of the "rational expectations" tendency. The language of economics and management tends to ignore any factors in policy success or failure that are associated with organizational limitations (such as time, scale and specificity) and to assume that organizations designed for one set of goals can be rapidly redeployed to answer another set of imperatives.

As mentioned earlier, all public policies that are systematically thought out include implicit theories about action, that if we do "x" then "y" will be the result. They are theories about how the world is organized, about how the relations between social groups are structured, about the forces creating overall economic and social patterns and of course about individual motivation, to name but a few of the dimensions. The new language of management has it made apparently possible to bring together into one corpus criteria used for evaluating policies in arenas where the state has played different roles, and where policies have been devised and operated with different theories of action. Its users have succeeded in making indisputable what are in fact highly diverse and debatable assumptions about how a society, in this case Australian society, works.

Trying to use a set of common concepts and a common language to describe, assess and make recommendations for change in very different arenas of public action forces policy thought to run along often inappropriately narrow channels. Taking a language developed in a very different field (the academic) further contributes to policy confusion because the language has not been created to solve practical problems. Further, the managerialist language reduces the likelihood of recognition of the legitimacy of particular values and political beliefs in the construction of public policies and inhibits appeal to such values as major guides for selecting action.

Where we used to use words and concepts such as "social justice" as the unifying language and criteria for action we now have efficiency and effectiveness. The latter concepts have their place but they need to be subject to guidance and direction, not to be the sole parameters for evaluation. Our policy theories need clearer definition. Finally, policies are usually the result of compromise and conflict rather than fact and consensus. Policy-making in modern societies is highly complex: the influences behind policy decisions are related to the positions of the players in the wider social and economic environment as well as to the organizational and properly political processes at work.

The Language of Management and Higher Education Policy in Australia

In the process of change policies for education – and for higher education in particular – have increasingly taken on an imperative rather than an exhortatory, stimulatory or permissive tone. The major reforms of 1987 transformed Australian higher education with little consultation with the constituencies. This was a political decision but one with an economic not a social justice motivation. Since that time, the Commonwealth government has become increasingly interventionist while using the rhetoric of "letting the institutions manage." The recent "quality" exercise in Australia is an excellent case in point.

The approach focuses on the following key terms: effective performance of the higher education system as reflected in the development and implementation of strategic planning, performance monitoring and review, according to agreed educational profiles for each institution. All universities were to have strategic management in place at the institutional level, involving the establishment not only of management but also information systems, for resource control and performance monitoring, on the presupposition that such systems are essential to accountability.

This approach to assessing the working of the universities has given rise to the creation of a whole new language unknown to university administrators who thought their role was to facilitate knowledge production and transmission. A recent document produced for the government was indeed forced to include a glossary to explain to readers such terms as management province, mission drift, niche migration and a host of different aspects of "quality" assessment, assurance, audit, control, culture, improvement, management and planning (Piper 1993:7). Quality management, the report goes on to explain, requires mission statements, value statements, and vision statements, aims, goals, objectives, targets and strategies. It requires rules and regulations, codes of practice, goal-setting, briefing and exhortation, staff performance review, training, incentives and rewards. It, of course, requires management maps and procedures for evaluating practice which in turn require sub-divisions designed to test efficiency, effectiveness, economy and policy evaluation and reference to the seven "Cs" – comprehensiveness, communication, cogency, coherence, consonance, constancy and consequence (Piper 1993). The author of the report admits that the "final proof of quality management is the quality of the organization, the merit of its mission and the efficiency with which it pursues that mission." However, "relying solely on that final proof may be impractical" (p. 33). The government has judged that "the quality of universities in general would be enhanced... by the widespread adoption of institutional quality assurance procedures. To this end, the minister's policy is to reward good quality management systems" (Piper 1993: 33).

In this list of management exhortations, transformed into imperatives by the promise of a share of an extra $70m, remarkably little attention is given to aspects of teaching learning and research that involve allocating more rather than less time and money. Thus students are asked to evaluate their existing courses but not to evaluate them against potential courses endowed with smaller classes, more individual tuition, greater interaction with staff actively engaged in well-funded research, not stretched by an ever increasing administrative burden and supported by excellent library facilities. In other words, students are being asked to evaluate courses supplied only within the current financial state, not to imagine an even better course. The quality of intellectual is nowhere mentioned. Nor is there any evaluation at all of what several studies have shown that students of an earlier generation valued as a central part of their university experience, namely, the time and space for thought, debate, personal development through relaxed interaction with peers and a strong sense of community among the student body (see *Cam,* June 1994).

The language of management has so far taken center stage in the ways in which universities are being forced to rethink their work and role, has taken so much of the time and space of staff, that it has taken over the whole effective higher education debate. Apparently intended for the implementation of agreed educational policies, it instead determines the agenda. Even more important, compliance with the organization edicts of managerialism has become the major language of justification and legitimation of their activities used by the universities themselves as they have been sucked into the dominant policy paradigm. The language and the imperatives disguised within it are transforming the organizational structures to which they apply and forcing organizational reconstruction of a common kind. While the rhetoric of politicians focuses on encouraging the diversity of the system and promotes a notion of university autonomy, the implementation of the policies in practice creates a powerful tendency towards uniformity and a unidimensional criterion of success.

Conclusion

This chapter has sought to make two essential points. The first is that education policy can only be understood when broader political concerns are taken into account. In the past this was a commonplace, visible in both the direction of policy selected and the language used for its justification. For much of the recent past western societies used the education system for social and political ends which were broader than the current focus on the economic. The use of the system for broader ends meant that policy progress was measured, to the degree that it was measured at all, through evaluations of a broader kind.

The second point is that in recent years the language of management has taken over additional stages of the policy process. Beginning as a language of option evaluation, the tenets of rational economics and managerialism have begun to play major roles in the creation of the agenda and thus in the choice of areas in which the government intervenes. These tenets have further shaped both the timing and the parameters of evaluation of the operation of complex social institutions, notably those of the education system. Since the goals of the system are increasingly defined as instrumental and narrow, so the criteria of evaluation have narrowed. Since quantification is of the essence of this approach, the establishments concerned are being forced to define their activities in ways which permit such quantification. While it is clear that publicly funded institutions should be accountable to the government as proxy for the taxpayer, it is less clear that it is ultimately beneficial to confine a multifaceted process within the bounds currently imposed. This is especially the case because education is an arena assigned multiple and difficult to reconcile goals by modern western societies. As policy-makers veer between favoring instrumental and expressive goals and new social needs appear, the institutions need to be able to retain the flexibility to respond effectively. It is thus imperative that higher education institutions be allowed to maintain a debate couched in other terms and to justify their activities using broader criteria.

The chapter is not intended, however, to stake the claim that universities, and, indeed, all education institutions, need to make for themselves. It is intended rather to suggest the reasons behind the present trends. It points out that the apparently "neutral" language of current policy discussion serves to narrow policy analysis by forcing attention on implementation issues and to take all eyes off a more diverse education policy agenda. As Simon Marginson says, budgetary and political cycles are short, something that encourages the obsession with efficiency at the expense of productivity (Marginson 1993). Quoting no less an authority than the OECD, Marginson reminds us that the main danger in education policy in the 1990s is the excessive emphasis on the short term at the expense of education's longer term contribution which is often indirect and less easy to measure than its costs (Marginson 1993). These costs which we may immediately measure may immeasurably cost us that which we cannot so measure.

References

Althusser, L. (1970), Ideologie et appareils ideologiques d'Etat, *La Pensée* 157, pp.3-38.
Bourdieu, P., and Passeron, J.C. (1970), *La Reproduction*. Paris: Editions de Minuit.
Bowles, S., and Gintis, H. (1976), *Schooling in Capitalist America*. London: Routledge and Kegan Paul.
Cam (June 1994), Interview with Past Students of Cambridge University, p.3.

EPAC (R. Clare and A. Tupule) (1994), *Australia's Ageing Societies.* Canberra: AGPS.

Ford, G. (1982), Human Resource Development in Australia and the Balance of Skills, *Journal of Industrial Relations,* Sept., pp. 443-453.

Foucault, M. (1977), *Discipline and Punish: The Birth of the Prison.* London: Harmondsworth.

Istance, D. (1985), *Education in the Modern World.* Paris: OECD.

Kuhn, T. (1962), *The Structure of Scientific Revolutions.* Chicago: Chicago University Press.

Marceau, J. (1989), The Australian Business Sector: Skills, Tasks and Technologies, in D. Pope and L. Alston (eds.), *Australia's Greatest Asset: Human Resources in the Nineteenth and Twentieth Centuries.* Sydney: Federation Press, pp. 220-238.

Marginson, S. (1993), *Education and Public Policy in Australia.* Cambridge: Cambridge University Press

Mathews, R. (1983), *Fiscal Equalisation in Australia.* Canberra: Centre for Federal Financial Relations, Australian National University.

Piper, J. (1993), Quality Management in Universities, Report Prepared for the Department of Employment, Education and Training. Canberra: AGPS

Pusey, M. (1991), *Economic Rationalism in Canberra: A Nation-Building State Changes its Mind.* Sydney: Cambridge University Press

Report of the Review Committee (1985), *Quality of Education in Australia*, Report. Canberra: AGPS

Rutter, M., Maughan, B., Mortimer, P., Ousten, J., and Smith, A. (1979), *Fifteen Thousand Hours.* Cambridge, Mass: Harvard University Press.

Schools Commission (1980), *Equality of Educational Opportunity. Diversity and Choice.* Canberra: Schools Commission and State Education Departments.

Stewart, J. (1982), Guidelines to Policy Deriviation, in S. Leach and J. Stewart (eds.), *Approaches in Public Policy.* London: Allen and Unwin, pp. 24-35.

Weiss, C. (1977), *Using Social Science in Public Policy Making.* Lexington, Mass.: Lexington Books.

The Subjectivity of Segmentation and the Segmentation of Subjectivity

Andrew Sturdy and David Knights

Introduction

In charting the social and historical constitution of the individualized "autonomous" self in western societies, Rose (1989) shows how our personalities, subjectivities and relationships arc the "socially organized and managed" (p. 3) objects of power. He draws upon the concept of "governmentality" (Foucault 1991) to highlight the relation between "knowledge," "beliefs" and the existence of "selves" in understanding the emergence of new conceptions and techniques of the self in the second half of the 20th century. In particular, he shows how the development of psychological theories and practices in World War II, notably the concepts of attitude, personality and the group, came to transform our very sense of ourselves – "the ways in which we interact… Our thought worlds… our ways of thinking about and talking about our personal feelings, our secret hopes, our ambitions and disappointments" (p. 3). This occurred through the application of such knowledges in programs to govern populations. For example, the management of subjectivity became central to organizations in pursuing increased productivity and harmony from employees (see also Hollway 1991). The capacities of individuals were also progressively incorporated into the field of public authorities in child, juvenile and family policies. Finally, Rose documents the proliferation of "expertise" in the form of counselors, social workers and personnel managers, or what he terms "engineers of the human soul" with techniques to "allow us" to construct, sustain and remodel the self (p. 3).

Such an analysis complements the work of Foucault and others (see Burchell et al. 1991) in showing how the development of the statistical and human sciences is intimately linked with that of new power mechanisms. In one sense, the aim of this chapter is simple and modest. By showing how the same psychological (as well as sociological) knowledges have also been deployed and modified in marketing practices aimed at knowing the consumer – "the inner person rather than the outward expression" (Beane and Ennis 1987: 22) – it calls for a more detailed, historical analysis – a genealogy of the "sovereign consumer." However, by focusing on market segmentation we also seek to demonstrate how aspects of marketing are instrumental in producing or reproducing a society of increasingly individualized subjects whose personal identity is founded upon specific forms of consumption and particular lifestyles. In examining the practices of both the segmenters and the segmented, we attempt to draw together Foucauldian literatures with the typically distinct traditions of organization theory and studies of a consumer society (Knights and Morgan 1993).

The chapter is organized as follows. First, we provide a brief introduction to market segmentation as a practice that seeks detailed "knowledge" of consumers and selectively deploys it in the design, delivery and promotion of products and services. The focus is on a particular form of segmentation based on consumer "lifestyles" using an example from the authors' research on financial services in the UK and France. Second, the marketing view that such activities are simply a consequence, and reflection, of social change towards a more segmented or "de-massified" social structure, is countered by drawing upon critiques which highlight the active role of advertising in creating or constituting individuals as consumers and transforming the nature of society. This literature is itself critically reviewed in arguing for an alternative approach to linking power, knowledge and subjectivity – through the concept of "governmentality." Such an approach is elaborated in the final section which consists of a brief exploratory account of the historical emergence of market segmentation as a technology for the regulation of subjectivity. Drawing on Rose's work in particular, the current form of segmentation practices, and therefore also of consumer society, is shown to be crucially dependent upon psychological conceptions of populations as aggregates of individual "wills" or "attitudes" and "motivations." Moreover, it is argued that segmentation comprises a combination of knowledges, each with its own governmental and constitutive trajectory.

Market Segmentation and the Consumer Society – A Financial Services Example

Social Change

There is a wide and, sometimes established, literature ranging from Bell (1970) to Beck (1992) documenting and assessing the post-war change in the social structure of western "class-societies" resulting from, or associated with, increased individualization. At the risk of conflating diverse perspectives, a common thread is evident: the decline of fixed status hierarchies ("status decay") and the emergence of a "freedom" in "choosing" from a range of shifting lifestyles whereby personal identity is increasingly associated with, and dependent upon, consumption (e.g. Bauman 1988; Bourdieu 1984; Featherstone 1987). For example, Beck's recent account of German society[1] documents how changes in the labor market primarily have given rise to an increasing freedom from the "traditional" social struc-tures of class, family, gender and occupation. This "liberation" coincides with a "reintegration" through adopting lifestyles which are dependent upon labor mar-ket position and consumption. The distinctiveness of this form of individualiza-tion compared to that of previous historical periods is seen to be associated with: a centralized state; concentration of capital; an increasingly tight division of la-bor; increased geographic and occupational mobility, and increasing consumption (Beck 1992: 127). Equally, the link between consumption and identity is by no means a new development. For example, status groups have been defined in terms of shared consumption patterns (e.g. see Weber 1948). However, consumption has become more diversified whereby the search for a degree of distinctiveness results in a multiplicity of identities through a highly differentiated set of consumer prod-ucts (Knights and Morgan 1993).

These social changes bring new forms of insecurity and risk. Beck points to the search for identity in a "detraditionalized" society and labor market depen-dency as well as developing his parallel thesis concerning the new global scale of ecological-technological risks. However, other conceptions of risk are largely ne-glected. For example, in France, post-war prosperity, social security provision and increases in average life-spans in the context of growing individualization have combined, it is claimed, to shift people's definition of security away from a "pas-sive" form of "risk" protection against potential "hazards" towards a more "ac-tive" security associated with individual autonomy and the achievement of "life-projects" (Foucault 1988; Paitra 1990; Mendras and Cole 1991). As we shall dis-cuss further, such changes are highly significant for financial services companies as well as state social policy.

The insured is going to look for the best trajectories in his life-cycle – less something against bad luck, more the optimization of well-being. To call on an insurer to manage a risk is no longer to guard against a chaotic succession of hazards but to optimize trajectories which have a relative certainty (Albouy and Ewald 1990: 12).

Not only are former "hazards," such as "dependency" in old age, becoming more certain, but the nature of security "needs" are changing.[2]

The Marketing "Response" – Segmentation

Since the war, a discourse of marketing has proliferated to represent and reproduce markets as consisting of increasingly fragmented and individualized, fluctuating and transitory consumer "needs" (see Knights et al. 1994). It is argued that com-panies have responded to the changes and should respond further in accordance with what has become known as the marketing concept – identifying and respond-ing to needs profitably (see Hooley et al. 1990: 7). In manufacturing industries in the USA and then elsewhere, the changes rendered product-led mass marketing and production and their associated technologies increasingly inappropriate[3]. An increasing variety of goods were produced in response (i.e. "tailored") to differentiated "needs" (a market segmentation strategy) and/or at least, delivery mechanisms and promotional messages for standard products were targeted according to different perceived requirements (a product differentiation strategy) (Smith 1956).

A similar development was advocated and followed in the service sectors including, more recently, financial services. Here, in both Britain and France it is currently claimed that a market orientation is being adopted and there are calls for this to expand by matching products and services to the more individualized "needs" or demands of consumers (Sturdy and Morgan 1993; de Moubray 1990; Philippe 1992). Moreover, as has been suggested, future financial services marketing will be concerned with responding to and constituting consumers in terms of new security "needs" based on realizing lifestyles and optimizing well-being. Before examining critically the claims of consumer-driven change theorists and practitioners, the practice of market segmentation is introduced by way of a contemporary example from French financial services.

In order to achieve market segmentation or even the tailoring of promotional messages, increasingly sophisticated market research and analysis has been used to identify consumer characteristics and needs and their location within given populations. Marketing literature documents varying approaches and techniques used in market segmentation (see Speed and Smith 1992; Beane and Ennis 1987 for reviews). In general, a market or population is divided on a basis or, typically, a number of bases which describe or, more often, can be related in some way to buying behavior. Ideally, the market divisions or segments should each be homogeneous in terms of the factor/factors under consideration. Also, they should be "accessible," "measurable," "actionable" and "substantial" as well as "profitable" (Kotler 1988) so that products, sales approaches and other information can be targeted/tailored with respect to them. Identifying appropriate "signs" of behavior and classifying distinct groups to which they are related provides the data to facilitate the achievement of the marketing concept through an efficient channeling of resources (Schauerman 1990).

A wide and ever-increasing range of factors are researched for use in segmenting the market. They are typically classified into three types: demographic, geodemographic and psychographic (see Joseph and Yorke 1989). Demographics include age, sex, socio-occupational group, income and family type and stage. The latter "family life cycle" concept consisted of a number of stages from "single" to "retired sole survivor" (i.e. assumes marriage) and has been subsequently modified to incorporate some "non-traditional" family forms (Murphy and Staples 1979). Geodemographics relate to neighborhoods and are derived from census data, with classifications combining variables including race and class (e.g. the "ACORN" groups in the UK). Psychographics refers to various personality traits and particular values, attitudes and behaviors or lifestyles (VALS). As we discuss below, it is claimed that psychographics gets "closer" to the nature and identity of individuals and supersedes socio-economic groups in reflecting the changed social structure.

In addition to the above three general categories, segmentations can be product/sector specific. Indeed, it is argued that this is the most useful application to marketers (Bowles 1987). For example, a "classic" French study in 1971 revealed two distinct behavior groups related to saving and spending – *les accumulateurs* and *les jouisseurs*, 39% and 61% of the population respectively (Zollinger 1985: 15). Now, companies make and use sharper distinctions. Crédit Lyonnais bank, for example, markets products on the basis of seven different saving/spending motivations, five "modern" and two "traditional." In addition, the "banking life cycle" is commonly used, charting periods of saving and borrowing against age for particular groups such as *cadres supérieur* and revealing a concentration of saving in the 45-65 age group, for example. Finally, segmentations may be tailored to specific companies' requirements including "micro-segmentation" – classifying existing clients. Frequently, companies will conduct or commission a number of studies and seek to combine their findings to provide a "truer" reflection of the market. This concern parallels the positivistic view that behavior is better "captured," the greater the range of methods used to "observe" it. Other concerns of practitioners, aside from cost and practicability, relate to the availability of data, how up-to-date it is and, in particular, the extent to which the bases or variables used are accurate predictors of the behavior (e.g. saving) in question (see Beane and Ennis 1987). Banks in particular with their large and "captive" client bases have the potential to collect massive amounts of information. Many are currently engaged in identifying and collecting customer information and transcribing it through IT into a usable form, adopting what is called a strategy of "relationship marketing." We now provide more detail of segmentation practices, particularly psychographics, and their application in financial services is by use of a case study company – Crédit Agricole bank.[4]

A Case Study of Segmentation

Crédit Agricole is a very large and, in France, well known retail bank with a strong rural and agricultural tradition. However, it has a wide range of customers, claiming an account in one in every three households in France and the largest branch network in all regions outside of Paris. Its success as a mainstream bank is attributed in the company to the "capture" of a high proportion of the post-war "baby-boom" generation as they reached adulthood in the late 1960s, and subsequently, satisfying their hitherto relatively "homogenous" needs as they progressed through the banking "life-cycle" (e.g. loans, housing, investments, life assurance and savings for pensions). However, its large and diffuse regionalized structure and concomitant Information Technology are seen as "costly" which, combined with a large "conservative" client base, has resulted in low profitability in relation to other banks. As we shall see, current strategies seek to address this perceived weakness. Its marketing is seen in the industry to be highly advanced, often acting as a leader, in product innovations for example (Cahier 1992). In this sense, it is a "leading edge," rather than a typical, player in the field of marketing within financial services (Sturdy and Morgan 1993).

The bank, in common with some others, has used the results of a psychographic study series on "Eurolife-styles" carried out by an agency, "CCA" (Centre of Advanced Communications). The study is seen by its users as comprehensive, citing the 24,000 interviews carried out in fifteen west European countries (60 regions) with 700 questions providing a range of 3,200 responses in each case. The questions and variables used are presented as covering, or capturing, the 3 elements of people's lives – opinions (rationality), feelings (emotion and dreams) and behavior (habits) – which colloquially correspond to the head, heart and body. Thus, it is claimed, a much richer picture of individuals can be gained than with, for example, demographic studies relating spending/saving patterns with socio-economic groups. Indeed, the "Eurolife-styles" study identified four sub-categories of financial behavior within the "cadres" occupational/social class.

One will understand better, for example, consumers of insurance by knowing what they consume in their leisure, on cars, how they raise their children, how they vote, what they believe (Cathelat 1991: 120).

Using a range of statistical techniques (e.g. cluster and multivariate analysis), responses are analyzed with a view to forming relatively homogenous and distinct groups or "clusters" of shared characteristics – lifestyle types.

In this case, 16 European "socio-styles" were created which were further grouped for practicality in commercial application into 6 "mentalities." Both sets of categories are identified and presented by their location on a pictorial map incorporating the measures of "materialistic-moralistic" along north-south and "dynamism-stability" along west-east[5] polar axes (see Figure 1). Each cluster or segment is given a commonsense name or "descriptor" which summarizes the nature of the characteristics shared. For example, in the "north-west" quarter (materialistic-dynamism) the "socio-ambitieux" ("go-ahead individualists") "mentality" is located comprising around 25% of the European population and three "socio-styles" – "Euro-Dandies..., Rockies, and Business." The latter are described as "yuppies" seeking power and money. By contrast, in the "north-east" the "Euro Prudent" are located – "resigned seekers of security" and so on.

The research on "socio-styles" is claimed to be dynamic as well as rich in that social trends can be identified by carrying out similar studies periodically, albeit with different interviewees. Indeed and as outlined earlier, the proliferation of differentiated groups with distinctive identities and behavioral characteristics has been a focus of western sociology for sometime but it is also clearly being seen as an important feature of market research. For example, it is claimed that in the

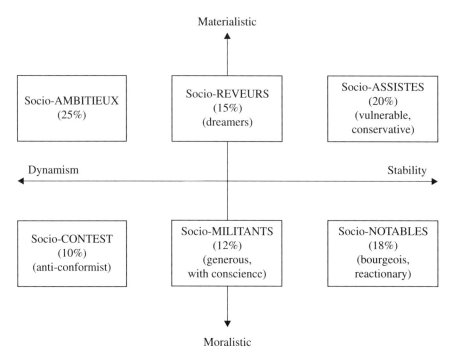

Materialistic

Socio-AMBITIEUX (25%)	Socio-REVEURS (15%) (dreamers)	Socio-ASSISTES (20%) (vulnerable, conservative)

Dynamism   Stability

Socio-CONTEST (10%) (anti-conformist)	Socio-MILITANTS (12%) (generous, with conscience)	Socio-NOTABLES (18%) (bourgeois, reactionary)

Moralistic

Source: Adapted from a Crédit Agricole marketing strategy document – original research by CCA, France.

Figure 1: European Social Mentalities (Percentages refer to approximate populations across 15 Wester European countries)

1950s there were only four or five "socio-styles" (and two "mentalities"), nine by 1970 and fourteen (and five "mentalities") in 1984. At the same time, apparently stable typologies exist across Europe which, for companies, highlights the possibility of marketing Pan-European products at target markets, regulations permitting (Langlumé 1992). The identification of such trends in social differentiation, particularly that of atomization, is used to promote segmentation as an essential marketing tool.

CCA claim that the "socio-styles" information is used by financial services companies to differing degrees. Most frequently, the messages in advertising and promotion (e.g. product literature) are partly informed by such segmentation. To a lesser extent it is used in new product development, matching products with perceived "needs" or risks and, occasionally, in distribution and sales training. For example, a training simulation computer package is available giving set phrases in response to signs from "clients" in relation to their segment location or lifestyle (see Cathelat 1991) – their identity. Crédit Agricole's use of "Euro-lifestyles" and other similar studies appears to be relatively advanced, particularly in relation to insurance companies. The behaviors and orientations of different segments can be matched with ranges of risk types (e.g. in relation to AIDS), available products, distribution channels/sales approaches, media (for promotions) and appropriate messages or images. Indeed, the ranges can be superimposed on to the "polar" segment chart with, for example, the "socio-ambitieux" group particularly associated with distribution through the "Mintel" (view data) network. Clearly, existing services and messages can be better targeted using such techniques. More significantly, they can also be re-designed and changed to meet better the "needs" of groups of potential and existing clients. For example, the lifestyles analysis informed the development and launch of a savings product in 1989, with 17 options regarding, for example, the periods of deposits, interest payments, and withdrawal penalties, built into the contract. It was targeted in two main directions – conservative segments in the "east" of the chart and relatively young people located further "west." Similarly, following the government's initiation in 1990 of a popular savings plan or "PEP," the bank adapted the basic product into six variations by combining it with other standard products such as housing savings, passbook accounts, unit trusts and other investments. This innovative range of differentiated mixed products was designed to match the perceived range of savings needs (e.g. security, rate of return, access, convenience) and to be targeted at different "socio-styles" or segments. For example, the two most conservative "mentalities," both well-off (south-east) and more vulnerable and poor (north-east), were targeted through regular income and free access product features respectively. By contrast, high rate of return products were positioned towards the less conservative groups. Other banks have also repackaged PEPs in a similar way such as Crédit Lyonnais' range, promoted as being "adapted to your objectives." Crédit Agricole has also used "socio-styles" in its communications. For example, in line with its corporate message that it is "not only a rural bank," the corporate logo was changed in 1988 to target those more "dynamic" (and younger) segments to the "west" of the chart. In relation to products, the name "PEP" was changed to "PEPS" partly because of its perceived phonetic advantages (like "Pepsi"). In addition, each product was "colored" in promotion material to coincide "psychologically" with the nature of the service and the target segments (e.g. blue for the investment-related product and green for regular income). Again, similar practices are carried out by other financial services companies. Crédit Lyonnais, for example, uses different images for each of its PEPs – a dove, an hour glass, a country house, an abacus and a father and son/grandson.

Crédit Agricole's marketing is only partly informed by the "socio-styles" analysis. Other segmentations and tools are used in combination such as the family, banking and product "life-cycles." Also, its existing clients are analyzed in relation to their usage of bank services and numerous other available criteria. Again, typologies are established and labeled (see Zollinger 1985). In addition to seeking simply to identify, respond to, and target different segments, increasing attention is being given to costs in the strategic marketing plans which are formulated with the aid of consultants analytical tools. A "differentiated" strategy is seen as most appropriate for a universal bank such as Crédit Agricole in an environment where consumer "needs" are increasingly diffuse. Such an approach is developed by the familiar management technique of measuring the "attractiveness" (profitability/ risk) for the bank of each segment and product and comparing these measures with its perceived strengths and those of its competitors. One result has been the hierarchical classification of clients' profitability for the bank into "stars," "dead weights" and "leeches." This partly informed a distribution strategy in the early 1990s. For example, the latter category are of modest profitability and do not need to be actively "courted" but have advantages for the bank such as cash flow and economies of scale. The distribution strategy was to develop three broad and seg-mented forms of distribution. Firstly, for simple, low "added-value" (profitability) products which are "bought" rather than sold, distribution was externalized – tele/ home banking, mailing/phoning, mobile sales units and distribution alliances. By contrast, the "second level" is for high-profitability products sold by specialists in a "made to measure" service closely matched to individual "needs." Finally the wide branch network was to be used to sell ranges of products, not distinguished technically (i.e. insurance or banking) but packaged and "colorized" according to the "needs" of client groups. Thus, in summary, marketing and segmentation, in particular, is increasingly central to activities in Crédit Agricole and other finan-cial services companies.

The Socio-Critique

We now seek to examine more critically these marketing practices and, in par-ticular, their implicit assumptions regarding the "sovereign consumer" to whom companies "respond" through identifying their changing needs and creating/tai-loring products and services. Even within definitions of the marketing concept, considerations of cost and profitability 'limit' the possible diversity of the prod-uct/service offers (Smith 1956). The "response" is therefore selective. Relatedly and despite claims to the contrary, established (non-tailored) products continue to be promoted *as if* they specifically meet individual or group needs (Knights et al. 1994). This is acknowledged among marketing practitioners, one of whom de-scribed this "personalizing" process as "mass marketing to units of one" and as an ideal to be pursued.

More importantly, however, the sovereign consumer to which companies sup-posedly respond is clearly as much an outcome as a condition of marketing prac-tices. Indeed within the more academic literature, this has not passed unnoticed and the "discipline" of marketing has been variously described as an "environ-mental shaping process" (Verbeke 1992; Savitt 1987). For example, in accounting for the tendency towards oligopolistic power or market concentration, the importance of constructing "entry barriers"; through links with suppliers for instance, has been highlighted as essential in securing market share.

Much marketing is about avoidance of competition and the dominance of markets – i.e. marketing benefits the firm *not by satisfying customers* but by establishing quasi-monopolistic power over them (Whittington and Whipp 1992: 19-20, emphasis added).

The shaping of the market is most blatant in relation to advertising (and selling practices) (Knights and Morgan 1993; Knights et al. 1993) where, again in the marketing literature, the "traditional" view was that it "was intended to shape the attitudes of the consumer and to cause subsequent sales" (Verbeke 1992: 1). This is particularly vivid in financial services, and life assurance especially, where consumers generally show little interest in the product (Knights et al. 1994) such that a continuing industry adage is that life assurance is sold and not bought (Newman 1984).

The role of advertising and sales in the constitution of a "consumer" or, even, "postmodern" society has been the focus of a critical literature that directly challenges marketing's self-image as responding to human "need" (e.g. Marcuse 1964; Baudrillard 1981). No doubt, their task is easier when people want what is being offered or promoted.

But:

when marketers claim to act merely as cultural barometers of the time period, they tell but half the story: 'reflecting' the values of target markets in pursuit of profits involves marketers in continuous maneuvering to refract meanings and reposition audiences in relation to their products (Goldman 1992: 43).

Goldman assesses the nature and impact of advertising in the USA since the 1970s. Following Baudrillard (1981), he focuses on the commodity sign – consumption has shifted from a concern with material utility or use-values to a consumption of signs which correspond to psychological utility or identity values. Advertising "teachers us to consume, not the product but its sign" (Goldman 1992: 19). It "invites us to step into the 'space' of the ad to try on the social self we might become if we wear the product image" (Goldman 1992: 3). Increasingly, the messages are "personalized" but also targeted according to "lifestyles" which has become a key category in product positioning (Baudrillard 1992: 54) as well as service delivery. For Goldman, the term reduces all life to a style – the product eventually becomes the lifestyle.

The development of advertising in this way is seen as a product of the need for capital to create new markets (and consumers) which is intensified as a result of diminishing returns to mass production and marketing consequent upon the proliferation of differentiated identities. At the same time, the constitution of consumers is not one of straightforward manipulation (cf. Marcuse 1964). Rather, a now familiar (e.g. see Willis 1990) dialectical, process is referred to whereby consumer resistance to, or adaptation of, advertising messages is responded to and re-incorporated and re-directed in a commodified form. Examples are the way in which expressions of urban youth counter-culture were appropriated in advertising "Levi's" jeans and how the political discourse of feminism, which rejected advertising stereotypes of women, became "reframed" into a discourse of style and independence. Finally, and more generally, rejection of the transparent advertisements of the 1970s has led to the use of increasingly ambiguous and opaque messages to retain consumer attention. A similar pattern is evident in financial services marketing where, as we have seen, "personalized" and lifestyle (cf. use-value) messages are increasingly used to counter consumer inertia – the Prudential's insurance advertising campaign of "I want to be...," representing a specifically vivid example of self assertive individual autonomy and a pluralized version of the "success ethic." Equally, one can see how the political discourse of environmentalism/morality has been appropriated and reshaped in relation to the marketing of "green"/"ethical investments."

Goldman (1992) argues that, in commodifying meanings, advertising reproduces social domination. By "numbing us" into an acceptance of the commodity form, social relations are atomized (or segmented) and "traditional forms of social reciprocity" are dissolved (Goldmann 1992).The apparent growth in the number of market segments and the concomitant claim of cultural pluralism are "ideological constructs" obscuring the underlying commodity logic (Goldmann 1992: 11). Targeted advertising has contributed to the decline of a class-based capitalist hegemony toward a fractured one, "grounded in the privatizing discourse of commodified desire" (Goldmann 1992:14). A similar perspective is adopted by Curtis (1988). However, his focus is not so much on the final images or signs of advertising but, closer to the subject of this chapter, the organizational practices of collecting and segmenting consumer data prior to the production of those images. In his account of the "information society," he highlights how developments in information technology have facilitated a massive growth in data collection and market segmentation. As with Goldman, the individualization or "demassification" of society is the product of segmenting individuals by "motivating factors" of opinions, beliefs and lifestyles. For Curtis, individual needs and motivations are learned through socialization from marketing media which appeal to people by providing a sense of belonging or identification that is, paradoxically, sought because of the alienating effects of individualization. However, the replacement of class divisions founded on property and kinship by "demassification" is more apparent than real. In contrast to Bell's (1970: 20) view of cultural pluralism based on lifestyles, segmentation is seen to obscure and reinforce economic inequalities by constituting individual motivations through the use of status distinctions (e.g. the variables used in cluster analyses). Inequalities become simply reflections of lifestyle differences between individuals. This stratification or "computer generated caste system" serves a control function, a "rationalization of consumption"

(Curtis 1988: 104) – individual motivation is managed and monitored through segmentation rather than homogenization (mass marketing) as before.

The accounts of both Goldman and Curtis provide a valuable corrective to the liberal view of marketing and market segmentation as politically neutral practices responding to sovereign individuals' needs and insecurities. For example, marketing reinforces existing social stratifications by rendering them "natural" and individualized as evident in the identification of a cluster in the socio-styles analysis discussed earlier – the "assisted/dependent": vulnerable, poor, defensive and conservative. Moreover, the practice of measuring the "attractiveness" (profitability) of particular individuals or segments and targeting and pricing products accordingly involves a selection process whereby, often, low income groups, for example, are effectively selected out. This is evident in insurance whereby premiums are increasingly differentiated or individualized according to perceived risks such that many people are effectively excluded by being priced out of the market (Knights et al. 1994).

Despite their contribution to a critical perspective on the practice of market segmentation, both accounts are limited in terms of their neo-marxist conceptual framework of power, knowledge and subjectivity. In particular, power is seen as repressive of subjectivity. For Curtis, social control is achieved through the possession of knowledge (of individual consumers) and manipulating motivations. It is assumed that socialization through marketing media is largely successful. For example, although it was noted how the conformity associated with mass marketing was resisted by consumers as a result of individualization processes, "the capacity to socialize sections of society into different values, attitudes and lifestyles" was seen to offer "stability to market segmentation" (Curtis 1988: 104). This portrays consumers as largely passive and predictable in relation to marketing communications. Similarly, Goldman talks of advertising numbing us into acceptance of its social logic. While he also incorporates a dialectical process of "hegemony, alienation and resistance" (Goldmann 1992: 2) associated with the crisis tendencies of capital (p. 13), it is not clear whether resistance arises from some sense of an autonomous self.

Relatedly, the new social relations of "cultural pluralism" and "freedom of lifestyles" and, therefore, the associated knowledges and media messages are seen as false. They are ideological constructs that mask and reinforce the "real relations" (Goldman 1992: 13) of the commodity form and the reproduction of social inequality and domination (see also Beck 1992). Finally, their explanation for the emergence of market segmentation is functionalist in character. It is explained in terms of its consequences for social control and the interests of capital. For example, Curtis argues that new technologies rendered segmentation a more economical form of social control than through homogenization – it is functional for the maintenance of social and material stratification.

Rose (1988; 1989) employs similar criticisms in outlining an alternative view of power, knowledge and subjectivity through the concept of government. He criticizes the "socio-critique" paradigm as it is applied to the development and use of human sciences. Firstly, rather than portraying knowledges of subjective life as false, Rose is concerned with how new truths are produced. Secondly, he criticizes the view that psychology is effective in dominating subjectivity as if there is a "freedom" to be constrained. In fact, psychological expertise stimulates subjectivity "promoting self-inspections and self-consciousness, shaping desires… fundamental to the production of individuals 'free to choose.'.." (1989: 4). Here, power is seen as enabling as well as repressive of subjectivity. Thirdly, while accepting that psychological techniques tend to support power relations, such a view neglects their new effects and the connections they produce between governing bodies and the "projects" of individuals. Finally, rather than explaining the origins and success of psychology and its applications in terms of the functions they serve for the state and control, Rose develops the wider Foucauldian concept of government. Briefly, the term refers to "a certain way of striving to reach social and political ends by acting in a calculated manner upon the forces, activities and relations of the individuals that constitute a (target) population" (Rose 1989: 4) or, more broadly, structuring the possible field of action of others (see Foucault 1991: 102-103). The concept is elaborated upon in the following section which outlines how extending such an approach to the government of consumers can better account for the emergence of segmentation and the connections between power, knowledge, subjectivity and an "atomized" social structure.[6]

Governing the Consumer

Michel Foucault is now well known for his work on the relationship between power and knowledge. In particular, he has shown how the development of human sciences was intimately linked with that of new power mechanisms.

> … the fact that societies can become the object of scientific observation, that human behavior became… a problem to be analyzed and resolved, all that is bound up, I believe, with mechanisms of power (Foucault 1988: 106).

For example, the "choice" of imprisonment as an essential mode of punishment in the late 18th century followed a long:

> … elaboration of various techniques that made it possible to locate people, to fix them in precise places, to constrict them to a certain number of gestures and habits (Foucault 1988: 104)

Others have followed a similar perspective in exploring the "government" of populations (see Burchell et al. 1991). For example, Hacking has shown how the growth and use of statistics in the 18th century helped to shape the form and, therefore, outcome of social sciences. Power is evident in the way in which the resulting classifications or models of human types come to define the boundaries of identity – new languages shape our lives, our reality.

Many of the modern categories by which we think about people and their activities, were put in place by an attempt to collect numerical data… The bureaucracy of statistics imposes not just by creating administrative rulings but by determining classifications within which people must think of themselves and of the actions which are open to them (Hacking 1991: 182 194).

An example given was the emergence of labels for the class structure from the first UK census and the factory inspectorate. We are concerned with the more recent classifications of lifestyles produced through the use of psychological concepts and market research in market segmentation.

In the same way, there is a literature showing how insurantial knowledges, such as those of actuarial science, were derived from gathering statistics and came to constitute risk and discipline populations. "Risk" is not only socially constituted by the way in which, with life assurance for example, privatized nuclear families with single breadwinners and dependents emerged historically. It also reflects a cultural, Western (Daniel 1992), preoccupation with rendering the future calculable and knowable – a principle of objectification (Ewald 1991; Knights 1988). In this way, insurance itself, as a technique of rational calculation, produces risks. As Ewald (1991: 200) observes: "By objectivizing certain [familiar or 'dreaded'] events as risks, insurance can invert their meaning: it can make what was previously an obstacle into a possibility."

Insurance helps to define security ("a possibility") and reinforce and reshape definitions of insecurity ("an obstacle"): "Each new measure of protection makes visible a new form of insurable insecurity" (Defert 1991: 215).

By reinforcing and constituting insecurity and offering a solution to it – the material and existential security from, for example, claims payments and "peace of mind" – insurance serves as a "moral-political technology" (Defert 1991: 215). It encourages "responsible" behavior from insured populations, e.g. state subjects, employees and consumers. It is also disciplinary, in the same way as with statistics, by locating individuals and defining them as risks:

[Insurance is]… a scheme of rationality, a way of breaking down, rearranging, ordering certain elements of reality…[it] individualizes, defines each person as a risk, but the individuality it confers is… relative to that of other members of the insured population – an average sociological individuality (Ewald 1991: 199, 203).

There are, once more, clear parallels between the practice described in the above quotation and that of market segmentation. For example one could substitute the words *"risk"* and *"insured"* with those of *"consumer type"* and *"market"* to account for the way in which individuals are located in relation to behavioral/psychological "clusters."

As we argue below, such parallels are by no means coincidental. Rather, they reflect how the history of knowledges of subjectivity including that of the financial services consumer are "bound up with programs which, in order to govern subjects, have found that they need to know them" (Rose 1989: 5) – populations are isolated and their characteristics selected, examined, inscribed and acted upon. In particular, in a brief sketch, the emergence of programs to govern the consumer through demographic and psychographic (lifestyle) segmentation is shown to be a combination and mutation of knowledges and practices which were themselves products of governmentality. For clarity of presentation, the account is organized in three sections which broadly correspond to, albeit overlapping, historical periods and forms of segmentation – demographic, psychographic and their "strategic" combination and application in contemporary financial services.

The Social Survey

According to market research literature, its practice in the form of the social survey began in the UK in the 1930s (Abrams 1951). Its "methodological roots" are recognized as being the philanthropic and early government social surveys of the late 19th and early 20th centuries (Downham et al. 1956; Moser 1958). Not surprisingly, these surveys are not seen as forms of government in themselves, but as objective tools for policy-making. Similarly, Hacking (1991) charts the emergence of the science of statistics from the 17th century onwards as an "avalanche of printed numbers" whereby attributes of the population (e.g. age, birth, death, habitation, employment) were inscribed in a numerical and usable form for the calculations of those in power (see also Rose 1989). However, as noted earlier, Hacking shows how the categories devised in measurement became meaningful labels such as social class and socio-economic categories (i.e. the bases of today's demographic segmentation). Governmental concerns to measure continued to develop in the 19th century with a particular focus on the living conditions and poverty associated with industrialization. Here, the market research literature personalizes its history by highlighting the poverty studies of Rowntree (1901), Booth (1902), Bowley and Burnett-Hurst (1915) and the town planning surveys of the inter-war period as landmarks in its development. Paradigms of inscription such as the family life-cycle (Rowntree) and the neighborhood concept (Booth)[7] as well as the continued extension of quantification of behavior (Booth) and sampling and interview techniques (Bowley) were "pioneered" (Moser 1958; Downham et al. 1956). Such innovations also informed, and were subsequently developed in the accelerated expansion of government social surveys during the "crisis" period of the second world war. For example the Food Survey was initiated in 1940, in the first instance, to examine the diet of the urban working class. Similar national surveys followed in sickness and consumer expenditure – the Social Survey began in 1941. As we discuss below, market research, which was little practiced during the war, drew on, and contributed towards, the extension of the social survey in the post-war period. The Market Research Society was formed in 1947 at about the same time as university statistics (applied economics) and sociology departments (e.g. LSE) were expanding the social survey method in relation to the income and savings and social mobility of the population, for example.

By the mid-1950s, market research was established and growing with around 2,000 people employed and an expenditure level of £3 million (Downham et al. 1956)[8]. The inscription paradigms of demographic segmentation (e.g. family and financial life-cycles) were being developed and extended (Clark 1955) from prior and continued governmental concerns to measure the material well-being of populations. However, the market research literature of the time observed some skepticism from practitioners (typically trained in economics or sociology) towards new developments focused more on the psychological condition of consumers – "motivation research" (Downham et al. 1956). We now turn to this new combination of knowledges in surveys and its significance for the regulation of the consumer society.

Battle for the Minds

Rose documents how the human problems of the second world war represented a new focus of scrutiny for governments in the USA and the UK – the "morale" of domestic, enemy and services populations. This concern, combined with the pre-war (and post-war) development of public (voter) opinion research conducted in the growing spirit of liberal "popular democracy," led to a number of developments in psychological theory and practice. For example, in 1939 Likert's work on public opinion in the US Agriculture Department was re-directed to enemy morale and soldiers attitudes. The resulting "Likert Scale" was to become one of the key tools for making attitudes quantifiable and meaningful. According to Rose (1989: 27):

Earlier psychological conceptions of the mass psychology of the mob... gave way to a notion of the populous as an *aggregate of individuals* with views and wishes that could be investigated by precise techniques and communicated to government by experts.

The new science of democracy also drew upon a new way of thinking about individual will... Individuals were moved by attitudes... [which] thus bridged the internal world of the psyche and the external world of conduct (emphasis added).

Similarly with the concept of personality, the use of psychiatrists in War Office Selection Boards saw their role change from the "keepers of lunatics" to examiners of the "normal" psyche and the resulting conduct of individuals. The wartime development of such research led to tests such as "Cattells 16PF" which, as with intelligence and testing in the previous war, enabled personality to be visualized, calculated and administered (Rose 1989: 46).

As noted in our introduction, Rose goes on to show how the new calibrations of "personality" and "attitude" produced new ways of calculating the link between subjectivity and administrative objectives in the workplace, the family, the consulting room and, we would add, the store or branch. This new expertise became effective in governing subjectivity not so much through the formal and coercive institutions of the state but in a more indirect way in keeping with the liberal democratic ideas of the time.

It achieves its effects… by way of the persuasion inherent in its truths, the anxiety stimulated by its norms, and the attraction exercised by the images of life and self it offers to us (Rose 1989:10).

In short, the psychological assessment such as the "measurement" of lifestyles and its use in marketing is self-disciplinary – "it makes persons amenable to having things done to them – and doing things to themselves – in the name of their subjective capacities" (Rose 1989: 7-8). Indeed, Rose also notes an increasing interconnectedness between work and "non-work" by showing how in contemporary employment "the primary image… is not that of the producer but of the consumer" (Rose 1989:102). This is translated into employment through workers' pursuit of a "quality of working life" for example.

Battle for the Markets

The post-war application of the concepts of personality and attitude into market research and segmentation paralleled the development of the other technologies of subjectivity discussed by Rose. Contemporary market segmentation, as illustrated in our case study, is clearly founded on the view of a population as an aggregation of individuals whereby inscription paradigms can render (buying) behavior predictable. Indeed, according to Wells (1975), psychographic segmentation developed in the 1960s directly from a combination of personality, motivation and social survey expertise. However, as we briefly suggest below, its practice is a combination of other knowledges with their own governmental and historical trajectories brought together in a battle for markets and consumers.

We draw the line at adopting the neo-marxian or "socio-critique" position outlined earlier whereby segmentation practices emerged in order to create new markets and sustain surplus value and/or control. Nonetheless, it is possible to argue that organizational requirements and existing practices are a condition (as well as consequence) of the growth of psychological knowledges – reshaping their methods, form and foci[9]. Indeed, in some marketing literature, segmentation is seen to have emerged as a result of managerial "needs" in responding to an external (market) environment rather than as the product of new ways of seeing that environment. In particular, increased competition (and/or market saturation), flexible production technologies and increased consumer sophistication and/or heterogeneity are typically cited as the conditions for a heightened marketing orientation[10]. Competition is the primary factor. For example, in insurance, the relevance of psychographics and other, now emerging, marketing practices was discussed and promoted in industry conferences in the 1970s, but only with the currently competitive market are such developments being practiced (Philippe 1992). However, their application does not simply involve measuring the psychographic characteristics of markets and segmenting them accordingly. As we have seen from our case study, the "attractiveness" of segments, distribution channels and products in terms of costs/profitability and competitor organizations are important foci. This suggests that accounting knowledge and other "management sciences," such as strategic management, are involved in a combination of knowledges. Rather than representing a tactical response to the market environment, both discourses have been shown to have their own history in the constitution of "market" (e.g. prices), consumers (e.g. value) and competition (Hopwood 1987; Knights and Morgan 1990a). Similarly, in insurance there is a parallel between long established techniques of risk assessment whereby individual risks are defined, measured and priced (or declined) accordingly and the market segmentation concept of matching (responding to) individual needs with personalized product offers (and prices). Indeed, it has been claimed in insurance marketing literature that the "triumph of the individual" in contemporary society means that a more general application of the insurance principle of assessing risks (security "needs") individually renders insurance and marketing a "marriage of reason" (Anon 1992)[11]. However and as noted earlier, insurance knowledges are also a medium and outcome of governmental programs to render populations and the future calculable and knowable – they produce risks. Moreover, as we have sought to demonstrate, the marketing notion of responding to individual needs or lifestyles neglects the constitutive role of marketing practice and the combination of psychological and other knowledges which it comprises.

Conclusion

In this chapter, we have shown, using examples from financial services, how market segmentation is increasingly deployed in the production, distribution and sale of goods and services. In particular, we focused on the growing use of psychographic or lifestyle classifications of consumer segments by French banks such as Crédit Agricole. The marketing view of such practices as a response to a changing social structure whereby "traditional" and broad identity groups (such as those based on occupation and social class) are less relevant and financial security needs relate more to achieving life-projects than minimizing "hazards," is criticized. Firstly, we draw on a range of conventional "socio-critique" literature. This highlights how the emergence of a more diffuse and dynamic social structure where identity is increasingly associated with consumption and lifestyles is a product, as well as a condition, of tailored and targeted advertising and marketing. Secondly, this literature is itself criticized by deploying an alternative approach to the power of segmentation to constitute consumers through the Foucauldian concept of "government" as it is applied by Rose (1989) and others.

In particular, we show that Rose's account of the post-war constitution of the individual self can be extended through an analysis of the production, modification and application of psychological knowledges in market segmentation. Rose (1989: 19) argues that:

One of the major contributions of the psychological sciences to our modernity has been the invention of techniques that make individual differences and capacities visible...

His examples of how the concepts of "personality" and "attitude" were developed and applied in post-war programs to govern populations within workplaces and through social policy and varying forms of counseling were supplemented in a brief historical account of the emergence of market research and its application in lifestyle segmentation. Crucial to these developments has been the conception of populations as aggregates of individuals with capacities that could be measured and acted upon. In addition, we show how the practice of market segmentation in financial services represents a combination and mutation of strategic, accounting and other financial (e.g. insurantial) knowledges with those of the human sciences each of which has been historically developed in governing or producing subjectivity. For instance, marketing practices elaborate and reinforce long established insurantial technologies in the classification of risk and constitution of "security" needs and, thereby, of consumers.

The disciplinary potential of market (e.g. lifestyle) segmentation in financial services is exercised in helping to define the boundaries and content of identity, particularly in relation to consumption, and in reinforcing the discipline associated with insurantial technologies and consumption of "security" products. In accounting for the extent to which segmentation and related practices and messages shape behavior and identity, power has been conceived as enabling as well as repressive of subjectivity. For example, segmentation can be seen to constitute the "norm" and facilitate the formation of self as a particular sort of subject – a consumer of security products and, more specifically, a particular type (cluster) of consumer. This is not, of course, to argue that subjects have come to use the precise labels of segmentation to describe themselves. Indeed, such a practice would conflict with a sense of distinctiveness and individual freedom. Indeed, the "willingness" of subjects to adopt identities of this form lies, as Curtis (1988) intimates, in the existential anxiety of individualization processes whereby people come to seek a sense of "belonging" but, at the same time and paradoxically, also a sense of distinctiveness and individual autonomy and control of their world (see also Becker 1972). For example, the marketing of "personalized" financial services clearly appeals to the latter while the use in advertising and promotion of familial images or those representing aspirations may also heighten the former. Moreover, marketing of financial services – "security products" directly appeals to, and helps constitute, individual securities and insecurities. The internalization of such messages is not a straightforward process however. Firstly, there is a tension implicit in seeking belonging and autonomy (e.g. individualism and solidarity). Secondly, and relatedly we have seen how marketing messages and practices are periodically resisted particularly in financial services. This reflects the way in which they may confront, rather than appeal to, prevailing or localized identities and insecurities (e.g. fear of hazards in relation to insurance). However, even in such a dynamic, power continues to be exercised in the constitution of identities, firstly in the incorporation of themes of resistance in subsequent and modified marketing messages and practices and secondly, in the act of resistance itself.

Our account has been exploratory in nature. Further research of an empirical nature is required to explore in more detail how knowledges have come to be combined, transformed and applied in governing the consumer. For example, Rose notes the frequently ad hoc nature of innovations in the development of psychological innovations (see also Hollway 1991). In addition, the correspondence of the observations of social scientists of an increasing plurality of lifestyles with constituting marketing practices requires further research. Other than in relation to advertising, the ways in which marketing practices and knowledge constitute consumer "needs" and identities have been neglected. As noted in the introduction, such neglect reflects the way in which knowledge itself has come to be segmented – the demarcation of organization and cultural theorists.

Notes

[1] Beck disclaims the applicability of his thesis to France and the UK. However, similar observations have been made of these countries (e.g. Mendras and Cole 1991; Featherstone 1987).

[2] A clear example of this shift is the way in which life assurance products have been promoted as, and have become, principally savings products rather than solely an insurance against financial losses on death (Knights 1988).

[3] The change in production technologies towards greater flexibility and its wider context has been widely discussed elsewhere (e.g. Wood 1989) not least in relation to Piore and Sabel (1984).

[4] The material used in the following account is drawn largely from internal company sources (e.g. interviews, documents and presentations) (see also Zollinger 1985; Cathelat 1991). This, combined with the paper's focus on formal marketing techniques, means that little attention is given here to those practices that are likely to limit the possibilities for "rational" and "systematic" management such as organizational "politics." However, such a neglect is not thought to detract from the arguments presented.

[5] Other axes can be used including the addition of a third dimension such as an "imaginative/serious" scale.

[6] In addition to the literature criticized above, there is a wide and growing literature on consumer culture from a different, cultural studies, tradition. Of particular relevance to our concerns is Featherstone's work on "lifestyle and consumer culture" (1987, 1991). He seeks to "go beyond" the distinct positions of postmodernist celebrations of consumption and lifestyles as autonomous spheres of pleasurable activity (e.g. Baudrillard 1981) and the counter view of them as manipulated products of mass society (e.g. Curtis, 1988). Following the work of Bourdieu (1984) on cultural taste and lifestyles in France and their correlation and interplay with the class/occupational structure, Featherstone highlights the role of intellectuals and the intermediary "petite bourgeoisie" (e.g. marketing, media and "helping" professions) in transmitting cultural tastes and lifestyles and a general interest in style – "symbol production…. the images and information celebrating style and lifestyles" (Featherstone 1987: 56-57). His analysis is explicitly at a "high level of generality" (Featherstone 1987: 56) and calls for more empirical study. It can be seen in parallel to the concern of this chapter in that we are concerned not so much with the occupants of intellectual and media strata nor the content of lifestyles and taste but with the emergence of associated calculative practices in knowledge production and its application within organizations.

[7] This was further developed in town planning surveys (e.g. Lock et al. 1947) and, later, in geodemographic market segmentation.

[8] These authors claim that given the different level and scope of economic activity between the UK and the USA, their market research activity was equivalent at this time.

[9] See Hollway (1991) for an example of this in the development of organizational behavior.

[10] See Smith (1956) for its emergence in consumer goods markets and Ennew et al. (1990) for its later development in financial services (cf. Knights et al. 1994).

[11] While this individualistic or actuarial approach of "to each according to their risks" conforms to an increasing consumer reluctance to share risks (e.g. non-smokers and life assurance), it conflicts with the insurance principle of mutualizing risks. It is more of a mutualization of *groups* (or segments) of risks (Roche 1990; Rothmann 1990). Moreover, it also conflicts with solidaristic values, which both compete and coexist with individualism (Mendras and Cole 1991: 117), in that certain groups/individuals are excluded by, for example, companies' selection of only the most profitable segments. It is claimed that this "segmentation-selection" tension may lead to a crisis of legitimacy for the insurance industry (Albouy 1992).

References

Abrams, M. (1951), *Social Surveys and Social Action,* London: Heinemann.
Albouy, F.X. (1992), A chacun selon ses risques directions, *CAPA,* (19), pp. 88-94.
Albouy, F.X., and Ewald, F. (1990), Le client, *Risques,* October, pp. 11-23.
Anon (1992), Marketing et assurances, un mariage de raison, *L'assurance Française,* 648.
Baudrillard, J. (1981), *Towards a Critique of the Political Economy of the Sign,* St. Louis: Telos.

Bauman, Z. (1988), *Legislators and Interpreters*, London: Polity Press.
Beane, T.P., and Ennis, D.M. (1987), Market Segmentation: A Review, *European Journal of Marketing,* 21(5), pp.20-42
Beck, U. (1992), *Risk Society – Towards a New Modernity*, London: Sage.
Becker, E. (1972), *The Birth and Death of Meaning*, Harmondsworth: Penguin.
Bell, D. (1970), The Cultural Contradictions of Capitalism, *Public Interest,* 21, Fall, pp. 16-43.
Booth, C. (1902), *The Life and Labour of the People of London,* London: MacMillan.
Bourdieu, P. (1984), *Distinction – A Social Critique of the Judgement of Taste,* London: Routledge.
Bowles, T. (1987), Does Classifying People by Lifestyle Really Help the Advertiser?, *Admap,* May, pp. 36-40
Bowley, A.L., and Burnett-Hurst, A.R. (1915), *Livelihood and Poverty,* London: King.
Burchell, G., Gordon, C., and Miller, P. (eds.) (1991), *The Foucault Effect – Studies in Governmentality*, Hemel Hempstead: Harvester.
Cahier, M. (1992), La Banque Verte: Leader en bancassurance selon, *Salomon Agence Economique et Financière,* 17 April, p. 4.
Cathelat, B. (1991), *Marketing et société risques,* 7, September, pp. 119-127.
Clark, L.H. (ed.) (1955), *Consumer Behavior Volume II, The Life Cycle,* New York: BYUP.
Curtis, T. (1988), The Information Society: A Computer Generated Caste System?, in Mosco, V., and Wasko, J. (eds.), *The Political Economy of Information,* Wisconsin: University of Wisconsin Press.
Daniel, J.P. (1992), Boudda et Confucius, même combat contre Sainte Barbe?, *Directions CAPA,* 12 June, pp. 24-25.
Defert, D. (1991), Popular Life and Insurance Technology, in Burchell et al. (1991), pp. 211-233.
Downham, J.S., Shankleman, E., and Treasure, J.A.P. (1956), A Survey of Market Research in Great Britain, in Edwards, F. (ed.), *Readings in Market Research,* London: British Market Research Bureau.
Ennew, C.T., Watkins, T., and Wright, M. (eds.) (1990), *Marketing Financial Services,* Oxford: Heinemann.
Ewald, F. (1991), Insurance and Risk, in Burchell et al. (1991).
Featherstone, M. (1987), Lifestyles and Consumer Culture Theory, *Culture and Society,* 4, pp. 55-70.
Featherstone, M. (1991), *Consumer Culture and Postmodernism,* London: Sage.
Foucault, M. (1988), On Power and Social Security, in Kritzman, L.D. (ed.), *Foucault. Interviews and Other Writings 1977-1984,* London: Routledge.
Foucault, M. (1991), Governmentality, in Burchell et al. (1991).
Goldman, R. (1992), *Reading Ads Socially*, London: Routledge.
Hacking, I. (1991), *How Should We Do the History of Statistics,* in Burchell et al. (1991).
Hollway, W. (1991), *Work Psychology and Organisational Behaviour,* London: Sage.
Hooley, G.J., Lynch J.E., and Shepherd, J. (1990), The Marketing Concept, Putting Theory into Practice, *European Journal of Marketing,* 24(9), pp. 7-24.
Hopwood, A. (1987), The Archaeology of Accounting Systems Accounting, *Organisations and Society*, 12(3), pp. 207-234.
Joseph, L., and Yorke, D. (1989), Know Your Game Plan – Market Segmentation in the Personal Financial Services Sector, *Quarterly Review of Marketing,* 15(1), pp. 8-13.

Knights, D. (1988), Risk, Financial Self-Discipline and Commodity Relations: An Analysis of the Growth of Life Assurance, *Contemporary Capitalism Advances in Public Interest Accounting*, 2(1), pp. 47-69.

Knights, D., and Morgan, G. (1990a), Management Control in Salesforces Work, *Employment and Society*, 4(3), pp. 369-389

Knights, D., and Morgan, G. (1990b), The Concept of Strategy in Sociology, *Sociology*, 23(3), pp. 475-483.

Knights, D., and Morgan, G. (1993), Organization Theory and Consumption in a Post-Modern Era, *Organization Studies*, 14(2), pp. 211-234.

Knights, D., Morgan, G., and Sturdy, A.J. (1993), Quality for the Consumer in Bancassurance?, *Consumer Policy Review*, 3(4), pp. 232-240.

Knights, D., Sturdy, A.J., and Morgan, G. (1994), The Consumer Rules? An Examination of the Rhetoric and Reality of Marketing in Financial Services, *European Journal of Marketing*, 28(3), pp. 42-54

Kotler, P. (1988), *Marketing Management Analysis, Planning, Implementation and Control*, New York: Prentice Hall.

Langlumé, P.M. (1992) (interview), Fidéliser, segmenter, globaliser directions, *CAPA*, (19), pp. 61-63.

Lock, C.M. (1947), *The County Borough of Middlesborough Survey and Plan*, Middlesborough: Middlesborough Corporation.

Marcuse, H. (1964), *One-Dimensional Man*, London: Routledge and Keegan Paul.

Mendras, H., and Cole, A. (1991), *Social Change in Modern France: Towards a Cultural Anthropology of the Fifth Republic*, Cambridge: CUP.

Moser, C.A. (1958), *Social Investigation*, London: Heinemann.

Moubray, G. de (1990), Le consommateur recherche une securité emotionelle, *Le Moniteur des Assurance*, 1095.

Murphy, P.E., and Staples W.A. (1979), A Modernized Family Life Cycle, *Journal of Consumer Research*, 6(June), pp. 12-22.

Newman, K. (1984), *Financial Marketing and Communications*, Eastbourne: Holt.

Paitra, J. (1990), De la securité passive à la securité active, *Risques*, 3 December.

Philippe, M.A. (1992), *La saga de la distribution directions*, CAPA, (19), pp. 46-51.

Piore, M., and Sabel, C. (1984), *The Second Industrial Divide: Possibilities for Prosperity*, New York: Basic Books.

Roche, P. (1990), Stratégie des sociétés d'assurance: segmentation ou selection, *Risques*, October, pp. 146-151.

Rose, N. (1988), Calculable Minds and Manageable Individuals, *History of the Human Sciences*, 1,pp. 179-200.

Rose, N. (1989), *Governing the Soul – The Shaping of the Private Self*, London: Routledge.

Rothmann, J.-M. (1990), Assurance et solidariteé – le point de vue des consommateurs, *Risques*, (October), pp. 85-88.

Rowntree, B.S. (1901), *Poverty: A Study of Town Life*, London: MacMillan.

Savitt, R. (1987), Entrepreneurial Behavior and Marketing Strategy, in Firat, F./Dholakia, N./Bagozzi, R.P. (eds.), *Philosophical and Radical Thought in Marketing*, Lexington: Lexington Books.

Schauerman, J. (1990), A New Basis for Segmenting the Corporate Banking Market, in Teare, R., Motinko, L., and Morgan, N. (eds.), *Managing and Marketing Services in the 1990s*, London: Cassel.

Smith, W.R. (1956), Product Differentiation and Market Segmentation as Alternative, *Strategic Journal of Marketing,* July, pp. 3-8.
Speed, R., and Smith, G. (1992), Retail Financial Services Segmentation, *Services Industry Journal,* 12(3), pp. 368-383.
Sturdy, A.J., and Morgan, G. (1993), Segmenting the Market – A Review of Marketing Trends in French Retail Banking, *International Journal of Bank Marketing,* 11(7), pp. 11-19
Verbeke W. (1992), Advertisers Do not Persuade Consumers; they Create Societies Around their Brands to Maintain Power, *Marketplace International Journal of Advertising,* 11, pp. 1-13.
Weber, M. (1948), *Selected Writings,* London: Routledge and Keegan Paul.
Wells, W.D. (1975), Psychographics – A Critical Review, *Journal of Marketing Research,* 12(May), pp. 196-213.
Whittington, R., and Whipp, R. (1992), Professional Ideology and Marketing Implementation, *European Journal of Marketing,* 26(1), pp. 52-63.
Willis, P. (1990), *Common Culture,* Milton Keynes: Open University Press.
Wood, S. (ed.) (1989), *The Transformation of Work?,* London: Unwin Hyman.
Zollinger, M. (1985), *Marketing Bancaire,* Paris: Durand.

From Concealment to Magnification: The Changing Social and Economic Agenda behind Homeworking

Michael Brocklehurst

Introduction

"The language which we use and which is directed to us embodies specific views – or 'theories' – of reality" (Fowler et al. 1979). Yet our use of language not only reflects social processes but simultaneously serves to legitimize these same processes. In such a way is meaning reinforced. The language use surrounding "work" is of particular significance because "work" is such a central activity. This chapter will use "homeworking"[1] and its contemporary variant "teleworking"[2] or "new technology homeworking" to explore the construction of the meaning of "work."

A concept such as homeworking is embedded in a network of related concepts which add meaning by providing contrast and context. Chief among these are concepts such as "employment," "unemployment," "leisure," "women's work" and "men's work" and the "private realm" and the "public realm." Homeworking itself needs to be broken down into its constituent parts of "home" and "work."

This chapter will attempt to show how the language use surrounding the concept of "homeworking" has served to disguise the real nature and extent of homework. In so far as traditional homeworking in the UK is concerned, this has led to its concealment; in so far as teleworking or new technology homeworking is concerned it has led to its exaggeration.

The chapter will start by tracing how the concepts of "home" and "work" have evolved since the 18th century before turning to examine how the terms are used today and the implications of contemporary usage. An attempt will then be made to gauge the extent of both traditional homeworking and new technology homework by drawing on published surveys and preliminary findings of the author's own research. The chapter will then proceed to account for the agenda behind new technology homework before concluding with some observations about the contradictions within the meanings given to "work" and its relationships to gender and the "public" and the "private."

The Concept of Work and Home in Eighteenth Century England

To understand both the historical and contemporary significance of homeworking requires tracing how the meanings of "home" and "work" have evolved.

Most members of an 18th century laboring household worked and most of this work would have taken place at home. The work would be intermittent and varied and only some of it would have been waged. As Malcolmson states:- "In most households an adequate subsistence depended on a complex of various forms of task-work and wage labor: regular, full-time employment at a single job was not the norm" (Malcolmson 1988: 48). This means that factories were virtually nonexistent at that time and, according to Chambers (1961: 21-22), did not become the dominant form in most industries until the last decade of the 19th century. Hence it was the household which was the central unit of production in 18th century England with domestic manufacture and farming of a small-holding often existing side by side.

Commentators disagree about the extent of wage labor at this time and generalizations are difficult because of wide regional disparities. Malcolmson (1988) considers it relatively unimportant. Kumar (1988) argues, however, that wage labor was predominant in the 18th century. Yet both agree that plurality and irregularity of occupations, organized around the home, was the norm. There was no clear distinction in terms of task content between waged and unwaged work; moreover wage work was sometimes paid for in cash and sometimes in kind.

The family economy also involved women and children in both waged and unwaged work. "The family economy was not normally centered around a single breadwinner: rather it was assumed that the family's sustenance would depend on the productive contributions of all its members, each of whom helped to sustain the whole" (Malcolmson 1988: 59). It is interesting to speculate if this period represents greater social and economic equality for women compared with what was to follow. Berg (1988), in reviewing the literature, concludes that not enough is known of women's working lives during this period to form any definitive conclusions.

The material basis for consciousness in the 18th century was thus very different from the 20th century. Work was not seen as something virtually synonymous with employment – least of all with employment outside the home, executed by males and constituting a singular, life long occupation or career. Indeed Kumar is critical of E.P. Thompson in this context. "Thompson's remark that, "the family was roughly torn apart each morning by the factory bell" (Thompson 1964: 416) is misleading, with its suggestion of a decisive fragmentation of family life, a radical separation of the spheres of work and family" (Kumar 1988: 157). If there is no concept of "employment" then there is no concept of "unemployment" either. The term "unemployed" did not assume its modern meaning in the Oxford English Dictionary until the late 1880s and the term was not a separate heading in Hansard until the early 20th century (Kumar 1988; Habershon 1986).

If "home" was the major location of work then "home" could not be distinguished from "work" and contrasted to a world of work which lay outside the home as is possible today. In fact the contemporary meaning of "home" with its connotations of comfort, privacy and intimacy, of a sanctuary against a harsh and impersonal public world of work, is a recent construction. Indeed the Japanese – lacking the concept – have found it necessary to import the term "praibashii." Such contemporary notions of "home" are first documented as occurring amongst the 17th century Dutch bourgeois and were taken up by their English counterparts in the 18th century (Rybczynski 1988). Bourgeois homes were by then no longer a place of trade and employed work – save for domestic servants. This enabled such homes to become places of leisure, for playing indoor games and reading novels. Diversions such as cards, billiards, embroidery, dancing and contemplation of one's garden all became popular for the first time. Although the home was a social place it also retained the element of privacy for its inhabitants. Visitors were screened and the system of calling cards was introduced to avoid the potential embarrassment of an unannounced visit. Within the home there were further layers of privacy, resembling the skins of an onion, culminating in each member of a well-to-do-family having his or her own room (Rybczynski 1988).

This world is captured in the novels of Jane Austen. Thus Mr. Woodhouse, when invited to meet Mr. Elton in Austens *Emma*, talks of: "The folly of not allowing people to be comfortable at home, and the folly of peoples not staying comfortably at home when they can" (Austen 1984: 91).

However it was to take at least another hundred years before such notions traveled down to working class homes. Firstly such homes had to be purged of "work." Secondly it required a reformulation of the concepts of "domesticity" and "comfort" so the concepts could be applied to the much smaller and poorer homes of the working class. It required the invention of "coziness."

Work and Home in the Twentieth Century

By the middle of the 20th century a very different conceptual relationship between the family and work had become established. On the one hand the relationship comprised a single, male breadwinner leaving the home behind to go out to undertake waged work in the public realm. On the other hand, the female stayed at home in the private realm, occupied with unpaid housework and child care.

The development of this new conception was fragmentary and uneven. The movement of waged work into factories varied across sectors and "putting-out" to homeworkers was still a dominant form of work organization in many industries until well into the 19th century. Thus hosiery in the East Midlands was still primarily a domestic industry up until the 1860s (Bradley 1986). Paradoxically,

early industrialization often resulted in an expansion of small-scale domestic industry (Pollard 1978; Samuel 1977).

The initial movement to a factory system did not immediately result in the con-
finement of women to the home. The early factory cotton industry employed far
more women and children than men (Berg 1988). Sometimes the family would be
employed en bloc – a common practice in the hosiery industry right up to the end
of the 19th century (Bradley 1986). It is as well to remember that agriculture was
still the most significant mode of employment accounting for nearly a quarter of
the occupied population at mid-century (Pollard 1978). Domestic service was also
significant and accounted for 40% of waged women workers at this time (Kumar
1988).

The gradual process by which married women were excluded from the labor force has been well documented (Oakley 1977). Protective labor legislation
against the employment of children and the differentiation of "childhood" as a
separate role from "adulthood" led to a decline in the numbers of children in paid
work and the child gradually assumed its modern role of dependent; this process
was reinforced by the growth of the school system and the Compulsory Education
Acts of 1870 and 1902. It was also emphasized that this dependency of children
required the attention of women. Simultaneously women's access to paid employment was being restricted by the Mines Act of 1842 and the Factory Act of 1847.

By the middle of the 19th century, a belief in female domesticity and marriage
as a full-time occupation was well entrenched amongst the middle class. Work
outside the home for women was seen as, at best, a misfortune and, at worst, a
disgrace. However it was a belief that did not diffuse to the working class until the
end of the 19th century (Oakley 1977). Kumar summarizes the trend succinctly:
"By 1911 only 10% of married women were employed compared to a quarter in
1851 and probably twice as much as that at the beginning of the 19th century"
(Kumar 1988: 164).

Attitudes towards the home were also percolating down through the class structure. Towards the end of the 19th century, the working class also began to perceive
the dwelling place as a home where each room had a function. Working class family life began to acquire the characteristics of privacy and of child centerdness. By
the 20th century, as Oakley notes, "the family itself has identified more and more
squarely with its physical location, the home. 'Home' and 'family' are now virtually interchangeable terms" (Oakley 1977: 65).

Contemporary Concepts of Home and Work: The Price to be Paid

Language use always carries a price. To choose to apply a set of concepts in one
particular way blinds the user to seeing the world in a different way. Different conceptual systems cut up the world in different ways but each user believes his or

her conceptual system or way of seeing is the natural way – one that holds for all times and places. It is taken for granted. What then are the costs of the contemporary meaning given to the concepts of "home" and "work"?

The sharp divide between home and work, between the private world of women and the public world of men, has influenced the development of social science. The presence of men typically defines a space as "public" and hence the province of sociology (Ardener 1978). It has been argued that the development of sociology has been dominated by men and only recently has this domination come under challenge. Men have concentrated on "the public domain, to the affairs of state and the market place" (Stacey 1980: 173). In Stacey's view both structural-functionalism and Marxism treat the public world of work as primary and the family as secondary. In structural-functionalism the family is a unit which contributes to society as a "whole" by providing the affective ties which enable the "male" to deal with the impersonal world of work. For Marxists, the family is exclusively concerned with reproduction, "to recreate materially, politically and ideologically, the social relations of production" (Gamarnikow and Purvis 1983: 2).

This characterization of the "private" as something marginal has led to a distortion in perceptions of certain social phenomena. Male violence in general – and the incidence of rape in particular – are often viewed as belonging predominantly to the public realm in spite of evidence showing how prevalent they are in the private sphere. As Gamarnikow and Purvis state, "it is this definition of violence which ideologically separates the two spheres and which thus obscures violence in the private sphere by defining it out of existence" (Gamarnikow and Purvis 1983: 5). The extent of child abuse has also been underreported until recently – in part because it contradicts so markedly the structural-functional claim that the family plays a vital "affective" function.

By contrast the view that something as socially significant as work can only take place in the public realm has become firmly entrenched. "Work" and "employment" have become interchangeable. Unwaged work, such as housework, does not count when it comes to constructing a curriculum vitae.

If work is associated with employment in the public sphere while women are seen as belonging to the private sphere, then women who take employment are short-circuiting the categorical system.

Allen and Wolkowitz observe how: "Women's waged work (both at home and outside it) is assumed to be temporary, intermittent and of secondary importance to the individual household and the economy as a whole" (Allen and Wolkowitz 1987: 4). These authors go on to document how current categorizations have underplayed the significance of traditional homeworking. If Marxism regards the home as the center of reproduction then it leaves no place for analyzing production located in the home. Feminist scholarship, in challenging the association of women as being part of a private, trivial world, has concentrated on women's waged work outside the home and paradoxically glossed over homeworking. In-

deed, when considering the home, feminists have stressed the unpaid work which
women undertake (Allen and Wolkowitz 1987).

The problem is that homeworking is a square peg in a world of round holes.
It fits neither the definitions of applied economics nor of industrial sociology nor
of the world of the full-time, nine-to-five working day. It brings together the two
concepts of home and work which most would rather keep apart; the dissonance
is resolved by simply not using or thinking about the concept. Thus homeworking has become marginalized or even something slightly freakish to be uncovered
periodically by investigative journalists.

Assessing the "Real" Incidence of Traditional Homeworking

This marginalization of homeworking has also spread to official attempts to measure its true incidence. The UK Census of Population in 1911 and 1921 asked people to report if they worked at home but the question was subsequently dropped
and did not reappear until 1971. The question has always been phrased broadly to
include small businesses, the self employed or freelancers as well as traditional
homeworkers.

Even in the years when the question has been included, census forms are completed by the head of the household who is likely to be male and who may well
operate with categories which dictate that "work conducted in the home" – particularly when carried out by women – is not a "real" job. Homeworkers themselves
may also have a variety of reasons for disguising what they do. They may themselves not see what they do as "work"; they may fear official reprisal such as the
loss of state benefits, deportation as "illegal immigrants," prosecution for using
domestic premises for industrial use etc. (Allen and Wolkowitz 1987).

The Annual Census of Employment also asks firms to report the use of homeworkers. However it only polls firms which employ in-workers so those firms
which exclusively employ outworkers are omitted. Firms need only supply information on workers who pay tax and who were employed in one particular week.
So the low paid and the casual worker – two groups likely to contain many homeworkers – are both omitted. As Allen and Wolkowitz conclude: "The vulnerability
of homework was, and continues to be constructed partly by the method of collecting statistical data used by official bodies" (1987: 11).

The British state indeed had recognized its own database was inadequate (Employment Committee 1981, 1983) and so initiated a research program on homeworking of which the National Homeworking Survey of 1981 was the outcome
(Hakim 1987). This study does attempt to provide clear-cut distinctions between
different types of home-based worker. It was based on the Labour Force Survey of
1981 which did ask respondents, who did not have a paid job in one given week, if
they ever did any occasional or casual work. This question certainly helped to in-

crease the reporting of homework. However the Labour Force Survey used a high number of proxy informants which augments the chances of male underreporting of female homework. A summary of the National Homeworking findings is given in Appendix 1.

An alternative method is to try and discover the incidence of homeworking in a particular area (Allen and Wolkowitz 1987) or a particular industry (Mitter 1986). Allen and Wolkowitz attempted blanket coverage of areas in West Yorkshire using local "non-official" interviewers. They found homeworkers at 1.2% of the houses visited (cf. the National Homeworking Survey figure of 0.9% in Appendix 1). If the houses where there was "no response" are eliminated then the population jumps to 2.6% although "no response" will often indicate that all family members go out to work.

Mitter (1986) uses an ingenious approach in examining the UK clothing industry over the period 1974-1982. Investment in this industry has fallen dramatically as has capacity utilization; yet labor productivity has gone up. Part of this can be explained by work intensification and part by marginal (and so less productive) operators being forced out of business. However, Mitter also draws attention to a third possible reason: the growth of unregistered small operations employing workers in small shops and in the home. Her reasoning is that the input measures (i.e. the number of workers in the industry) are collected by Census of Employment Data which come from large firms which are then adjusted. But if the proportion of small unregistered producers are growing, then this adjustment will lead to underreporting of the numbers employed. However, the output figures are collected from different sources and are rising. Since increasing numbers of workers are hidden, then the gain in productivity is not real. This period also saw a buoyant market in second-hand sewing machines which provides reinforcement for the theory of a growth in homeworking (Rainie 1984). Mitter estimates that the Department of Employment's official estimates of "72,000 manufacturing homeworkers for the UK as a whole" would have to be substantially increased; there may be this number in London alone.

There are of course dangers in blowing up figures for a locality or industry – which may well be atypical – to produce national figures. Nevertheless such studies do tend to suggest a considerable underreporting of the true extent of traditional homeworking.

Assessing the "Real" Incidence of New Technology Homeworking

One of the earliest proponents of new technology homeworking was Toffler (1980: 212) who quoted industrialists as saying that 25% to 50% of the workforce could do most, if not all of their work at home. In the UK, Clutterbuck and Hill (1981) were claiming that by the year 2000 "a considerable proportion of employees will work from home, most of them with a computer terminal of some kind for all or part of the week" (1981: 19). Other studies in the latter part of the 1980s appeared to confirm this trend of substantial growth. The National Economic Development Office reported that it was predicted that 10-15% of the UK workforce would be working from an electronic office in the home by 1995 and 20% by 2010 (NEDO 1986: viii). The Henley Centre for Forecasting estimated in 1988 that, if it depended on the nature of the job, almost half the workforce could be doing some telecommuting by 1995 (quoted in the Sunday Times, article "When Homework Comes of Age," 28 April 1988). Other sources were even prepared to put figures on the current extent of new technology homeworking. Thus Forester (1987: 162) states there has been: "A steady increase in homeworking over the last decade especially among white collar workers to 1.7 million or 4% of the workforce by 1985." In 1988 the Director General of the Confederation of British Industry (CBI) was on record as saying "some 2 million people are currently working from home with the aid of a telephone or a fax machine or a computer which can signal directly to the computer in the office or factory. The number could easily double to 4 million by 1995 – roughly one in six of the working population" (CBI News Release "Go to work-by Phone" 3 August 1988).

When these claims are examined carefully they do not tell such a convincing story. Many of the above sources rely on "expert" testimony rather than quantification (Toffler 1980; Clutterbuck and Hill 1981). Indeed Kinsman (1987: 24-6) regards this as a virtue. "Statistics can incorporate a spurious sense of uncertainty into an analysis of future projects because so often a mere extrapolation of today's curve is a poor guide to the shape of tomorrow's urban community. It is perhaps better to depend on the weight of informed qualitative opinion than on the quantitative evidence of the past – hence the reliance here on a panel of the expert and the experienced." On closer examination many of the studies such as the Henley study are only indicating the potential of new technology homeworking. Even the precise figures given for present numbers are suspect. Forester (1987) does not give a source and implies that these 1.7 million are all new technology homeworkers – it seems likely he is referring to the figure for all home based workers including those living at home and those with live-in jobs (see Appendix 1).[3] One could also be cynical about the figures quoted in the CBI press release since it goes on to publicize a conference jointly sponsored by the CBI and British Telecom on working from home. What then is the true picture?

The National Homeworking Survey of 1981 gives a detailed breakdown of the principal occupations of non-manufacturing homeworkers. (See Appendix 2. The occupations which lend themselves to new technology homeworking are marked with an asterisk.) Even if one assumes that everyone in these occupations was working as new technology homeworker, then the number of such workers in 1981 was no more than 80,000.

Another approach is to find out how many households have a computer at home which could be used for work. The British Social Attitude Survey of 1985 found only 0.5% of economically active households had a computer installed at home with a telephone linked to a mainframe; this would suggest that the number of such homeworkers was then between 10,000 and 15,000. Although 3.8% of households had a word processor, it is probable a large proportion of these would not be used for paid work (survey quoted in Hakim 1987: 250). These figures stand in stark contrast to the estimates of alleged "experts" given above and fit with the critical case study evidence available at the time (Brocklehurst 1989a).

More recent research indicates that, if there has been any recent growth in new technology homeworking, it has been very slow. The author conducted research in 1991 and 1992 to try and uncover new technology homeworking projects. There has been a steady growth amongst the highly skilled professional workers although frequently such workers only work some days at home and retain an office presence. (An update on the case reported in Brocklehurst 1989a noted how the company concerned – a critical case in that it possessed all the features likely to encourage new technology homeworking – had over thirty workers in 1992 in this mode compared to only three in 1988.) However exhaustive attempts to uncover clerical new technology homeworkers have only discovered eighty such workers working for five different employers.

One interesting finding is that the constraints appear to be on the demand side. Every case researched revealed that the employer has been inundated by applications whenever the firm has advertised new technology homeworking jobs; this applies as much before the current recession as during it. This is confirmed by other recent research which suggests that interest in new technology homeworking is higher in the UK than in West Germany, France and Italy (Huws et al. 1990).

What explanation can be offered for this significant gap between the claims made about the prevalence of new technology homeworking and the actual incidence?

The Agenda behind New Technology Homeworking

New technology homeworking is seen as a "convenient" solution to a wide range of "problems" which presently preoccupy "First World" industrial nations. Claims are made that the escalating costs of commuting in terms of energy, time and stress and the high costs of inner city business locations could all be reduced by new technology homeworking (Toffler 1980; Handy 1984). Developing such homeworking could help unleash the "information economy" and offset the worrying decline in manufacturing in countries such as the UK (Handy 1984). The "solution" of new technology homework is seen as taking advantage of one of the "success" stories of modern industry: the falling costs and increased capabilities of modern telecommunications technology. New technology homeworking is thus presented as a dramatic illustration of the economic system's self-healing properties and provides a balm to those who find "social engineering solutions" – and other more radical solutions to societal ills – unpalatable.

There is also a humanist/ecological variation of new technology homework. Toffler's image of the "electronic cottage" (Toffler 1980) has become a defining concept for many – a world of "small is beautiful" and a contrast with urban blight. Williams (1981: 69) has played on the same image: "Human beings can be made whole again, working and living in the same community. Microelectronics offer the opportunity of reuniting the family and making commuting an obsolete and unnecessary activity." Here we have a golden, mythical and organic past and future, both tantalizingly just out of reach.

Others such as Robertson (1985) see new technology homework as a mechanism for permitting a decentralization and democratization of work: "Whereas the technology of the industrial age drove work out of the home and the neighbourhood and deprived most people of the freedom to control their work, the technology of the post-industrial age will make it possible to reverse this trend."

This stress on the "home" and the "neighborhood" enables new technology homework to be seen as a means of shoring up the family, as a way of resolving the alleged conflict between on the one hand, the feminization of the labor force and, on the other hand, the moral concerns about the "decline" of the family and the alleged decline in behavioral standards of youths and adolescents. The argument runs that, if women must work, then it is better they do so at home and preferably on a part-time basis. This is in spite of evidence that new technology homework and child care make uneasy bedfellows (Brocklehurst 1989b). Both Robertson (1985) and Handy (1984) welcome the growth in part-time work. Toffler (1980: 219) sees his electronic cottage leading to lower divorce as does Williams (1991). The community too will see a new lease of life as families no longer need to relocate. A new job will involve no more than unplugging from one computer and plugging in to another.

Behind this propagation of new technology homework lies a drive for privatization in all its forms. Some instances are the stimulus given to owner occupation in the 1980s and the encouragement of people to retreat to the cozy world of family and to turn their backs on the deteriorating public realm – a world of rising crime and vandalism, of declining transport and cuts in public spending on nursery care. It is as if new technology homeworking is being seen as a way of shoring up the private realm, of strengthening it in order that the private may take the pressure off the inadequacies of the public realm.

New technology homeworking is pictured as a positive sum game. It thus takes its place in a long tradition of futurology which sees conflict being resolved by technology (Bell 1961). To quote Toffler: "the leap to a new production system in both manufacturing and the white collar sector and the possible breakthrough to the electronic cottage promises to change all the existing terms of debate making obsolete most of the issues over which men and women today argue, struggle and sometimes die" (Toffler 1980: 223).

The same process is seen at work in two related concepts. Roszak (1986) has noted how the concept of "information" has been elevated in status. He argues that the belief has taken hold in many circles that when confronted with a problem – particularly one involving conflict – all that is required is more information. Information is an end-product of an increasing number of enterprises and looks set to become more significant than consumable goods and services in the UK (Handy 1984). Others have noted how "flexibility," of which new technology homework is often given as an example, carries the same positive consensual aura (MacInnes 1987; Pollert 1991).

Conclusion

This chapter has attempted to trace the evolution of the meaning attached to work within one country and how that meaning forms part of a wider web of meaning linked to concepts such as "the public" and "the private" and "male" and "female." This web provides a mutually legitimizing process which helps to fix the meaning of each individual concept. Yet conceptual systems contain contradictions. In this chapter homeworking and its over- and under-reporting has been used to demonstrate such a contradiction. While women were being excluded from the labor force during the later part of the 19th century and the first half of this century, then it did not serve to draw attention to their role as workers. Homeworking as one of the few avenues open to married women – particularly those with dependents – was thus ignored. Home was seen as something separate from the contamination of work and a place where women were expected to make the major contribution. However in the 20th century, as the feminization of the labor force continues – over 71% of women of working age are now economically active in the UK compared to only 63% as recently as 1979 (Employment Gazette 1992) – it becomes increasingly hard to retain the notion that women workers are working in some sort of intermittent, transitory and secondary role. It is of note that women's role in taking prime responsibility for domestic duties has remained more or less a constant over the past century (British Social Attitudes 1992); it is the way these responsibilities have to be combined with women's paid work which has changed.

New technology homework may provide a convenient rhetorical device for resolving the contradiction since it permits the notion of women working while retaining the link between the female and the private realm.[4] There is thus an incentive to exaggerate its importance. In contrast to this rhetoric, the small growth of new technology homework indicates that this "solution" is not on the agenda for most British women.

Appendix 1: Distribution of Home-based Work

		All home based workers 658,250		Total 1.7million or 7% of the labor force
			plus another 750,000 living at work & with live-in jobs	
		All home-based workers excluding childminers, etc. 630,000		
Childminding & related work done mainly at home both for single & 2+ clients (all women) 27,000	Working at home (mainly women) 229,800		Working from home as a base (mainly men) 400,800	plus another 284,000 in construction road haulage & family workers

	No.	% of all working at home	% of total labor force
Manufacturing homeworkers			
– single employer	40,000	17.4	0.16
– multiple employers	18,750	8.2	0.08
– total	58,750	25.6	0.24
Other homeworkers			
– single employer	66,270	28.8	0.23
– multiple employers	104,780	45.6	0.43
– total	171,050	74.4	0.66
Total homeworkers	229,800	100.0	0.90

Source: National Homeworking Survey 1981, in Hakim (1987) (England-Wales only).

Appendix 2: Principal Occupations of Non-manufacturing Homeworkers

---

A. Working for single employer

Teachers (marking, preparation of course material)	6,000
Local government	3,000*
Systems analysts and programmers	1,000*
Key-punch operators	1,000*
Typists/secretaries	15,000*
Non-retail clerks and cashiers	21,000*
Mail-order agents and collectors	6,000*

B. Working for multiple employers

Telephone canvassers/sales representatives & agents	5,000
Import/export	3,000*
Retail sales	8,000*
Management consultants	1,500*
Accountants	7,500*
Architects	3,000
Hairdressers/beauticians	1,500
Commercial artists and illustrators	12,000
Journalists, writers, authors, translators	16,000
Professional and related in education, welfare and health (not otherwise classified)	21,000*

---

* Indicates could be involved in new technology homeworking.

Source: National Homeworking Survey 1981, adapted from Hakim (1987).

Notes

[1] Homeworking is defined here as "the supply of work to be performed in domestic premises which offers the highest degree of flexibility to the employer." This definition stresses that homeworking is principally a form of waged work; its location is secondary. The intention is to eliminate the self-employed freelancers who work for a range of clients. In practice the employed/self employed distinction is hard to draw as sometimes one or both parties prefer the designation "self-employed" even though the homeworker has almost all the characteristics of a conventionally waged worker.

[2] The phenomenon whereby employees work at home using a computer is easily comprehended. The most commonly used terms are teleworking (Huws et al. 1990, Stanworth and Stanworth 1991) or telecommuting (Kinsman 1987). However these terms also include any remote working with a computer and not just work at home. This chapter is specifically concerned with work at home and so the term "new technology homework" is preferred. The definition then is "the supply of work to be performed in domestic premises and involving a computer which offers the highest degree of flexibility to the employer."

[3] It is interesting to note how Forester is now far less bullish about the prospects for new technology homeworking (see Forester 1988).

[4] Huws (1991), in tracking the various images of new technology homeworking makes a similar point. She notes how one particular image works to reconcile the conflict of "women as paid labor outside the home" with "women as unpaid labor inside the home."

References

Allen, S., and Wolkowitz, C. (1987), *Homeworking: Myths and Realities*, MacMillan, London.

Ardener, S. (1978), Introduction, in Ardener, S. (ed.), *Defining Females: The Nature of Women in Society*, Croom Helm, London.

Austen, J. (1984), *Emma*, Everyman Edition, Dent, London.

Bell, D. (1961), *The End of Ideology: On the Exhaustion of Political Ideas in the Fifties*, Collins, New York.

Berg, M. (1988), Women's Work, Mechanisation and the Early Phases of Industrialisation in England, in Pahl, R. (ed.), *On Work: Historical, Comparative and Theoretical Approaches*, Blackwell, Oxford.

Bradley, H. (1986), Work, Home and the Restructuring of Jobs, in Purcell, K., Wood, S., Watson, A., and Allen, S. (eds.), *The Changing Experiences of Employment: Restructuring and Recession*, MacMillan, London.

British Social Attitudes (1992), *Social and Community Planning Report*, Dartmouth Publishing, Dartmouth.

Brocklehurst, M. (1989a), Homeworking and the New Technology: The Reality and the Rhetoric, *Personnel Review*, 18(2).

Brocklehurst, M. (1989b), Combining a Career with Child Care – Is New Technology Homeworking the Way Forward?, *Women in Management Review and Abstracts*, 4(4), pp. 5-11.

Chambers, J.D. (1961), *The Workshop of the World*, Oxford University Press, Oxford.

Clutterbuck, D., and Hill, R. (1981), *The Remaking of Work*, Grant Macintyre International Management, London.

Employment Committee (1981), Homeworking, House of Commons, First Report from the Employment Committee Session 1981-82 and Minutes of Evidence (HC 1980-81) 188i to 188vii, HMSO, London.

Employment Committee (1983), The Work of the Department of Employment Group, Minutes of Evidence, HC 1981: 213ii, HMSO, London.

Employment Gazette (1992), Women and the Labour Market, Results from the *1991 Labour Force Survey*, 100(9), HMSO, London.

Forester, T. (1987), *High Tech Society: The Story of the Information Technology Revolution*, Blackwell, Oxford.

Forester, T. (1988), The Myths of the Electronic Cottage, *Futures*, 20 June.

Fowler, R. and Kress, G. (1979), Rules and Regulations, in Fowler, R., Kress, G., Trew, A., and Hodge, R. (eds.), *Language and Control*, Routledge and Kegan Paul, London.

Gamarnikow, E., and Purvis, J. (1983), Introduction, in Gamarnikow, E. (ed.), *The Public and the Private*, Heinemann, London.

Habershon, J. (1986), Perspectives on the Experience of Unemployment, PhD Thesis (unpublished), University of London, London.

Hakim, C. (1987), Home-based Work in Britain, Department of Employment Research Paper 60, HMSO, London.

Handy, C. (1984), *The Future of Work*, Blackwell, Oxford.

Huws, U. (1984), The New Homeworkers: New Technology and the Changing Location of Work, *Low Pay Unit*, 28.

Huws, U. (1991), Telework Projections, *Futures*, 23(Jan.-Feb.), pp.19-31.

Huws, U., Korte, W.B., and Robinson, S. (1990), *Telework: Towards the Elusive Office*, John Wiley, Chichester.

Kinsman, F. (1987), *The Telecommuters*, John Wiley, Chichester.

Kumar, K. (1988), From Work to Employment to Unemployment: The English Experience, in Pahl, R. (ed.), *On Work: Historical, Comparative and Theoretical Approaches*, Blackwell, Oxford.

MacInnes, J. (1987), *Thatcherism at Work: Industrial Relations and Economic Change*, Open University Press, Milton Keynes.

Malcolmson, R.W. (1988), Life and Labour in England 1700-1800, in Pahl, R. (ed.), *On Work: Historical, Comparative and Theoretical Approaches*, Blackwell, Oxford.

Mitter, S. (1986), Industrial Restructuring and Manufacturing Homework: Immigrant Women in the UK Clothing Industry, *Capital and Class*, 27.

NEDO (1986), IT Futures Surveyed. A Study of Informal Opinion Concerning the Long-Term Implications of Information Technology, Technology and Society, HMSO, London.

Oakley, A. (1977), *Housewife*, Penguin, London.

Pollard, S. (1978), Labour in Great Britain, in *Cambridge Economic History of Europe*, 7 (Part 1), Cambridge University Press, Cambridge.

Pollert, A. (1991), The Orthodoxy of Flexibility, in Pollert, A. (ed.), *Farewell to Flexibility*, Blackwell, Oxford.

Rainie, A. (1984), Combined and Uneven Development in the Clothing Industry: The Effects of Competition on Accumulation, *Capital and Class* (1).

Robertson, J. (1985), *Future Work*, Gower, London.

Roszak, T.(1986), *The Cult of Information: the Folklore of Computers and the True Art of Thinking,* Pantheon, New York.

Rybczynski, W. (1988), *Home: A Short History of an Idea*, Heinemann, London.

Samuel, R. (1977), Workshop of the World: Steam Power and Hand Technology in Mid-Victorian Britain, *History Workshop*, 3 (Spring).

Stacey, J. (1980), The Division of Labour Revisited or Overcoming the Two Adams, in Abrams, P., and Lewthwails, P. (eds.), *Development and Diversity: British Sociology 1950-1980*, Allen and Unwin, London.

Stanworth, J., and Stanworth, C. (1991), *Telework: The Human Resource Implications*, Institute of Personnel Management, London.

Thompson, E. (1964), *The Making of the English Working Class*, Victor Gollancz, London.

Toffler, A. (1980), *The Third Wave*, Collins/Pan Books, London.

Williams, S. (1981), *Politics Is for People*, Penguin, Harmondsworth.

Part II
Management and Meaning at Work

Corporate Culture and De-Institutionalization: Implications for Identity in a Brazilian Telecommunications Company

Suzana Braga Rodrigues

Introduction

The notion of organizational culture has received considerable attention in organizational studies in recent years. In contrast to the 1960s and the 1970s when attention was focused on the rational utilitarian behavior of those acting in organizations, recent studies have focused on the subjective and emotional side of organizational life (Smircich 1983; Turner 1990; Gagliardi 1990; Frost et al. 1991; Alvesson and Berg 1992; Alvesson and Willmott 1992; Fineman 1994). As some authors suggest (Turner 1990 and Morgan 1986), the failure of western organizations to reproduce Japanese productivity levels by transplanting their management techniques has revealed the importance of cultural background in the sense of exposing the difficulties in transferring that tacit (Faulkner 1994), uncodified knowledge (Boisot and Liang 1992) embedded in techniques which is inseparable from culture.

The study of growing Asian economies has raised scholarly curiosity about socially institutionalized non-orthodox forms of behavior which can also result in organizations which are competitive under a market order, despite western understanding of what constitutes technically ideal forms (Orrù et al. 1991). In drawing attention to cultural factors, the institutionalist approach has demonstrated, the relevance of myths and rituals in the creation of a stable organizational logic (Meyer and Rowan 1991; DiMaggio and Powell 1991) even if prescriptions of normal rationality and technical efficiency have indicated otherwise, and have showed, in addition, how organizations can abandon traditional practices (Oliver 1992) despite their members' opposition.

The emphasis on the institutionalization of values and behavior in organizations through building of corporate cultures appeared associated on the one hand with declining quality in American industry in the 1980s (Turner 1986), and on the other, with the high estimation of Japanese companies as examples of organizations which maximize staff commitment. Though postmodernity seems to be awaiting a Japanization of the industrial world (Clegg 1992; Oliver and Wilkinson 1992) which is based on the ability to manage groups and on collectivism (Hofst-

ede 1992), the West, conversely, witnesses the emergence of the "new age" of sacred individualism; an increasing concern with autonomy, self-development, and
self fulfilment (Heelas 1991). Furthermore, we have the fact that excessive preoccupation with the question of personal security, involving concepts such as "false
consciousness" and "alienation," usually denotes the waning power of modern organizations to provide it, as stated by Berger et al. (1973). Such realignment of
organizational studies around culture, therefore, cannot be understood separately from changes in western societies, such as the strengthening of individualism
(Pascale 1985) and the sacralization of self (Heelas 1991) which apparently conflicts with the logic of collectivism predominant in Asian organizations. Neither
can it be understood apart from the contradictions of capitalism itself. Bell (1991)
argues that because of economic demands, modern organizations are unable to ful-
fil needs of individual self-realization which have become central to western culture. In this context, the emergence of corporate culture as a notion central to management seemed ideal, apparently, allowing for the reconciliation of the emotions
and the subjective – the unpredictable and intangible, but undeniable, dimensions
of organizations – with their rational requirements. In other words, it permitted the
integration of the symbolic with the rational and strategic, by proposing to manage
the symbolic, and thus, bringing the unmanageable under control.

Corporate culture presumes that a strong culture is a consistent organizational state achievable by the construction of shared meanings through managing
symbols, rituals, myths and creating heroes (Deal and Kennedy 1982; Allen and
Kraft 1982; Sathe 1985). The underlying assumption is that a strong and unitary
culture generates a greater return on investment (Saffold III 1988); productivity would be improved by creating a favorable climate and greater job satisfaction (Ouchi 1981). Within this approach, socialization into organizational values
is a necessary solution to control uncertainties derived from individual idiosyn-
crasies and, therefore, it is an "inescapable necessity for organizational effectiveness" (Pascale 1985: 29). As Rose (1989: xi) argues, the psychological imperative
of work became as important as the economic; "work itself is a means of self-
fulfillment, and the pathway to company profit is also the pathway to individual self-actualization." Nevertheless, the potential of a strong corporate culture to
generate meanings for employees' identity, and management's capacity to create
a homogeneous organizational culture through shared meanings has been largely
overstated and overestimated.

This paper argues through an in-depth case study of a Brazilian telecommunications company that managerial strategies to foster an organizational culture may
oppose employees' attempts to achieve individual identity. It shows that when
an organization tries to introduce a new corporate culture that opposes already
institutionalized values, this may lead to de-institutionalization and induce a redefinition of employees' involvement. By analyzing the characteristics of the organizations subcultures, those of the parent company and the top management,
for example, this paper suggests that, under these conditions, some categories of

employees (e.g. engineers) adopt different forms of affective distancing from the corporate culture while re-affirming that of the parent company's. In the very process of trying to stimulate individual identification with the organization, corporate culture may, paradoxically, create the opposite situation, i.e. "distancing" of employees or identity crises.

Corporate Culture and Identity

Research on organizational culture and on corporate culture in particular, has emphasized the homogeneity of culture (Pfeffer 1981; Pettigrew 1985; Albert, Whetten 1985; Schein 1986; Hampden-Turner 1990) and its cohesive function rather than its divisive potential (Gregory 1983; Meek 1988; Sackmann 1991; Fleury and Fisher 1989; Rose 1988); its integrative capacity and power to build shared meanings rather than resistance (Rodrigues and Collinson 1992); its capacity to generate meanings for individual identity rather than its potential to degrade identity.

The emphasis on the capacity of a culture to build consensus and shared meanings diverts attention from the importance of internalization (Berger and Luckmann 1976) and from the processes whereby a culture uses its available means (e.g. rituals) to supersede occupational or personal identity as the primary source of meanings for the individual (Warren 1990; Deetz 1992). It also diverts attention from its divisive (Gregory 1983) nature and its dependency on power relations and games, for the culture that unifies is also the one that separates (Bourdieu 1991; Foucault 1977).

The discussion whether a culture exists only as part of the individuals' conscience or whether it is recognizable only as shared meanings expressed by its artifacts, seems to be an old debate that goes back to Marx, Weber and Durkheim. Though the dilemma of whether, in cultural studies, primacy is accorded to subjective beliefs or objectified entities, seemed superseded by Berger and Luckmann's "Social Construction of Reality," much of the recent debate on culture still centers on the process of individuals seeking meaning versus the impact of the external social forces that the individual experiences as constraints (Wuthnow 1987; Alexander and Seidman 1991).

This debate about the interplay between agency and structure (Collier 1993; Apter and Garnsey 1992), and about masculinity and power at the workplace, have fostered the person as the agent of the production and reproduction of meanings (Knights 1990; Collinson et al. 1990; Knights and Collinson 1985; Collinson 1992; Deetz 1992). It draws attention to the importance of identity as a notion that explains why, how, and to what extent an individual incorporates meanings and then acts to reinforce them, or instead chooses not to incorporate them. Individuals may choose organizational routines and confirm rituals if they think this would

contribute to secure identity (Knights 1990), or learn how to reify external meanings as a strategy to cope with conflicting identities (Deetz 1992). Alternatively,
they may decide to withdraw commitment (Rodrigues 1991) and take refuge in
de-identification or detachment (Berger et al. 1973) or even distance themselves
by subtle and disguised forms of resistance (Rodrigues and Collinson 1992; Linstead 1988).

Furthermore, the strategy by which a culture defines itself as a dominant culture
is a political process. In the process of defining their own identities through building meanings for their intended patrons, dominant cultures define not only the sacred and the profane but also the included and the excluded (Bourdieu 1991). In
its strategy to create unity around a definition of reality, a dominant culture creates a hierarchy of the social world; it not only defines what people are and have to
be, but it also "makes and unmakes groups" (Bourdieu 1991: 221). Thus, a dominant culture, through its symbolic power, not only provides meanings for people
to make sense of reality, guiding what they see and believe, but also creates meanings for identities in the sense that it supplies definitions of what they are.

Bourdieu (1991: 221) suggests that the unity of a dominant group can be
foamed by the principles of "di-vision," whereby a group creates a consensus
around the principle of hierarchization and the distinction between insiders and
outsiders. By using their resources and means, agents "invest" their interest and
objectified representations (emblems, flags and images) in the definition of reality. They use their symbolic power "to sanctify," "to sanction," "to consecrate,"
and to show people what their places are and what they are worth. This notion of
culture, therefore, makes the concept of identity closely related to culture since it
is this process of definition and separation that makes identity recognizable and
distinct. It also brings the notion of culture close to that of power since the latter
not only translates a culture but, by its acts of power confirms and reinforces it.

As Foucault (1977) suggests, the use of power makes identity visible and distinct. By separating individuals and bodies, by registering "presences and ab-
sences," by differentiating individuals and creating hierarchies, power defines
what individuals are and must be. His notion of an invisible and pervasive power
network, the ideal power of the Panopticon, highlights the relevance of the internalization of power control, suggesting the significance of the interaction between
power and culture to the definition of identity. The distribution of places does not
depend on people occupying these positions: "the perfection of power should tend
to render its actual exercise unnecessary... this architectural apparatus should be
a machine for creating and sustaining a power relation independent of the person
who exercises it: in short,... the inmates should be caught in a power situation of
which they are themselves the bearers" (Foucault 1977: 201). It is in the sense that
power need not be embodied, that it homogenizes individuals into groups, that the
notion of power integrates better with the notion of culture.

Therefore, the use of power becomes more effective when it is able to create
symbolic means (e.g. an organizational culture) which encourages members to in-

ternalize values and disciplinary procedures that will provide them with identity and identification (Foucault 1977). A corporate culture is infused with symbolic power in the sense that it is able to impose a structure of classifications as natural, in a concealed way. According to Bourdieu (1989), an intrinsic characteristic of symbolic power is that it realizes its symbolic potential by displacement, that is, its effectiveness stems from the fact that it usually presents itself to the audience in a transmuted and concealed form. This permits power to impose classifications and categorizations under the appearance of religious and philosophical taxonomies. Furthermore, the effectiveness of classifications depends on specific acts of power such as punishment and reward mechanisms (Foucault 1977).

One way by which power makes classifications appear natural is by creating ceremonies and rituals of confirmation of its own superior identity. As Scott (1990) suggests, scripts of subordination continuously confirm power "by rules about language, gesture, tone and dress" (Scott 1990: 31). By adopting a subordinated attitude, acts of deference, attentive listening and encouraging smiles, "subordinated" individuals confirm not only their own "inferior identity" but also endorse the "superior identity" of "the powerful." Nevertheless, this paper does not intend to suggest that power shapes identity in an inexorable way. One contribution of subjectivity theories is to show that individuals can either re-affirm an attributed identity or not (Scott 1990, Knights 1990, Collinson 1992). According to Scott (1990: 5), subordinated attitudes and behavior are commonly public "transcripts" or misrepresentations that do not correspond to "hidden scripts." Behind the scenes the "dominated" tend to defend their subjective identity and social space via cultural responses by creating linguistic disguises, ritual codes and various forms of symbolic resistance. Escape into fantasy (Cohen and Taylor 1992; Thompson and McHugh 1991), development of alternative involvement outside the workplace universe (Thevenet 1993), and distancing (Knights and Collinson 1985; Collinson 1992) constitute usual responses to external pressures on identity.

Hence, the possibility of creating a strong culture depends on the construction of mutual representations; on the one hand on the consent and confirmation by "consumers" and on the other, on the capacity of this culture to generate meaningful values for them. The meanings advanced by a culture should make sense for "consumers" and provide their symbolic and material goods. As Collinson (1992: 29) points out, in the experience of the self as both "separated and yet related to the natural and social world" human beings may invest in a dominant or subordinated strategy: may choose either to become enactors or to be subjects in the world, in which latter case they can reinforce control and corporate strategy. Thus, culture and identity are interrelated and interdependent as each needs the other as a source of meaning.

At the individual level, identity emanates from the meanings an individual attributes to interaction with socially diverse groups, e.g. the family, the peer group, the schools. The significance of each varying in accordance with how it confirms and fosters the the individual's self perception (Tajfel 1978). Social psychologists view social identity as a subjective phenomenon whereby the individual definition of self is based on a comparison with others. According to Tajfel (1978: 3) identity is the "individual's knowledge that he belongs to certain social groups together with some emotional and value significance to him of group membership." This suggests that identity needs to be continuously informed by environment and culture. The individual, nevertheless, makes use of this information in a way that makes sense to him. Goffman's concept of "performed self" (Goffman 1956) suggests that individuals usually act in social interaction in order to improve their self concept. The content of an individual's evaluation of others should be favorable to his self-image and self-concept. Thus, while relationships with others inform self definition, self definition, in turn, guides and sets the parameters for ideas regarding others. As Berger (1966: 111) mentions, "one identifies oneself as one is identified by others." The dependency of identity on culture or on "significant others" makes it vulnerable to the absence or disappearance of those "significant others," whether they be a person, a group or an espoused value system that an individual has internalized through contact in an organization, or during a person's lifetime (Child and Rodrigues 1993). The dual experience of self as distinct from and, at the same time, integrated with the social world, and as both subject and object, creates ambiguity and makes identity a precarious concept. This results in an inherent need for confirmation which draws the individual into a continuous quest for security (Collinson 1992), and/or into an imaginary world of a performing self or a missing past (McCall and Simmons 1966; Cohen and Taylor 1992). In strategies to preserve identity one can usually, but not intentionally, confirm and reinforce those values one does not necessarily agree with (Knights 1990).

At the macro level, the organization can engage in strategies which can encourage individuals to choose between incorporation and abandonment of meanings, between a subordinate or an active position. It can use its main representations (rituals, myths and stories) both to enforce the sense of collectivity by confirming identity, or alternatively it can reinforce collective feelings by dissolving or degrading identity. As Trice and Beyer (1984) suggest, rites of degradation dissolve social identities at the same time as they reaffirm the importance of organizational values and defend their boundaries, making public who belongs and who does not. As Bourdieu (1976) puts it, rituals have the effect of confirming those who exercise power as well as those who have to obey. Their joint functions involve enforcing the organizational values by establishing distinctions. And by determining who are the insiders and who are the outsiders, they fulfill their political logic.

In using rituals of degradation, the organization chooses to reaffirm and separate its identity from "others," whereas in enhancement rituals it chooses to associate and identify with "others" (e.g. as in graduation ceremonies). In showing its distance from "others," these rituals dissociate the organization from their "failure," while in the case of enhancement rituals, managerial strategy involves sharing "others'" success and linking it to the organization, by suggesting that it is part of corporate identity (Trice and Beyer 1984). Both cases, nonetheless, imply power confirmation. As Berger et al. (1973: 86) suggest, when an organization tries to enforce values which clash with those relevant to securing individual identity, it paves the way for de-institutionalization; in other words, the organization weakens its power over the individual. It creates an occasion for a definition of an identity "apart from and often against the institutional roles."

Individuals are linked to the organization through role performance and it is by performing roles that they attribute meaning to self (Foote 1951; Burke and Tully 1977) and reiterate the organizational values. When corporate strategies affront meaningful values for identity, or go against already institutionalized values, role performance comes to be experienced as a struggle between a subjective and an objective identity (Berger et al. 1973). Individuals can show that they reject these changes by cognitively distancing themselves and withdrawing commitment from these roles or from the organization. The multiple attachments of individuals to roles, institutions and situations inside and outside the workplace universe vary in intensity and in the degree to which they overlap. This allows space for accommodation of identity; by negotiating his involvement, an individual may be committed to the work but not to the organization; or alternatively, to certain dimensions of the workplace universe (e.g. colleagues) but not to the work itself or the organization. Accordingly, the work itself and other dimensions of the workplace may or may not operate as competitive sources of meanings for identity in an independent way. In other words, the way in which identity is defined and re-defined in a negotiated transaction with the environment (Thompson and McHugh 1991) will depend on subjective perceptions or meanings attached to the workplace and the organization universes.

The case study discussed in this paper describes a situation wherein management, in its attempts to diffuse a corporate culture, enforced values that apparently affronted internalized individual values. Instead of creating unity, this kind of strategy had the paradoxical effect of encouraging individuals to withdraw and detach themselves from the organization. At the organizational level it fostered division into subcultures and the emergence of a counterculture (see Rodrigues and Collinson 1992). The study suggests that the values advocated by the corporate culture clashed with values institutionalized by the organization's founders and leaders (the parent culture). Initially, the paper describes the case study methodology; secondly, the characteristics of the parent culture and corporate culture; thirdly, it discusses the process of de-institutionalization which occurred in the organization, and finally, it analyses the implications of de-institutionalization for employees' identity.

The Case Study

The empirical material is drawn from a larger study of organizational culture designed to probe the multiplicity of cultures that can simultaneously exist over time within particular organizations (Rodrigues 1991). The research focused on a state telecommunications company (Telecom[1]) within the Brazilian telecommunications system (Telebrás[2]). The latter is a government holding company that owns and controls each separate organization in the system.

From its inception until 1985, when the civilians took office, the military had held the key management positions in these companies. Usually, the top echelons of management in these companies were officers or had been educated in a military school. This generated an inter-institutional isomorphism (Meyer and Rowan 1991) in the telecommunications industry, grounded in the military culture (clear hierarchy and rules, rigid norms, discipline, etc.) and in the engineering dream of an organization without people (Child 1985).

In Telecom, beginning in 1979, strategic decision-making became the responsibility of a new management structure (the managerial council). This initiative was intended to pave the way for a civilian board which took complete responsibility only in 1985. Their strategy was to replace the old autocratic approach with what they defined as a pluralistic, liberal managerial style. New management intended to create a corporate culture based on these principles, aiming, apparently, to build up support for the effective operation of the managerial council, which had barely met during the military regime, and to buffer union activism within the organization.

The original study (Rodrigues 1991) involved an analysis of the relationships between three organizational subcultures: the parent culture, the corporate culture and the counterculture. The study of the interrelationships between the corporate culture and the counterculture has already been the subject of another paper (Rodrigues and Collinson 1992). Consequently, this present chapter concentrates primarily on the interactions between the two former subcultures and the implications for engineers' identity.

The analysis of the empirical data presented below examines the main characteristics of the organizational culture during the period of military domination (parent culture), the top management practices adopted to infuse the values of "new management" (the corporate culture) and the employees' response to these managerial initiatives to transform Telecom from a military autocracy into a more democratic organization.

The organization had approximately 7,500 employees during the period of data collection (1988-1991). The company had 7 board members, and 216 people in managerial positions, 21 of whom were in the higher positions, 268 engineers and the rest comprising clerical staff and manual workers.

This study adopted an anthropological approach of researcher immersion in everyday practices of the research site from 1988 till 1991. Research interviews were conducted with 60 line managers and engineers; 5 managing directors; 12 ex-managing directors and retired employees; and the president of the company. These interviews were supplemented by a detailed analysis of company dossiers and documents. In addition, research interviews were conducted with 4 local union officials, 1 national union officer responsible for telecommunications, 5 key organizational members and 3 human resource managers. A detailed analysis was also conducted of every edition of the trade union newspaper, entitled *The Goat*, from its creation in 1979 to the completion of the research in 1991.

While the analysis of the interviews with previous directors and retired employees informed the shaping of what constituted the main values of the parent culture, interviews with managers and engineers helped to capture the content and strategies of the corporate culture and its conflicting nature. Data from all categories, nevertheless, were used to make sense of each subculture.

The telecommunication's company dossiers contained registers of the history of the industry as seen by people who had experienced it. By examining 386 documents the researcher selected dossiers of 25 leaders and founders of the industry, as assigned by Telecom and according to stories and sagas found in those documents. In using this information, the researcher constructed 25 professional biographies. The data from the personal interviews with some of the founders and leaders (12) was also used to make sense of the biographies. These biographies included information on their professional experiences as heads or leaders of companies, posts they had occupied and data about their qualifications. This biographical data, together with interview data, was used to capture the main characteristics and strategies of the parent culture. Details of this data can be found in Rodrigues (1991). The following analysis concentrates on the often conflicting and political nature of discourses in the interviews related to a still extant parent culture and a corporate culture which was seen as illegitimate by the employees.

The Parent Culture

The analysis of the biographical data of the telecommunications industry founders and leaders revealed not only the kind of values they espoused but also the tight links which existed between the military and telecommunication engineers in these organizations. These links permitted the institutionalization of the parent culture core values inter and intra-organizationally in the telecommunications system.

Military management at Telecom was based on scientific management, formalization and routinization of tasks. They emphasized technical competence by reassuring the primacy of technical criteria over the political in decision-making, and they attributed a special importance to the technical department, mainly formed by engineers. Politics for the military was considered illegitimate; "it is parochial, divisive and above all it is not based on expertise" (O'Donnel 1979: 81). The parent culture created awards for technical inventions and innovations as well as ceremonies for their public delivery. Earlier members of telecommunications companies remembered the founders of the industry as myths, for what they had achieved and for the values they enforced: those of hard work, honesty, and achievement.

Routines in telecommunications companies were imbued with technocracy which had a ritual significance in the organization. Stanley (1981) has defined technocracy as an ethos that emphasizes the importance of technical control and language in problem solving. Other studies suggest that technocrats base their power on the neutrality of the technical discourse and decision-making. They believe that emotional problems prevent reaching a rational solution and that conflict is dysfunctional (Martins 1974; O'Donnell 1979). They negate political reason while elevating technical rationality; politicians are cunning while engineers are virtuous. Technocracy, according to Burris (1989), is an important cognitive base produced by engineering training institutions which finds in bureaucracies a propitious terrain for their reproduction.

The story of the telecommunications industry in Brazil and also this research suggest that engineers were the main supporters and consumers of the military culture for two principal reasons. The military and the telecommunication engineers had a common educational background. Technocracy, bureaucracy and rigid disciplinary procedures were values shared in Brazilian telecommunications' schools. The educational links between the military and telecommunications engineers were maintained even when civilian schools were created; they had people of military background on the staff and, usually, students had had work experience under the supervision of an officer. The process of professionalization impacted on telecommunications organizations in terms of a "normative isomorphism" and by reproducing rules and discursive practices which tended to mirror those of the educational institutions (DiMaggio and Powell 1991:67).

Military officers and engineers also controlled a power network and positions which they shared in rotation. The officers usually occupied important posts in state companies while the technocrats were invited to occupy relevant posts in public administration (Dreifuss 1981). This created a favorable context for institutionalization and mythification of technocracy as a powerful organizational ideology and granted a cultural isomorphism across companies.

When the civilians took office they not only designed strategies to differentiate themselves from the military personnel and their culture, but also attempted to undermine the values of the parent culture, in particular technocracy and meritocracy (Rodrigues 1991). From 1985 onwards the assignment of board positions followed political party affiliations and the appointment of higher and lower management was made in accordance with the coalition they belonged to; management and their corporate culture was seen by employees, and engineers in particular, as illegitimate (Rodrigues and Collinson 1992). As will be seen later, many of the parent culture values were still alive in the organization while strategies and values enforced by the corporate culture were seen as an affront to these "inherited values."

The Corporate Culture

When the civilians took over the organization in 1985, they planned to introduce a completely new corporate culture, aiming to change the organization's internal and external image. Motivated by changes at the level of society which demanded a more democratic state and authority and by a highly active union which required better working conditions and employee participation, managers tried to create an alternative corporate culture. The new management intended to construct a new organizational identity completely separate from that which has prevailed under military domination; one that was less militaristic and autocratic and more liberal and democratic. Accordingly, they decentralized decision-making and encouraged employee involvement through the managerial council. They also took from the past what they thought would be useful to their purposes: they created integration rituals; they revived the happy family metaphor and created a new one, the open door policy. Their intention was to create meanings for the employees identification with Telecom by portraying a positive image of a democratic, caring and considerate organization (Rodrigues and Collinson 1992).

The corporate culture proposed a new disciplinary regime which was apparently more flexible, but on the other hand, introduced greater ambiguity; norms could be subject to negotiation with management and would be enforced by participative managers who were willing to communicate and listen.

In its strategy to define a new philosophy, top management defined not only the included and the excluded but also created degrees of inclusion according to proximity to the inner group. The promise of a pluralist organization involved the intention to acknowledge the union as a legitimate representative of the employees. To achieve its intentions to unify and integrate workers under the new philosophy and to expand its influence and control, top management transformed supervisory functions into lower management. By categorizing lower supervisory functions as managerial, top managers tried to increase the number of allies at the same time that it established limits for union participation and influence. Managers were not allowed to support the union, and were expected to articulate justifications of top managers' practices and strategies. By training all managers to disseminate the new managerial culture, top managers tried to create mediators for their values. They also encouraged subordinate managers to take responsibility for solving work-related problems, primarily those regarding the need to improve working conditions. According to top managers this would reduce the power of the union in its role as mediator between the workers' needs and the organization.[3]

Telecom's culture followed the principles and descriptions of any dominant culture in a Foucauldian sense: it designed strategies of agglutination, created rituals of integration, and trained mediators – those who would be in charge of reaffirming its principles and making sure they were followed in the day to day life of the company. They created new disciplinary procedures to transmit the message of a more flexible and participative management and even produced a new creed which could justify their actions and at the same time their election to, and continuation in managerial positions. They emphasized the political criteria for selection and promotion and for decision-making in general. These strategies, nevertheless, did not ensure cultural hegemony in the organization. Paradoxically, instead of generating unity it fostered the emergence of a counterculture, one that elaborated derogatory metaphors of management and the organization (Rodrigues and Collinson 1992), a subculture of engineers who found that traditional company values were being undermined and "vandalized" and a group of managers who resented having been excluded.

Dissent and De-institutionalization

Oliver (1992) defines de-institutionalization as disruption of consensus around organizational values and practices. She links de-institutionalization to legitimacy crises in organizations leading to discontinuity of habits and customs.

In Telecom's case, although the corporate culture was seen as being more pluralist than the parent by creating the opportunities for employee participation, it did not achieve its planned hegemony, not even the necessary agglutination to secure legitimization among the managers. The corporate culture bearers were seen as cunning and Machiavellian. Most engineers viewed top managers as forming an "impermeable layer" in the Foucauldian sense of an ubiquitous capillary network of supporting and integrating relations. The corporate culture was seen as a weapon used by top managers to guarantee and justify their power positions. "The corporate culture is the patrimonialistic product of a group of managers" said one engineer[4]. Thus, managers' attempts to create political dependencies by constructing a propitious "organizational field" to ensure a faithful network of interests (Clegg 1989: 204) seemed to be quite a visible strategy in this organization. According to lower managers and engineers the corporate culture definition of "the included" was very narrow: "power in the organization is in the hands of nine managers; they act to protect the interests of their own group," "one is promoted only if one belongs to this inner group" for "they include and exclude people as they please."

Managers themselves admitted in interviews that their managerial philosophy concealed strategies of worker and union control. The union in its turn claimed that the corporate culture had been introduced in the organization to manipulate and control the employees and, as a response, metaphors had been created to oppose and demystify those of the corporate culture. As described in detail in Rodrigues and Collinson (1992) the organization was portrayed by the union as a "flying train," as a "circus" and even as "a disguised military organization." The open door policy was portrayed by the union newspaper as "the open door to the street."

The corporate culture was seen as illegitimate and so were its bearers. Employees disagreed mostly with the criterion used by the corporate culture to create what Clegg (1989: 5) calls "circuits of power": "Managers are only in their positions because of their political affiliations and alliances," "they promote their friends and relatives" and "bring people to work in the organization who have no other qualifications but being their friends."

Managers, nevertheless, created justifications and explanations for their behavior and values, thus fulfilling the logic of all managerial cultures as Bendix (1970) points out. Being asked by the researcher how they would define a "good manager" they replied that one did not necessarily have to have technical qualifications in the area. However, "he or she would necessarily have to be able to deal with political demands and human beings." "The fact that an employee has a technical qualification in engineering does not guarantee that he will be an effective manager," "managerial qualities are essential, nevertheless."

According to Oliver (1992), political, social and functional pressures can trigger a de-institutionalization process. Changes at the macro-political level, such as the introduction of democracy in the country were fundamental in dismantling the political network between the technocrats and the military. With democracy, technocrats withdrew their political support for the military, thus breaking the macro and micro institutional networks and weakening technocracy as the ideal solution for managing state organizations.

However, even more important for de-institutionalization was the fact that the new corporate culture was unable to generate consensus. Management practices, according to managers themselves, engineers and the union, introduced ambiguity and contradicted the messages of corporate culture and eroded the sense of community identification and loyalty to the organization. The fact that management gave primacy to political criteria over technical concerns, created gaps of credibility in management, for the parent culture had institutionalized technocracy as a myth itself, by transforming it into an organizational attribute which was diffused and disseminated by ritual and learning (Freund 1969).

De-institutionalization, therefore, implied, fundamentally, a problem of meaning. In other words, the organization was not seen by the employees as a place for fulfillment of occupational identity or for professional development, as will be discussed below.

Telecom's Corporate Culture and Identity

The enduring nature of identity and its concomitant volatile essence suggest that individuals draw meanings for their identity from their past social experiences, as well as by performing their current social roles. Identities are embedded in a historical past; as Strauss (1959: 164) puts it "individuals hold membership in groups that are themselves a product of a past." Likewise, they tend to evaluate interactions within a group on the basis of their contribution to a positive self-image. Thus, a group has a particular significance to an individual if it represents experiences which he values and has an emotional significance for him.

The parent culture of Telecom seemed to have this kind of significance, in particular for the engineers. As the interview data suggest, the parent culture had an emotional and affective value for the engineers because of positive experiences they had shared in the past. The isomorphism of the parent culture renovated itself in the technical department through learning. Engineers' discourse seemed to reproduce similar relations of meanings. When they joined the technical department most of them were 25 years of age and "their job was to make the company grow," said one of them. Employee turnover was low, thus favoring transmission of the parent culture isomorphically to the technical department.

By contrast, the corporate culture seemed ineffective in conveying meanings to the employees, in general, and to the engineers in particular. In the 1980s, government money for the expansion of state companies started to shrink, which forced telecommunications companies to redefine their mission as soleley service-providing organizations, abandoning other activities such as design and construction, research and development, etc. In addition to that, top management lack of legitimacy (in the eyes of the employees) had weakened the power of corporate culture to provide meanings for identity. The institution that was once able to provide meanings and stability for the employees had become, in their eyes, incohesive and deprived of feasibility, chiefly because management strategies had generated ambiguity about the limits of sacred and profane practice, in the sense that employees had always been taught "not to be contaminated by the 'political' in their judgment or decisions." As Martins (1974) puts it, technocrats attribute a supreme value to technical knowledge and construct their legitimacy based on the ideological neutrality of their own discourse; technical criteria are unbiased, as they are founded on reason and rationality.

Interviews with managers suggested that the technical department was able to construct an isomorphism based on similar symbolic resources and discourses. They defined the uniqueness and the isomorphism of the technical department in the following way: "in this organization there was an engineering disease," "the technical department is formed mostly by engineers," "they are an elite; they have the best people, the best salaries, the best working conditions." "They are more integrated and unified than the rest of the organization."

Accordingly, technocracy was not only a moral code that served as a guideline for "right and wrong." It had a taken for granted superiority over all other forms of rationality, enforced by the parent culture at the top and reiterated at the operational level by the engineers and technicians. It was the engineers' distinction as the holders of this "rare competence" that linked them to power during the military. This distinction was reaffirmed in the organization's public rituals (e.g. award ceremonies) and in taken-for-granted assumptions that it was this category that should take positions of power in the organization and in the telecommunications system in general. When new management took power, not only did they suspend these rituals, but by adopting an ideology that was insensitive to the superiority of technical rationality they excluded the engineers from power and simultaneously impeded their association with it. Through its discursive practices, new management de-legitimized beliefs in the distinction of the engineering group and apparently, de-institutionalized its historical link to power.

In its strategy to impose itself as the dominant culture, corporate culture withdrew the positive work-related meanings for the engineers' identity. As Tajfel (1978) mentions, an individual remains a member of a group if it makes a positive contribution to his or her identity. If the group fails to provide security for the individual identity by generating positive meanings for self-image, he/she tends to leave it, even if only psychologically (Tajfel 1978). When an organization fails to provide the desirable niche to lodge identity, the individual may choose other alternatives to cope with the ambiguity of the information coming from the environment.

Role distancing (Snow and Anderson 1987) is a situation whereby an individual avoids identification with and attachment to a particular role or institution. In Telecom, many subordinate managers and engineers in particular, emphasized their detachment from the organization, which they stressed was collective and not personal. As one engineer put it "the employees are not loyal to this organization as they used to be." "People are alienated as far as this organization is concerned," "there is no motivation to work in this organization" were frequent remarks found in the interviews with engineers.

Another way individuals can express their cognitive and emotional distance from roles and institutions is by categorizing and stereotyping. Categorizing consists of placing, locating, defining a group or a person, while stereotyping commonly involves describing groups by using derogatory metaphors (Tajfel 1978; Strauss 1959). In Telecom, engineers responded by negatively valuing managers. Managers were portrayed by engineers as "nepotists," "patrimonialists" and "corrupt," while management practices were classified as "insulting," "revolting" and "unstimulating" (see Rodrigues and Collinson 1992, for details).

The sense of self worthlessness and resentment (Scheler 1961) were embedded in the respondents' statements. One engineer's comments illustrate this point:

The work of the technical department does not have the same value for the organization any longer. Management pretends it makes a decision based on rationality and on what the technical department had recommended. Nevertheless, after working very hard on a project we find out that our recommendations have been neglected. First they consider how their decisions will influence their political career. Secondly, they worry about what the local politician might think (Scheler 1961: 21).

Both group worthlessness and resentment seemed to be feelings difficult to rec-oncile with the organization's present power relations. They denoted a sense of 'impotence and moral impoverishment'. As one engineer pointed out, "it is all re-volting but I feel I do not have the power to change things."

In coping with these changes the engineers re-defined their own subjectivity by using strategies of accommodation. Displacement was a strategy by which they negotiated their identity in their relationship with the environment. Interest and involvement possibly move to other locations and work related issues may be-come marginal in terms of their relevance as source of meanings for identity. In the words of one manager: "Motivation here is low; people are trying to do other things and others are resigning and moving to other places." Another form of dis-placement occurs when the employee withdraws organizational involvement and loyalty while directing commitment to social aspects of work (e.g. towards par-ticular groups and colleagues). As another manager commented: "Loyalty here is associated with particular people and groups, but not with the institution, as it used to be before." As Thompson and McHugh (1991) suggest, members of a group tend to look to themselves as a source of meanings when their identity is under external threat.

Alternatively, individuals may try to secure identity by "embellishment" (Snow and Anderson 1987: 1359) whereby they select from "the collective memory" (Halbwachs 1968) those elements that could contribute to a positive self concept. In other words, they tend to exaggerate the past. In the case of Telecom, employ-ees appealed to the parent culture for meanings. Although they recognized that the military culture was not a solution that would now work or that would be useful in the present, they tended to mythify the past. Statements such as "fifteen years of military regime created a culture of loyalty to the organizations," "the bad sol-dier was not allowed to stay in the organization by the military," "in the past all employees felt part of the organization and behaved accordingly," were common in the interviews with employees.

Conclusions

This case study suggests that culture, power and identity are closely interrelated, in the sense that they nurture meaning for each other. An organizational culture, by reaffirming the values and ideologies that distinguishes one group from any other also constructs the legitimate basis of this group. By bestowing it with a positive distinction this culture also confers power to a group and simultaneously feeds its members' identities. Power serves to elevate identity since it provides an illusion of unproblematic recognition. More precisely, the character of power is to arbitrarily define the identity of "others." Power has the effect of rendering subordinates insecure about their performances (Knights 1990), and induces in its bearers the illusion of superiority in the sense that it contributes to extending a network of people with vested interests willing to confirm their subordination, or the "superiority" meanings and feelings of the power holders.

At an individual level, if management neglects the organizational representations of those values that bestow identity on a group by interrupting their reiteration in rituals and ceremonies and by withdrawing resources that foster their existence, they weaken their legitimacy and the basis of this group status and in consequence, the justification for their power.

It is at this point that role-based social identities and personal identities are interdependent. Because of the insertion of social roles in the context of social and power relations, they affect other dimensions of self, such as self-image, need for recognition and the stability of the occupational biographical trajectory (Dubar 1992, Demazière 1992).

In this case study, these role-based social identities were linked to the occupational status of engineering and its power in the organization. De-institutionalization of its interface with status and power by demeaning and debasing technical rationality has fostered identity insecurity. Engineers' lack of trust in the organization's capacity to provide meanings that could support feelings of continuity and stability of their biographical experience induced detachment and alienation from their organizational and occupational roles (distancing, displacement), together with attempts to re-assemble identity (embellishment).

In summary, organizations are mediators of meaning for individuals' careers and achievements. However, if an organization restrains chances for professional advancement it also diminishes, in turn, the opportunities for employee involvement, as Child and Rodrigues (1993) point out. A manager or an employee who feels that the organization does not fulfill professional expectations or considers his personal identity demeaned by the corporate culture will probably not be a mediator of this culture in performing his role in the organization. Accordingly, the same strategies that a corporate culture uses to integrate and produce unity, can paradoxically foster formation of subcultures and individual detachment.

An organizational culture, therefore, can only be understood within a relational and political dimension. This study suggests that an organizational culture can only make sense within a field of symbolic production wherein different agents fight to impose their definition of reality. By defining what is considered sacred and legitimate, it confers distinctions defining those who belong and those who do not and, in this way, confers power and the right of groups to exist socially or not.

Therefore, an organizational culture arranges and re-arranges "relations of meanings and membership, and in this process it empowers and disempowers agencies' capacities" (Clegg 1989: 224) This study suggests that a corporate culture can contribute to making the use of power unobtrusive by fabricating meanings and justifications for management action. Power, on the other hand, makes those meanings integrative by constructing networks of interests and alliances that will be defined in terms of those meanings (Clegg 1989: 204). Thus, both culture and power interact in the construction of a propitious symbolic field for mutual reproduction.

In the example given in this chapter, corporate culture partially fulfilled this logic but was, as yet, unable to generate isomorphism. By neglecting some myths and fabricating others that conflicted with strong institutionalized ones and by failing to create legitimacy for membership criteria, it generated a context of greater uncertainty and ambiguity of identity. Contradictions between "membership" and meaning prevented corporate culture from achieving its desired legitimacy.

This study suggests, in addition, that corporate culture and institutionalization do not always occur together, nor do they imply the same process of meaning construction. As part of a managerial program designed by particular managers, corporate culture's existence hangs on the empowerment and disempowerment of these managers. An institutionalization process is depersonalized, as Meyer and Rowan (1991) suggest, and implies a much stronger and stable process of value internalization due to its interconnectedness with social relations in general. In organizations, therefore, a corporate culture is usually superimposed on institutionalized parent values that may or may not support it. The success of a corporate culture may depend on how one matches the other. If a corporate culture advances values conflicting with those already internalized, it also creates reasons for its own failure.

De-institutionalization implies, in addition to the factors mentioned by Oliver (1992), a "missing power"; in other words, it is triggered by failure of acts of power to create meanings for commitment with the organization and the workplace. This study suggests that de-institutionalization occurs when a new philosophy or culture is unable to obtain the necessary legitimacy to replace old values, which in their turn, are not as useful under the new circumstances and in the new environment. This creates a political and motivational vacuum that neither the new philosophy nor the old is able to fill.

Though this research concerns one case study, its findings reflect changes that occurred frequently in many other Brazilian state companies: those that had military personnel on their boards, and telecommunications companies in particular. It also reflects the de-institutionalization process and consequent individual detachment that has been occurring recently with increasing frequency in the recent Brazilian history of public organization.

Notes

[1] Pseudonym.
[2] Pseudonym.
[3] Some managers showed clearly what their views were on the managerial strategy.
[4] According to Schwartzman (1982: 23) a patrimonialist system develops and maintains itself through political co-optation. It is a fragile political system because it creates a superior subordinate relationship – between those who belong to the dominant group and aspirants to this. Usually, a dependent relationship is developed based on symbolic exchanges (e.g. favor versus a temporary inclusion in the group).

References

Albert, Stuart; Whetten, David A. (1985), Organizational Identity, in L.L. Cummings and B.M. Staw (eds.), *Research in Organizational Behavior*, vol. 7: 263-295. Greenwich: JAI Press.

Allen, F.R.; Kraft, C. (1982), *The Organizational Unconscious: How to Create the Corporate Culture You Want and Need*. Englewood Cliffs, NJ: Prentice-Hall.

Alexander, Jeffrey C.; Seidman, Steven (1991), *Culture and Society: Contemporary Debates*. London: Cambridge University Press.

Alvesson, Mats; Berg, Per Olof (1992), *Corporate Culture and Organizational Symbolism*. Berlin, New York: Walter de Gruyter.

Alvesson, Mats; Willmott, Hugh (1992), Critical Theory and Management Studies: An Introduction, in M. Alvesson and H. Willmott (eds.), *Critical Management Studies*: 1-20. London: Sage.

Apter, Terri; Garnsey, Elizabeth (1992), *Rethinking the Constraints on Women: A Social Enactment Approach*, Cambridge: Clare Hall.

Bell, Daniel (1991), Modernism, Postmodernism, and the Decline of Moral Order, in J.C. Alexander and S. Seidman (eds.), *Culture and Society: Contemporary Debates*. London: Cambridge University Press.

Bendix, Reinhard (1970), The Impacts of Ideas on Organizational Structure, in O. Grusky and G.A. Miller (eds.), *The Sociology of Organizations: Basic Studies*. New York: Free Press.

Berger, Peter L. (1966), Identity as a Problem in the Sociology of Knowledge. *European Journal of Sociology*, 7: 105-115.

Berger, Peter L.; Berger, Brigitte; Kellner, Hansfried (1973), *The Homeless Mind: Modernization and Consciousness*. London: Penguin.

Berger, Peter L.; Luckmann, Thomas (1976), *The Social Construction of Reality: A Treatise in the Sociology of Knowledge*. London: Penguin.

Boisot, Max; Xing Guo Liang (1992), The Nature of Managerial Work in the Chinese Enterprise Reforms. A Study of Six Directors. *Organization Studies*, 13(2): 161-184.

Bourdieu, Pierre (1976), Les modes de domination. *Actes de la Recherche en Sciences Sociales*, 2(3): 122-132.

Bourdieu, Pierre (1991), *Language and Symbolic Power*. London: Polity Press.

Burke, P.; Tully, J. (1977), The Measurement of Role Identity. *Social Forces*, 55(4): 881-897.
Burris, Beverly H. 1989, Technocratic Organization and Control. *Organization Studies*, 10(1): 1-22.
Child, John (1985), Managerial Strategies, New Technology, and the Labour Process, in D. Knights, H. Willmott and D. Collinson (eds.), *Job Redesign: Critical Perspectives on the Labour Process*. London: Gower.
Child, John; Rodrigues, S. (1993), The Role of Social Identity in the International Transfer of Managerial Knowledge through Joint Ventures. Paper presented at the 11th EGOS Colloquium, Paris.
Clegg, Stewart R. (1989), *Frameworks of Power*. London: Sage Publications.
Clegg, Stewart R. (1992), Postmodern Management? An Inaugural Address to the University of St. Andrews, St. Andrews.
Cohen, Stanley; Taylor, Laurie (1992), *Escape Attempts: The Theory and Practise of Resistance of Everyday Life*. London, Routledge and Kegan Paul.
Collier, Jane (1993), Research into Women in Organizations: Some Philosophical Issues. *Research Papers in Management Studies*, 11, Cambridge.
Collinson, David; Knights, David; Collinson, Margaret (1990), *Managing to Descriminate*. London: Routledge.
Collinson, David (1992), *Managing the Shopfloor: Subjectivity, Masculinity and Workplace Culture*. Berlin, New York: Walter de Gruyter.
Deal, Terrence E.; Kennedy, Allan A. (1982), *Corporate Cultures: The Rites and Rituals of Corporate Life*. Reading, MA.: Addison-Wesley.
Deetz, Stanley (1992), Disciplinary Power in the Modern Corporation, in M. Alvesson and H. Willmott (eds.), *Critical Management Studies*. London: Sage.
Demazière, Didier (1992), Les identités des chômeurs de longue durée. *Revue française de sociologie*, October-December: 33-34
DiMaggio, Paul J.; Powell, Walter W. (1991), The Iron Cage Revisited: Institutional Isomorphism and Collective Rationality in Organization Fields, in W.W. Powell and P.J. DiMaggio (eds.), *The New Institutionalism in Organizational Analysis*. London: The University of Chicago Press.
Dreifuss, René A. (1981, 1964) *A conquista do Estado: ação pol'tica, poder e golpe de classe*. Petrópoles: Vozes.
Dubar, Claude (1992), Formes identitaires et socialisation professionnelle. *Revue française de sociologie*, October-December: 33-34
Faulkner, David (1994), *International Strategic Alliances: Cooperating to Compete*. London: McGraw-Hill.
Fineman, Stephen (ed.) (1994), *Emotion in the Organizations*. London: Sage.
Fleury, Maria Terezea Leme; Rosa M. Fisher (1989), *Cultura e poder nas organizaçoés*. Sao Paolo: Atlas.
Fleury, Maria Tereza Leme (1986), O simbólico nas relações de trabalho: um estudo sobre as relações de trabalho na empresa estatal. Tese de livre docência Sao Paulo: USP/FEA.
Foote, Nelson N. (1951), Identification as a Basis for a Theory of Motivation. *American Sociological Review*, 16: 14-21.
Foucault, Michel (1977), *Discipline and Punish: The Birth of the Prison*. London: Harmondsworth.

Frost, Peter J.; Moore, Larry F.; Louis, Meryl R.; Lundberg, Craig C.; Martin, Joanne (1991), *Reframing Organizational Culture*. London: Sage.

Freund, Julien (1969), *The Sociology of Max Weber*. New York: Vintage.

Gagliardi, Pasquale (1990), *Symbols and Artifacts: Views of the Corporate Landscape*. Berlin, New York: Walter de Gruyter.

Gregory, Kathleen L. (1983), Native View Paradigms: Multiple Cultures and Cultures Conflicts in Organizations. *Administrative Science Quarterly*, 28, pp 359-376.

Goffman, Erving (1956), *The Representation of Self in Everyday Life*. Doubleday: Anchor Books.

Halbwachs, Maurice (1968), *La Mémoire Collective*. Paris: Presses Universitaires.

Hampden-Turner, Charles (1990), *Corporate Culture: From Vicious to Virtuous Circles*. London: The Economist Books.

Heelas, Paul (1991), The Sacralization of the Self and New Age Capitalism, in N. Bercrombie and A. Warde (eds.), *Social Change in Contemporary Britain*. Cambridge: Polity Press.

Hofstede, Geert (1991), *Cultures and Organizations*. London: McGraw-Hill.

Knights, David; Collinson, D. (1985), Redesigning Work on the Shopfloor: A Question of Control or Consent?, in D. Knights, H. Willmott and D. Collinson (eds.), *Job Redesign: Critical Perspectives on the Labour Process*. London: Gower.

Knights, David (1990), Subjectivity, Power and the Labour Process, in D. Knights and H. Willmott (eds.), *Labour Process Theory: Studies in the Labour Process*. London: Macmillan.

Kondo, Dorinne K. (1990), *Crafting Selves: Power, Gender, and Discourses of Identity in a Japanese Workplace*. Chicago: The University of Chicago Press.

Linstead, Steve (1988), Jokers Wild: Humour in Organisational Culture, in C. Powell and C.E. Paton (eds.), *Humour in Society: Resistance and Control*. London: MacMillan.

Martins, Carlos E. (1974), *Tecnocracia e Capitalismo: a prática dos técnicos no Brasil*. Sao Paulo: Brasiliense.

McCall, George J.; Simmons, J.L. (1966), *Identities and Interactions*. New York: Free Press.

Meek, V. Lynn (1988), Organizational Culture: Origins and Weaknesses. *Organization Studies*, 9(4): 453-473.

Meyer, John W.; Rowan, Brian (1991), Institutionalized Organizations: Formal Structure as Myth and Ceremony, in W.W. Powell and P.J. DiMaggio (eds.), *The New Institutionalism in Organizational Analysis*. London: The University of Chicago Press.

Morgan, Gareth (1986), *Images of Organizations*. London: Sage.

O'Donnell, Guilhermo (1979) *Modernization and Bureaucratic Authoritarism*. Berkeley: Institute of International Studies.

Oliver, Christine (1992), The Antecedents of Deinstitutionalization. *Organization Studies*, 13(4): 563-588.

Oliver, Nick; Wilkinson, Barry (1992), *The Japanization of British Industry: New Developments in the 1990s*. London: Blackwell.

Orrú, Marco; Biggart, N.W.; Hamilton, Gary G. (1991), Organizational Isomorphism in East Asia, in W.W. Powell and P.J. DiMaggio (eds.), *The New Institutionalism in Organizational Analysis*. London: The University of Chicago Press.

Ouchi, William (1981), *Theory Z*. Cambridge, MA: Addison-Wesley.

Pascale, Richard (1985), The Paradox of Corporate Culture: Reconciling Ourselves to Socialization. *California Management Review,* 27(2): 24-41.

Pettigrew, Andrew M. (1985), *The Awakening Giant.* Oxford: Basil Blackwell.

Pfeffer, J. (1981), Management as Symbolic Action: The Creation and Maintenance of Organizational Paradigms, in L.L. Cummings and B.M. Staw (eds.), *Research in Organizational Behavior,* 3. Greenwich: JAI Press.

Rodrigues, Suzana B. (1991), *O Chefinho, o Telefone e o Bode: autoritarismo e mudança cultural no Setor de Telecomunicações.* Thesis subbmitted for the title of Professor at Universidade Federal de Minas Gerais, Brasil.

Rodrigues, Suzana B.; Collinson, David L. (1992), Metaphors of Control and Resistance: Subversive Humour in a Brazilian Workplace. Paper presented at the British Academy of Management Conference, Bradford.

Rose, Nikolas (1989), *Governing the Soul: The Shaping of the Private Self.* London: Routledge.

Rose, Nikolas (1992), Governing the Enterprising Self, in P. Heelas and P. Morris (eds.), *The Values of the Enterprise Culture: The Moral Debate.* London: Routledge.

Rose, Randall A. (1988) Organizations as Multiple Cultures: A Rule Theory Analysis. *Human Relations,* 41(2): 139-170.

Sackmann, Sonja A. (1991), *Cultural Knowledge in Organizations: Exploring the Collective Mind.* London: Sage.

Saffold III, Guy S. (1988), Culture Traits, Strength, and Organizational Performance: Moving Beyond Strong Culture. *Academy of Management Review,* 13(4): 546-558.

Sathe, Vijay (1985), *Culture and Related Corporate Realities: Text, Cases, and Readings on Organizational Entry, Establishment, and Change.* Homewood, Ill: Richard D. Irwin.

Schein, Edgar H. (1986), *Organizational Culture and Leadership: A Dynamic View.* London: Jossey-Bass.

Scheler, Max (1961), *Ressentiment.* Glencoe, Ill: Free Press.

Schwartzman, Simon (1982), *Bases do Autoritarismo Brasileiro.* Rio de Janeiro: Campus.

Scott, James (1990), *Domination and the Arts of Resistance.* London: Yale University Press.

Smircich, Linda (1983), Concepts of Culture and Organizational Analysis. *Administrative Science Quarterly,* 28: 339-358.

Snow, David A.; Anderson, Leon (1987), Identity Work Among the Homeless: The Verbal Construction and Avowal of Personal Identities. *American Journal of Sociology,* 92(6): 1336-1371.

Stanley, Manfred (1981), *The Technological Conscience: Survival and Dignity in an Age of Expertise.* Chicago: Phoenix.

Strauss, Anselm (1959), *Mirrors and Masks: The Search for Identity.* Glencoe, Ill: Free Press.

Tajfel, Henri (1978), *Differentiation between Social Groups: Studies in the Social Psychology of Intergroup Relations. European Monographs in Social Psychology,* London: Academic Press.

Tajfel, Henri (1982), Instrumentality, Identity and Social Comparisons, in Henri Tajfel (ed.), *Social Identity and Intergroup Relations, European Studies in Social Psychology.* London: Cambridge University Press.

Thevenet, Maurice (1993), L'implication et la relation entre l'individu et l'organisation. Paper presented at 17. ANPAD, Salvador, Bahia, Brasil.

Thompson, Paul; McHugh, David (1991), *Work Organizations.* London: MacMillan.

Trice, Harrison M.; Beyer, Janice M. (1984), Studying Organizational Cultures through Rites and Ceremonials. *Academy of Management Review,* 9(4): 653-669.

Trice, Harrison M.; Beyer, Janice M. (1991), Cultural Leadership in Organizations. *Organization Science*, 2(2): 149-169.

Turner, Barry A. (1986), Sociological Aspects of Organizational Symbolism. *Organization Studies*, 7(12): 101-115.

Turner, Barry A. (1990), The Rise of Organizational Symbolism, in J. Hassard and D. Pym (eds.), *The Theory and Philosophy of Organizations: Critical Issues and New Perspectives*. London: Routledge.

Warren, Mark (1990), Ideology and the Self. *Theory and Society*, 19: 599-634.

Wuthnow, Robert (1987), *Meaning and Moral Order: Explorations in Cultural Analysis*. London: University of California Press.

Patterns Of Meaning: Institutionalization and Circumstances[1]

Clóvis L. Machado da Silva and Valéria Silva da Fonseca

Introduction

A review of specialized literature has shown an increasing utilization of principles of contemporary institutional theory to explain the delimitation of structure and organizational actions. From this perspective, an organization, seen as a component of a relationship system in a specific field, is affected not only by technical and financial matters, but also by normative factors of legitimacy. According to Meyer and Rowan (1983), as well as Scott (1983, 1987), institutional rules have substituted for technical norms in environmental specifications of organizational functioning and performance. In this sense the idea of institutional environments, and their influence on the construction of meaning, concerns the type of social context liable to orient the development of organizations.

We share a large part of the arguments formulated by institutional theory, yet, nonetheless, the assumption as to the inexorable homogenization of organizational practices through the force of conceptions sustained in a common environmental arena is, to some extent, questionable. Some researchers have shown that, in spite of the modeling influence of institutional rules, organizations can take on different forms. In a comparative study of two organizations in the American publishing industry, Fombrun (1989) for example, has observed that, despite similarities in size, age, technology and compliance to the same environmental requirements, temporary adjustment among internal pressures of a technical, economic, political and cultural nature has led to differentiated structural configurations. Implicit in this understanding is the importance of considering the interference of other dimensions in the definition of structure and organizational actions, as proposed by Oliver (1988), Fombrun (1989), and Aldrich (1992).

This chapter seeks pertinent theoretical principles. On the basis of on a conceptual framework stemming from an interpretive approach, organizational structure, conceptualized as depending on the reciprocal relationship between formal attributes and interactive patterns, is intermediated by interpretive schemes leading to understanding and action in the face of institutional pressures. As time elapses, interpretive schemes may suffer alterations. Alteration occurs because of pres-

sure from environmental disturbances, and from characteristics peculiar to each
organization (which we will define as situational circumstances in the context of
this chapter), which may upset the coherence of structural arrangements (Giddens
1976; Ranson et al. 1980; Greenwood and Hinings 1988). The relationship between organization and environment develops according to interpretation by the
agents of institutional demands; moreover, the configuration of contextual pressure results in patterns of meaning that shape organization forms.

Taking into account the implications of these dimensions for organizational performance, we investigated a privately owned Brazilian organization that faced
change in its formal arrangement, because of conformity between institutional rules and situational circumstances. While being aware of Scott's arguments
(Scott 1983) concerning the context of the inter-organizational field as the level of analysis most adequate for understanding the organization-environment link
(implying the use of the comparative method), we chose a case study to understand cognitive aspects of the formulation of organizational practices. However,
we maintain the concept of homogenization to provide an explanatory foundation.

Environmental Forces and Organizations

The concept of formal organizations as systems of rules and rationally ordered activities has guided organizational theory since the first studies on Weber's concept
of bureaucracy. As DiMaggio and Powell (1983) have pointed out, "bureaucracy
remains the common organizational form." In this perspective, rules of rationality have become an institutionalized set in modern society, a socially built and
frequently shared conception regarding the effectiveness of organizational functioning. This notion has developed into a strong element to define patterns of interaction and organizational meanings. From the viewpoint of Meyer and Rowan
(1983), this dominance has contributed to creating a true "rational myth." As a
consequence, modern organizations are sustained by belief systems that emphasize the importance of rationality. Their legitimacy in the public eye often depends on their ability to demonstrate rationality and objectivity in action (Morgan
1986).

This historic process of predominance of bureaucratic characteristics seems to
show how a system of beliefs and values can become a product of social interaction (Berger and Luckmann 1967) and can orient organizational action as long as
it involves a definition socially legitimated as real. The nature of organizational
procedures depends, along with other factors, on a system of beliefs and values
and on working relationship developed in this system, in terms of elements legitimated both inside and outside the organization. The nation-state, the market,
the professional associations, and so on – all contribute to creating and dissem-

inating new rational myths. Changes in the institutional environment, therefore, cause changes in the organizational routine.

Meyer and Rowan (1983) believe that organizations function by incorporating previously defined and socially rationalized orientations, which contribute to the legitimacy of their activities and to their survival regardless of efficiency and its production demands. Organizations adopt many programs, policies and technologies through the force of contextual orientation, as manifestations of rules and meanings embedded in structures built and institutionalized in society (Giddens 1976). In this way, having to face environmental uncertainty, competition among organizations turns not only toward resources and customers but also toward institutional legitimacy, making for more homogeneous practices in a particular organizational domain (DiMaggio and Powell 1983; Meyer and Rowan 1983). This modifying effect following environmental characteristics, or, as defined by Hawley (in DiMaggio and Powell 1983), isomorphism, derives from coercive, mimetic and normative mechanisms, causing homogeneity of organizational actions belonging to the same organizational field.

According to Dimaggio and Powell (1983), coercive isomorphism is the result of formal and informal pressures, exerted by one organization on another that happens to be in a condition of dependence. In the face of common legal and political environment, organizational action may come about as a response to governmental policies. In Brazil, for instance, one observes, in consequence of financial adjustment measures enforced by the administration of President Fernando Collor de Mello (1990-1992), such as the reduction of financial assets and the "deindexation" of the economy, Brazilian firms faced with the need to develop projects of modernization and rationalization, to cope with the resulting recession in the domestic market. The imposition of procedures and standardized rules can also occur in authority relations, as in the case of adoption, by a subsidiary, of operating procedures compatible with the policies handed down by the head office of the firm. Coercive isomorphism, however, may not necessarily result from conscious choices, since once confronted by a shortage of information, an action may be carried out according to socially established rules, at least for the purpose of maintaining the legitimacy of an organization in its field.

The second mechanism of isomorphic change is mimetic, based on the adoption by the organization of structural arrangements and procedures developed by other organizations, to minimize the uncertainty resulting from technological problems, conflicting objectives and institutional demands. So, action models may be incorporated indirectly, through the transfer and turnover of personnel, or directly by hiring consultant firms, for example. Organizations may also show mimetic behavior by observing the success of other organizations in the same line of activities. The popularity of Japanese management models, especially, stimulated imitation among North American corporations, and more recently among Brazilian organizations, as a means of increasing productivity by perfecting production quality and, in this way, maintaining institutional legitimacy.

DiMaggio and Powell (1983) also suggest that the degree of professionalization is an important factor to consider in understanding pressures resulting from environmental isomorphism. Professionalization involves the sharing of a set of rules and work routines by members of a given occupation. Universities, associations, and training institutions represent some of the transmitting vehicles of normative rules of professional action, disseminated on the organizational level through recruitment, selection and promotion. Normative isomorphism leads to common forms of interpretation and action in the face of organizational problems and demands, institutionalized in an occupational subculture.

The influence of each one of these institutional mechanisms in organizational action might occur, regardless of any apparent evidence of increase in internal efficiency. Isomorphism, thus, is an advantageous mechanism for organizations, since similarity facilitates inter-organizational transactions and favors internal functioning through the incorporation of socially accepted rules. By demonstrating that it acts according to shared collective rules, an organization conquers outside recognition and assures its further development, thus creating better opportunities for expansion through maximizing its capacity to obtain resources and adopt possible innovations (DiMaggio and Powell 1983; Meyer and Rowan 1983).

Yet, awareness that organizational structures are subject to isomorphic pressures does not eliminate the possibility of an action on the part of the organization to attain a certain level of autonomy and control over environmental conditions, as it seeks to reach its objectives and maintain its best interests. This capacity, particularly observed in organizations powerful enough to be capable of influencing strategically their network of relations, creates demand for their products – either through formal and informal inter-organizational arrangements, or by setting their aims directly in the competitive environment. In this sense, even the attempts at organizational control develop within a normative order, formed within the institutional environment. Therefore, it is conformity, more than performance, that determines the survival of organizations (Meyer and Rowan 1983).

An Interpretive Account of Organizational Action

Aldrich (1992) observes appropriately that "organizations are in environments, but environments are also in organizations, as the institutionalists remind us." This interdependence reflects the basis for the development of modern sociology, delineated under a more dynamic view of the formation of social order, whose application to organizational theory resulted in interpretive/cultural approaches.

Although it is beyond the scope of this chapter to discuss the theoretical-methodological variations characteristic of research undertaken from the interpretive perspective, we should point out that, underlying this paper is the premise that organizations are cultures (Smircich 1983). As such they compose sets of rules and conceptions, formed by the dissemination of provinces of meaning manifested in symbolic patterns, as for example myths, rituals, stories, and reflect the organizational identity. To outline an understanding like this, one must conceive of organizational life, according to Ranson et al. (1980), Riley (1983), Bartunek (1984), Barley (1986), among others, as a product of permanent reciprocity between action and structure.

Ranson et al. (1980), taking as the main point of departure the ideas of Giddens (1976) and Schütz (1972), insist on going beyond the traditional dichotomy between structural framework and interactive patterns that prevails in the field of organizational studies. They suggest an interdependent analysis based on the visualization of organizational structure "as a vehicle constructed to reflect and facilitate meanings [that] describes both the prescribed frameworks and realized configurations of interaction, and the degrees to which they are mutually constituted and constituting" (Ranson et al. 1980).

The prescribed framework portrays the formal arrangement of roles and hierarchic levels, of rules and proceedings, that define the normative patterns of activities. Nevertheless, daily routine requires occasional operation and application of these patterns to situations not foreseen in the structural framework. Such an established fact suggests a continuous reinterpretation of rules and actions, resulting in emergent patterns of interaction. This idea of organizational structure, seen as stemming from the connection between normative and emergent interactive patterns, intermediate by a set of values, ideas or interpretive schemes, is one we endorse (Ranson et al. 1980; Greenwood and Hinings 1988).

We understand interpretive schemes as assumptions resulting from the mental elaboration and filing of perceptions of objects from the concrete world of reality, that operate as frames of reference, shared and often implicit, of events and behavior presented by organizational agents in different situations (Ranson et al. 1980; Bartunek 1984; Fonseca and Seleme 1991). In making it possible to incorporate knowledge coming from external perception, interpretive schemes guide the standardization of activities within structure by elaborating interactive organizational patterns. Structure is thus a manifestation of the alignment of interpretive schemes, and consequently of actions, whose existence depends on the practices and interactions that compose it.

Interpretive schemes consolidate in provinces of meaning. Understood as Schütz (1972) and Ranson et al. (1980) do, a province of meaning suggests interpretive expressions shared and maintained through the congruence of individual and/or group interpretation. Through the articulation of values and interests, these provinces of meaning guide actions and make for a legitimate configuration of the structural framework. Structuring, therefore, "is a process of generating and recreating meanings, one in which organizational members wish to secure their 'provinces of meaning' (Schütz 1967) within the very structure and working of the organization" (Ranson et al. 1980: 5).

An understanding and internalization of the meaning of organizational practices involves the capacity of agents to reorder structure through interaction according to values and interests. Values consist of the most evident representation of interpretive schemes. For Parsons (1951) a value is "an element of a shared symbolic system which serves as a criterion or standard for selection among the alternatives of orientation which are intrinsically open in a situation." As a general category endowed with cognitive components, a value is manifest as a rationalization of rules of conduct, adopted by agents or members of social subgroups, that impel and integrate actions (Jacob et al. 1962; Fonseca 1992).

In the organizational context, the emergence and consolidation of a system of values result, according to Gagliardi (1986), from the complexity and differentiated distribution of information and power within the structure itself. In this perspective, values influence the delimitation of the organizational design, by indicating, for example, operations and arrangements perceived as priorities, as well as when forming the image to be transmitted to the outer context of what expectations exist for the organization (Deal and Kennedy 1982). In short, values reflect the dimensions considered important for organizational functioning and development.

The sharing of values by organizational groups is conducive to legitimizing the process of structuring of structure, if values as guides of interactive patterns, along with interests, favor the adoption of certain actions in organizational functioning. For Lukes (1974) the idea of interest involves a sense of assessment, coherent with the distribution of scarce resources and with the professional and personal intentions of organizational agents. As "interested action" (Ranson et al. 1980), it relates to the satisfaction of needs, immediate or future, and to the motivation to develop and assure a distribution of status and authority, to maintain or increase positions of gain. Thus the articulation between values and interests makes explicit the intentions underlying conduct and reflected in organizational practices.

The ability of individuals to protect their interests depends on the degree of commitment to the interpretive scheme prevalent in the organization. The predominance of a particular interpretive scheme, as well as the extent of commitment of the agents, is a result, therefore, of the existing power relations, as specifically associated with a link between values and interests. Even though organizational structure implies limitation of hierarchy and control, this very articulation is conducive to obtaining advantages and privileges. Different groups seek to make their own interests predominate, and as they succeed, these interests become a reference for other organizational agents, that may or may not share them. The process of domination occurs because the dynamics of interests allow the participating groups to disseminate their provinces of meaning. In this way, if the proposals of a given group are implemented and they get favorable results, it is possible that their province of meaning may become institutionalized and thus become the dominant pattern of orientation for the conduct of organizational agents (Ranson et al. 1980; Greenwood and Hinings 1988; Fonseca and Seleme 1991).

Greenwood and Hinings (1988) suggest that interpretive schemes generate values regarding three main vectors of organizational activity: "(1) the appropriate domain of operations, i.e. the broad nature of an organization's *raison d'être*; (2) beliefs and values about appropriate principles of organizing; (3) appropriate criteria that should be used for evaluating organizational performance."

The set of values about organizational form and domain allows for the continuous creation of meanings of organizational structure and processes. However, the quality of transformation intrinsic to the idea of structuring, as well as the dynamics of association among various internal factors, reflect the possibility of these values emerging in a disconnected manner, or even in competition, causing changes in the organization.

On the other hand, this also suggests the existence of situational circumstances that constrain the configuration of normative and emergent interactive patterns, in such a way as to call for a new organization response. Ranson et al. (1980) distinguish two types of contextual constraints: (1) organizational characteristics, mainly size, technology, and resource distribution; (2) environmental characteristics, such as elements of socio-economic infrastructure and institutional rules.

It is appropriate to mention here the pertinence of the criticism made by Willmott (1981) and Whittington (1992) toward Ranson et al.'s (1980) conceptualization of environmental factors, as forms of contextual constraints. For these authors the introduction of this category in a model based on the theory of structuration (Giddens 1976) becomes redundant, since the idea of reproducing structure involves a social totality. Thus any allusion to external contextual constraints is possible only when related to environmental events, and not as part of a temporal model. It is in this sense that we use the principles of institutional approach in this chapter; in a contrary sense to Ranson et al. (1980) who consider it as a source of impact on the organization. Situational circumstances, understood as nothing more than periodic and intense environmental disturbances (a radical transformation in the principles regarding government jurisdiction, for example), can influence structural adjustment, thus promoting organizational changes. In addition, the contingent dynamics of interrelationship of internal organizational characteristics, such as size, technology, or even the form of ownership, can influence action directly.

For Barley (1986), the dynamic structuring of structure evolves in a sequential manner, through the link between the realm of action and the institutional realm. The institutional realm, defined as the idealized interactive patterns originating from past practices, serves as a basis for the daily practices of the agents. The realm of action involves present arrangements for coping with current events.

The structuring process assumes, according to (Barley 1986), temporal phases that got started as a result of exogenous alterations that gradually accumulate in the memory of the organization. These alterations, introduced in the institutional realm, pressure action, which, in turn, shapes the activities of the organization. Institutional patterns, therefore, provide programs of action and interpretation at the beginning of each temporal phase, and actions lead to modifications in the organization within each phase. Structures of signification, domination and legitimization govern this process, as intervening factors in establishing reciprocal rules and interpretations of contextual constraints (Giddens 1976; Riley 1983; Barley 1986; Fonseca and Seleme 1991).

Scripts carry the interchange between institutional realm and the realm of action (Barley 1986), or equivalent interpretive schemes (Ranson et al. 1980) that reflect the interactional ordering of internal reality. Situational circumstances may provoke, in this way, a structural incongruence, pointing to the need for a modification or redefinition of patterns of meaning.

Hinings and Greenwood (1988) observe that, although values constitute the basis for interpreting contextual conditions, power and commitment are determining factors in the intensity of the change, due to the struggle undertaken among the different groups or organizational agents to protect their interests in the configuration of the organizational structure. Hence, interests and dependencies of power effectively influence the alteration of organizational structure, inasmuch as a situational circumstance can cause a strategic reorientation, when it involves a break in the coherence between interpretation and action. This very dynamic can also result from the loss of legitimacy of prevalent values in the organization. In this case, new interpretive schemes emerge and, as a result, new organizational structures. Therefore, structural differences emerge among organizations subjected to the same contextual constraints, result of the definition of the prescribed and interactive patterns of activities that justify a given organizational configuration. In this perspective, interpretive schemes become essential elements as a source of organizational coherence (Greenwood and Hinings 1988).

A Case in Point

A privately owned family firm in the metal-mechanical business located in southern Brazil provided the site for research. The organization location is in a small city in the south of Brazil, known nationally for the high degree of development of its industrial area, especially the textile and metal-mechanical sectors. Colonized by immigrants of European origin, this region contains a great quantity of middle-sized organizations, whose ownership and management are under the complete or partial control of one or more families. Looking at this context, we infer that this kind of leadership has played a very decisive role, both symbolic and substantive, in the growth of the region's economy, acting not only as a source for generating normative rules but as a parameter of reference for other family ownership organizations located in that area, in view of the success of the undertakings.

Data collection occurred over a period of eight months. The researchers looked for changes in the structural framework over a retrospective period of five years of the organization's life, i.e. from 1988 to 1992. Data relating to formal configuration, production, technology and other organizational elements came from consulting procedural manuals and organization's reports. We consulted specialized magazines and newspapers, searching for information about institutional factors, as well as the situational circumstances extant at the time of the research. A major technique of data collection was a focused interview with the presidents, chief executives and mid-managers of the organization under investigation. We managed identification of interpretive schemes through studying the values of agents. In addition, we sampled opinions regarding the components of some dimensions considered representative in the specialized literature on organizational design. In this way we wished to observe the meanings conferred on the elements of form and organizational domain, the combination of which reflects the value given to a specific arrangement, as, for example, a traditional managerial system or a more professional system. The association of values with organizational arrangements made it possible to verify the existing interpretive schemes and their relation to the actions carried out within the structural dimension of the organization under study.[2]

Founded in the early sixties by two brothers, the organization researched began its activities with the production of electronic parts and, shortly after that, went into the metal-mechanical business, manufacturing auto parts. In the eighties, with the second generation of the family on the management staff, it enlarged its facilities, modernized its machines and equipment and turned toward external markets through exportation. In addition, it began to diversify its products, thus increasing its share in the market of auto parts, and specially in the replacement market. At present, counting only on domestic capital, this organization distributes its products throughout the Brazilian states, and exports them to around thirty-two countries. It is a middle-sized organization, with about 500 employees, who manufacture a large number of its products on order, and holding around 70% of the domestic market. The founders still remain in control of the organization; relatives and descendants occupy the high hierarchical levels[3].

In the early phase of operation, the organization displayed a structural configuration characterized by informality and by a high degree of centralization. As a small organization it had a stratified and fluid hierarchy, which conceived of functional relations as based on personalized rules and procedures. The owners acted as presidents, as directors, and even as middle managers directly supervising the performance of those occupying positions in mid-management and operational levels, and distributed in turn among the areas of sales, production and technical assistance.

Seeking consolidation in a specific field, the organization concentrated on producing a single line of products, manufactured and commercialized according to specifications pre-established by its customers. To this end, it subsequently introduced a technology of continuous flux and adopted, in market terms a predominantly proactive orientation toward his competitors. In this sense, it showed a tendency to "harmonize" with contextual circumstances, by creating competitive advantages that could make it possible to face the constant fluctuations in the Brazilian economy, and obtain legitimacy and environmental support.

Based on its dependence on customer's needs, the organization became increasingly oriented toward obtaining high quality in the productive process. This factor enabled it to achieve a position of relative tranquility in terms of sales, and that allowed it, at the end of the eighties, to develop a diversification of products within the already existing line, as well as to direct a part of its production to the international market. Stability of demand and the beginning of mass production made increased specialization necessary in the technical and organizational areas, leading to the reformulation of the structural framework that prevailed during the entrepreneurship stage. The organization continued to function according to classical standards, within a high degree of centralization of decisions, due specifically to two circumstances – family ownership and the simultaneous exercise of the presidency by two members of the same family. Past structural reforms aimed at promoting not only organizational normalization but also professional training for the descendants of the founders, who previously occupied mid-management positions before taking on the three new directorships. This stimulus to specialization represented a preparatory step toward both professionalizing and managing the future process of leadership succession in the organization.

Yet, the alteration in the formal hierarchy has contributed to the reproduction of power relations, manifested in the strong influence exerted by one of the founders in the definition of organizational practices. The successful implementation of his decisions has contributed, eventually, to the legitimizing of his values, conferring on him, according to his interests, the authority to entrust to one of his relatives the responsibility for the command of the industrial directorship, which has come to hold control over some essential areas of the organization. This orientation expresses itself in the delimitation of organizational form according to principles of a traditional or paternalistic management system.

Configuration at the organizational level has a parallel at the macro-society level, in the very socio-political formation of Brazil. Present Brazilian reality is shaped by a politically oriented capitalist system, whose commanding staff manifested itself according to its own interests, in leading and supervising the actions of the economic and financial sectors. Administering the country from a centralized perspective, the political community has instituted a kind of power with a patrimonial pattern, legitimated on a traditionalist basis (Faoro 1987). In these terms, the nation-state appears as the fundamental generating source of institutional rules, when providing through "authorized" or "imposed" (Scott 1987) mechanisms the normative conditions for the social functioning.

The economic measures put into practice within each new government, as conjunctural models drawn up with the intention of easing, on a short term basis, problems that are already chronic, such as inflation, range all the way from financial and monetary prescriptions to direct control of public organizations and interference in private ones. Even the aggravated political and social crises in Brazil in the late seventies, that led to the return of a civil president in the middle eighties, did not reduce state control, inasmuch as they broke out around the interests of the political community.

From this viewpoint, installation of these policies, we believe, occurs in the organizational field according to institutional patterns characteristic of the existing functional order in Brazilian society, whose chief manifestation, mainly over the past ten years, consists in establishing conjuncture economic models. On the other hand, the premises contained in the severe economic-administrative plan implemented by the administration of President Fernando Collor de Mello (1990-1992) had deep repercussions in the actions of organizations operating in various industrial sectors, and fit the definition of environmental disturbance. In other words, the expectation of oscillations in the Brazilian economy expressed itself as an institutional orientation, but the nature of the measures promulgated constituted a situational circumstance.

Based on liberal discourse and governmental control, the measures of economic adjustment of the Collor administration aimed at, among other factors, modernizing Brazilian industry by means of increasing quality and productivity. Nevertheless, the confiscation of financial assets and the "disindexation" of the economy led the country into deep recession. The unexpected growth of inflation and interest rates, decreased both industrial production and the employment level. Faced with consequent reduction in the volume of business, organizations had to cope with innumerable difficulties, and tried to act to assure their survival – for example, by cutting costs and general expenses, to compete in the market with prices below those offered by their competitors. In this context, even the oligopoly of the automobile industry was shaken. Weakening the impact in the organization under study, a great part of its production went to the replacement market and only a small part to the automobile industry itself. The still rising demand in this type of market, along with the high export rate, made it possible, in a fairly short time, for the organization to recover from possible losses stemming from the decline in sales, experienced by the majority of private firms in this period.

Faced with the restrictions on financial resources offered by the government, and having maintained its conditions for competition, the organization sought to expand the degree of differential in relation to the suppliers, redirecting its investments toward modernization of the production processes. Following a mimetic tendency, the president of the firm, along with the directors, visited organizations in Japan, the United States, Germany and other European countries, with the aim of seeking knowledge about technological production systems, as well as finding prospective customers. At the same time this action sought better adaptation to the rules contained in the new government plan, in the sense of coming up to an international level of quality, raising productivity, and also, unanticipatedly, providing the possibility for organizational agents to perfect their professional performance, especially among candidates for leadership positions. The orientations of leadership aspirants accorded with the expectations disseminated in society and with the opportunities for profit, investment and professionalizing the organization.

The adjustment between institutional patterns and situational circumstances (both internal and external) favored the emergence of new sets of meanings in the symbolic organizational universe, congruent with a more developmentalist philosophy. This led to the implementation of modernizing actions, such as a program of strategic planning, a system of management information, a system of quality management in accordance with international norms, modernization of the factory area, and promotion of the capacity of human resources in the organization, among others things. As a consequence, it led to, almost naturally, a reformulation of the structural framework in October 1992. Maintenance of the same hierarchical stratification and a redistribution of the organizational units, mainly on the middle level, occurred as a result of these changes[4].

The research evidence shows an attempt at accommodation between bureaucratic logic and traditional logic, expressed in the maintenance of the same dependencies of power. A member of the family with very little professional formation achieved command of a newly created department[5]. The change in the structural framework, as an instrument of power, showed not only the possibility of promoting innovation but also that it was a means for perpetuating positions in organizational structuring. We observed both the ability to maintain the legitimacy of an interpretive scheme and the ability to protect certain interests, by commitment to the values and ideas underlying such domain.

From this perspective, the introduction of actions favoring a change of interactive patterns, such as those mentioned above, may not necessarily imply an immediate alteration of patterns of interpretation, inasmuch as the founders (or rather, one of them in particular), still constitutes the main source of institutionalization of values in the organization. As Bartunek (1984) argues, even if the leaders do not propose alternative orientations, they are the ones who open up the possibility of reorientation to processes and structures, by legitimizing the expression of private orientations.

Regarding organizational change, we observed the occurrence of increasing progressive incremental alterations. Their cumulative effect merely redefined the formal arrangement of the organization over time, not necessarily effecting radical modifications. In spite of institutional demand and emerging external constraints, the force of internal circumstances, such as maintaining the interests of the family, are reflected in the delimitation of its characteristics. In consonance with Hinings and Greenwood (1988), we affirm that although organizational actions are subject to institutional demands, selective perception of situational circumstances, bounded by power relations, frames their basis.

Conclusion

Undertaking an investigation premised on principles of institutional theory and the interpretive approach, we observed the structuring of organizational structure occurring as a product not only of institutional demands but also of the relationship between interpretive schemes and situational circumstances. Yet, coterminous with this analysis, another facet of the reality of organizations began to emerge as one that was equally relevant to the understanding of them – namely, the dependencies of power. We would, in consequence, accede to those views that stress the importance of coupling power/institutions (Clegg 1990).

Rather than differentiated access to material and structural resources (Ranson et al. 1980), the dynamics of domination in the organization under study, structured as a principle of command-obedience, sustained characteristics of the structural framework, including the distribution of authority, mainly by the standardization of the set of values that guide action (Pfeffer 1981). Although ownership and position conferred power and legitimacy on the founders, since people usually follow their decisions, due to their rank in the hierarchy, the force of tradition allowed them to maintain dominance, as a shaper of patterns of meaning of structural arrangements, the perpetuation of which depended on the ability to solve problems and to create rules and positions assuring reproduction of their aims. Thus the founders' power consisted of the ability to utilize their values to legitimate their own actions, to maintain or expand certain interests. Consequently, leaders reinforced their role in the formation and institutionalization of values in the organization. Evident examples of leaders, identified with founders who shaped the basic conceptions of the symbolic universe of the organization, recur in a large portion of specialized literature, mainly that grounded on an interpretive approach. From this literature our analysis took shape. The mimetic nature of leadership structuring process is evident. Leadership thus delineates itself through imitation. To the process of the structuring of organizational structure, therefore, we add the reflex of the evolutionary history of the social leadership itself.

Notes

[1] We would like to thank Stewart Clegg for his editorial work on this chapter.
[2] Qualitative analysis proved to be the principal method of data assessment, using document analysis and preliminary techniques of content analysis as well as simple descriptive statistics used as a technical resource. Due to the contextual limits imposed by the frame of a single chapter, we present only limited empirical findings, those of importance for the argument we develop here.
[3] The founders play a key role in the organizational biography. People of humble origin and with very little educational background, they transmitted and maintained, during their administration, a set of meanings based on preserved ideas and values, such as

hard work, effort and dedication, which became an implicit reference for the definition of the organizational form.

[4] The reserach identified the following sequence of events: the Department of Accounting and the Department of Finance merged in a department called Controllership, and the Department of Supplies created out of the Department of Logistics, both of which now link to the Industrial Directorship. With the aim of extending trade relations into the international market and expanding its domestic market share, the marketing sector became directorially represented, assisted by a unit of Research and Dissemination. Furthermore, a relationship of functional authority became instituted between the Technical Directorship, responsible for the development of products, and the Industrial Directorship, responsible for their manufacture, through the Production Department.

[5] In this way, with a new formal arrangement the Technical Directorship became strongly linked to the Marketing Directorship, identifying marketing opportunities, and to the Industrial Directorship, where the factory is located.

References

Aldrich, Howard E. (1992), Incommensurable Paradigms? Vital Signs from Three Perspectives, in Michael Reed and Michael Hughes (eds.), *Rethinking Organizations: New Directions in Organization Theory and Analysis*, pp. 17-45. London: Sage.

Barley, Stephen R. (1986), Technology as an Occasion for Structuring: Evidence from Observations of CT Scanners and the Social Order of Radiology Departments, *Administrative Science Quarterly*, 31(1), pp. 78-108.

Bartunek, Jean M. (1984), Changing Interpretive Schemes and Organizational Restructuring: The Example of a Religious Order, *Administrative Science Quarterly*, 29(3), pp. 355-372.

Berger, Peter L. and Thomas Luckmann (1967), *The Social Construction of Reality*. New York: Doubleday.

Clegg, Stewart R. (1990), *Modern Organizations: Organization Studies in the Postmodern World*. London: Sage.

Deal, Terrence and Alan Kennedy (1982), *Corporate Culture: The Rites and Rituals of Corporate Life*. Reading, MA: Addison-Wesley.

DiMaggio, Paul J. and Walter W. Powell (1983), The Iron Cage Revisited: Institutional Isomorphism and Collective Rationality in Organizational Fields, *American Sociological Review*, 48(2), pp. 147-160.

Faoro, Raymundo (1987), *Os donos do poder: formação do patronato brasileiro*. Rio de Janeiro: Globo.

Fombrun, Charles (1989), Convergent Dynamics in the Production of Organizational Configurations, *Journal of Management Studies*, 26(5), pp. 439-458.

Fonseca, Valéria Silva da and Acyr Seleme (1991), Configuração estrutural da decisão: um modelo explicativo, Paper presented in the 15th Annual Meeting of the National Association of Postgraduate Programs in Management, Belo Horizonte, Brazil.

Fonseca, Valéria Silva da (1992), Estrutura de decisão: um estudo de caso em uma organização catarinense, Paper presented in the 16th Annual Meeting of the National Association of Postgraduate Programs in Management, Canela, Brazil.

Gagliardi, Pasquale (1986), The Creation and Change of Organizational Cultures: A Conceptual Framework, *Organization Studies*, 7(2), pp. 117-134.

Giddens, Anthony (1976), *New Rules of Sociological Method*. London: Hutchinson.

Greenwood, Royston and C.R. Hinings (1988), Organizational Design Types, Tracks and the Dynamics of Strategic Change, *Organization Studies*, 9(3), pp. 293-316.

Hinings, C.R. and Royston Greenwood (1988), *The Dynamics of Strategic Change*. New York: Blackwell.

Jacob, Philip E., James J. Flink and Hedvah L. Schuchman (1962), Values and their Function in Decision-Making, *American Behavioral Scientist*, 5, pp. 6-38.

Lukes, Steven (1974), *Power: A Radical View*. London: MacMillan.

Meyer, John W. and Brian Rowan (1983), Institutionalized Organizations: Formal Structure as Myth and Ceremony, in John W. Meyer and W. Richard Scott (eds.), *Organizational Environments: Ritual and Rationality*, pp. 21-44. Beverly Hills, CA: Sage.

Morgan, Gareth (1986), *Images of Organization*. London: Sage.

Oliver, Christine (1988), The Collective Strategy Framework: An Application to Competing Predictions of Isomorphism, *Administrative Science Quarterly*, 33(4), pp. 543-561.

Parsons, Talcott (1951), *The Social System*. Glencoe, Ill.: Free Press.

Pfeffer, Jeffrey (1981), *Power in Organizations*. Boston: Pitman.

Ranson, Stewart, Bob Hinings and Royston Greenwood (1980), The Structuring of Organizational Structures, *Administrative Science Quarterly*, 25(1), pp. 1-17.

Riley, Patricia (1983), A Structurationist Account of Political Culture, *Administrative Science Quarterly*, 28(3), pp. 414-437.

Schütz, Alfred (1972), *The Phenomenology of the Social World*. London: Heinemann.

Scott, W. Richard (1983), The Organization of Environments: Network, Cultural, and Historical Elements, in John W. Meyer and W. Richard Scott (eds.), *Organizational Environments: Ritual and Rationality*, pp. 155-175. Beverly Hills, CA: Sage.

Scott, W. Richard (1987), The Adolescence of Institutional Theory, *Administrative Science Quarterly*, 32(4), pp. 493-511.

Smircich, Linda (1983), Concepts of Culture and Organizational Analysis, *Administrative Science Quarterly*, 28(3), pp. 339-358.

Whittington, Richard (1992), Putting Giddens into Action: Social Systems and Managerial Agency. *Journal of Management Studies*, 29(6), pp. 693-712.

Wilmott, Hugh C. (1981), The Structuring of Organizational Structure: A Note, *Administrative Science Quarterly*, 26(3), pp. 470-474.

International Corporate Governance: Who Rules the Corporation?

Thomas Clarke and Richard Bostock

Introduction

Questions concerning corporate governance have become more pressing than at any time since the 1930s, when Berle and Means' *The Modern Corporation* (1932); and James Burnham's *The Managerial Revolution* (1941) discussed the implications of the separation of ownership and control, and the professional managerial impact upon corporate direction. Now, as then, public trust in the efficiency and reliability of the governing structures of industry suffers from a lack of confidence. Contemporary concerns include the effect of the radically changing pattern of the distribution of share ownership upon corporate direction; the large scale corporate collapses of the recent past, often despite healthy recent audit reports; a consequent concern with the standards of the audit and accountancy profession (Cadbury 1992); the lack of accountability, disclosure, and transparency of boards to shareholders (Monks and Minow 1991); concerns over the adequacy of board structures and processes (Lorsch and MacIver 1989; Mace 1972); the quality of directorial competencies; the apparent lack of corporate social responsibility; the destabilizing impact of the growth of merger and acquisition activities (Pound 1992); the short term basis of corporate performance measures and resulting decision-making; excessive executive compensation despite poor performance (Gregg et al. 1993); the spate of business fraud; and the evident weakness of corporate self-regulation. These problems, exacerbated by the development of more complex corporate structures, in part a result of modern corporate law, create a modern corporate reality that lags behind the problems encountered (Hopt 1984).

The purpose of this chapter is to examine some of the background to the contemporary concerns regarding corporate governance, to elaborate a simple classification of the existing corporate governance systems, to suggest areas where convergence in systems of governance, under the influence of recent pressures, may occur, and, where divergences are likely to remain. It is not the concern of this chapter to question more fundamentally matters of ownership and control, inequality, or the structure and operation of corporate capital. Issues of such profound significance are beyond the scope of this chapter, which represents only an attempt to reflect current thinking on corporate administration and regulation.

Accountability

The large scale collapses of major corporations such as Maxwell's MGN and MMC, BCCI and Polly Peck when all appeared to be going well adds urgency to the call for higher standards of corporate governance and the requirement of greater accountability to be able to detect such fraud. In an increasingly international and global economy (Dicken 1992; Oxford Analytica 1992) with infinite numbers of stakeholders effected, the demand for change is considerable. Of particular concern is the scope available for creative accounting and the lack of homogeneity between company audits. Such variations within countries are perfectly legal and international variations in accountancy standards further exasperate this lack of harmonization. Despite such criticisms, in the final analysis legal responsibility remains firmly with the board of directors whose responsibility it is to prepare the annual accounts showing a true and fair view of the state of the company. (The fact that in Europe itself accounting standards differ markedly in the interpretation of a "true and fair" view, suggests any form of international regulation will remain in infancy for some time to come.)

At the heart of the corporate governance debate is the concern over the lack of accountability of board's of directors to shareholders, and more recently in the view of stakeholder theory to society in general. As the magnitude and international spread of corporations increase, their decisions impact universally and unevenly throughout the industrialized world. The requirement for accountability to shareholders in the form of stockholder theory, is extended to the need for accountability to a wider section of society in the form of stakeholder theory (Freedman and Reed 1983). At present it is possible to argue corporations are accountable to neither sets of interests (Monks and Minow 1991), hence the corporate governance debate and the argument for statutory regulation to replace self-regulation. However the degree of accountability to different groups varies nationally. The German system of labor representation, in the form of co-determination, and the Japanese system of corporate governance, both align with stakeholder theory. Accountability to a wider section of society predominates as the norm. In contrast, the Anglo-Saxon system, with accountability foremost to the shareholder, adheres to stockholder theory.

The concern with board structures and processes has been on the agenda since the pioneering work of Myles Mace in the 1970s, developed further in the 1980s by Jay Lorsch and Elizabeth Maciver. In the eyes of the law the board of directors has control over management and is there to oversee management and hold it accountable to shareholders, and, in the German and Japanese model, society. However, in reality executive management often dominates the board which merely acts as a rubber stamp. This is often seen in the over-powering and domineering Chief Executive Officer (CEO) and Chairman. As a result suggestions to reform boards of directors most frequently address the strengthening of directors powers relative to that of the CEO/Chairman (Pearce and Zahra 1991). Domination of boards by one or two executives is a problem that recurs in all systems of corporate governance, but the checks and balances against it are probably weakest in the Anglo-Saxon system practiced in the UK and US, where boards in the past often confined themselves to largely nominal functions. It was this inertia in responsible boardroom activity which the Cadbury Report on the Financial Aspects of Corporate Governance (1992) sought to address in the UK.

In comparison such concerns are not so widespread in the German model where, to a degree, the two-tier board system contains management power and acts as a check upon any excesses. Within such a system labor representatives are represented on the supervisory board and can oversee management and its actions. In addition banks who hold a big stake in German industry and often act as trustees for individual shareholders prevent individual managers from becoming too autocratic and over-powering.

In the Japanese model top management fill the board giving a relatively unaccountable board structure (Viner 1993). However monitoring is exercised by banks who through cross-shareholding's and implicit contracts hold a majority stake in Japanese industry (Kester 1992a). It is also a system that relies heavily on trust. However many recent developments have began to question Japanese corporate governance and like the other systems it is in transition. Such developments include the internationalization and globalization of business and the resulting influence of international institutional investors (Baladi 1991). This interest group of powerful investors including the big pension funds is becoming more active and changing board structures and processes internationally. They are demanding greater accountability, transparency and information. The success of the Japanese system causes problems in that it results in a vast accumulation of wealth. As a result of this, and due to the globalization of financial markets, Japanese industry no longer needs to rely on the banks to such a degree: thus the monitoring role they used to provide is in jeopardy:

Displacement of traditional relational contracting between companies and banks by price-driven, deal orientated financing imposes great stress on the traditional Japanese corporate governance system. Because this displacement is being driven by the inexorable globalization of Japanese financial markets, the stress is not likely to subside (Kester 1992: 187).

Finally the recent spate of frauds questions the very heart of the Japanese system, in so far as trust undergirds it.

Mergers and Takeovers

The 1980s phenomenon of merger's and acquisitions, leveraged buy-outs and management buy-outs, very much an Anglo-Saxon phenomenon, brought with it many problems (Pound 1992). This debt financed era, seen by some as short term, lacked concern for stakeholders at large: a form of individual greed that lead to anti-takeover devices like poison pills and thus an entrenched, inefficient and conceited management who lacked accountability. It was after all the ultimate form of market orientated capitalism with the ultimate price being paid now due to the over gearing of the 1980s. However others saw it as a form of market orientated control that kept management in its place.

The 1990s have seen a sharp reduction of such activities and has witnessed what John Pound has described as the "Politicization of Corporate Governance." Here the emphasis is more on communication between companies and their shareholders. "The emerging weapon in the fight for corporate control: debate not debt" (Pound 1992: 83). This has shown itself in the increasingly active role shown by major institutional investors (Lipton 1992):

In the 1990s politics will replace takeovers as the defining tool for corporate governance challenges, and a marketplace of ideas will replace the frenzied activity that dominated the financial market place in the 1980s. In the transaction-driven market of the past, corporate raiders used junk bonds and other financial tools to take control of their targets. In the new market place of ideas, debate will replace debt as active shareholders identify specific operating policies for their target corporations and then invent new mechanisms to get their message across to management (Pound 1992: 83).

As he points out such a new political mechanism does not depend on the availability of financing. Indeed such an approach has occurred because the old system is no longer viable. "This new form of governance based on politics rather than finance will provide a means of oversight that is both far more effective and far less expensive than the takeovers of the 1980s" (Pound 1992: 83).

The 1980s phenomenon of mergers and acquisitions did not occur to the same extent in Continental Europe or Japan. The reason being their corporate governance systems protect companies from hostile predators. The main protection against such actions is the high percentage of cross-shareholdings. Many Japanese and German companies, where shares, held by banks or friendly associate companies, remain stable in their ownership, form a long term stable shareholding base. This makes it extremely difficult for a predator to get majority control. In Japan "Keiretsu" developed this to an art form. These are groups of companies confederated around a major bank, trading company, or a major industrial corporation and interacting within the context of close, stable, co-operative commercial relationships (Kester 1992b). Similarly, industrial groupings dominate the German industrial sector. This system, criticized by the United States as anti-competitive and as breaking US anti trust laws (Kester 1992b), nonetheless mirrors some aspects of corporate action in America. In the 1980s many American companies put up barriers to protect themselves from takeovers in the form of poison pills and staggered boards to deter predators.

Directors Pay and Performance

The issue of director's pay has become a subject of some interest particularly in the US and UK. Indeed there appears to be a diminishing relationship between directors pay and corporate performance (Gregg et al. 1993). These authors found that in large companies in the United Kingdom over the 1980s and early 1990s the rate of growth of directors remuneration was very high (about 20% per year on average) and very weakly linked to performance. They also found that during the 1988 to 1991 recession very high pay awards were received despite very poor corporate performances. As a result they come to the conclusion that corporate growth is an important determinant of the change in directors remuneration. This might help to explain the large number of mergers and acquisitions in the 1980s.

In the United States executive pay is becoming a central issue but despite attempts to curb excessive compensation, director pay is still on the increase and tends to lack any form of relationship to performance. However, boards are beginning to take more interest and concern in this issue (Byrne 1993). It could, however, be argued that remuneration committees which are seen as one of the answers still lack total independence (Kochan and Syrett 1991). One solution of bringing in external consultants to help remuneration committee's would further appear to be a step in the direction of more objective assessment and is a trend which is on the increase.

In comparison in Japan in the past year or so many leading companies have announced cuts in pay for their chief executive officers. For example at Fujitsu Ltd, some executives have seen their compensation slashed by up to 35%; at Hitachi Ltd., 15%. "When company results are down, managers have to take responsibility and accept such cuts," said Takahiko Shinohara, a managing director at Hitachi. Japanese chiefs averaged $872,646 in 1991, about a quarter the pay of their American counterparts. Looked at by other measures, the disparities in American and Japanese pay are equally stunning. In Japan, the CEO makes less than 32 times the pay of the average factory worker, and 26 times what the typical school teacher earns. In the US, that gap is considerably wider: roughly 157 and 113 times, respectively (Neff 1993).

Cultural Influences

Corporate governance varies as a result of differing ideologies, histories, political beliefs, social, economic and other factors. This lack of compatibility at present is well summed up by Klaus Hopt and Gunther Teubner (1985: v):

> To be sure, a transplantation of one national approach to another country is not easily achieved, since the various approaches to corporate social responsibility are intimately connected to national economic and social structures and to political and cultural traditions.

Despite this, convergence is still possible as they go on to indicate:

> However, it might still be possible for each country to learn something from the others: with each country avoiding misjudgments made, or implementing, where feasible, ideas developed in other countries by carefully adapting the diverse national experiences to their own particular institutional traditions (Hopt and Teubner 1985: v).

It is not possible to transplant corporate governance from one country to another. However it may be possible to develop some general principles, as Jonathon Charkham, adviser to the governors of the Bank of England suggests: "We should not seek to transplant them, but to identify the various ways in which the universal principles of sound corporate governance can be applied. This will help us pinpoint and correct the weaknesses in our own system" (Charkham 1992: 8).

Governance systems do not arise complete and mature, they evolve over time. The Anglo-Saxon system is very much based on the individual and short-term market orientation. In contrast the German and Japanese models are more orientated around groups and long-term implicit trust relationships (Kester 1992b). Indeed Bimal Prodhan (1992), who has looked at the possibility of transferring either the UK-US type or German-Japanese form of corporate governance to eastern Europe talks of the disturbances such transfers can cause. He comes to the conclusion that the exportation of Anglo-US style corporate governance to such countries is likely to result in tragedy. As a result, while businesses have become increasingly international, their corporate governance systems have become less so, and there are possibly inherent dangers of attempting to make them conform to an inappropriate model.

UK Corporate Governance

The British corporate governance system is based upon individualism, competition and short-termism and a belief in market orientated capitalism. The key players in this model are the institutional investors, for example the big insurance companies and pension funds. These groups are potentially the UK's most powerful shareholders. Until recently these owners of British industry have played merely a passive role in the companies they own (Younghusband and Wilson 1990). This could be said to be changing with shareholder activism on the rise in the 1990s, though as recently as 1989, Johnathon Charkham in a Bank of England discussion paper concluded that shareholders have for the most part withdrawn from playing actively even the limited part the UK Companies Acts gave them and that boards of directors have been dominated by management. It is not that shareholders did not have the power to influence management, although they are at a disadvantage, but more the fact that the will was not there. As long as they were making short term profits there was no need to question management.

This passive role started to change in the late 1980s when the extent of merger and acquisition activity removed executive management further from any effective shareholder control. This undermined further any conception of shareholder democracy that still existed, alienating shareholders from the decision-making process. This along with management buy-outs, leveraged buy-outs and general capital restructuring has obliged institutional investors to play a more active role in their involvement in corporate matters. Indeed institutional shareholders are increasingly seen as having the capacity to decide whether power remains with executive management. Stratford Sherman (1988) sees power slowly shifting back to shareholders again. Hence there is clearly a new willingness of institutional investors actively to influence the management of the companies they own. This has clearly shown itself in Investment Protection Committees (IPCs) and Institutional Shareholder Committees, which have also helped to increase shareholder protection.

A number of proposals have sought to try to redress the balance and bring back accountability to the corporation. In the Anglo-Saxon system this has involved supplementing executive directors with further representation of independent non-executive directors. Independent representation on the board will help to separate the management function from that of the supervisory function, bringing the Anglo-Saxon model closer into line with that of the European model. One of the problems of such a system is that although independent and serving on other companies' boards, independent directors are often CEOs of their own companies. One of the solutions to this problem advocated but not as of yet implemented is the idea of the professionalization of directors (Gilson and Kraakman 1993). This would entail independent directors whose full time job it is to serve on boards. This may also help to alleviate the accusation often leveled at directors that they lack the time and knowledge to run the companies they direct (J. Lorsch and MacIver 1989, and others). Precisely whom or what independent directors might represent is another question.

Along with the independent director has come further moves to change the structure of the Anglo-Saxon board to make it more accountable. This includes the setting up of various committees of mainly independent non-executive directors to oversee important board decisions. These include audit committees, remuneration committees and nomination committees. The audit committee is used as

a further check on the accounts and statements of the company. The audit committee chooses the companies auditors and has a critical role to play in ensuring the
integrity of the companies financial reports. This involves reviewing the half-year
and annual financial statements before submission to the board and dialogue with
the external auditors providing a neutral link between the company and its external auditors (Cadbury 1992). In the light of recent criticisms of directors pay, the
remuneration committee provides a more objective value of executive pay and
prevents management from setting their own pay. However, the problem is not
completely solved as independent non-executive directors are executives of other companies and their decisions are not therefore impartial. Finally nomination
committees can be seen as a partial guard against the nepotism of the past where
the CEO/Chairman had the freedom to choose his own board and successor. Indeed it could be argued that it was this board process that helped to create boards
without teeth or power.

There are also legal checks, for there may be cases when institutions are not
able to influence the board. For example in a hostile situation when the institution is concerned that the board is not acting in the best interests of the company,
they may consider the possibility of requesting an extra-ordinary general meeting
(EGM) at which to propose a resolution for the removal of one or more of the existing directors and the appointment of additional directors who are sympathetic
to the institutions concerned. A number of members acting together holding not
less than 10% of the paid up capital which carries voting rights has the power to
request an EGM to propose a resolution. For example to remove existing directors. At any general meeting institutions through their corporate representatives
can ask questions of the board which relate to the business of the meeting. The
use of proxies means the views of institutions should be made known even if they
have not attended (Younghusband and Wilson 1990).

However, despite this, accountability is lacking and the shareholders are at a
disadvantage to management. This is clearly shown in the fact that in order to lay
a resolution with a company a shareholder must pay for its circulation (Simpson
1990). Shareholders have a restricted role to play in the UK, but are hitting back,
and the big institutions are beginning to question this limited role. Also, accountability, which is at the heart of the corporate governance debate, is becoming a key
issue. This is being reflected in the increasing importance being given to board
structures and particularly independent directors and board committees. How effective such a body which lacks both time and information can be is yet to be seen.

Finally one of the major criticisms of the UK model of corporate governance
is its short term horizons and perspectives. Indeed institutional investors are often accused of being short term investors and lacking any concern in the companies they own. The rise in importance of pension funds which by their very nature
are long term may help to reverse this trend. However, most large institutional investors have index investment formulae which demand a certain return or recom-

mend sales of shares. A more active long term role is the only viable alternative (P. Drucker 1991).

Short term pressures to perform result in managements main concern with short term profits and quarterly dividends. As a result stock market share prices are kept up at the expense of longer term investment in capital, training and research and development. This short-sighted approach has often been suggested as the principal reason for Britain's recent industrial failure. The 1980s mergers and acquisitions fever was a classic illustration of short-term market orientated capitalism. One of the remedies often cited is that of the German and Japanese systems of corporate governance. Here there is a much heavier reliance on cross-shareholdings and bank involvement (Kester 1992b). Under such systems there is less concern on stock market value and more on long term interests of the company and its many stakeholders. This more stable long term base is seen by many as a superior model of corporate governance. How viable it would be in such a totally different historical and social setting is questionable (Charkham 1992).

US Corporate Governance

Like the UK model of corporate governance the American model is based on the unitary board. As a result this has often led to a management dominated board which lacks accountability. Restructuring boards to give them a greater degree of accountability has been achieved by introducing a majority of non-executive directors. The problem with such board structures is well analyzed by Jay Lorsch and Elizabeth MacIver (1989) in their book *Pawns or Potentates – The Reality of America's Corporate Boards.* Their research of US boards shows the limited value of such a board structure. For example, they found outside directors have limited time, knowledge and expertise in the companies they direct. They also lacked group cohesion and consensus on goals, and group norms were against criticizing the chief executive officer. In contrast there is the power of the Chief Executive Officer who has great knowledge and expertise of the company and controls the agenda, meetings and information. In the past he/she has also selected the directors.

The remedies to this problem of management domination have been the increasing use of committee's on boards which have been chaired by non-executive directors. For example audit, remuneration and nomination committees. These have helped to take some of the decisions and power out of management hands and particularly that of the chief executive officer, who can no longer decide his/her own pay and choose his/her own board.

Another check on management power can be seen to be the more active role being played by shareholders. This major change in US corporate governance has seen the evolution of institutional investors from that of a passive role either ignoring voting, or voting with management, to that of questioning managements power and decisions. This has resulted in some big investors, for example public pension funds, using their power to bring about constructive changes. A good example being CALPERS, the Californian public pension fund. This new found interest in voting and corporate governance to date has been largely confined to American companies but as Baladi (1991) indicates, as they start to put larger amounts in foreign capital markets, they will probably take a more active interest in the corporate governance of their non-US holdings.

These changes have mainly been due to developments in the 1980s, for example, the growth of institutional holdings, with American institutions now owning more than 45% of outstanding US equities and this figure is growing (Heard 1990). There has also been a proliferation of voting issues that have had economic impacts. For example, the takeover boom of the 1980s saw the proliferation of anti-takeover amendments to corporate charters and by laws, poison pills, golden parachutes and other defensive measures which were designed largely to deter or defeat value-enhancing bids. These may have helped top management but they were not in the shareholders' interest. They had harmful effects on shareholder value and need shareholder approval. Institutional activism has been on the rise and public pension funds in particular have become a pro-active force in corporate affairs. This has become a necessity as the size of capital they have committed makes them virtual prisoners of the market. As a result they have shown few inhibitions in confronting management.

Many activist public funds have joined together to form a council of institutional investors including 50 or more institutions worth $300 bn. (Heard 1990). This provides a forum for institutions to exchange ideas and information and coordinate strategy. They see themselves as the owners of America's companies and as entitled to participation in major financial issues and other important structural questions. Indeed, over the years they have taken some significant actions. A number of their shareholder proposals have been successful and they have gained shareholder support, for example voting on poison pill defenses. As public pension funds become more expert in soliciting support for their proposals, the impact of their efforts will probably grow.

Such developments mean that public funds can now influence the composition of the board. Some corporate management are not happy with this institutional interest but the challenge seems to have resulted in a more active stance and improvements in corporate performance. It is possible that this public fund interest and activism will spread to the private institutional investors but this is not the case to date.

There has been a dramatic rise in ownership of non-US equities by American investors, for example, total American holdings in foreign securities more than doubled between 1979 and 1987 and exceeded $1 trillion according to data by the Investor Responsibility Research Center. Pension funds accounted significantly for this growth and this trend is likely to continue. Even so such investments are small amounts in comparison to what they own, and they have only started going abroad. However, this trend is likely to accelerate dramatically as Baladi (1991) indicates. This has resulted in an institutional interest in shareholder rights regarding their foreign stock. Such interest groups have recently raised a host of questions about their rights as shareholders in non-US companies, from curiosity about how to vote proxies in non-US companies to inquiries about decision-making, including rights associated with nomination and election of directors. It remains to be seen exactly how this interest will play out, but major Japanese and European companies should prepare themselves for more active involvement by US institutional investors in the future. The pension funds, in particular, could be a major force in changing corporate governance systems and shaping international corporate governance (Baladi 1991; Drucker 1991).

The public pension funds have been the most active and vocal institutions on corporate governance matters. Some of the larger state funds, for example New York and California (CALPERS), have established special units within their investment departments to monitor corporate governance matters affecting their portfolio companies. Public funds have been leaders in a variety of governance initiatives. However, others have been more cautious in asserting themselves on corporate governance issues, for example banks who do not want to offend for profit motive reasons. They are, however, beginning to take a more independent role in voting. In comparison corporate pension funds remain largely unwilling to play an active role in corporate governance while foundations and endowments actively pursue social issues such as South Africa but not corporate governance issues.

To conclude on institutional investors, they did become more active in the 1980s and this has been shown in their willingness to use shareholder proposals. The big institutions have tended to focus on a selection of poorly performing companies to get their message across (Kochan and Syrett 1991). These funds are also supporting changes in the Securities and Exchange Committee's (SEC) proxy rules that would give shareholders much greater access to the proxy to put proposals before other shareholders, ridding them of their present disadvantage. In the past decade two contradictory trends seem to have occurred. On the one hand there has clearly been an erosion of shareholder rights while on the other institutional investors have begun to re-assert themselves and play a more active role in corporate governance. Whether the latter will prevail and is here to stay is yet to be determined.

If shareholders interests do prevail, the question remains, what will be the criteria for investment? Will the existing narrow, financially based performance measures continue and be further intensified? Like its British counterpart, American corporate governance failure is often cited as due to its short time horizon, as Michael Porter insists, "The US system first and foremost advances the goals of shareholders interested in near-term appreciation of their shares even at the expense of the long term performance of American companies" (Porter 1992: 67).

Porter and many others see America's industry failing as a result of a lack of investment in research and development, employee's training and skill development, supplier relations and so on. This short term shareholder dominated perspective which creates highly fluid investment is very different to the German and Japanese model which recognizes the importance of secure investment and the longer term, for the benefit of all concerned.

German Corporate Governance: A European Perspective

The German system of corporate governance is fundamentally different from that of the Anglo-Saxon system described above using the examples of Britain and America. This is shown in their two-tier management structure comprising of the "Vorstand" or management board which is entrusted with the day to day running of the company, and the "Aufsichtsrat" or supervisory board whose job is to supervise the management board when necessary and to participate in long term strategic decisions (cited in Lufkin and Gallagher 1990). This helps to prevent the abuses of management dominated boards of the unitary board system of the Anglo-Saxon model. On the supervisory board there are both shareholder and employee representatives controlling the managing board, increasing accountability to a greater range of stakeholders and reducing institutional pressures upon boards of directors towards short term decisions and allowing for longer term strategic planning.

This system of corporate governance has the longer term interests of the company at heart and like the Japanese system of corporate governance accountability can be seen to be to a wider range of interests than solely to that of shareholders, hence the two tier board system. The longer term interests of the company are demonstrated in greater investment in plant, equipment and intangible assets for example corporate training than occurs in the Anglo-Saxon models (Porter 1992). As a result, less emphasis is placed on share dividends which tend to be lower than in America and the United Kingdom and more on the long term viability of the corporation. This low return on shareholdings is not seen as a problem by the major shareholders in German industry who are the banks and have other business relationships with the companies they invest in. Apart from their shareholdings, German banks are also creditors and help debt finance industry. However, this acceptance of a low return on the stock market may be about to change with the rising influence of the international institutional investor. Such powerful interest groups, which include the large American public pension funds, have already started to indicate their disapproval of low returns on the capital markets. If German industry wants to attract more foreign capital it may well have to show more interest in its capital returns. In doing this the Germans will have to try to satisfy the shareholder without jeopardizing the long term interests of other stakeholders.

At present the German capital markets do not match Germany's world economic status. For example, at the end of 1991 market capitalization was DM 596.5 bn. whereas in the United Kingdom it was DM 1,507.4 bn. As a proportion of GNP it was only 23% in Germany as opposed to 89% in the United Kingdom (E. Schneider-Lenne 1992). This is likely to change as it is likely to grow in importance. Low reliance on capital markets has resulted in fundamental differences between this system and that of the Anglo-Saxon model:

> With so many differences between the German capital markets and their transatlantic and cross-channel counterparts it is not surprising that corporate governance in Germany is totally different from that in the US or UK in that shareholder activism by large institutions, hostile takeovers and shareholder involvement in management are less prominent in Germany (Schmalenbach 1990: 110).

The two basic reasons for these differences can be seen in the legal structure of German public companies with their two tier boards as opposed to the unitary board of the Anglo-Saxon model and the structure of shareholdings in Germany with the banks controlling the majority of shares. The reason for this is that banks own their own shares and also look after and vote for private and corporate investor's shares. For example, in 1988 shares with a nominal value of DM 65 bn. were deposited with banks (cited in Schmalenbach 1990). Banks can vote vast numbers of shares which they do not own giving them significant power at general meetings of shareholders. This is shown by the fact that on average banks collectively represent more than four fifths (82.67%) of all votes present in the meetings (Baums 1992). They tend to support management, making shareholder activism contrary to this by other parties futile. Banks tend also to be lenders which helps to explain this support and their interest in the long term.

The votes of the banks as discretionary proxies is very important in the context of corporate governance. The problem is that the banks voting power is much greater than their economic share. Also, as lenders they are not so interested in the short term but more the long term. Banks could also be seen to stifle shareholder activism by others and there is always the danger that although they are supposed to vote in the interest of shareholders they may not always act in the shareholders interest (Baums 1992), thus self interest may prevail as Adam Smith would argue:

> From this it may seem that the banks seek to prevent corporate governance being exercised by shareholders in German companies. This is not the case. The decisive factor is that the shareholders are apparently not aware of, nor interested in fully exercising their rights. The banks are simply the beneficiaries of such habit (Schmalenbach 1990: 117).

Shareholders can take an active role in the life of a company if they are willing to do so, however due to the two tier board system their influence on the day to day business decisions will be limited. There is nothing to stop them from exercising their rights in general meetings and in appointing representatives on the supervisory board. Although German company law may not encourage corporate governance by shareholders it should not be seen as an obstacle. Indeed it is argued that the quietness of the market for corporate control is caused by the fact that shareholders are not interested in pursuing their rights. They are seen as happy with banks exercising their votes on their behalf, usually in accordance with the proposals of the management. There are no legal or economic reasons to prevent a shareholder from rallying other shareholders to support him in an attempt to actively exercise corporate governance. To date there are few such cases but this is not to say that such attempts will be fruitless.

As well as a lack of shareholder activism there is also less of a market for hostile takeovers. In general it can be said that it is not the regulatory framework which discourages such practices in Germany (Schneider-Lenne 1992) but rather the structure of shareholdings and, perhaps, the maximum voting rights clauses in the Articles of Association of certain companies. There are, for example, preference shares with no voting rights which are gaining popularity. It is also possible, but not usual, to put limitations on voting rights. Finally, clients who deposit with banks can give voting instructions but if they do not, as is usually the case, the banks can vote as they feel fit. However as Nicholas Kochan and Michael Syrett (1991) point out, hostile takeovers look increasingly likely in Germany, a phenomenon confirmed by Ellen Schneider-Lenne (1992), partly due to Germany's relatively low share prices. This process is ever more likely with the internationalization of business and thus the internationalization of takeovers.

In conclusion, while the German corporate governance system with its supervisory board, with both shareholder and employee representatives on it, is in many ways a superior governance system to that in the Anglo-Saxon world, there are some inherent problems. For such a system ignores the interests of small shareholders, is over-secretive and is ill designed to cope with the pressures of international investment or the global market for companies. The biggest influence will be international forces; in other words, the shaping of corporate governance by the globalization of the financial and corporate markets. Despite these problems, which are solvable, the advantages of the German system of corporate governance, like that of the Japanese system, can be seen in its use of industrial groupings, implicit contracting and extensive cross-shareholdings which are all relationship orientated and finally in the financial sectors close links with industry.

Japanese Corporate Governance: An Asian Perspective

This system of corporate governance which is closest to that of the German system, but still very different, has been described by Nicholas Kochan and Michael Syrett (1991: 91) as "perhaps the most remote and exotic of any of the developed world." This can perhaps be seen in its heavy reliance on trust and implicit contracting and a relationship orientated approach to corporate governance. Like the

German system, there are also close ties between banks and industry and a web of cross-shareholdings making hostile takeovers virtually impossible:

One of the many comparative strengths of Japanese Corporate Governance has been the systems hostility towards hostile takeovers. Japanese corporations can conduct business without building defenses that could preclude the accumulation of valuable assets or inhibit long term research and development strategies (Viner 1990: 27).

As a result Japanese industry can concentrate on the long term interests of the company and invest in research and development, capital, employee training and skills development etc. The ability to invest, Michael Porter has argued, has given Japanese industry a competitive advantage. This system, like the German one which concentrates on the long term interests of many stakeholders at the expense of short term returns for stockholders only, is fundamentally different from the Anglo-Saxon model and many would argue is eminently superior. However, the increasing activity of international institutional investors may well change this, demanding greater returns on their investments. If this occurs Japan will have to try to balance the interests of shareholders without jeopardizing the long term interests of the company which at present are well served.

Although hostile takeovers are unusual, particularly foreign ones, mergers are not that unusual. They tend to be with businesses in the same industry and more commonly within the same group. This is particularly likely to occur if a member within a group is in financial difficulties, resulting in a merger with a company within the group. This is very different to the Anglo-Saxon merger phenomenon of the 1980s when diversification was the main aim, often with devastating results. However, recently Japanese companies have been diversifying into unrelated areas often resulting in conflicts of interest between different stakeholders, something which did not happen in the past (Kester 1992a). At present acquisitions are far more unusual than mergers but Aron Viner (1990) suggests that in the future an increasing number of Japanese companies will not be able to survive in Japan's fiercely competitive environment and will be looking abroad for friendly buyers. One of the major constraints on this could be the extraordinary high prices of Japanese corporate shares.

One of the major features of Japanese corporate governance is the reliance on cross-shareholdings. Nichon Keizai Shimbun estimates that for the nation at large nearly 200 trillion yen of stock is held under reciprocal shareholding agreements (Kester 1992a: 57). Some have argued the influence of such a mechanism is decreasing (Viner 1990). Corporate governance in Japan is in transition with the final outcome yet to be decided. Yet, as Aron Viner points out, cross-shareholdings are likely to remain a keystone of the Japanese stock market and of Japanese corporate governance for some time. This close web of shareholders helps management give primary attention to the long term and decision-making, instead of pursuing short term profits to satisfy the fleeting inclinations of institutional investors. Also, stable cross-shareholdings is the main takeover defense of Japanese companies.

There has undoubtedly been a growth in merger and acquisition activity in Japan recently. For example, the number of acquisitions of Japanese companies during the past decade has increased dramatically, but is still low in comparison to the United States and the United Kingdom. This trend is seen by some as likely to sharply increase with the globalization of markets making a process of increased acquisition activity an intrinsic part of business practice in Japan (Viner 1990). Those who see acquisition activity sharply increasing argue it will be for specific reasons, for example, for employees benefit, not shareholders, and will not involve unfriendly acquisitions. In other words it will stay distinctively Japanese. As such it will only occur in those industries facing crisis with the buyer stepping in to solve the problems of the acquisition target. This trend along with the internationalization trend may result in major companies being acquired by foreign interests in the 1990s.

There are, as briefly mentioned, other forces which are likely to change Japanese corporate governance in the 1990s. For example, growing competition in the capital markets will discourage institutional investors from keeping low yielding equities in their portfolios. This process has began in Japan and could weaken Japan's obsession with capital gains at the expense of dividend yield. If this occurs institutional investors could gradually adopt American strategies including the practice of selling blocks of shares to potential hostile bidders. This process is ever more likely with further breakdowns in trust and a decreasing emphasis on cross-shareholdings, with buy-outs now occurring.

In the past, Japan's huge institutional investors including the life insurance companies and banks have not been too keen to exercise their influence on company management unless it was facing financial or other difficulties, and then any influence tends to be behind the scenes. Toru Ishiguro (1990) argues this passive shareholder approach is changing and investors are increasingly becoming less friendly towards management. The big institutions are starting to realize their obligations to maximize shareholder value. Thus long term institutional shareholdings and cross shareholding of shares by several or a group of companies, which used to guarantee management a reliable bases of control over the company, may no longer continue to be as reliable as before. It can be seen from this that the Japanese environment for corporate governance is changing and is expected to continue to do so, with, perhaps, a move towards a greater Americanization of Japanese corporate governance? Will Japan become more accountable to the shareholder? Will the outside director come to the Japanese board and monitor and advise inside executive directors thus moving the Japanese system of corporate governance more towards the Anglo-Saxon model, as Bob Tricker suggests (Kochan and Syrett 1991)? This is the way Shigeru Watanabe and Isao Yamamoto, two Nomura Research Institute analysts, believe Japanese corporate governance should be going (Watanabe and Yamamoto 1993).

Corporate governance issues have now become conspicuous in Japan. Japan is becoming fully integrated within the international financial world and having to adapt both its social and regulatory systems. The way it changes will be of interest and importance for the international financial and industrial community at large.

Conclusion

This chapter has shown that systems of corporate governance vary as a result of differing histories, cultures, social beliefs and ideologies. As a result, different countries' corporate governance systems can broadly be put into one of three categories, that of the Anglo-Saxon model as represented by the UK and USA, the European model as represented by Germany, or the Asian model as demonstrated by Japan.

The Anglo-Saxon model has been shown broadly to represent a market for corporate control based on market orientated capitalism, with a particular interest in the short term and thus a concern with stock market return for shareholders. As a result, one of the major concerns with the system has been its obsession with short term returns for a minority of stockholders at the expense of long term gains for a wider variety of stakeholders. This argument has been particularly strongly promoted by Michael Porter who argues that it has led to a lack of investment, both tangible and intangible, in the US and UK. Other major concerns include sudden unexpected collapses, fraud, the lack of corporate accountability, inadequate board structures which have resulted in management dominated boards, excessive director compensation despite poor performance and a perceived lack of directorial and board room competency. As a result, shareholder activism, particularly amongst the large institutional investors, is on the rise.

In comparison the European and Asian model as represented by Germany and Japan are very differently structured. These systems rely heavily on trust and implicit contracting with cross-shareholdings and a close reliance between banks and industry providing a stable long term base. Here the emphasis is on the long term interests of the companies' many stakeholders. This has resulted in a greater value being put on investment at the expense of short term profits for the owners of capital. However, both systems, like all corporate governance systems, are under pressure as a result of international economic forces and are in a state of transition. For example, low dividend payments are coming under attack as large international institutional investors, for example large American pension funds, start looking abroad and demanding higher returns on their investment. Global and international forces are helping to shape corporate governance systems.

Other internal and external forces are also changing the system. For example, there is less emphasis on cross-shareholdings, which are seen as anti competitive by others within the international community. This has resulted in a less stable long term base and some signs of a more active market for corporate control. The success of the Japanese system has also helped to bring about change and what

could be seen as a more western approach. For example, excess cash has been used
to diversify and speculate on the financial markets. As a result, Japanese industry
has become more detached from banks thus removing any accountability that existed. This removal of industries' main monitor has also resulted in money being
used for managers' and employees' advantage, not shareholders', as opposed to
representing all interests as in the past. There have also been examples of breakdowns in trust. However, it must be remembered that these changes are at present
on a small scale and do not necessarily represent the final outcome.

It can be concluded from this chapter that corporate governance is in a state of
transition with the strongest force being the internationalization and globalization
of financial markets. Strategic management, in terms of corporate governance, increasingly constitutes its realm globally. Consequently, the balance of power between states and corporate actors is shifting, perhaps irrevocably?

References

Baladi, A. (1991), The Growing Role of Pension Funds in Shaping International Corporate
Governance, *Benefits and Compensation International,* October, 21, pp. 8-12.
Baums, T. (1992), Takeovers vs. Institutions in Corporate Governance in Germany, The
Oxford Law Colloquium, 9-11 Sept. (unpublished papers).
Berle, A. and Means, G. (1932), *The Modern Corporation and Private Property,* MacMil-
lan, New York.
Burnham, J. (1941), *The Managerial Revolution: What is Happening in the World,* The John
Day Company, New York.
Byrne, J. (1993), Executive Pay: The Party Ain't over Yet, *Business Week,* April 26, pp. 38-
59.
Cadbury, A. (1992), *The Committee on the Financial Aspects of Corporate Governance,*
Burgess, London.
Charkham, J. (1989), Corporate Governance and the Market for Companies: Aspects of the
Stakeholders' Role, Discussion Paper no. 44, Bank of England, London.
Charkham, J. (1992), Corporate Governance: Lessons from Abroad, *European Business
Journal,* 4(2), pp. 8-16.
Cox, L. (1990), Investing Institutions Start to Flex their Muscles in the US Boardroom,
Multinational Business UK, 3, p. 1-8.
Dicken, P. (1992), *Global Shift: The Internationalization of Economic Activity,* Chapman,
London.
Drucker, P. (1991), Reckoning with the Pension Fund Revolution, *Harvard Business Re-
view,* March-April, pp. 106-114.
Freedman, R and Reed, D. (1983), Stockholders and Stakeholders: A New Perspective on
Corporate Governance, *California Management Review,* 25(3), pp. 88-106.
Garratt, B. (1993), Directing and the Learning Board, *Executive Development,* Special Edi-
tion.
Gilson, R. and Kraakman, R. (1993), The Case for Professional Directors in "The Fight for
Good Governance," *Harvard Business Review,* Jan.-Feb., pp. 76-83.

Gregg, P, Machin, S. and Szymanski, S. (1993), The Disappearing Relationship between Directors Pay and Corporate Performance, *British Journal of Industrial Relations*, 31(1), pp. 1-9.

Gregory, G. (1989), A Stake in Japan, *Management Today,* November, pp. 109-112.

Heard, J. (1990), Institutional Investors and Corporate Governance: The US Perspective, in *International Corporate Governance*, ed. by Lufkin, J. and Gallagher, D. (1990), London, Euromoney Publications.

Hopt, K. (1984), New Ways in Corporate Governance: European Experiments with Labor Representation on Corporate Boards, *Michigan Law Review*, 82(April-May), pp. 1338-1363.

Hopt, K and Teubner, G. (eds.) (1985), *Corporate Governance and Directors Liabilities: Legal, Economic and Sociological Analyses on Corporate Social Responsibility*, Walter de Gruyter, Berlin, New York.

Ishiguro, T. (1990), Japan, in *International Corporate Governance,* ed. by Lufkin, J. and Gallagher, D. (1990), Euromoney Publications, London.

Kester, C. (1992a), *Japanese Takeovers: The Global Contest for Corporate Control,* Harvard Business School Press, Harvard.

Kester, C. (1992b), Industrial Groups as Systems of Contractual Governance, *Oxford Review of Economic Policy,* 8(3), pp. 24-44.

Kochan, N. and Syrett, M. (1991), New Directions in Corporate Governance, Business International Limited, Report No. 2137, London.

Lipton, M. (1992), Takeover Bids and United States Corporate Governance, The Oxford Law Colloquium, 9-11 Sept 1992.

Lorsch, J. and MacIver, E. (1989), *Pawns or Potentates – The Reality of America's Corporate Boards,* Harvard Business School Press, Harvard.

Lufkin, J. and Gallagher, D. (1990), *International Corporate Governance,* Euromoney Publications, London.

Mace, M. (1971), *Directors: Myth and Reality,* Harvard Business School Press, Boston.

Mace, M. (1972), The President and the Board of Directors, *Harvard Business Review,* March-April, pp. 37-49.

Monks, R. and Minow, N. (1991), *Power and Accountability*, Harper Collins, London.

Muzruchi, M. (1983), Who Controls Whom? An Examination of the Relation Between Management and Boards of Directors in Large American Corporations, *Academy of Management Review,* 8(3), pp. 426-435.

Nader, R., Green, M. and Seligmin, J. (1988), Who Rules the Corporation, in *Ethical Issues in Business: A Philosophical Approach,* ed. by Donaldson, T. and Werhane, P., Prentice Hall, New York.

Neff, R. (1993), What do Japanese CEOs Really Make?, *Business Week,* April 26, pp. 42-43.

Oxford Analytica (1992), *Board Directors and Corporate Governance: Trends in the G7 Countries Over the Next Ten Years,* Oxford Analytica, Oxford.

Pearce, J. and Zahra, S. (1991), The Relative Power of CEOs and Boards of Directors: Associations with Corporate Performance, *Strategic Management Journal,* 12, pp. 135-153.

Porter, M. (1992), Capital Disadvantage: America's Failing Capital Investment System, *Harvard Business Review,* Sept.-Oct., pp. 65-82.

Pound, J. (1992), Beyond Takeovers: Politics Comes to Corporate Control, *Harvard Business Review,* March-April, pp. 83-93.

Price, M. (1989), Activism on the Rise Overseas, *Pensions and Investment Age,* 17(October), p. 66.

Prodham, B. (1992), Ownership and Control: An International Perspective, *Management Accounting,* July-August, pp. 50-53.

Rechner, P. and Dalton, D. (1991), Research Notes and Communications. CEO Duality and Organizational Performance: A Longitudinal Analysis, *Strategic Management Journal,* 12, pp. 155-160.

Schmalenbach, D. (1990), Federal Republic of Germany, in *International Corporate Governance,* ed. by Lufkin, J. and Gallagher, D., Euromoney Publications, London.

Schneider-Lenne, E. (1992), Corporate Control in Germany, *Oxford Review of Economic Policy,* 8(3), pp.11-23.

Shapiro, I. (1988), Power and Accountability: The Changing Role of the Corporate Board of Directors, in *Ethical Issues in Business: A Philosophical Approach*, ed. by Donaldson, T. and Werhane, P., Prentice Hall, New York.

Sherman, H. (1991), Governance Lessons From Abroad, *Directors and Board*, 15(3), pp. 24-28.

Sherman, S. (1988), Pushing Corporate Boards to Be Better, *Fortune,* July 18, pp. 58-67.

Simpson, A. (1990), Overview of UK Corporate Governance, in *International Corporate Governance,* ed. by Lufkin, J. and Gallagher, D., Euromoney Publications, London.

Smith, A. (1961), *An Enquiry into the Nature and Cause of the Wealth of the Nations,* Merrill, Indianapolis.

Tricker, B. (1990), Corporate Governance: A Ripple on the Cultural Reflection, in *Capitalism in Contrasting Cultures,* ed. by Clegg, S. and Redding, S., Walter de Gruyter, Berlin, New York.

Tricker, B. (1992), Impressive, Inscrutable but not Incorruptable, *Director,* 45(7 Feb.), pp. 56-60.

Viner, A. (1990), Mergers, Acquisitions and Corporate Governance in Japan, in *International Corporate Governance,* ed. by Lufkin, J. and Gallagher, D., Euromoney Publications, London.

Viner, A. (1993), The Coming Revolution in Japan's Board Rooms, *Corporate Governance – An International Review,* 1(3), pp. 112-119.

Watanabe, S. and Yamamoto, I. (1993), Corporate Governance in Japan: Ways to Improve Low Profitability, *Corporate Governance: An International Review,* 1(4), pp. 208-225.

Younghusband, V. and Wilson, I. (1990), United Kingdom, in *International Corporate Governance,* ed. by Lufkin, J. and Gallagher, D., Euromoney Publications, London.

Part III
Identity in Management

Gender Stereotypes and their Impact on Management Processes

Gill Palmer

Introduction

Women are increasing their numbers in higher education in commerce and business, and we have seen the slow growth of women in middle, if not top, management positions (Berthoin Antal, Izraeli 1993; Still 1993). The slow flow of women into what were once predominantly male positions creates social and structural tensions. In the context of this volume's concern with the construction of our understanding of management, this chapter puts the argument that the tensions surrounding the movement of women into traditionally male, managerial positions are affecting the way that management itself is perceived and analyzed.

Within the managerial literature there are now discussions about differences between masculine and feminine managerial styles (Aburdene and Naisbitt 1992). Androgynous management is recommended in prescriptive managerial texts (Rizzo and Mendez 1990) and the management of cultural assumptions and cultural diversity are recognized as major issues for the development of leadership and management skills for the next generation of managers. In the context of these discourses, the whole nature of the management process can be put under review.

The managerial and popular interest in women in management has therefore raised questions about our understanding of management and of managerial process at work. It can be argued that management education and thought has traditionally been associated with philosophies and values of elitism and the maintenance of existing social structure and status. However, there are signs of a developing new sociology of management that can assess the managerial strategies of disadvantaged social groups, and review the dynamics of managerial processes subject to these social and cultural changes. The development of these studies of management can challenge the social conservatism of management as a discipline, and broaden our understanding of the management process itself.

The Conservatism of Traditional Conceptions of Management and Management Education

The development of management education has features that distinguish it from other forms of university education in the English speaking world. These features tend to enhance a social conservatism that is even more marked than that found in the field of organization theory (Mills 1986).

Degrees in management are of relatively recent origin, and have been heavily influenced by the development of the North American MBA. As masters degrees, the MBA took a particularly practical and general form. The content was primarily shaped to add a basic expertise in allied social sciences to executives who had a scientific or engineering education. MBAs therefore contained undergraduate material on economics or psychology, and introduced allied disciplines like accounting, strategic analysis and personnel management. The content was introductory, but heavily allied to practical experience. As a product the MBA degree did not fit easily into traditional university structures built to cater for a progression of specialist undergraduate, honors and postgraduate classes.

Secondly, the market for management education was distinct. It was expected that management education would only be relevant or available for students who had already reached senior management positions. At this time these were typically middle class, white men from private industry. Given the career structures of this cohort of people at this time it was expected that these mature students would be able to devote 2 years in mid-career to full time study.

MBAs differed from other university degrees both by the nature of their teaching and their student intake. These differences were often compounded by ideological conflicts about the academic validity of the new field of management as a discipline, and policy conflicts over management academics' concern to build close links with the local industrial or business community, in particular, to use university facilities for consultancy. In many colleges these organizational tensions were addressed by separating management education from the mainstream of university activity. Business Schools or Graduate Schools of Management were established, sometimes with separate funding relationships or Boards to incubate the new form of education and give management educators some separation from the normal university administrative controls.

Universities have changed since separate units were required to ease the introduction of management education. The pressures of recession and government policy have made universities more familiar with commercialism. Across all the disciplines of academic life, closer links have developed with business and industrial communities. Management education itself has become more mature and extensive as a subject of study. It has always been multi-disciplinary, but as new fields arise, for example in business ethics, marketing or business communications, the value of close links with a wider range of traditional university disciplines has become more apparent.

The old assumption that management could not be studied by students without direct managerial experience has also been challenged by the market. Undergraduate courses are now common, and the thrust of Australia's Industry Task Force on Leadership and Management Skills is the need to spread management training throughout the workforce, and even into secondary schools. In many of these contexts, management can become a broad education in the social sciences with a vocational focus. With the widening student market for management education within the universities, the proportion of women students has shown a sharper increase than for many other non-traditional courses. (Figures published by the Australian Federal Department of Employment, Education and Training in their 1993 Higher Education Profiles show roughly 50% of females in the undergraduate courses in commerce in Australia.) Management appears to have become a favored choice for many who have traditionally suffered discrimination in the workforce. If management education is a route to social mobility for some disadvantaged groups, then the exclusive, elitist image of management education is bound to be challenged. The "think manager, think male" stereotypes (Berthoin Antal and Izraeli 1993: 63) create dissonance.

In summary, management education is undergoing many changes. We have seen the integration of management into mainstream university education. University-based management education is no longer simply a professional and post-graduate "top-up" to other, more "genuine" forms of academic training. It has become broader based, incorporating many new subjects and interests, for both undergraduate and post-graduate students. Changes in this market, and in market for continuing, post experience management education has encouraged the development of new methods of delivery and course structure to ease access to management education for those who are in no position to take the traditional, two year, full time MBA. It is in the context of these changes in management education that we see the academic development of a new sociology of management (Reed 1989).

New definitions of management stress the importance of managing cultural diversity and the need to develop more flexible, less conservative images of the management process.

There are many arguments for the need to change images of management to make management practice and process more sensitive to cultural diversity. Berthoin Antal and Izraeli (1993) discuss four that advocate more women in management. Arguments often stress the more efficient utilization of resources to be gained from the better use of half the population's talents, skills and education. However,

the impact of the competitive advantage argument depends on whether managers at the corporate level really believe women managers are an economic asset. It is questionable whether deep-rooted prejudices against women's leadership abilities and statistical discrimination are responsive to such rational arguments – especially when there exists a self-fulfilling prophecy that the absence of women in management signifies their lack of suitability (Berthoin Antal and Izraeli 1993: 70).

In West Germany, Switzerland and France *demographic* arguments were once put that the anticipated shortage of highly qualified males would increase the value of women in management. However West German women who used this argument found in 1989 that the fall of the Berlin Wall altered this logic, and policies to make childbearing more attractive may be adopted as an alternative option. *Leadership characteristics and styles* are of perennial interest to management, and female characteristics once thought to disqualify women from management are currently lauded as particularly appropriate for meeting new management challenges. Many proclaim the "feminine qualities" needed for management now as: co-operativeness and the ability to integrate people without dependence on status hierarchies, the ability to listen, or to motivate people through non-monetary rewards, to name but a few. Although the logic of this feminine leadership argument is intended to be women friendly, it carries the risk of a new form of stereotyping. And to date, some companies appear more willing to invest in training programs to help men "become more feminine" than to hire the women themselves (Berthoin Antal and Kresbach-Gnath 1988). Recent studies associate leadership with behaviors of dependency and responsiveness of both leaders and followers, showing that leadership is dependent on others perceptions (Denmark 1993). Placing leadership in a group and social context and seeing leadership style as a function of the exchange between leaders and their followers limits the applicability of arguments based on "feminine" leadership styles. Berhoin Antal and Kresbach-Gnath finally discuss the *entitlement argument*. They suggest that of the four types of argument, the claim to entitlement and ethical logic has been used least over the past decade in Europe, in contrast to the significance the claim to equal opportunity as a civil right has had in the USA. Political reasons, associated with socialism and systems of industrial relations, are suggested to explain the difference. However, now, given the problems that have been found with the other three arguments, the entitlement argument may be on the rise in Europe (Berthoin Antal and Izraeli 1993) as well as Australia.

If women do maintain the pressure for a presence within management, then studies of management will need to incorporate an understanding of gender, and this chapter seeks to advance that end.

Sociology of Management

Sociological perspectives encourage the construction of management as processes of social control, as power and influence systems. If management is an aspect of social control, one significant question becomes "who manages whom?" If management is an aspect of social control, then it should be seen in terms of group and social dynamics, not simply in terms of individual "managers" competencies and skills. Students of labor relations and labor processes have long studied the power relationships between managers or employers representatives and subordinate classes of workers. Within the discipline of industrial relations, an interest in managerial process has been stimulated in the 1980s and 1990s by the spread of enterprise bargaining, and the growing interface between industrial relations and human resource management. The disciplines of industrial relations and human resource management have been integrated by focusing on the strategies of different actors (Gardner and Palmer 1992). With this approach, management becomes identified as a process of social control that is not explained simply by the activities of people with "management" in their job titles. The process of managerial control is shaped by the influence, initiatives and reactions of many actors. Employees, workgroups, trade unions as well as managers, the representatives of employers, industrial and arbitration tribunals, government departments and agencies, external lobby and political groups and the courts all have a role. They may all influence organizational recruitment and selection, training and development, financial and non-financial rewards, disciplined termination and the organization and control of the work itself.

If management is conceptualized as a process of social control which may be used by different groups for different purposes, there are many implications for the study of management and gender. Various actors may shape the managerial process, and various actors may act to entrench or remove gendered relations at work.

How should we analyze managerial processes in terms of social control? Reed identifies three different perspectives on management which have theoretical significance for a sociology of management (Reed 1989). He distinguishes between technical, political and critical perspectives. Technical perspectives see management as a tool to efficiently achieve organizational goals. Under this perspective, management is defined as consisting of a set of rationally designed technical rules which ensure efficient administration, production and financial control. Much of the literature of managerial prescription has been based on the elaboration of technical managerial controls. Underlying the technical perspective are assumptions of social control based on rationality. Rational managerial processes will establish an efficient, harmonious order, that will be accepted as legitimate and effective.

Under Reed's second, political perspective, management is viewed as a political process concerned to resolve conflicts in a situation where many stakeholders are likely to dispute the criteria on which organizational effectiveness should be judged. In place of the rational, co-ordinated machine, this perspective sees a plurality of competing groups and coalitions. Instead of focusing on organizational rules and structures, this perspective focuses on the sectional interests of individuals and groups. Actors are identified, who may have different objectives, different strategies to achieve their various goals, different access to power and resources. The political perspective focuses on sources of conflict, power plays and influence systems and the strategies and mechanisms by which conflict can be resolved. Reed suggests that the underlying assumption of the political perspective is that there is a plurality of interests and power bases. The political process of management requires the skills to establish a relatively stable negotiated order.

Finally, Reed contrasted the technical and political with the critical perspective. The critical perspective is skeptical of the claims of the technical approach to guarantee a rational-legal or bureaucratic order, and the claims of the political perspective to guarantee a stable, negotiated, peace. From the critical perspective, management is seen as the instrument of dominant social groups. Management acts to advance and protect the economic and political interests, not just of organizational ruling elites, but of the dominant socio-economic strata in the society. The underlying assumption about the managerial objective under this perspective is the maintenance of privilege.

Gardner and Palmer (1992) and Dawson and Palmer (1995) have developed Reed's sociological perspectives on management to distinguish between "administrative, political and cultural managerial processes" and skills. In this chapter, these three categories of management process are related to the problems of gender stereotyping. Reed's technical perspective is re-labeled to become "administrative processes." This change in name is justified in order to link with Weber's theory of bureaucracy. Weber's (1947) work on bureaucracy still provides many powerful sociological propositions to explain how "rational legal" administration can structure behavior at work. Reed's political perspective translated without difficulty into the concept of political processes and skills. All the processes of negotiation, alliance building and the analysis of dependency and power come under review (Pfeffer 1981). Reed's third, critical perspective was revised and replaced in terms of the discussion of managerial processes and skills, by the concept of cultural processes. Reed argues that under the critical perspective, managers are best seen as "merchants of morality." "They act as the conduits for a... logic that has to be obscured, hidden and distorted in some way or another through the promulgation of various ideological mystifications" (Reed 1989). In this sentence, Reed referred to economic logic, and he goes on to discuss managerial behavior that reinforces class. However any system of privilege can provide a logic (e.g. based on caste, religion, gender, sexual privilege...) on which managerial controls can be built. The critical perspective opens up the need to discover and judge the assumptions of moral order on which management rests. Any social structure, or system of privilege, may be maintained, supported or challenged by managerial processes. The management of moral order can involve, not just the administration of formal rules, or the political negotiation of compromise, but the establishment and support of cultural assumptions which legitimize or delegitimize social regulations. This links to the increasingly popular managerial literature on culture. Many current managerial prescriptions about organizational culture cannot be simply categorized in terms of administrative or political processes.

The management of cultures is associated with the construction of meaning through image management and communication skills. The concept of culture has a multitude of definitions. Most managerial uses focus on organizational cultures defined in terms of the attitudes, values, assumptions and beliefs found within organizations. Managerial literature usually implies that these organizational cultures are (or can, or should) be constructed by management (Grint 1991). However, cross-cultural studies take a more societal view and include social artifacts, such as national education and training systems or political structures in the definition of culture (Joynt and Warner 1985). Lundberg's (1989) framework suggests a three-layered construct in which core values, ideologies and assumptions underlie strategic beliefs which in turn become visible as symbols, language and patterns of conduct and behavior.

Culture builders and culture managers can be powerful mobilizers of organizational action and resistance. How should the power to manage culture be studied? Weber assessed the culture building power of certain personalities. He discussed non-bureaucratic, or non rational-legal forms of authority under the concept of charisma. His charismatic "heroes" exercised the power to gain obedience and loyalty by mobilizing moral commitment. The managerial "excellence" prescriptions now seek a similar outcome, but through socially constructed or managed activity, which is not dependent on particular individual's characteristics (Peters and Waterman 1982; Ouchi 1981; Kanter 1983 and 1989). This focus on the social creation of moral commitment has been emphasized in recent years by the recognition of cultural difference, for example between Japan and the West, the growth of multi-culturalism, and by movements for equal rights. The shaping of culture can be seen as a sociological, small or large group activity. Organizational culture may be managed by management and other social actors at work. The role that the dominant culture plays in supporting, modifying or subverting particular administrative or political strategies should be the subject of study.

Gender, Gender Stereotypes and Managerial Processes

In what ways are these managerial processes affected by gender, and in what ways are these processes used in maintaining or challenging the management of gendered stereotypes at work?

Administration and Gender

Weber's theoretical work has been reviewed in the context of modern feminism. Sydie notes that Weber's action framework, and his definition of power are sex neutral. However the ideal type model of patriarchy formed what was seen as a "natural" structure of male dominance at the base of the other ideal types of domination he identified, including bureaucracy (Sydie 1987).

Research on women in management uncovers many difficulties faced by women when the ideas about authority assume male characteristics and when male supremacy is seen as normal. Female authority is often defined as illegitimate in terms of the rationality that is accepted as normal (Brenner et al. 1989; Hearn and Parkin 1988). In these situations, women in authoritative roles will not be granted the usual acceptance (Kanter 1977), and there will be problems associated with the reluctance of followers to accept the authority usually attached to formal organizational status (Denmark 1993). Sexual harassment and political attack can become socially supported strategies to reassert the status quo (Di Tomasco 1986; and Sheppard 1986). Formal administrative structures that are supposedly designed, as Weber noted, to guarantee managerial control through strictly rational, universalistic, criteria and decision-making, can become suffused with particularistic biases about gender.

If administrative procedures were gender neutral, then the proportion of women in the labor force might be expected to be related to the numbers of women in management, and the entry of women into managerial positions might be expected to show a linear growth, with the rise of women in the workforce. International evidence supports neither proposition (Berthoin Antal and Izraeli 1993). Indeed when Alpern traces the history of women in the labor force of the USA, she concludes that they have advanced their status in time of war, only to fall back in peacetime, and that occupations change with feminization. Clerical, secretarial work, which had been an avenue of upward mobility for men lost that role as women entered the profession (Alpern 1993). Something other than administrative neutrality is affecting the statistics that emerge.

Bureaucratic administrative processes do not prevent the emergence of a gendered division of labor. On the other hand women can and do use bureaucratic techniques to challenge patriarchal discrimination. Socially disadvantaged groups have often used "rational-legal" argument to support campaigns for social change. Trade unions found their claims for wage justice or shorter hours gained greater acceptance and were more likely to result in permanent change if they were sold with bureaucratic arguments, for example on precedent, comparability and seniority. Such arguments were used to incorporate union demands into new structures of shared or negotiated control that altered, but did not replace, the bureaucratic regulations (Palmer 1983; Gospel and Palmer 1993). Discriminated groups argue efficiency and justice to back claims for equity. They seek the imposition of bureaucratic, rational legal regulations. For example, unions and lobbyists for women and minority groups seek bureaucratic selection criteria and formal recruitment, reward and discipline systems as a way of enforcing non-discriminatory decision-making. In her analysis of strategies used by women to work within masculine organizational cultures, Pringle discusses the reformist strategies adopted by Australian femocrats. Femocrats have been defined as women whose bureaucratic organizational roles have been created by the various state and federal Equal Opportunity laws. These women "constantly monitor the perils of co-option and assimilation against their feminist agenda for change through some (but how much) compromise." Women who work in this challenging but somewhat uncomfortable position describe their tactics as follows: "camouflage" whereby they hide an activist agenda by first working hard to gain respect from the organization; the "double agent" tactic, and finally, the "pincer" movement between the pressure within and the pressure without (Pringle 1992; see also McKinlay 1990). Similar problems faced the early union representatives who worked to establish industrial relations systems of collective bargaining or compulsory arbitration. They balanced radical and reforming agendas against a perceived need to gain legitimacy and acceptance from those they were trying to influence. Rational-legal arguments were backed by economic sanctions and the combination of these two strategies were used to build new industrial relations structures which established negotiated rules on the economic terms of employment.

Advocates of gender equality therefore use bureaucratic, rational legal arguments, but they have mobilized political, rather than industrial or economic, sanctions in their campaigns. This has led to the use of legislation and administrative policy-making, rather than bargaining or market mechanisms to implement change.

Politics and Gender in Management

For bureaucratic arguments to be successful, some political strength seems necessary. Women who seek organizational influence network within the organization. They lobby for political support outside. Political activity is needed if they are to challenge the established norms of behavior at work (Rizzo and Mendez 1990). The political perspective on management therefore provides the channel for studying the political resources that accrue to gender, and the extent that organizational power plays are used to further interests and objectives derived from gendered stereotypes.

Power can be exercised by individuals, small informal groups, organizational units, groups or organizations in the environment, state agents and governments. There are also many sources or bases of power. On the issue of gender in management, political activity across the full range of political processes is likely to be found.

At the most personal and individual level, sexual relations at work can involve organizational politics. Sexual attraction can be one of the power resources used to pursue interests at work. Mainiero (1993) studied co-worker reactions to publicized office romances, to find that hierarchical romances could provoke strong negative reactions from co-workers who believed that the uneven organizational power resources of the partners would be exploited to the detriment of others. Co-workers were more willing to tolerate lateral peer romances, because the danger of "illegitimate" exploitation was seen to be less. However, hierarchical romances may prove successful for the participants, and fears associated with this form of politics clearly lie behind some of the tensions surrounding the promotion of more women at work.

At more general, institutional and organizational levels, the successful implementation of non-discriminatory policies established by corporate or government administration often requires strong political support. Administrative dictate is rarely sufficiently powerful to establish organizational change. Collinson et al. (1990) study the impact of British anti-discrimination legislation after a 20 years history. They find evidence of widespread ignorance or evasion of the legal principles. The importance of political alliances between professional EEO officers, personnel professionals and trade unionists was very evident, in the one example where a complaint against discrimination was successful.

Another factor very relevant to political process is the access to the decision-making-power held at higher levels of business and government administration, and the impact this has on the opportunities of others. Some positions of high status for previously discriminated groups can provide mentoring opportunities. The need for women in senior positions to empower other women is emphasized by all advocates of women in management (Denmark 1993; Yancey Martin 1993).

The political support of "numbers" is also crucial to claim legitimacy for unfamiliar assertions. Numerical strength lends credibility to the value of an argument both to waverers on the claimant's side and to the more sympathetic of outsiders. Isolated women or minority representatives do not have the social resources to re-socialize groups to accept or conform to different points of view (Collinson et al. 1990). Notions of legitimacy lead on to our final management process, the management of culture.

The Management of Culture and Gender

Assumptions, values and ideologies lie at the core of the concept of culture. Traditional work and social roles are stereotyped by gender, and assumptions and values which provide the ideological support to these stereotypes have a powerful impact. As Farley (1993) puts it, "the idea that men are leaders and women are helpers is deeply rooted... it will take massive transformation to dig it out" (p. 102).

Culturally supported sex discrimination can negate the implementation of the equal opportunity policies that are established as a result of administrative and political action. There are many studies of the impact of sexist values and beliefs on managerial processes. The impact of sexist attitudes on recruitment and selection (Collinson et al. 1990), job evaluation or performance appraisal (Burton et al. 1987) as well as on the division of labor and remuneration. Managerial decisions are often taken in the light of assumptions about natural or appropriate behavior for women or men (Baker 1991, Tables 1 and 2). Indeed Mills argues that organizational theory itself needs to be reassessed in the light of an improved understanding of the impact of culture on gender (Mills 1988). Much prescriptive managerial literature now takes the establishment of non-discriminatory assumptions and beliefs as the hallmark of achieving new, improved organizational cultures (Aburdene and Naisbitt 1992).

In what ways can a study of the cultural constraints or advantages that affect women in management influence a sociology of management? Much has been done to provide women with new understanding, and new strategies for use at work. Various forms of cultural discrimination which detract from women's ability to manage have been extensively documented (Kanter 1977; Marshall 1987; Davidson and Cooper 1992; Baker 1991). Gender stereotypes are found to limit the culturally approved communication and interpersonal influence methods used by men and women, and these cultural expectations are so strong that they influence the way identical behavior is perceived.

Studies of gender bias in management are resulting in prescriptions, eagerly sought by female managers, designed to change the implicit assumptions that women do not seek public power, or that their influence strategies are affiliative rather than instrumental. The implications of this work for men, and for our notions of management are still to be fully explored. However we now see the slow growth of interest in problems of masculinity, and the impact of cultural stereotypes on men (e.g. Brittan 1989).

Culturally approved dependency models may make the traditional woman dependent on a man for economic and physical protection, but they have also made the traditional man dependent on women for the maintenance of ethical and emotional values and domestic support. It is in these areas that studies of the influence of gender on organizational culture still has some way to go, before the full impact of this area on the study of management is clear.

Conclusion

Received social expectations about management and managerial behavior are being challenged as a result of the changing education and recruitment policies which give more access to women in management. The tension felt by women as they enter these non-traditional roles is stimulating a body of research and writing on managerial women, and on management.

The role of management in supporting or challenging dominant social structures has rarely been placed on the curriculum, and management education has traditionally had a conservative image, closely aligned with the protection of existing social structures. The development of management education has been heavily influenced by the attempt to copy the MBA model of the USA, in a context which encouraged separate, specialist business schools. These separate academic structures promoted the exclusion of a range of academic disciplines, for example philosophy, sociology or political theory from management discourse. This separation gave management education some protection from critical analysis.

Recent developments towards a sociology of management open opportunities to study the managerial process in terms of its impact as social influence, and to study the nature of the social controls prescribed in managerial theories. Gender analysis adds a rich new vein of theorizing which can be added to this development. In academic or intellectual terms, the advantages of this integration could be considerable. However, its impact on the social standing of academic structures and careers will no doubt depend on wider structural forces. Whether the greater feminization of management theory will empower the discipline, by addressing broader social issues, or whether it will be seen to contribute to the redefinition of management as a marginalized, service activity in support of external (male) power-holders, remains to be seen. No doubt this will depend, not on our academic endeavors, but on the role that women are perceived as playing in wider social formations.

References

Aburdene P. and Naisbitt J. (1992), *Megatrends for Women*, New York, Villard.

Adler, N. and Izraeli, D. (eds.) (1988), *Women in Management Worldwide,* New York, M.E. Sharpe.

Alpern, S. (1993), In the Beginning, A History of Women in Management, in Fagenson, E. (ed.), *Women in Management: Trends, Issues and Challenges in Managerial Diversity*, Newbury Park, Sage.

Baker, M. (1991), Reciprocal Accommodation: A Model for Reducing Gender Bias in Managerial Communication, *The Journal of Business Communication*, 28(2), pp. 113-130

Berthoin Antal, A. and Izraeli, D. (1993). A Global Comparison of Women in Management, in Fagenson, E. (ed.), *Women in Management: Trends, Issues and Challenges in Managerial Diversity*, Newbury Park, Sage.

Berthoin Antal, A. and Kresbach-Gnath, C. (1988), Women and Management. Unused Resources in the Federal Republic of Germany, in Adler and Izraeli (1988).

Brenner, O. Tomkiewicz, J. and Schein, V. (1989), The Relationship between Sex-role Stereotypes and Requisite Management Characteristics Revisited, *Academy of Management Journal* 32, pp. 662-669.

Brittan, A. (1989), *Masculinity and Power*, Oxford, Blackwell.

Burton, C., Hag, R. and Thompson, G. (1987), *Women's Worth, Pay Equity and Job Evaluation in Australia*, Sydney, AGPS.

Clutterbuck, D. and Devine, M. (1987), *Businesswoman: Present and Future*, MacMillan, London.

Collinson, D., Knights, D. and Collinson, M. (1990), *Managing to Discriminate,* Routledge, London.

Connell, R.W. (1987), *Gender and Power: Society, the Person and Sexual Politics*, Cambridge, Polity Press.

Davidson, M. and Cooper, C. (1992), *Shattering the Glass Ceiling: The Woman Manager*, London, Chapman.

Dawson & Palmer (1995), *Quality Management: The Theory and Practice of Implementing Change*, Melbourne, Longman.

Denmark, F. (1993), Women, Leadership and Empowerment, in *Psychology of Women Quarterly* 17, pp. 343-356

Di Tomasco, N. (1986), Sexuality in the Workplace: Discrimination and Harassment, in Hearn et al. (1986).

Fagenson, E. (ed.) (1993), *Women in Management: Trends, Issues and Challenges in Managerial Diversity*, Newbury Park, Sage.

Farley, J. (1993), Commentary to Section II, Historical and Global Issues, in Fagenson, E. (ed.), *Women in Management: Trends, Issues and Challenges in Managerial Diversity*, Newbury Park, Sage.

Gardner, M. and Palmer, G. (1992), *Employment Relations: Industrial Relations and Human Resource Management in Australia,* Melbourne, MacMillan.

Gospel, H. and Palmer G. (1993), *British Industrial Relations,* 2nd edition, London, Routledge.

Grieve, N. and Burns, A. (1986), *Australian Women: New Feminist Perspectives*, Oxford, Oxford University Press.

Grint, K. (1991), *The Sociology of Work*, Oxford, Polity.

Hearn, J. and Parkin, W. (1988), Women, Men and Leadership: A Critical Review of Assumptions, Practices and Change in the Industrialized Nations, in Adler and Izraeli (1988).

Hearn, J., Sheppard, D., Tancred, Sheriff P. and Burrell, G. (1986), *The Sexuality of Organization Theory,* London, Sage.

Joynt, P. and Warner, M. (eds.) (1985), *Managing in Different Cultures*, Bergen, Universitetsforlaget.

Kanter R.M. (1977), *Men and Women of the Corporation*, New York, Basic Books.

Kanter, R.M. (1983), *The Change Masters: Corporate Entrepreneurs at Work,* London, Allen & Unwin.

Kanter, R.M. (1989), *When Giants Learn to Dance: Mastering the Challenges of Strategy, Management and Careers in the 1990s,* London, Allen & Unwin.

Kaplan, G. (1992), *Contemporary Western European Feminism,* London, Allen & Unwin.

Lundberg, C. (1989), Working with Culture, *Journal of Organizational Change Management,* 1(2).

Mainiero, L. (1993), Dangerous Liasons? A Review of Current Issues Concerning Male and Female Romantic Relationships in the Workplace, in Fagenson, E. (ed.), *Women in*

Management: Trends, Issues and Challenges in Managerial Diversity, Newbury Park, Sage.

Marshall, J. (1987), Issues of Identity for Women Managers, in Clutterbuck, D. and Devine, M. (eds.), *Businesswoman: Present and Future*, London, MacMillan.

McKinlay, R. (1990), Feminists in the Bureaucracy, *Women's Studies Journal*, 6(1-2), pp. 72-95.

Mills, A. (1986), Gender, Sexuality and Organization Theory, in Hearn et al. (1986).

Mills, A. (1988), Organization, Gender and Culture, *Organization Studies* 9(3), pp. 351-369.

Morgan, G. (1980), Paradigms, Metaphors and Puzzle Solving in Organization Theory, *Administrative Science Quarterly*, 28, pp. 601-607.

Morgan, G. (1986), *Images of Organisation,* London, Sage.

Ouchi, W. (1981), *Theory Z: How American Business Can Meet the Japanese Challenge*, Reading, MA, Addison-Wesley.

Palmer, G. (1993), *British Industrial Relations,* London, Allen and Unwin.

Palmer, G. (ed.) (1988a), *Australian Personnel Management,* Melbourne, MacMillan.

Palmer, G. (1988b), Human Resource Management and Organizational Analysis, in *Australian Personnel Management,* Melbourne, MacMillan, 148-63.

Peters, T. and Waterman, R. (1982), *In Search of Excellence: Lessons from America's Best-run Companies*, New York, Harper & Row.

Pfeffer, J. (1981), *Power in Organization*, Marshfield, MA, Pitman.

Pringle, J. (1992), Survival or Success? Ways of 'Being' for Women in Organisations, in Olsson, S. (ed.), *The Gender Factor*, Palmerston North, Dunsmore Press.

Reed, M. (1989), *The Sociology of Management*, Hempstead, Harvester Wheatsheaf.

Rizzo, A. and Mendez, C. (1990), *The Integration of Women in Management*, Westport, Quorum.

Sheppard, D. (1986), Organization, Power and Sexuality: the Image and Self Image of Women Managers, in Hearn et al. (1986).

Still, L. (1993), *Where to from Here? The Managerial Woman in Transition*, Chatswood, Business and Professional Publishing.

Sydie, R.A. (1987), *Natural Women, Cultured Men,* Milton Keynes Open University Press.

Weber, M. (1947), *The Theory of Social and Economic Organization*, New York, Free Press.

Williams, C. and Thorpe, B. (1992), *Beyond Industrial Sociology*, Sydney, Allen and Unwin.

Yancey Martin, P. (1993), Feminist Practice in Organizations: Implications for Management, in Fagenson, E. (ed.), *Women in Management: Trends, Issues and Challenges in Managerial Diversity*, Newbury Park, Sage.

Corporate Image, Gendered Subjects and the Company Newsletter: The Changing Faces of British Airways

Albert Mills

Introduction

Sexual discrimination at work lies not only in discrimination against women but in the social construction of womanhood (and manhood) itself (Calás and Smircich 1992); not simply in the overt sexist act of the individual but in the deep-rooted organizational processes and structures that constitute "systemic discrimination" (Abella 1984). Recognition of this increasingly frames inquiry, leading to research into the relationship between organizational cultures and the social construction of gender (Burrell 1984; Mills 1988; Morgan 1988). This approach exposes the way certain aspects of an organization's culture contribute to sexual discrimination. In that vein, this chapter sets out to examine the role of the company newsletter in the construction of discriminatory images. In-depth content analysis of the company newsletters of British Airways from 1926 through to the present allows exploration of this issue. Company newsletters can play a key role in projecting discriminatory images and in a way which approves them and renders them mundane. As such organizational members need to pay careful attention to the role of the newsletter in translating or otherwise challenging the culture of the organization.

Organizational Culture, Corporate Image and Discrimination

Analyses of the role of organizational culture suggest that leaders play a key part in the process of framing discriminatory behavior at and that their influence is experienced through a number of processes and artifacts – including policy (Morgan 1988), strategic planning (Morgan and Knights 1991), organizational rules (Mills and Murgatroyd 1991), organizational discourse (Ferguson 1984), stories (Martin 1992), metaphors and language (Riley 1983), socialization (Cox 1986), organizational signs and symbols (Meissner 1986).

Recent attention has focused on the role of corporate image – in particular the production of corporate materials – in the development of discriminatory images (Tinker and Neimark 1989). Broadly defined, corporate image refers to "the impression the culture makes on its environment" (Alvesson and Berg 1992); the mental picture that clients, employees and others associate with a particular organization. In that regard, corporate image is a particularly interesting aspect of an organizational culture in that it helps us to understand something of what/who is valued in the organization – especially by the organizational leaders. That impression is usually the result of a combination of factors that arise out of the interactions of organization members and the decision-making of organizational leaders.

Company materials, including annual reports, advertisements, in-house newsletters and external magazines, are an important medium for translating the culture of an organization into visual images: each developed to serve specific purposes. Corporate materials provide literal images (textual, photographic, design) of the company that have the capacity to approve and render mundane discriminatory images and practices. As such corporate materials provide a rich source for viewing a company's image and it is on this narrow aspect of image-making that the chapter focuses.

Image Making: Intent, Context and Subjectivity

In order to understand the impact of corporate materials on discriminatory practice and subjectivity we need to understand something about the intent of those materials and the context in which they were introduced. Tinker and Neimark (1987) make the case that corporate materials, specifically annual reports, "are not passive describers of an 'objective reality'; but play a part in forming the world view or social ideology that fashions and legitimizes women's place in society." "Corporate informational" services can be seen as ideological instruments that promote policies, beliefs, attitudes, and practices perpetuating the inequality of women and other disadvantaged groups, an approach that has been criticized for over-stressing the deliberate and conscious nature of company-generated values (Mills 1993).

Burrell (1987: 91), on the other hand, understates the potential impact of corporate materials on "others" and their sense of self in the argument that

company reports may be best seen as material for the internal consumption of in-house accountants (rather than for any external audience). They are 'accounts' of action and belief used to legitimize, to the writers, their own activities. As such they are attempts to develop self-control and self-discipline whether or not the author is conscious of this. In other words, the attempt at political manipulation in company reports may be self-directed rather than other-directed.

In his stress on self-directness Burrell (1987) underplays the fact that corporate materials contribute to a visual mirror of the world in which we live and, regardless of intent, can serve – by exclusion through denigration – to influence the way people come to view themselves. As several studies have suggested, the hegemonic power of organizational leadership is due to a combination of conscious and unconscious (Gramsci 1978), intended and unintended (Merton 1949), and deliberate and emergent (Mintzberg et al. 1986) actions.

The work of Ferguson (1984), Morgan (1988) and Morgan and Knights (1991) – each in their own different ways – have been influential in drawing attention to the importance of organizational and social discourses in the shaping and acceptance of leadership thinking and action, and in the construction of gendered subjectivities. This body of work goes beyond Tinker and Neimark's (1987) concern with the "legitimization of women's place" and examines the relationship between discriminatory organizational arrangements and the organizational construction of gender.

Drawing on this latter approach, it can be argued that (1) company materials need to be examined for their perceptions of womanhood and manhood, of which "legitimate social place" is but one of several defining aspects, and (2) that those perceptions need to be understood through the framework of the key social and organizational discourses of the time.

British Airways and the Development of the Company Newsletter

British Airways (BA) is one of the world's oldest and leading airlines, with roots going back to 1919. Company production of an in-house newsletter is almost as old – dating back to June 1926 with the introduction of the *Imperial Airways Monthly Bulletin* ('Bulletin').[1] This simple one-page affair was designed to inform staff about timetables, fares and route developments. It also included items on "passengers of note" and other comments concerned with building pride in the airline.

Over the next five years staff numbers grew tenfold and the newsletter was expanded in size and scope. At the end of 1930 the 'Bulletin' was replaced by the weekly *Imperial Airways Staff News* ('Staff News') which, in addition to company "information," carried items on personnel, including company-related issues of recruitment, posting, promotion, achievements, and retirements and individual issues of engagements, marriages, births, and deaths. The 'Staff News' also carried editorial comment concerned to encourage staff to follow a particular course of action or way of thinking (see Exhibit 1).

In March 1936 the *Imperial Airways Weekly News Bulletin* ('News Bulletin') was published alongside the 'Staff News' in order to separate company and industry news from personnel items. The existence of two newsletters provided more

> The knowledge is common that at the present moment the nation, indeed the whole
> Empire, is passing through a very serious crisis, for at no period of its history has its
> financial stability been more gravely threatened than at the present moment. This dan-
> ger threatens us all, whatever be our position. In short it is a case of 'work or starve' –
> there is no other course open to any of us.
> [Editorial, Imperial Airways Staff News, no. 40, 11th Sept. 1931]

Exhibit 1:   Let Us Act and Think Imperially

space to expand on items of interest but it is clear from analysis of the differences
that the company failed to create two distinctly different products: the 'News Bulletin' constantly carried personnel items and the 'Staff News' continued to report
on general company and industry affairs.

In 1940, Imperial Airways was reformed as the British Overseas Airways Corporation (BOAC) and the 'News Bulletin' and 'Staff News' gave way to a single in-house newsletter – the *British Overseas Airways News Letter* ('News Letter'); recombining company, industry and personnel reporting. Following the Second World War the 'News Letter' was produced as a magazine and it maintained
that format through several name changes – (*Speedbird* 1946; *BOAC Review and
Newsletter* 1950-51; *BOAC Review* 1951-67) until March 1967.

In January 1959, BOAC introduced a two paged broadsheet – *BOAC News*
('News'). In a "first issue message," the Managing Director set out some of the
thinking behind its introduction (Exhibit 2):

> In an enterprise as fast moving and as widespread as ours it is difficult for management
> to keep staff currently advised about what is going on. This broadsheet is being pub-
> lished in an attempt to meet this difficulty. So far as is possible it will contain factual
> information and explanation only: and it will be written in what I hope will found to
> be an interesting and readable style.
> BOAC News will normally appear on a Friday and will be available free of charge to all
> members of the staff. I hope that, by keeping everyone more in the picture about what
> we are doing and why, it will do much to promote a better sense of common purpose
> and a better team spirit throughout the corporation.

Exhibit 2:   A Rationale of Common Purpose

Over successive years the 'News' focused on internal company issues and included items specifically designed to motivate and shape employee behavior. An
article in the October 16th, 1959 issue clearly spelt out the role of the new broadsheet (and the 'Review') in the thinking of management, placing it in the context
of a broad policy of personnel development (Exhibit 3).

From November 1961 much of the direct motivational material was channeled
through a column entitled "From The Managing Director's Desk." In April of

'Responsibility for the whole field of human relations.' This phrase in the terms of reference of the Director of Personnel and Medical Services... has created much interest and discussion among people in B.O.A.C...

Broadly speaking, it means that BOAC is improving its use, as effectively as it can, of modern theories of personnel management – striving even more to treat the individual as a human being and as a business asset of even greater value than the expensive machinery which he uses...

More and more the provision of a form of organization in which the human being can work with the highest morale is being recognized in industry as a job for the scientifically trained expert. Psychologists and sociologists are conducting research into what makes a man happy, what induces him to increase his output, what causes him to feel resentment, or what causes him to lose interest in his work.

The personnel officer who can fully interpret and handle these matters is not yet widely established – but he is coming along. Until he arrives the practical experience and knowledge of the personnel officer must be allied to the psychologically trained doctor, with his close contact with humanity in all its aspects, to work for the emergence of the optimum intimate approach to personnel handling.

One can see this pattern of approach in B.O.A.C... The experts believe that the passing of information and plans, decisions, research and thinking up and down the line of authority will do much to improve the worker's knowledge of an interest in his work and will foster a feeling of security that is considered to be one of the basic requirements of a properly balanced personnel policy. Management at top, middle and lower levels should lose no chance of explaining these things in person to their staff.

'BOAC News' helps to fulfill this function but while it is a useful aid, particularly at this stage, it is no substitute for personal contact between management and staff.

Exhibit 3:   Good Human Relations – A Sociological Problem

1967 BOAC stopped producing the 'Review' and the 'News' became the primary internal source of company news and views.

In 1946 B.E.A. was established (out of a division of BOAC into separate European and "Overseas" companies) and it immediately set up its own in-house journal. In the process the company consulted the editors of "various old-established house journals" including the editor of "Shell Magazine" who provided a number of useful insights. In the first edition of the *BEA Magazine* Sir Harold Hartley, the company's first chairman, set out some of the main aims of the magazine (Exhibit 4):

One year later a senior management review of the 'Magazine' assessed that too little space was being given over to the activities of staff. Commenting on "The Future of the BEA Magazine," a 1947 editorial (Christmas issue) announced that,

In accordance with the desire of the General Manager (Staff and Services) the Magazine will in future devote more space to articles on the work, hobbies and social activities of the staff and less to matters of external interest.

> The magazine will tell you what B.E.A. is doing and what are its aims; it will tell you of our successes and mistakes. It will be something to which you can all contribute ideas; it will help us to know one another even if we are far apart, and you must help to make it something of which we can all be proud.

Exhibit 4:   Knowing and Feeling Pride in Each Other

In 1948 financial constraints led to threatened closure of the magazine, but this was averted through the introduction of a cover charge. Despite the new charges sales were soon running at 90% of production.

Although the magazine emphasized a focus on staff affairs it remained an important platform for management. As the company chairman, Lord Douglas, was to express to readers in 1952: "In its pages, the management is pledged to give full information to you of the plans and progress of our airline." This was done in part through the introduction, in February 1949, of a regularly featured "Chief Executive's Page." The views of the General Manager, the chairman and the Chief Executive not withstanding, the editor felt the need to proclaim that, "Thanks to the broad-minded policy of the Management the magazine enjoys a very large degree of independence..."

BEA Magazine continued in production until 1972 and the merger of BEA and BOAC into British Airways. Between 1972 and 1976 the magazine continued under different titles, including BA's *European Division Magazine* 1972-73 and *Topline* 1974-76, before giving way to the all-company, newspaper-formatted, *British Airways News* 1973.

Images of Gender

Analysis of the in-house newsletters of British Airways and its predecessors, from 1926 onwards, indicate that they were a vehicle not only for the production of items of "company interest" but also of images of gender. Through specific foci and emphases, silences and exclusions, direct comment and presentation, airline company newsletters lent themselves to the shaping of specific images of "men" and "women" and approved organizational/occupational associations.

Specific Foci and Emphases: The Changing Faces of British Airways

Over time one group or other has come to dominate the pages of BA's newsletter. Pilots, senior managers and administrators, stewards, stewardesses and other uniformed female staff have been among the central figures highlighted by the newsletter over the years. Which group received particular attention and when was a feature of the time, the company strategy, and the peculiar interests and concerns of the newsletter editor.

Within BA stewarding was exclusively a male occupation until 1946, piloting was restricted to men until 1987 and it was very rare to find a female senior manager/administrator until the early 1980s. By focusing on the activities of pilots, senior managers/administrators, and stewards the company – through the newsletter and other materials – served to emphasize the importance of those groups to and within the company. The fact that they were almost always males served to stress the importance of men as opposed to women in British Airways.

Following the Second World War BA hired its first female flight attendants and steadily increased the number of uniformed female staff on its payroll. Both factors were recorded in the company newsletter but in a different way to that of the reporting of male-associated activities. While there were individual news items on the introduction, recruitment, and training of stewardesses, most of the reporting has been in the form of photographic material that has tended to trivialize the work of those involved.

Through a series of particular foci and emphases the newsletter has managed to produce a series of images that associate men with heroism, leadership, experience, reliability, technical knowledge and skills, authority and power, and women with beauty, glamour, sexuality, domesticity, and caring. It has not only reproduced traditional notions of men and women but contributed to the production of new discriminatory images. The impression that only men can pilot airplanes, for example, was largely created inside the commercial airline industry.

The pilot, as a central part of the core technology, has always been a key figure in company materials. At various times particular images of the pilot have been produced to advertise the safety, reliability and normalcy of flight, and the pages of the newsletter have been filled with associated images.

In the early days of commercial flying, when people were more wary of flying, the company drew on several images of the pilot as a means of reassurance. The "heroic flyer" was one early image. Drawing upon the pilot's World War I associations, the company attempted to sell the idea that potential passengers could feel safe in the hands of an experienced and courageous pilot. To this end, Imperial Airways produced signed photographs of its pilots for distribution by each to his passengers. As the company became concerned to de-emphasize the link between courage and flying a new image was produced – that of the "man of experience." Here the emphasis shifted to the pilot's years of flying and company experience and the number of air miles flown (Mills 1995).

Company strategy and the centrality of piloting to the airlines has been reflected in the pages of the newsletter over time, with numerous articles, photographs and cartoons on the activities of the pilot. The fact that the overwhelming majority of the images produced were of male pilots served to reduce the association between maleness and piloting to the level of the mundane: an unquestionable fact of life!

Senior managers/administrators have always dominated the pages of the company newsletter. It has always been made clear that the newsletter is a vehicle for the communication of senior management views and policy. But the newsletter has also focused on the activities of various senior managers and, from time to time, has produced a series of articles which 'introduce' a particular senior administrator and "explain his role" in the company. Through a wealth of material focused on the activities of the male administrator, the newsletter helped to render mundane the association between masculinity and management.

In the history of BA there has not been one single women Chief Executive, Managing Director, or "Chairman" (sic). It was 1939 before the company appointed its first female manager, and she, as "Women's Staff Supervisor," was strictly in charge of other women. In 1943 the first woman was appointed to the Board of Directors and when she retired in 1945 it was twenty-one years before another woman came onto the Board (of BEA). As late as 1978 there were no women to be found in the ranks of the "senior management levels" and only seventeen (2.06%) female "senior staff" out of a total of eight-hundred and eight. Too often the newsletter's reporting of female managers and their activities was too little, too trivial, too late or too condescending and sometimes they just gave up on the idea that there were women managers. These images, as a result, helped to confirm the masculine associations with management (Exhibit 5).

The steward became an important symbol of BA in the period 1928-45. In the late 1920s a number of European airlines began to compete with each other and with other modes of luxury travel (i.e. first-class rail and ocean liners) in terms of service. Adopting existing practice in other areas of luxury transportation, British Airways hired male stewards to provide a service in the air.

In 1930, United became the world's first airline to hire female stewards and slowly but surely other world airlines followed suit. By the mid-1940s flight attending had become a female-associated occupation. But BOAC was one of the last international airlines to employ woman and for almost twenty years (1928-46) it was exclusively the male steward who was featured in the company's advertising materials and newsletters.

The stewardess was introduced into the employ of BOAC in 1946 on 'an experimental basis' (Bray 1974). At the beginning the company worked hard to "desexualize" the stewardess image – fearing that their new hiring practice might be seen as pandering to the US trend of selling glamour rather than service. To that end, the new female members of the cabin crew were titled "stewards," and issued with uniforms (complete with collar and tie) that closely resembled the war issue as worn by the male stewards. The newsletter dutifully reported the company strategy but almost immediately went its own way – missing little opportunity to present the female stewards as "glamour girls." The overall result was summed up by a female employee who complained that,

Too Masculine

What Makes a Manager?

In the first place management is damned hard work, It means taking responsibility and being accountable for that responsibility . It means working all hours and frequently disrupting one's private life. It means a great many sacrifices both personal and financial. And above all it means commitment to the job.
He must be…
[BA News, no. 403, 18th Dec. 1981]

Too Late.

The First Woman for Board

Miss Jennifer Tanburn is to join the Board of British Airways on January 1, her appointment on a part-time basis was announced on Wednesday…
She is the first woman to serve on the Board.
[BA News, 21st December 1973]

In fact, Pauline Gower was the first female Board member 30 years earlier, and Alice Munro had served on the Board of BEA from 1966-73 – AJM.

Too Trivial and Condescending

She's Bright, Beautiful and the Boss

Jennifer Clay has every right to look happy as she takes it easy on the stairs of her Belgravia home. She was appointed Sales Training Manager BATL on May 1 – another victory for the feminist camp in British Airways.
How do people react to such a young, beautiful and highly intelligent lady boss?
'People are naturally suspicious of a female manager,' says Jennifer 'but… once they see that you know what you are doing they become more confident about your all-round ability…'
[BA News, No. 23, 24th May 1974]

Too Ignorant

Executive Magazine Launched With a Bang

The new Executive Magazine is launched with a bang – The occasion: The introduction of a new deal for the businessman – and the woman behind him.
[BA News, No.18, 19th Apr. 1974]

Exhibit 5: Images of Woman and Management

Your chauvinistic editorial policy… will do nothing for the female staff striving to get on in the company. It will only perpetuate the impression that women are decorous purposes and are unable to do any job as well as a man (Letter to the editor, *BA News*, "Letters page," no. 348, 7th Nov. 1980).

Silences and Exclusions

Much of the imagery in British Airways has been framed by a deep-rooted and often narrow sense of heterosexuality. The mundane reproduction of heterosexuality has been achieved in a number of ways, including the presentation of "typical men" and "typical women" in certain ways; the routine reporting of engagement, marriage, and birth announcements; advertising campaigns built around the notion of the "typical" family; the constant reproduction of material focused on heterosexual (nuclear) family groups; and the use of eroticized female display aimed at an heterosexual male audience (Exhibit 6). Throughout its history the company newsletter has remained silent in regard to any type of sexual preference or family life which did not conform to its own narrow view of the "typical" family.

In terms of exclusions, the newsletter contributed over the years to management resistance to the recruitment of female stewards and pilots. The newsletter did not only reproduce images of existing (male) stewards and pilots but, from time to time, included copy which questioned the potential of women to serve in either role (Exhibit 7).

Despite the fact that BA have been hiring female pilots since 1987 they have yet to feature a woman pilot in any of their advertising campaigns and the newsletter has yet to treat female pilots as normal – preferring to record "record firsts" rather than the routine activities of women pilots.

[BEA Magazine, no. 285, March 1973]

SO LONG SONIA! A familiar face is missing from Bealine House, where she has been resident for fifteen years—the lady in question being SONIA BROWN, now Sonia Evans since her marriage to Mike at Uxbridge Registry Office last month. Sonia, who was for many years with Personnel at Bealine and, latterly, as a Job Evaluation Officer, is seen with the happy groom (3) signing the register.

The ceremony was followed by a call at Bealine House to receive the good wishes of her former colleagues—and it turned out to be quite a farewell party!

Back from their honeymoon in the United States, Mr. and Mrs. Evans are now in residence in their new home at Lakenheath.

[Topline, 2/11, Nov. 1975]

Exhibit 6:   Images of Heterosexuality

– Stewards

Victualling Her Way to Matrimony

[Report of a letter received by Imperial Airways' Paris Office "the other day, from a young lady at Versailles". The letter is reproduced with some amusement at the thought of a female steward]

Could you not take me on board one of your company's aircraft as stewardess? This is why....I would like to join [my fiance in Biltire] so that we could be married. The air trip to Geneina via Cairo and Khartoum is too dear for me. As a stewardess, however, I could work my passage out there...

My suggestion will probably surprise you. It is useless to tell you how happy I should be if you would care to consider it. [IA, Staff News, 9/9, 3rd March 1939]

[At the height of the Second World War when BA were recruiting large numbers of women they steadfastly refused to hire female stewards]

STEWARDS-TO-BE

These boys are the youngest employees of the Corporation. At the ages of 14, 15, and 16, they are being trained by the Catering Branch for their duties as Stewards. Owing to the shortage of man-power in war-time, they are preparing for jobs which in peace-time were open only to young men over the age of 21.

[BOAC, News Letter, Nov. 1942]

– Pilots

Book Reviews

A most useful book for any boy who has ambitions to fly as an airline pilot has just been published by Edmund Ward Ltd. In their 'Men of Action' series, it is entitled 'Airline Pilot' and is written by Eric Leyland with the co-operation of B.O.A.C.
[BOAC Review, Mar. 1957]

Your Chance to Fly Engineering Officers Needed

Engineering officers are to be carried, as at present, on current B.O.A.C. aircraft and on those on order for the future...
To fill these positions, however, the Corporation needs well qualified men.
[A full-page ad., BOAC Review, Nov. 1957]

Hats Off to Concorde's First Lady

By Alice Dunhill, Reuters

AT HEATHROW: British Airways Capt. Barbara Harmer, 39, became the first woman civil supersonic pilot Thursday when she flew a Concorde from London to New York.

[BA News, No. 949, 26th March 1993]

Exhibit 7:   The Exclusion of Female Stewards and Pilots

Comment and Presentation

From the beginning, the company newsletters have (re-)produced comment on 'the typical' 'women' and 'man.' But those comments changed to some extent over time and depending upon changing social and organizational discourses.

In its earliest years (1927-39) the airline displayed a limited concern with women. The company employed less than a handful of women in 1924, and although that number had grown to 500 by 1939 it still represented less than ten percent of the airline's workforce. As a matter of policy female employees were almost exclusively recruited from the middle and upper classes. In this same era the company's advertising was centrally focused on the middle- and upper class male passenger but limited attempts were made from time to time to attract female passengers from the same elite strata. Newsletter comment of the time reflected this limited class and gender focus. Through the pages of the newsletter middle-class womanhood was associated with shopping trips and fashion (Exhibit 8) compared to a rich store of male images associating masculinity with business, technical knowledge, heroism and piloting (Exhibit 9).

Ladies Only

On arrival at Croydon recently of the regular afternoon Paris shopping service, it was noticed that the twelve passengers were all ladies. This is only another indication of the fascination that flying has for women, and the increasing popularity of the Paris shopping service.
[Imperial Airways Monthly Bulletin, July 1927]

Romance of Air-Borne Freight

Samples of women's ever-changing fashions are now rushed for long distances by air. The other day a hot new style which had been designed in London was, within 24 hours of its creation, en route by air to Salisbury in Southern Rhodesia, more than 6,000 miles away.
[Imperial Airways Weekly News Bulletin, no. 2, 31st March 1936]

Exhibit 8:   Feminity Flys Fashionably

In a number of ways newsletter references associated women with a limited number of tasks and capabilities. Rank ("captain") and authority ("manager") was only ever associated with the names of male employees; women were always described as "Miss" or "Mrs." but men were reported by full name (e.g. "Fred Hards") or initials ("E.W. Bailey"); the phrase "the wife of" was often used to refer to the married partner of a male passenger or employee, while the term "the husband of" never appeared in print: the typical passenger and employee was assumed to be male! In terms of airline occupations a survey of the newsletters for the period show men associated with one-hundred and fifteen different jobs – including accountant, booking clerk, electrician and first officer, and women asso-

---

Imperia's Men to the Rescue

News of a thrilling eleventh-hour rescue by sailors from the motor yacht Imperia... A notable feature of the rescue was the very skilful handling of the boats by the boatswain and sailors in very difficult conditions. The whole episode was witnessed from the shore by female relatives of the crew of the motor-boat, who were in a state of prostrate anxiety as they saw their menfolk threatened.
[Imperial Airways Staff News, no. 9/9, 3rd March 1939]

Exhibit 9:   An Image of Heroism and Manhood

ciated with only thirteen jobs – including stenographer, secretary, telephonist, and teleprinter operator. Four jobs were associated with both men and women – journalist, junior clerk, machinist, and typist.

Images of womanhood changed during the war years (1939-45) as the company quadrupled the number of female staff it employed; by 1942 the company's two thousand female employees constituted thirty-four percent of all its UK-based staff. In this era women moved into a range of jobs previously held by men, including a limited number of supervisory and managerial positions. It was a time when the changing role of women in the company was moving faster than the traditional attitudes to womanhood and this produced several mixed and ambivalent images (Exhibit 10).

When the war called to Miss J. Applebee she put the cover on her typewriter in the Technical Development Branch... [and] joined the A.T.S. [Auxiliary Training Service].
[B.O.A.C. Newsletter, no. 14, March 1941]

There are now twenty-five industrial women employed at Bath Factory some of whom came forward during the last war and are now once more helping to defeat the same enemy. There seems no doubt that these women are definitely capable of undertaking a man's job efficiently and well.
[B.O.A.C. Newsletter, no. 21, October, 1941]

Exhibit 10:   Girls in Battledress

Following the war, there are two distinct periods in the presentation of womanhood. In the first period (1946-1960) official company policy centered on de-emphasizing glamour while focusing on the professional image of female uniformed staff. While the newsletters reported this approach they increasingly used a series of images which focused on the bodily beauty of selected uniformed staff. In the second period (1960-75) these latter emergent images of womanhood triumphed over official concerns with desexualization, and official policy in practice and image merged as the company began to use eroticized images of womanhood to sell airline seats (Mills 1994).

In the immediate post-war era the newsletter could still draw upon warfare as a reference point for manhood (Exhibit 11), but as the years rolled forward the newsletter editors resorted to a more traditional utilization of female sexuality to stress male virility (Exhibit 12).

Some of our staff, who left the Corporation as messenger boys, junior clerks, or apprentices, have come back as R.A.F. Wing Commanders or Squadron Leaders, Naval Commanders, or Army Lieutenants, Colonels and Majors, and in lesser commissioned ranks. They have grown into men with experience of the world...
[BOAC News Letter, no. 7, October 1946]

Exhibit 11:   The Men Who Came Back

The B.O.A.C. figure entirely surrounded by lovelies is Catering Assistant H. Seddon, of New York. Occasion was the opening of the new 'sheeprun' built at La Guardia air terminal, attended by representatives of all airlines on the North Atlantic route. Having then no stewardess, the Corporation supplied a steward; the other airlines stewardesses. Local humorists described the set-up as the 'B.O.A.C. Harem.'   *Picture by 'Aviation' magazine*

[B.O.A.C. News Letter, no. 10, January 1947]

Exhibit 12:   "B.O.A.C. Harem"

Womanhood seems to have presented more of a problem to the newsletter editor and his staff. Before the war, women had been described in brief terms (e.g. Miss Morris of Accounts). During the war the greatly increased number of female employees needed explanation, as seen in the number of newsletter stories focused upon the new and greatly expanded range of task taken on by women. In the post-war period the number of female employees continued to climb (2,840 by 1946) and this was reflected in the newsletter. Without the benefit of a wartime rationale the newsletter simply drew on the device of producing an increased number of photographic images of (now, uniformed) female staff. Women were an evident part of the airline but that evidence was viewed through a series of inane images. Now and then the newsletter included an extended commentary on the work of a female employee, but this tended to be focused on extraordinary women or tasks and served to reinforce the impression that 'women's work' was normally trivial. Even here the newsletter could not resist references to the woman's bodily appearance (e.g. "slim," "dark curls"). This was to become a growing trend over the next fifteen years.

An increasing emphasis on beauty and a concern with the body became a key aspect of the reportage on women within the newsletters of the airline and this trend was reinforced by a number of airline practices. From 1948 beauty competitions became a regular feature of company (both BOAC and BEA) life, and the respective newsletters played an important part in their promotion. Steadily items on women were accompanied by descriptors such as "lovely," "blue-eyed," "blond," etc. A 'women's page' in the BOAC News Letter appeared and featured articles on fashion, hair care and make-up. Nonetheless, the presentation of female sexuality was produced through images that suggested a 'wholesome' or 'proper' type of femininity – the 'girl next door type' who is pretty but not overtly sexy (Exhibit 13)!

The emphasis on the body steadily grew to the point where overt bodily sexuality became synonymous with femininity in the pages of the newsletter. A 1954 cartoon in the BEA Magazine (no. 73, November) signaled the changing view of sexuality. In the cartoon a female flight attendant is drawn curvaceously – with large breasts bulging out of a tight-fitting uniform – while three other women are drawn as plain and plump and one – commenting on the 'attractive female' – is saying to the others: "And here, girls is Miss Andya Ticketova to show us how we shall all look in our new uniforms."

In this era, the focus on the body took several forms. In terms of ritual, beauty contests proliferated throughout the company and the industry. References to female employees increasingly, from about 1958 onwards, included (manufactured) descriptions of hair ("brunette") and eye ("blue-eyed"), coloring, bodily size ("petite") and shape ("shapely") and overall attractiveness ("pretty"). In November 1962 bodily measurements began to appear – informing the reader of the breast, waist and hip measurements of selected women. March 1962 saw the beginning of occasional articles and reports which commented on women's bodies in some form or another – focusing on such things as exercise to improve breast size and weight loss. Visual presentations of the new interest in the body included the development of pin-ups in the magazines of BEA (beginning Dec. 1957) and BOAC (beginning Jan. 1958). Posed pictures of females in swim suits were frequent throughout the 1960s – to be replaced briefly by a fascination with 'hot pants' in 1971! Drawing upon the popularity of the mini-skirt, an increasing number of newsletter photographs involved posed shots designed to 'show off' a female leg. This reached its apex in 1967 with a newsletter competition which showed five

Hair Commentary	Marianne – Her Page
The B.E.A. mädchen in uniform, now such a familiar figure all over Europe, besides being expected to look pleasant and attractive, has to conform also to very strict rules as to smartness and the wearing of her uniform. [BEA Magazine, no. 66, March 1954]	As I see it, passengers look to us for reassurance and if we look sloppy and rather disinterested they are inclined to think that our appearance is indicative of the efficiency of BEA... [A] neat, cheerful appearance spreads confidence among the passengers. B.E.A. gives us a uniform to wear and, though it may have its faults... it is up to us to do our best with it. Nail varnish is not to be worn according to the book but if you should... wear it, for goodness sake be sure there are no chips... [BEA Magazine, Women's Page, no. 75, January 1955]

Exhibit 13: A Smart Uniform Appearance

pairs of female legs and faces which the readers were asked to match up. There were no prizes offered, only the 'thrill' of taking part. Images of female nakedness were introduced in cartoon form in May 1962, and developed through a shot of a naked women in a bath in 1970, a stewardess in a Playboy see-through negligee (1972), and a semi-naked woman sun-bather in a 1974 British Airways advertisement. Various cartoons suggested that stewardesses (and other uniformed staff) were 'free and easy.'

This increasing eroticization to some extent matched changing sexual mores and to some extent changing organizational practices and attitudes. Inside the company, organizational practices contributed to a developing eroticization through changes in flight attendant training and presentation, and in new advertising images. Between 1963 and 1969 stewardess training dramatically shifted towards an emphasis on beauty and charm (Exhibit 14) and from around 1965 advertising campaigns began to be built around overt sexuality, with the utilization of female bodies – usually in bikinis, mini-skirts, or other forms of 'revealing' attire.

By the early 1970s the woman's movement was making itself felt in a number of ways and the airline industry – as a prominent purveyor of degrading forms of female sexuality – was far from immune. In Britain and the US, stewardesses were to the fore in challenging sex discrimination (Hochschild 1983; Nielsen 1982). This was reflected in the columns of BA's newsletter in contradictory ways.

From the late 1960s through to the late 1970s, the newsletter was constantly announcing new breakthroughs as women entered jobs that had previously been for men only, including engineering (1966), sales (1970), senior and chief stewarding (1974), management (1974) and Board membership (1974). Over the same period the newsletter began to do feature articles on the work done by women.

Often reports on female breakthroughs were couched in terms of a debate with the discourse of women's liberation. When, in 1969, BEA appointed its first and only female station superintendent (at the Scottish post of Barra) the headline read "[I]n Barra it's a Woman's World." The following year the *BEA Magazine* played on the same theme when appointing its first woman sales representative, announcing "It's not Always a Man's World." BOAC, on the other hand, preferred headlines such as "Four Women in a Man's World," which heralded the fact that the company had employed four women to work in the work study department. When British Airways appointed its first female Sales Training Manager the newsletter hailed this as "a victory for the feminist camp in British Airways" (see Exhibit 5). By 1975 BA News was resorting back to the "It's a Woman's World" type of headline. From time to time, articles on female advancement seemed more aimed at discounting feminism than anything else. But it was not a one-sided debate and in recent years a number of feminist letters and contributions have appeared in the newsletter, challenging both company practices and the newsletter's discriminatory way of viewing reality (Exhibit 15).

The Changing Face of British Airways and the Role of the Newsletter

In the 1980s and 1990s British Airways continued to employ an increasing number of women managers. In 1991 the company joined with several other major UK organizations in a campaign – Opportunity 2000 – aimed at increasing the number of women managers at all levels. Whether the company succeeds in its aims or not will depend on several things – not least of which will be the commitment of senior management and their willingness to tackle not simply the numbers of women employed but the cultural rules which have for so long discriminated against women.

Policy alone will not be enough to deal with the deep-rooted discriminatory practices and discourses which exist within organizations in general and British Airways in particular. It is not simply a question of numbers (how many women, and what percentage of key positions) but how those numbers are viewed, discussed and imagined. In 1976, following the passage of Sex Discrimination legislation, BA developed a policy statement aimed at providing equal opportunity regardless of sex.

Beyond this top management did very little to change the cultural practices and discourses of the organization which render inequities mundane. Had senior management examined the character of the company image-making processes (adver-

> The curricular for B.O.A.C. stewardesses reads like a course for perfect wives including, as it does, the preparation and presentation of meals and refreshments, the care of babies, young children and invalids, first aid, cocktail mixing, dietetics, deportment and beauty care.
> [B.O.A.C. News, Issue 248, 13th Dec. 1963]
>
> *Beauty Spot*
>
> Up until last season Cabin Crew Training courses were mixed then segregation was tried on an experimental basis. This proved a success and this season, for the first time, stewards and stewardesses are being trained separately. In the past stewardesses were expected to have the same technical knowledge as stewards, ie., capacity of tanks and positions of stopcocks. However, this knowledge was very rarely put to full use as, by the very nature of the division of duties on board an aircraft, any work relative to this was done by stewards. It was thus decided that the new entry of stewards this season should still learn the full technical details of an aircraft, whereas stewardesses would concentrate on those subjects which were more realistic with their duties.
> The job of an airline stewardess is generally regarded as one of the 'glamour' occupation. Whether you agree, or disagree, with this it does mean that any girl who does the job is on show and has to look her best for a considerable period of time – and an airline passenger can be very critical indeed, women by pulling somebody to pieces or by slightly envying their turnout, men by being pleased at having an attractive young woman to look at.
> [Included in the five week training course will be sessions in the grooming workshop; deportment; make-up application; personal hygiene – care of feet and legs; correct manicure, care of hands and nails, skin, and the importance of make-up.]
> [BEA Magazine, no. 237, March 1969]

Exhibit 14:   Making Women's Work

tisements, annual statements, corporate image, and the in-house newsletter) they would have found a series of counter-productive actions.

While there can be no doubt that BA has made a number of significant steps in the direction of promoting women to management they continue to do so against a background of continued discriminatory images of women. The typical image of women in the pages of *British Airways News* continues to be one which is utilized in support of male image-making (e.g. one male senior manager surrounded by several female subordinates), which portray women as decorous and occupying a relatively low position of power, authority and status. It is still true that very few female managers ever appear in the newsletter and it is rare to find the work of a female manager profiled.

Airline chiefs have had little hesitation in radically tackling the organizational culture of their company to achieve a better service orientation: Sir Colin Marshall put each and every employee through a training program in the 1980s and put an end to many vestiges of the old BA culture which was seen to inhibit the

Newsletter

The Women's Lib Lady Seeks A Fare Deal

This women's Lib business has gone about as far as it can go. All the way to New Zealand, in fact. Our sales people in Auckland report getting a most indignant call from an anonymous lady who was terribly uptight about the advertising of 'family excursion fares.'

Why, she wanted to know, were they advertised as full fare for father, half fare for his wife and so on? Why not full fare for the wife and half for the husband? It was gently pointed out to her that the full fare was normally applicable to the head of the household – and that was usually a matter for domestic assessment.

They did think of asking: who's paying for the flight anyway? But, with admirable restraint, they resisted the temptation.

[BOAC News, no. 213, 4th June 1971]

Viewpoints

This is the year sex equality became law in Britain. Today we turn the spotlight on two women who didn't need the law…

Long before 'women's Lib' became fashionable, Ouida Huxley developed promotional ideas, since widely copied, that treated the woman passenger as a traveller in her own right.

The Mother Who Is Going Back to School

This month, within days of the Equal Pay and Sex Discrimination Acts becoming law in Britain, a woman from British Airways will attend a specific management training course for the first time.

[When asked if she would like to attend:]

'My goodness what will I do with the children? was the first thing that came into [her] head.'

BA News, no. 105, 9th January 1976

Women's Viewpoints

Grace Leaves with a Plea: Give Women a Chance

On the eve of her retirement after 27 'very happy' years with the airline Grace McCoy, Promotional Material Superintendent with overseas division, has some interesting things to say on behalf of her colleagues.

'Perhaps one day British Airways may have a woman member on the Board.' That is the hope of 55 year old Grace…

'As we all know the airline business is very much a man's world… yet there are many jobs in this world that a woman can do equally well, and often better than a man.'

'But,' she warns, 'it is a hard fight. A woman has to be twice as good as a man in any job in order to prove her worth.'

Grace is strongly against bra-burning women's lib and believes emphatically that women should always retain their femininity".

'However," she says, "I do think that we have got to have more faith in our capabilities. We have got to realize that we need not always be content with being the power *behind the throne."*

Why Should Women be Rank Outsiders?

I have read in your pages that a new female uniform is soon to become available . . . I hope that the opportunity will be taken to change the rank markings for women so that they are as prominent and easily recognizable as those worn by men.

[Female employee, letter to the editor, BA News, No. 164, 11 Mar. 1976]

Don't Let Baby Stop Us Working

Come on, British Airways, how about leading the way in creating an increase in productivity – for the good of your staff, your future and the future of Britain? How? By creating creche facilities of course!

[Female contributor to "Points of View", BA News, no. 160, 11 Feb. 1977]

Proud to Be a Woman

I do not consider myself a bra-burning women's libber, but for a while now a habit of British Airways News has me flaming. I refer to your paper's constant throwback to the dark ages in referring to those of the female sex as "girls" while the males pictured are "men."

[Female employee's letter to the editor, BA News, no. 181, 15th July 1977]

Exhibit 15:   Debates with Feminism

aim of 'customer orientation' (Hampden-Turner 1990). If gender discrimination is to be seriously tackled a similar set of radical changes are needed. The company newsletter is a good place to start. It both reflects and produces the organization's culture and if we can understand the particular forces which shape any given set of images then we have at least half a chance of dealing with the root of the organizational construction of discrimination.

Note

[1] Between 1924-1939 the forerunner of BA was called Imperial Airways.

References

Abella, J.R.S. (1984), *Equity in Employment. A Royal Commission Report*. Ottawa: Ministry of Supply and Services Canada.

Alvesson, M. and P.O. Berg (1992), *Corporate Culture and Organizational Symbolism*. Berlin, New York: de Gruyter.

Bray, W. (probably 1974), *The History of BOAC 1939-1974*. Camberley, Surrey: BOAC-Wessex Press.

Burrell, G. (1984), Sex and Organizational Analysis. *Organization Studies*, 5(2): pp. 97-118.

Burrell, G. (1987), No Accounting for Sexuality. *Accounting, Organizations and Society*, 12: pp. 89-101.

Calás, M.B. and L. Smircich (1992), Using the "F" Word: Feminist Theories and the Social Consequences of Organizational Research, in *Gendering Organizational Analysis*, edited by A.J. Mills and P.Tancred, pp. 222-234. Newbury Park, CA: Sage.

Cox, M.G. (1986), Enter The Stranger: Unanticipated Effects of Communication on the Success of an Organizational Newcomer, in *Organization Communication: Emerging Perspectives*, edited by L. Thayer. Norwood, NJ: Ablex.

Ferguson, K.E. (1984), *The Feminist Case Against Bureaucracy*. Philadelphia: Temple University Press.

Gramsci, A. (1978), *The Modern Prince and Other Writings*. New York: International Publishers.

Hampden-Turner, C. (1990), *Corporate Culture. From Vicious to Virtuous Circles*. London: Hutchinson.

Hochschild, A.R. (1983), *The Managed Heart. Commercialization of Human Feeling*. Berkeley, CA: University of California Press.

Martin, J. (1992), *Cultures in Organizations. Three Perspectives*. Oxford: Oxford University Press.

Meissner, M. (1986), The Reproduction of Women's Domination, in *Organization Communication: Emerging Perspectives*, edited by L. Thayer, pp. 51-67. Norwood, NJ: Ablex.

Merton, R.K. (1949), *Social Theory and Social Structure*. Glencoe, Ill.: Free Press.

Mills, A.J. (1988), Organization, Gender, and Culture. *Organization Studies*, 9(3): pp. 351-69.

Mills, A.J. (1993), Managing Subjectivity, Silencing Diversity: Organizational Imagery in the Airline Industry, Paper presented in the Symposium "Is the Melting Pot Boiling Over?," Eastern Academy of Management, Providence, Rhode Island, May 6-8.

Mills, A.J. (1994), Dueling Discourses – Desexualization versus Eroticism in the Corporate Framing of Female Sexuality: Images of British Airways, 1945-60. Paper presented at the annual meeting of the British Sociological Association, University of Central Lancashire, Preston, April.

Mills, A.J. (1995), Strategy, Sexuality, and the Stratosphere: Airlines and the Gendering of Organizations, in *Gender Relations in Public and Private: Changing Research Perspectives,* edited by S. Lyon and L. Morris. London: MacMillan.

Mills, A.J. and S.J. Murgatroyd (1991), *Organizational Rules: A Framework for Understanding Organizations.* Milton Keynes: Open University Press.

Mintzberg, H., J.P. Brunet, et al. (1986), Does Planning Impede Strategic Thinking? Tracking the Strategies of Air Canada from 1937 to 1976, in *Advances in Strategic Management,* edited by R. Lamb and P. Shrivastava. Greenwich, CN: JAI Press.

Morgan, G. and Knights, D. (1991), Gendering Jobs: Corporate Strategies, Managerial Control and Dynamics of Job Segregation. *Work, Employment and Society,* 5(2): pp. 181-200.

Morgan, N. (1988), *The Equality Game. Women in the Federal Public Service (1908-1987).* Ottawa: Canadian Advisory Council on the Status of Women.

Nielsen, G.P. (1982), *From Sky Girl To Flight Attendant.* New York: ILR Press.

Riley, P. (1983), A Structurationist Account of Political Culture. *Administrative Science Quarterly,* 28: pp. 414-437.

Smircich, L. (1983), Concepts of Culture and Organizational Analysis. *Administrative Science Quarterly,* 28: pp. 339-358.

Tinker, T. and Neimark, M. (1987), The Role of Annual Reports in Gender and Class Contradictions at General Motors 1917-1976. *Accounting, Organizations and Society:* 12(1), pp. 71-88.

Function of Meaning and De-Differentiation of the Labor Process for Agent's Identity

Ioanna Tsivacou[1]

Introduction

The starting point for all contemporary systems research with an emancipatory interest in organizations is the work of Checkland (1990). Systems researchers who try to incorporate an emancipatory rationality usually adopt a critical philosophical perspective in its multiple unfolding from Kant to Habermas. For instance, one refers to the "critical systems heuristics" of Ulrich (1983), to the efforts of Jackson (1985, 1988) and Flood (1990) to include in their method the Habermasian emancipatory interest, to Oliga's (1990) model of power and ideology, and to the "interpretive systemology" of the University of Los Andes (Fuenmayor and Lopez-Garay 1991). Contemporary systems researchers intervene in formal organization problems, applying claims and assumptions that allow participative and discursive methodologies to function emancipatorily for all those affected by the organization.

Checkland's (1990) position is that systems methodologies do not intervene in the real world, but use models to interpret the perceived world of the participants as a process of methodology. Through this double representation, they gain insight into reality. Thus, methodologies address interpretations as meaning formation, and they conceptualize emancipation as "emancipation from hidden presuppositions" (Flood and Ulrich 1990), or as "the uncovering of the constitution of the 'trap' (in Vicker's terms) as a precondition for the liberation from the power structure" (Fuenmayor and Lopez Garay 1991).

It may be argued that all discursive systems methodologies accept the division of the organizational process into two domains. According to second order cybernetics assumptions (Maturana 1987; Von Foerster 1979), these comprise the operational domain, where organizations are constituted by the participants' moment-to-moment interactions, and the information domain, where participants function as observers of their own interactions, and, "through recurrent coordination of co-ordination of actions (i.e. language)" create "a consensual domain of actions, or shared reality: the organization" (Espejo 1993). Thus, organization is not pre-sumed to be a sociological entity that should be studied, but to be a conceptual entity derived from the interpretative models of the participants.

Systems methodologies are models, or interpretative schemata, constructed within the informational domain, to make sense of the operational domain. In the terms of this chapter, this is "double representation." The first representation is that of reality as represented in the informational domain, while the second one is the rerepresentation of the former, as systems models attempt to objectify it. Historically, representation and rerepresentation played major roles in the constitution of scientific knowledge. The difference between the representations of this kind and the historical representations of the 16th and 17th century, described by Foucault (1973), is that knowledge now tries to represent or to symbolize meaning structures, while in the previous centuries knowledge used representation for the ordering and displaying of things in space-time dimensions.

Today, systemic models are not the representations of actual things or relationships, but the representation of figurative forms of an already objectified reality. The arrangement of this objectified reality in conceptual activity systems (as, for example, in soft systems methodology), composes a higher level of abstraction than the depiction of real events in statistical tables and lists. The systems models are empty forms (signifiers) which revitalize independently of their referent. What is interesting in the methodology's process is the relationships between the models, one signified by the constitution of rules that govern a content of action already consolidated in the models. The most significant and revolutionary element is in the use of oral language that undermines the logic of representations.

Obviously, language, and especially the particular form that it takes in rational discourse, plays a central role in discursive methodologies. While language probably is not considered only as a medium for the transference of meaning but also as the area where meaning is constituted, it seems that methodologies originated from emancipatory ideals rely on rational discourse as able to grasp all the nuances of human action. However, while rationality is dealt with by systems researchers – especially those occupied with the policy of emancipation – the same cannot be said for the theme of subjectivity and identity.

Even when the policy of emancipation focuses on the subjective level, systems researchers have not yet provided a thorough analysis of the historical, structural or agency presumptions responsible for the shaping of subjectivity and identity in modern organization. By deduction, the formation of meaning and the actual conditions of its context of development, also remain unadressed. From their writings, especially Flood's, Jackson's and Oliga's, it is obvious that they accept power relations in the organization as responsible for the constitution of consciousness. However, they do not proceed to an analysis of the way that these power relations influence subjectivity and identity.

Consider these representative recent examples. Flood (1990), adopting Foucault's analysis, gives a more concrete view, according to which subjectivity does not owe its existence to a transcendental essence of human being, but it is the product of power-resistance relations. Knights and Willmott (1989) develop a similar view. Fuenmayor, more than the others, contributes significantly to the interpretation of subjectivity and especially of "identity" and "otherness" (Fuenmayor 1991b). Nevertheless, he places the whole argument in a philosophical perspective, to found, on behalf of the systems movement, an onto-epistemology able to explain the notion of "wholeness" (Fuenmayor 1991a). Therefore, to our knowledge, issues concerning the social formation of meaning and identity of the agent are not treated in his writings.

One appreciates the sociological awareness of systems theoreticians and practitioners who belong to the realm of "critical systems thinking." At the same time one wishes to contribute to a different perspective for the critical assessment of emancipatory methodologies. Consequently, the present chapter deals with the analysis of the function of meaning in contemporary complex organizations. Of course its scope is neither the extensive nor the exhaustive analysis of such a subject. It brings in to the systems field a problematique that remains both alive and debatable within sociological thought.

One starts from the recognition that the identity of working people is a synthesis of several social identities interconnected in different space-time relations. Trying to put forth the identity of the agent of a postmodern organization and trying to clarify the influence of the function of meaning on this identity, does not mean a devaluation of other identities. In the case of managerial interventions, or at least those guided by an emancipatory interest, it sheds light on some characteristics developed in those organizational processes constructed under the guidance of functionally defined meaning. To deal with this subject we use Luhmann's theory for the function of meaning and Clegg's inferences for modern organizations. The core of the argument that is derived is based on two notions of "differentiation." It is proposed that these define the contemporary individuality of the agent in two ways. First, the functional differentiation of the society in social subsystems (Luhmann 1990a); second the de-differentiation of the production sphere (Clegg 1990).

The next two sections delineate the formation of meaning, subjugated to the reproductive and functional rationality of the social system, as well as the de-differentiation of the labor process. Subsequently, it discusses the impact of these processes on the agent's subjectivity/identity. The final section outlines the physiognomy of an artificial domain for emancipatory systems methodologies.

The Function of Meaning

Contemporary society is functionally differentiated (Luhmann 1983). Institutionalist theorists (Friedland and Alford 1987; Scott 1987) accept the differentiation of society in social spheres with different belief systems and different types of

social relations. However, in Luhmann' s perspective the functional differentiation of the subsystems of a society is the dominant principle of systems building.
In these subsystems (legal, domestic, political, economic, educational, religious,
etc.), the exchanges in and among them are not carried on by a common symbolism, one that regulates the significations for the whole society, but by a grid
of meaning that sub-systems themselves define. In this way, each system sets its
boundaries with the other systems.

According to Luhmann (1990a) social and psychic systems (i.e. individual
consciousness) are meaningfully constituted systems, distinguished by the mode
through which they arrive at a meaning-based reproduction: the social, using communication, and the psychic, using consciousness. Communications can be realized only through a structural coupling among organizations and between organizations and psychic systems, considering psychic systems as parts of the social
system environment.

In both cases, of psychic and of social systems, selection is accomplished with
the comparison between expectations and the plurality of possibilities. Meaning carries this comparison, as Luhmann argues. Otherwise, social systems select from a horizon of potentialities that part actualized through experience. This
broader world of potentialities is socially and historically produced: we imagine
it as a pool of "latent" meaning. The realization of selected experience occurs
through a process that grasps part of latent meaning and makes it emerge in consciousness.

In both kinds of systems (psychic and social), meaning functions to choose possibilities that the system actualizes, as well as the non-possibilities remaining outside of system boundaries. Every system of meaning approximates the complexity
that it seeks to regulate by negating meaning superabundant to its understanding,
its systematicity. Based on this selected part of meaning social systems create a
shared meaning structure through which communication occurs. It is this internal sharing of meaning that provides the necessary context for the development of
other elements of action, related to material conditions; in other words, permitting
action to realize and express its transformative character. If the function and the
appearance, or the emergence, of meaning is selective, this selectivity is based upon the capacity of meaning to constitute identifications and negations (Luhmann
1990a: 35).

Luhmann's overall analysis concerning the foundations of selectivity in consciousness does not concern us here. The interest is in the functional aspect of selectivity and how it operates in a social system. Behind the constitution of meaning there is a social context which regulates conditions for the function of meaning. In a world in which meaning explodes in order to identify continuously new
and emergent forms of existence, where selection is rendered possible, social context restricts the explosion.

We choose from the moment that we discover the similarities between compared objects or experiences. However, if meaning needs a linguistic domain in

order to become operational, it seems that in a formally organized world, the linguistic code, in its plurality, is not an appropriate means to secure identifications. In formal organizations, and in functionally differentiated social systems, the selection of possibilities that facilitate the coordination of action and direct the purposive-rational attitude of the system should be based on some other symbolic media. On the one hand, these media satisfy the criterion of simplification concerning selectivity, contributing to the bypassing of complexities posed by linguistic, culturally defined, communication; on the other hand, they contain as a criterion the strategic influence of decisions on the participants in the formal organizations or systems. Such symbolic media are the well known "symbolic media of interchange" of Parsons (1970; see also Parsons and Platt 1973), or as they are better conceptualized and called by Habermas (1987), "steering media."

These media, because they are able to assimilate the differences and restore symmetries in an asymmetrical world, have been raised to the status of general media of equivalence of values; thus, "general equivalents." In Marx (1976) the exchange values of merchandises derived from the analysis of production, in order to become effected, are based on "abstract labor." Money is the "general equivalent" for the valuation of this labor. In Baudrillard (1972) the medium is the "sign," which emerges primarily from the consumer field and has become the "general equivalent" of virtually every human action. In Habermas (1991), the life world (i.e. the space where the processes of cultural reproduction, social integration and socialization take place) is in retreat and the steering media of money and power have taken over its position.

The values of every social sub-system of a differentiated society are internally homogenized through their subjugation to a general medium of equivalence. Consequently, meaning can reveal and select identities. The above "general equivalents," used by the meaning mechanism, formulate first the selectivity behavior of the social system and second, the homogenization of personal experiences through the structural coupling between the social system and the psychic system. The latter implies the adaptation of individual consciousness to identifications and selections imposed by the social system as necessary for its survival and evolution. The degree of success of this homogenization is dependent on the strength of structural coupling between social and psychic system.

The reduction of any value to a "general equivalent" presupposes, of course, historical processes of development occurring in the social system: processes that transform a common symbolic medium to a general measure and counterpoise of values. (Whether these historical processes concern production or consumption lies beyond the horizon of this chapter.) The social system accomplishes its auto-production and auto-organization through a symbolic medium. Its rationality is governed hereafter by a code, and one argues, this rationality rules the institutionalization of practices in the organizational context. Commodities and services may take the form of exchange values, either as signs and codes, emergent under the structural behavior of a system that functions both to provide relations between

components and rules for their interactions. Relations that determine the reproduction of the system's properties and confirm the order and the unity of the system.

The above mentioned interpretative scheme does not deny that the structure of
coding, even while represented as operative, also implies cognitive notions. We
believe that this is a phenomenon connected with the social system, that it is, on
one hand a structural context of human action, and on the other hand, a product
of this action.

The argument developed here, of the general equivalents or of a homogenizing
and homogenized code, brings in the institutional perspective an approach already
developed in macro-sociological domains. The systems of belief distinguished in
the social spheres by institutional theorists coincide with the rationality that social
systems promote in order to maintain their survival and autoproduction.

Environmental agents impose their will on the organizational context by means
of power and legitimization or through control of funding resources (Scott 1987).
Empirical findings from institutional theory enhance macro-sociological claims
that steering media (or general equivalents) aid the organization adapt to the pre-
requisites of system integration (Habermas 1987). Steering media are anchored in
formal norms and rules from which organizational action draws its legitimization
in order to try and secure cultural neutrality.

The structural coupling of human beings with organizations, and consequently
with their social system and its coding, is confirmable in the regularities and particular patterns of action that they display. Such membership roles, rules, goals,
objectives, procedures, ceremonies, are cultural regularities enacted in the organized context. They establish social relations dictated by the general equivalents.
Surveillance and obedience, authority relations and personal ties, formalize and
standardize through cultural regularities. In this way, cultural regularities constitute not only a repertoire of structures available to human beings for the realization
of their intentions (Swidler 1986), but also constitute channels for the entrance of
meaning of the environment (or of the social system in which organization is embedded) in the organizational domain. Namely, they are used as means for the circulation of a socially constituted and institutionalized meaning. Human being represents a unity, or individuality, in the organizational domain. This human being
participates also in other domains of existence that introduce behaviors generated elsewhere to the organizational domain, independently of whether these other
domains overlap. Our interest is in the way that an agent's identity is constituted;
hence, we propose to address the changes that identity may undergo in postmodern formal organization.

De-Differentiation in Modern Organizations

Clegg, in his book *Modern Organizations* (1990) provides a deep analysis of organizations in the era known as postmodernity. This text caps a literature on new organizational types, formed in post-industrial society, that expands greatly from the middle of the sixties (Bennis 1966). The description of these types usually focuses on the impact that the variables of human labor and technology have on organizational forms (Heydebrand 1989). The terms used to describe the new types, such as "decentralized," "flexible," "robust systems" (i.e. computer integrated systems (Koppel et. al. 1988), or "post-bureaucratic," derive from analysis of this impact.

Other terms have had widespread currency. We prefer not to use other widely disseminated terms such as "flexible" organization (Atkinson 1984) because we wish to refer not only to production and marketing flexibility but also to employment flexibility, especially to various forms that the labor force takes in modern organizations (Wilkinson 1981; Handy 1984). Pollert's (1988) critique of the model of the "flexible firm," particularly with respect to its employment situation, one of permanent or short term contracts, job sharing, part-time or temporary work, raises many doubts concerning the empirical evidence for the model. In contrast, the term "de-differentiated" used by Clegg (borrowed from Lash 1988) is preferable for two reasons: the one is that in this word the main difference of postmodernity versus modernity, which is a matter of signification (Lash 1988), is implicitly mentioned. The other is that this word semantically refers to the division of labor and to the labor process in general. This suggests that our intention is to pay attention to the anthropocentric view and to the changes that this view has been undergoing in actual postmodern organizational situations, through the alteration of working practices. Clegg's main interest, focused on the decrease in differentiation (translated as a process of de-differentiation), manifested in the production level and the debates that it provokes, not only in the theory of organizations, but in the broader context of the social sciences, captures this broader canvas.

The concept of de-differentiation emerges from research usually conducted on the shop floor or in manufacturing. We are referring to writers such as Kenney and Florida (1988), Clegg (1990), Williams et al. (1987). Despite different considerations about the impact of the division of labor on organizational control, they agree that new technology has led to de-differentiated, de-demarcated and multi-skilled (for some de-skilled) work, as well as to restructuring of organizational practices in more flexible forms. The college-educated worker or employee emerges as an agent better able to handle new computerized equipment, to promote new management profiles, and to motivate innovation. The complex interactions of this agent with other organizational variables become the subject of study of management theory, oriented towards advancing the ideal of efficiency.

In regard to human values, a long debate exists in the social sciences centered on the value of efficiency. Critical systems thinkers, in management sciences, especially those using systems methodologies, raise explicitly or implicitly many questions concerning new attitudes in the work process. Some of these questions, related to the manifestations of subjectivity/identity in agent's, require clarification here. Especially, these include changes associated with meanings embedded in radically changing locales of production. The phenomenon of de-differentiation increases the possible forms in which meanings appear, especially due to the modifications imposed on action contexts by information technology. The computerization of productive and administrative work has made electronic texts the focus of action, instead of a workplace that required participation in a common work process (Zuboff 1988). This alteration of work practices, as Zuboff (1988) describes, effects radically both oral culture and patterns of cognition. The chief effect is in the direction of a transfer of emphasis from bodily to mental effort.

The transfer of emphasis from bodily to mental effort increases cognitive capacity but it is not evident that it enhances human partnership and social engagement. The subjugation of the work process to a systems rationality bound up with power relations through the "general equivalents," continues to be a serious impediment to the opportunities offered to human subjectivity by information technology. High technology and associated abstract forms of work permit a flexible restructuring of organizational operations. However, the differentiation of the social systems, and their institutionalized function of meaning, continue to detach relations of meaning from technology, as they couple with the internal requirements of the social and, therefore, the organizational system.

Research conducted in organizations in the service sector in Greece confirms this phenomenon of de-differentiation. These research findings add to inferences other researchers reach concerning service organizations (Baron and Bielby 1984). This leads one to conclude that, even in countries that are late-comers to modernity (countries not at the front-line of the post-capitalist world), like Greece, service delivery organizations, or the social overhead capital sector (advertising, media, research centers, cultural industries, consultancy offices, etc.) may already constitute a de-differentiated sector. Perhaps this is further evidence that supports Clegg's (1990) hypothesis that no necessity attaches to the stages of history: that modernity may quite easily be "skipped" from the premodern stage, and that, as in the case of Benetton, there may be some advantages to such a progress.

In the case of Greek service delivery organizations the "cadre" today is not the abstracted specialist of Weber's (1978) depiction but the person who develops multi-skilled capacities, able to control a broader domain of organizational activities. The trend toward the decentralization of management sciences, noticed by Lee et al. (1989) is accompanied by experts, called "self-starters," familiar with management sciences, such as decision problems, computer support, planning, etc., a phenomenon widespread in Greek organizations. The power of expertise acquires a new dimension as the current need is not for a simple generalist, but for a multi-expert person, a skilled generalist (Jaikumar 1986).

The Self-Identity of the Agent in a De-Differentiated Labor Process

Since at least the publication of *Capital* the ideology of de-differentiation traverses social thought as a critique of differentiation and of the division of labor. However, it is only recently, that this ideology became a public value, as more de-differentiated organization of both knowledge and practice increases.

Structural coupling occurs between both human systems and organization, as well as between organizations and the social system. In this coupling, possibilities are subject to a logic of homogenization, achieved through the "general equivalents." Simultaneously, due to de-differentiation of jobs, one has a proliferation of experiences. These lead to a multiplicity of interpretive schemes and meaning structures through which one may grasp the totality of meaning that circulates in the social system. It is at this point that one transforms non-possibilities into possibilities. The "general equivalents" act as regulators of meaning. They constitute experience and attempt to homogenize possibilities that facilitate selection. They do not behave as barriers to an increased selective ability so much as to homogenize possibilities, which, while increasing their quantity, inhibit the expression of their multi-semantics in consciousness.

The linkage of decreased differentiation with increased selectivity also enriches, potentially, the common pool of meaning. In this way it might contribute to the formation of a collective consciousness that finds support in a commonality of meaning. Alternatively, modern, multi-skilled individuals in organizations signified by "general equivalents" may develop instrumental rationality to a higher degree, thus controlling the complexity of the social system in which the organization is embedded.

De-differentiation touches two dimensions of the agent; that of the agent as a bearer of meaning and that as a bearer of labor power. Both of them influence self-consciousness, on the one hand, and social awareness on the other: namely, all that is implicitly signified in the notion of subjectivity. Subjectivity is an ambiguous term of modernity and is construed here according to the meaning attributed to it in Abercrombie et al. (1984) as "The self-conscious awareness of subjects." By "identity" we mean the objectification of subjectivity in distinctive forms. Social practices constitute subjectivity, as these forms are recognized by agencies in the social environment. It is the reflexivity of the self back on to those forms in which subjectivity vests (and invests) itself that is termed subjectivity.

Knights and Willmott (1989) have observed a "fetishism" of identity where processes of commodification and solidification disregard the social process of their constitution. Knights and Willmott, drawing upon Foucault's analysis of disciplinary mechanisms and power-knowledge strategies, return the theme of subjectivity to the sociology of organizations. We believe that their positions have many similarities with those of critical system thinkers. Other researchers occupied with subjectivity/identity in the workplace (Burawoy 1979; Cockburn 1984), also enrich critical system thinking in its efforts to create not only rational, but also an emancipatory management. Nevertheless, as held here, analyses of the function of meaning and the "general equivalents" mechanism, enlighten the problem of subjectivity in contemporary organizational contexts through a different perspective.

The domain where the interplay between society and subjectivity takes place is consciousness (Berger and Luckmann 1985). We are of the same mind regarding consciousness as contemporary cognitive scientists (Varela et al. 1991; Jackendoff 1987; Minsky 1986). Consciousness is not a unified background for the multiplicity of experiences. It is rather a continuous flux of inner appearances caused by different events and formations. Self, according to the above mentioned scientists, derives from the causal coherence and integrity of these appearances. Consciousness is the place where meaningful subjective reality constitutes itself and where the reflexivity of the self hypostatizes self-identity. Thus, self-identity is the closure of a self-referential psychic system (Luhmann 1990b: 116) that is able to integrate the different elements of its reproduction in a self-organizing process occurring in the different domains, or subsystems, of society. Thus are integrated in an emergent self-identity the different personal identities that this psychic system shapes as it connects with the differentiated subsystems of society.

The self-identity of the agent of today's de-differentiated organizations, created by selected experience, could be characterized as more complex, since it emerges in consciousness through the grasp of a wider meaning, acquired during a less differentiated work process. Self-identity is incarnated in a wider consciousness than in a more divided universe of meaning.

Let us first address how this self-identity constitutes itself in the processes of everyday life, before turning to the constitutive process in organizations.

One important argument comes from within the mindfulness/awareness tradition, concerning the "enactive cognitive approach to experience." This emphasizes the importance of the other: "the so-called self occurs only in relation to the other... because self is always codependent with other..." (Varela et al. 1991). It is only with the other that self enacts the world. It is in the eyes of the other that ego faces its own identity. Ego cannot acquire a self-identity without perceiving its reflection in the other's gaze. My identity is found in the other, i.e. expectations inducing my actions are defined by the others' expectations. Ego, satisfying the others' expectations, aims at an identity that the other appreciates positively, and that ego then receives through the gaze of the other. However, as I need to perceive myself in the other, so the other has the same need. From the respective needs of each subjectivity, shared understanding can be created. As Merleau-Ponty says, "in the absence of reciprocity there is no other ego" (Merleau-Ponty 1992). Situations of common experiences arise and this is the phenomenon of structural coupling between living organisms that the biologist Maturana (1987; Maturana and Varela 1980) calls "love."

Now we shall turn to the contemporary processes that construct self-identity in formal organizations. Consider the archetype of the worker. The contemporary manufacturing worker confronts automated self-contained cells of machine tools, controlled by computers (Kenney and Florida 1988). She/he does not recognize the self in another ego, but stands alone in front of a mechanized world. Even in service delivery organizations the dominant rationality is that of computer programming and not a rationality driven by the intention to actualize expectations of the self through a mutual understanding of the other's expectations.

The independence of the knowing individual is defined beyond its position in a community of working people. His/her eagerness for computer knowledge, for a close inquiry into it, is an endless thirst for the infinity of information. This is a mental journey through the interminable combination of technological forces, one which can only ever proceed without reaching a satisfactory end. In this launching of the self to the infinite the other does not exist. There is only a self which presupposes the other, but who does not share the world with the other. There are individuals who presuppose society, but they feel they do not reside in that society, as they ordinarily engage the world at work.

This mental journey could only stop when ego meets the other. Only in this context could knowledge find its natural boundary. The presence of the other does not allow such a narcissist identity to emerge but contributes to closure of the multiplicity of identities at the disposal of an individual in a differentiated society. This kind of knowledge is not based on information but on shared understanding. This means it is based on thorough observation of the other, so self is able to break the circularity of its selfishness. The restless trip to the infinite space of information is finished and the self can repose, secure in the common boundary with the other. In this repose the individual conceives the constitutive identities of self and the process of their integration.

On this point our position is opposed to optimist views concerning workers subjectivity in the information organization (Zuboff 1988). The problem is not the communication that may develop around a computer screen, but the absence of the kind of intentionality that occurs "behind" a face-to-face interaction. It is in the intercourse of human relationships that the world is constituted. It is a world enacted through human action. However, the intentionalities behind a face-to-face interaction are always larger than those that a purposive action binds within its boundaries. Intentionalities always slide out from under the constraints that purposive action imposes on them. Action selects a part of intentionality and in this way rationalizes and reifies a part of human interactions. In this way, action offers to the flux of consciousness reified human relations invested with the form of things. That part of intentionality that selection (or, as previously analyzed, the function of meaning) was not able to reify, shapes that part of consciousness that maintains the non-reified character of human relations. It is in this part that Ego can receive the other.

The common search for the solution of a problem raised by an electronic text cannot be considered adequate as an approximation of relations between individuals. Dialogue, in this case, is not developed between them, but between them and the computer. The "other" is in this case the text and the expectations of the other are the expectations of the electronic text.

The increase of de-differentiation increases the selectivity of the agent in front of a world objectified in symbolically functioned technological means. The worker (or employee) of a high-tech competence comes in contact not with many aspects of reality, but with many representations of this reality. Moving alone in a symbolic world, she/he does not approach this world with curiosity and playfulness but is motivated by values dictated by "steering media" or "general equivalents" to conquer and manipulate it. So the function of meaning must coincide with the rationality of the "general equivalents." Meaning, even if transferred by symbols, cannot be disconnected from its action context. The actualization of meaning acquired through a logic of homogenized selectivity is associated with the satisfaction of success or domination, not with that of mutual understanding and pleasure. An intelligible mind, in these conditions, seeks satisfaction through revealing the mysteries of textualization rather than dwelling, intertextually, within a speaking community of language. Such textual satisfaction is reflected not in the eyes of the other, but in the pale mirroring of a computer-screen.

The new position of the individual in a contemporary textualized work context has different impacts from that described by Lukács (1968). According to Lukács, the worker of the 20th century is the supervisor of a rationalized work process. The particularities of the worker are presented as sources of error in a planned and well-designed operation. He (for the person is invariably constructed in the male voice) is an individual who constrains his freedom in the name of the functional use of a technologically organized work process. By contrast, the de-differentiated worker assimilates to the description that Kallinikos (1992a: 116) has reserved for the instrumental activities of modern organizations: "rather than being the mechanical enactment of the recipes embedded in machines and standardized bodies of knowledge" he could "constitute a tangle within which ambiguity, interpretation and choice feed on one another." The increase of experiences does not establish in consciousness a socially recognized identity. Instead, it contributes to the emergence of a psychology of Narcissus in the sphere of production, until now something manifested only in the consumption sphere.

In Christopher Lash's (1980) work one finds a thorough analysis of the phenomenon of Narcissus in modern society. However, this analysis confronts narcissism as a strategy that the individual designs to defend against increasing environmental adversity. Lash describes it in terms of the individual who, for fear of communication, stands against the world. He/she is the human being, who has lost his/her historical continuity. In front of a risky society this individual turns to him/herself, seeking the necessary security and self-esteem that society denies.

Our conceptualization of narcissism is slightly different. It is not grounded on a psychoanalytic view, although it represents some similarities with the secondary narcissism described by psychoanalysts (Freud 1963; Renard 1969; Dessuant 1983). In secondary narcissism, libido, by means of an alternating motion, is removed from the objects of an external world and returns to the subject (Dessuant 1983). This kind of narcissism could be characterized as a psychic backwardness, where the individual projects again into him/herself the image with which she/he has invested objects with meaning. In this way an identification of the Ego with the other is observed.

An initial narcissism precedes the secondary one. During the initial narcissism the individual constitutes the Ego as a reflection of his/her image in the eyes of the other. As long as this image is positive, the individual is reconciled with and loves him/herself. During his/her biological and social development the initial narcissism is blunted and the narcissist libido is turned toward the ideal of Ego (Freud 1969). Something that should not be forgotten is that this psychoanalytical situation is observed in a social environment where ideals are dictated by concrete and historically produced social relations regulated by symbolic codes, or by general equivalents. It is this kind of self-esteem, with a narcissist origin, that provokes feelings of delightfulness. It is a self-esteem backgrounded on a coherent, distinctive self. The more social recognition is invested in an objectivity where the person of the other is identified with the ideal of ego, the more self-esteem (of an ego invented and in the same time generated by psychoanalysis) could be involved in a creative sentiment.

Today, the conditions appropriate for this older form of ego idealism are often absent. Social recognition nowadays takes the form of social success, derived from wealth and power. Signs of such a success are only commodities; the person of the other disappears completely. This situation, where the ideal of Ego is fulfilled by the admiration of the self of a skillful and de-differentiated individual, has overwhelmed the contemporary social system. It deals with the domination of an individual able to integrate and to manage a textualized work process, and dominated by virtue of their capacity to do so. One might say, persuasively, that their capacities invite their domination. It is a process where the conceptual abilities of the individual to explore the intrinsic capabilities of a computerized technology, to reveal its significations, and to control its forces, provide the illusion of panoptic reasoning. The narcissist individual is reborn. Hence, narcissism generates today in the production sphere, not in consumption where Lash located it: here it is probably enhanced and manifested but its "natural home" is no longer there.

It is in the organizational domain that the individual retires their eyes from the other person and turns them on the observation of the self. It is here that the possibility for self-reflection is undermined by the tendency for self-observation. On the organizational level, the psychic system, enclosed in the connectedness of structures and pressed by systemic rationality, proceeds to choices driven by a homogenized meaning. So, the increase of choice is at the end an increase of information and not an increase of understanding. If these lifestyles have the forms of consumerism, i.e. the form of appearances, these appearances are the outward expressions of a self-identity created in the area of the organization. In this domain we find the root-definitions of consumer lifestyles that the individual assumes in the private milieu defined by personal activities (Giddens 1991).

Back to Emancipation

According to the above analysis, emancipation could be considered as the restoring of the other in consciousness. Emancipation, in this case, would mean the withdrawal from self-observation and the re-establishment of a situation where subjects could share their experiences and elucidate in common their perceptions concerning the cultural and natural world.

There is an overwhelming form of management of discursive rationality in the postmodern world that evolves from modernity. It is one which obliges existing meaning to limit its potentialities in the selectivity of future meaning. Emancipation should reveal an area where the selectivity of meaning would not yet have started its instrumental march. It would render an organizational domain where the de-differentiated experiences are not yet subjugated to the domination of the "general equivalents." It would be a domain where, as Levinas (1988) argues, signification precedes "meaning-giving" (*Sinngebung*) and meaning is the other person.

Is it possible under the self-maintenance rationality of formal organizations? Surely not. Narrative forms of knowledge (Brown and Duguid 1991), where established in the organizational area, subordinate themselves to formal language mechanisms. Only an artificial domain, constructed purposively, could gather the properties mentioned above. Such an artificial domain would be constructed in parallel with the organizational one, where the rules of the latter would be fully reversed. This domain cannot be other than that of a play. Surely this domain cannot be that of a formal system?

Systems methodologies, as a "representation system," defined by a given context, content and process, could be designed to secure a place of "openness" of one subjectivity to the other. We live in a world of simulations and artifacts, so only through virtual conditions can human beings create the terms of their shared understanding. In an artificial environment the sharing of experience most often takes the obligatory forms of a game in which individuals, playing with symbols and representations, try to comprehend a world constituted by themselves.

In the informational domain of the organization, referred to in the introduction, system methodologies apply. Not in the operational domain, where meaning plays its functional role, but in the domain of the observer, where representations of representations take place. There is no reason to transpose in this domain the instrumentality of the operational one. On the contrary, a part of the informational domain could be regarded as an artificial space in which the official rules of the organization could be ignored and the rules of play established.

Our intention is to substitute systems methodologies as forms of representation of a more abstract level, with play, as representation of a lower level. That means to replace representations of rules imposed on an objectified reality, by play, conceived as representation of real things and relations. We agree with Dandridge that " the ability to create or to respond to presentational symbolism is akin to the ability to play " (Dandridge 1986: 164). It is an ability motivated to direct the organizational work context from the abstract to the concrete, thus restraining the perpetual trajectory of the individual towards the abstract.

We know that the number of organization analysts who support the ideal of "playing" in the sphere of organizational activities continuously increases (March 1976; Guillet de Montoux 1983; Erickson 1978; Dandridge 1986; Kallinikos 1989). However, we disagree with those who propose the form of play for different patterns of action, such as decision problems, computer support, planning, to increase initiative and creativity. For example, March (1976) declares play as an instrument of intelligence. This detaches from play those characteristics that define it as an "irrational" activity of human life, that join the rational human being with the other creatures of the world. Play is subordinated to the instrumental function of meaning that dominates the formal organization. Work and play might seem integrated, but, instead, a controlled play is created, one that tries to improve the quality of work life but that does not create emancipatory conditions in the work place. Such perspectives distort the nature of play. As Huizinga (1949) says, play has some special properties. Chief among these is the sensation of illusion.

When the player enters the world of play she/he has the sensation that she/he enters in a magic world, as in fairy-tale, but she/he knows that rules have to be respected. Rules are respected because play is viewed as a process, and rules ensure the normal fluidity of this process. However, rules do not substitute for symbols and symbols are not empty of content. Rules are the frame in which rituals are enacted and the play process unfolds. It is a process quite opposite to that of the work, which is outcome-oriented. Play is a process where the splitting of means from ends occurs, leading to an uncoupling of meaning from its instrumental use, trying to restore the disturbed relationship "sense" and "reference."

In an inspired presentation, Kallinikos (1992) attempts to reveal this relationship, and that of the history of representations, through the symbolic language of a play, using in his analysis fragments from Italo Calvino's novel *Invisible Cities*. Chess, the play of Calvino's personages, is not the kind of play here suggested. We are not referring to games where rules and calculation, rather than chance, regulate the probabilities (Huizinga 1949). Play is here connected with what Bowman (1978) calls spontaneous play (of childhood) and not with the structured play (of adulthood). "Fun" is the biggest satisfaction that play offers, as it is disconnected to the steering media of money and power. Engagement (Huizinga 1949) is the provocation and compensation for the winner in play and does not correspond to the premium, or price, or praise, namely to symbols connected with money or power, the "general equivalents." In the symbolic forms of play that human beings explore during childhood they establish in their consciousness the unity of the world (Miller 1973). In play also, communicative interests unfold their primary dynamics.

The artificial recreation of play conditions in the "system" of systems discursive methodologies will animate, perhaps, an organizational context where the agent of a contemporary organization will recover a lost ability. In such a representational system, language accomplishes what Levinas (1988) describes as its uncoupling from the practical side (work) and its coupling with expressiveness. The agent, playing and communicating with the other, far from the homogenizing logic of a functional meaning, will find the opportunity to reinstate the other in his/her consciousness. A person who is able to receive and welcome the other, even playing, is able to retreat from the psychology of Narcissus. To do so is to restore his/her emancipatory interest and with it, rewind the desire "for a human autonomy, but not autonomy that, for the absence of solidarity, results in loneliness;... a human solidarity, but not solidarity which for the absence of autonomy, results in oppression" (Bauman 1988). A desire wished for, perhaps, finally to be realized in real life and not in the artificial world of the play.

Conclusion

The chapter, motivated by critical system thinking, sought to include an "emancipatory interest" in discursive and participative systems methodologies. The main focus was on the process of constitution of the agent's identity in contemporary formal organizations. In particular, it focused on the function of meaning and particular practices in the postmodern labor process, their impact on agent subjectivity, and, consequently, on identity.

The chapter did not analyze power relations behind the institutionalized mechanisms of meaning and the patterns of action dominant in formal organizations. Critical system thinking considers emancipation exactly as the enhancement of self-reflection about these power relations. The main scope of the article is thus to clarify extant processes in the organizational domain that hinder consciousness in this self-reflection.

In postmodern organizations, due to the de-differentiation of the work process, opportunity for the enrichment of circulated meaning, and an increase of meaningful expectations, exists. The function of meaning, aelectivity, chooses between phenomenal possibilities and impossibilities, controlled by the general media of equivalence of values (the well known steering media of Habermas) constituted as money and power. Media, homogenizing possibilities that facilitate selection, lead to an impoverishment of meaning. The agent under these contradictory conditions increases the quantity of his/her experiences, without strengthening his/her internal links with the social and natural world. At the same time, due to computerized labor processes and to the replacement of his/her bodily capacities by mental ones, she/he loses contact with the other person. The individual, who does not recover in consciousness the other person's gaze and who thus remains alone, is constrained to demonstrate multiskilfulness only as Narcissus: for your eyes only, where the you is also the I that looks and is reflected back in the screen that writes. Emancipation restores consciousness of the other and disengages identity from the psychology of Narcissus, a looking glass self that gazes obsessively at a small screen, in which it sees itself mirrored.

The conditions of emancipation cannot be realized in the operational domain of the organization but in the informational one, where systems methodologies take place. However, restoration of the other cannot be actualized either by language coupled with instrumentality or by meaning controlled by steering media. Pleasure and fun must be the measure of participation in methodologies. Their intention should be the reconciliation between Ego and other, if the emancipatory interest is to be pursued by these methodologies.

The present argument is an outline in need of further exploration and grounding in empirical data. However, a "Manifesto for a theory of drama and irrational choices" published by Howard et al. (1993) in *Systems Practice*, is a persuasive contribution in support of the general argument. Many people wish to turn away from the representational rationality of codes, from the homogenized logic of the general equivalents, from pre-arranged selections, restoring forms of play to the organizational context. Howard and colleagues invite us to join them in their endeavors, as people who believe in the introduction of strategies of play into formal organizations. Discursive systems methodologies provide an opportunity to accomplish such an endeavor.

Note

[1] I would like to thank Stewart Clegg for the work that he did as 'language-editor' on this chapter.

References

Abercrombie, N.S., S. Hill and B.S. Turner (1984), *Dictionary of Sociology*, Penguin, London.

Atkinson, J. (1984), Manpower Strategies for Flexible Organizations, *Personnel Management*, August.

Baron, J.N. and W.T. Bielby (1984), The Organization of Work in a Segmented Economy, *American Sociological Review*, 49, pp. 454-473.

Baudrillard, J. (1972), *Pour une critique de l'economie politique du signe*, Gallimard, Paris.

Bauman, Z. (1988), Is there a Postmodern Sociology?, *Theory, Culture and Society*, 5, pp. 217-238.

Bennis, W.G. (1966), *Changing Organizations*, McGraw Hill, New York.
Berger, P. and T. Luckmann (1985), *The Social Construction of Reality*, Penguin Books, England.
Bowman, J.R. (1978), The Organization of Spontaneous Adult Social Play, in M.A. Salter (ed.), *Play: Anthropological Perspectives*, Leisure Press, West Point, New York.
Brown, J.S. and P. Duguid (1991), Organizational Learning and Communities of Practice: Toward a Unified View of Working, Learning, and Innovation, *Organization Science*, 2, pp. 40-57.
Burawoy, M. (1979), *Manufacturing Consent*, Chicago University Press, Chicago.
Checkland, P. (1990), *Soft Systems Methodology in Action*, J. Wiley, Chichester.
Clegg, S.R. (1990), *Modern Organizations*, Sage, London.
Cockburn, C. (1984), *Brothers: Male Dominance and Technological Change*, Pluto Press, London.
Dandridge, T. (1986), Ceremony as an Integration of Work and Play, *Organization Studies*, 7, 2, pp. 159-170.
Dessuant, P. (1983), *Le narcissisme,* Presse Universitaires de France, Paris.
Erickson, E.H. (1978), *Toys and Reasons*, Marion Boyars, London.
Espejo, R. (1993), Domains of Interaction between a Social System and its Environment, *Systems Practice*, 6.
Flood, R.L. (1990), *Liberating Systems Theory*, Plenum, New York.
Flood, R.L. and W. Ulrich (1990), Testament to Conversations on Critical Systems Thinking between Two Systems Practicioners, *Systems Practice*, 3, p. 729.
Foucault, M. (1973), *The Order of Things: An Archeology of Human Sciences.* Vintage Books, New York.
Fuenmayor, R. (1991a), Between Systems Thinking and Systems Practice, in R. Flood and M.C. Jackson (eds.), *Critical Systems Thinking*, Wiley, Chichester.
Fuenmayor, R. (1991b), The Selfreferential Structure of an Everyday Living Situation: A Phenomenological Ontology for Interpretive Systemology, *Systems Practice*, 5, pp. 449-472.
Fuenmayor, R. and H. Lopez-Garay (1991), The Scene for Interpretive Systemology, *Systems Practice*, 4.
Freud, S. (1963), *Essais de psychanalyse,* Payot, Paris.
Freud, S. (1969), Le Narcissisme, in S. Freud, *La Vie Sexuelle,* Presses Université de France, Paris.
Friedland, R. and R. Alford (1987), Symbols, Structures and Institutional Contradictions, paper presented at the conference on "Institutional Change, Center for Advanced Study in The Behavioral Sciences," Stanford, CA.
Giddens, A. (1991), *Modernity and Selfidentity*, Polity, London.
Guillet De Montoux, P. (1983), *Action and Existence: Anarchism for Business Administration*, Wiley, New York.
Habermas, J. (1987), *The Theory of Communicative Action,* 2, Polity, Cambridge.
Habermas, J. (1991), *The Theory of Communicative Action,* 1, Polity, Cambridge.
Handy, C. (1984), *The Future of Work*, Blackwell, Oxford.
Heydebrand, W.V. (1989), New Organizational Forms, *Work and Occupations*, 16, pp. 323-357.
Howard, N., P. Beanet, J. Bryant. and M. Bradley (1993), Manifesto for a Theory of Drama and Irrational Choice, *Systems Practice*, 6, 4.

Huizinga, J. (1949), *Homo Ludens: A Study of the Play Element in Culture*, Routledge, London.

Jackendoff, R. (1987), *Consciousness and the Computational Mind,* The MIT Press, Cambridge MA.

Jackson, M.C. (1985), Social Systems Theory and Practice: The Need for a Critical Approach, *International Journal of General Systems*, 10, pp. 135-152.

Jackson, M.C. (1988), Some Methodologies for Community OR, *Journal of Operational Research Society,* 39, 8, pp. 715-724.

Jaikumar, R. (1986), Postindustrial Manufacturing, *Harvard Business Review*, 6, pp. 69-76.

Kallinikos, J. (1989), Play and Organizations, in Jackson, M.C. Keys, P. and Cropper, S.A. (eds.), *Operational Research and the Social Sciences*, Plenum, New York.

Kallinikos, J. (1992a), The Significations of Machines, *Scandinavian Journal of Management,* 8, 2, pp. 113-132.

Kallinikos, J. (1992b), Decontextualized Accomplishment: Representation is Technology, International Conference on "Technologies of Representations," University of Warwick, Warwick.

Kenney, M. and R. Florida (1988), Beyond Mass Production: Production and the Labour Process in Japan, *Politics and Society*, 16, 1, pp. 121-158.

Knights, D. and H. Willmott (1989), Power and Subjectivity at Work: From Degradation to Subjugation in Social Relations, *Sociology,* 23, 4, pp. 535-558.

Koppel, R., E. Applebaum and P. Albin. (1988), Implications of Workplace Information Technology: Control, Organization and Work, and the Occupational Structure, *Research in the Sociology at Work*, 4, pp. 125-152.

Lash, C. (1980), *Culture of Narcissism*, Abacus, London.

Lash, S. (1988), Discourse Or Figure? Post Modernism as a Regime of Signification, *Theory, Culture and Society*, 5(2-3), pp. 311-336.

Lee, S.M., Y.K.Cho and David L. Olson (1989), The Decentralization of Management Science and the Birth of Selfstarters, *Journal of Operational Research Society*, 40, 4, pp. 323-331.

Levinas, E. (1988), *Totalite et infini: erssai sur l' exteriorité*, Nijhoff, La Haye.

Luhmann, N. (1983), *Struttura della societa e semantica,* Laterza, Roma.

Luhmann, N. (1990a), Meaning as Basic Concept, in *Essays on Self Reference*, Columbia University Press, New York.

Luhmann, N. (1990b), The Individuality of the Individual: Historical Meanings and Contemporary Problems, in *Essays on Self Reference,* Columbia University Press, New York.

Lukacs, G. (1968), *History and Class Consciousness,* The MIT Press, Cambridge, MA.

March, J.G. (1976), The Technology of Foolishness, in March, J.G. and J.P. Olsen (eds.), *Ambiguity and Choice in Organizations*, Universitetsforlaget, Oslo.

Marx, K. (1976), *Capital*, 1, Penguin, Harmondsworth.

Maturana, H. (1987), Everything is Said by an Observer, in Thompson, W.I. (ed.), *Gaia: A Way of Knowing*, Lindisfarne Press, New York.

Maturana, H. and F. Varela (1980), *Autopoiesis and Cognition*, Reindel, Dodrecht.

Merleau Ponty, M. (1992), *Phenomenology of Perception,* Routledge, London.

Miller, S. (1973), Ands, Means, and Galumphing: Some Leitmotifs of Play, *American Anthropologist,* 75, 1, pp. 75-87.

Minsky, M. (1986), *The Society of Mind,* Simon and Schuster, New York.

Oliga, J.C. (1990), Power Ideology Matrix in Social System Control, *Systems Practice*, 3.

Parsons, T. (1970), Some Problems of General Theory in Sociology, in McKinney, J.C. and Tiryakian, E.A. (eds.), *Theoretical Sociology, Perspectives and Developments.* Appleton Century Crofts, New York.

Parsons, T. and G. Platt (1973), *The American University.* Harvard University Press, Cambridge, MA.

Pollert, A. (1988), The Flexible Firm: Fixation Or Fact?, *Work, Employment and Society*, 2, 3, pp. 281-316.

Renard, M. (1969), Le Narcissisme, in *La theorie de psychanalytique,* Presse Université de France, Paris.

Scott, R. (1987), The Adolescence of Institutional Theory, *Administrative Science Quarterly*, 32, pp. 493-511.

Swidler, A. (1986), Culture in Action: Symbols and Strategies, *American Sociological Review*, 51, pp. 273-286.

Ulrich, W. (1983), *Critical Heuristics of Social Planning: A New Approach to Practical Philosophy*, Haupt, Berne.

Varela, F., E. Thompson and E. Rosch (1991), *The Embodied Mind,* The MIT Press, Cambridge MA.

Von Foerster, H. (1979), Cybernetics in Cybernetics, in Krippendorff, K. (ed.), *Communications and Control in Society*, Gondon and Breach, New York.

Weber, M. (1978), *Economy and Society: An Outline of Interpretative Sociology*, University of California Press, Berkeley.

Williams, K.A., J. Williams Cutler and C. Haslam (1987), The End of Mass Production?, *Economy and Society*, 16, pp. 405-439.

Wilkinson, F. (ed.) (1981), *The Dynamics of Labour Market Segmentation*, Academic Press, London.

Zuboff, S. (1988), *In the Age of the Smart Machine*, Basic Books, New York.

Part IV
Constituting Tomorrow's Management

Postmodern Management[1]

Stewart Clegg

Introduction

One hesitates before addressing the "postmodern": is it appropriate to address phenomena which might seem almost alien and certainly exotic, to some, at least, of an audience for a management text? The problems that one faces do not end there. Some who might find the notion of the "postmodern" congenial enough might also find the notion of "management" alien; in addition there is the matter of the "postmodern" seen from the perspective of management. Additionally, one writes in times when the gatekeepers of "management" as a discipline are sounding a retreat from the more theoretically reflexive concerns of some sociologists in favor of fortifying the intellectual keep, hoisting the drawbridge, and rallying, opportunistically, to the flag of pragmatic paradigm consolidation as a political rather than an intellectual end-in-itself (Pfeffer 1993). There ought to be, then, ample opportunity indeed, to offend almost everyone, in such a conjuncture of unlikely bedfellows as management and the postmodern.

Yet, none of these terms are transparently evident. It is not immediately clear what any of them signify. Perhaps an initial definition of some key terms is an appropriate point of departure. I shall begin with the more concrete and then move to the more abstract. Management, conventionally, is concerned with coordination, communication and control of relations between people, technologies, materials, markets and so on. Management is studied from a number of disciplines, rather as the body is approached in the study of medicine. In each case the social sciences are central. Social science refers to the general field in which is situated the study of social reality. By disposition, habit and training sociology is the social science discipline which I draw on most centrally, although not exclusively, in the analysis of organizations and management. Sociology, as I understand it, seeks to provide an explanatory and interpretive understanding of the meaningful qualities of everyday social life, the structures and processes whereby the meaningfulness of a particular reality is socially constructed, transmitted and changed, the ways in which the rules, routines and regularities of the social order are constituted, breached, and understood.

Social science can illuminate many areas of substantive focus when it is applied to management. One issue stands at the core of management: the theoretical understanding of the concept of power and its empirical analysis in organizations, across different social settings (Clegg 1989; Clegg et al. 1992), because management, as "handling, direction, control" necessarily involves relations of power: getting others to do things. The focus on power characterizing this chapter sees the socially constructed practices of management and organization as forms of economic and other action. Like all social practice one is inclined to see management and organizations as constituted in culturally embedded ways (Granovetter 1985). An example may serve to make this clear. Patterns of consumption persist in many advanced industrial societies which are highly culturally specific and have important implications for the structure of management and organizations. In France, for instance, the structure of the bread industry and its organization and management is distinctly different from that of the corporate dominance of an industrial foodstuff industry which is achieved in the UK and elsewhere. The small-scale, essentially local and artisanal mode of production creates not only a unique product – perishable baguettes rather than shrink-wrapped bread – but a very different industry structure to go with it. Rarely have these embedded particularities been addressed adequately by theorists of management and organization.

The Modern and the Postmodern

What of the concerns of postmodernism and the postmodern? Perhaps these are a little too unfamiliar, unsuitable, or even a trifle too "radical" for an audience of a "management" book? Might not an audience with such auspices think sociology dubious at the best of times and in tandem with "postmodernism" sufficiently notorious as to convince themselves witness to the worst of times? In a sign of what is, perhaps, a cussed nature, the gnawing criticism represented by such musing was almost sufficient to confirm me in my chosen course. Yet, I need not have fretted. Any doubts that I might have entertained were soon to be vanquished. Relief was at hand, in the unlikely form of a trade journal. The trade was that of education; the journal was *The Times Higher Education Supplement*.

If one may be forgiven a pun, it was indeed a relief to find that one obtained succor from unequivocally Higher authority. It was in an editorial of January 17, 1992 on "A Postmodern Social Science" in *The Times Higher Education Supplement*. The topic of postmodernism was publicly lauded as the cutting edge of social science. Contributions by Howard Newby, the Chairman of the ESRC – the Economic and Social Research Council, and Anthony Giddens, Professor of Sociology at Cambridge, were the occasion for the editorial imprimatur. Professor Newby argued the well-established case that sees the centrality of social science to our new understanding of intellectual and technological change – precisely because it is able to challenge two central ideas in the dominant natural sciences tradition. The first is that science has its own self-sustaining logic, standing outside particular social and economic contexts. The second is that innovation is largely a linear science-led phenomenon, beginning with the uncovering of basic principles and issuing in their practical (and profitable?, it asks, as an aside) applications. By contrast,

Professor Newby infers… that the intuitive eclecticism typical of the best social science may be better able to make sense of, and so influence, the complexities of innovation, intellectual and other, under modern conditions (*The Times Higher Education Supplement*, January 17, 1992: 12).

The Times Higher Education Supplement attaches an immediate rider, however: perhaps one ought not to be addressing "modern conditions": "maybe postmodern is better."

The reference to the postmodern is prompted by an article by Professor Anthony Giddens in the same issue which

discusses the drift from modernity, a set of ideas, values and institutions firmly anchored by an organizing reason, to postmodernity which implies a dissolution of these scientific and cultural forms. The reflexivity demanded by this transformation may come more easily to the social sciences with their less determinate and more ambiguous knowledge than to the natural sciences more deeply attached to objective, that is context-free, truths, or even the humanities with their instinctive commitment to notions of culture, worth and discrimination (*The Times Higher Education Supplement*, January 17, 1992: 12).

The matter could not be put with more clarity. *The Times Higher Education Supplement* elaborates its characterization of the contemporary social science scene further. Social science, it suggests, is today characterized by "a reflexivity arguably superior to the more restricted scientism… once espoused which takes it beyond the old frontiers of modernity," a reflexivity marked by "a populism, a lack of respect for academic propriety, a celebration of 'enterprise'"(*The Times Higher Education Supplement*, January 17, 1992: 12). A position combining reflexivity and a lack of respect for academic propriety is one that I take to be an admirable point of departure. That it can also claim enterprise is an additional bonus.

In gaining one's bearings, some terms newly central await definition (Giddens 1992: 21). First, there is "modernity," "that cluster of social, economic and political systems brought into being in the West from somewhere around the 18th century onwards." "Postmodernity," by extrapolation thus refers to the incipient or actual dissolution of those social forms. Both modernity and postmodernity should be differentiated from "modernism and postmodernism." Modernism refers to a particular ensemble of

cultural or aesthetic styles, visible in various realms such as architecture, the plastic and visual arts, poetry and literature,… developed in conscious opposition to classicism; it emphasizes experimentation and the aim of finding an inner truth behind surface appearances.

Postmodernism, supposedly, is in some part a recovery of a classical, romantic outlook. It is not a reversion to tradition, because tradition today is just as defunct as is the truth for which modernism strove. Postmodernism is decentred; there is a profusion of style and orientation. Stylistic changes no longer 'build on the past,' or carry on a dialogue with it, but instead are autonomous and transient. Any attempt to penetrate to a 'deeper' reality is abandoned and mimesis loses all meaning (Giddens 1992: 21)

While useful, Giddens' definition only catches part of the issue of "postmodernism." New genre and styles of analysis enable us to analyze familiar phenomena as less familiar. Looked at this way they (are seen as if they were and thus) become a "different" phenomena. Using an unusual and unfamiliar style of analysis can have this effect. Yet, difference comes not just from different ways of seeing familiar phenomena. Instead, a concern with difference may arise from the changing empirical world.

In the world of management and organizations the first alert that something different might be abroad came from the ever-prescient Peter Drucker (1957) as well as from the recent contributions of Bauman (1987, 1988a, 1988b, 1989, 1992) in which he makes the crucial distinction between a "postmodern" analysis and an analysis of "postmodernity." While the former concerns the issue of "style" that Giddens identifies, the latter concerns less the genre of analysis and more the analysis of phenomena in themselves. Bauman suggests that characteristically "modern" aspects of empirical reality are changing increasingly in ways that are discontinuous with the recent, modernist, past. Modern times are being superseded, not just in genre and style of analysis, but also empirically and materially, an analysis which he makes with particular reference to markets and consumption. Empirically we may think of the matter in terms of an epochal periodization in which the premodern slowly dissolves into the modern and the modern slowly dissolves in to the postmodern, each leaving residues and traces in the new history in which it is inscribed. One may think of it in the terms shown in Figure 1.

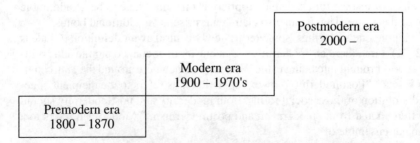

Sources: Peter Drucker (1957, 1992) identifies crucial "points of transition" in historical business climate which Boje and Dennehy (1992) later clarify as above.

Figure 1:   Empirical Modernism and Postmodernism in Management and Organization

The empirical, epochal characterization suggests a first axis for consideration that can be seen in Figure 2.

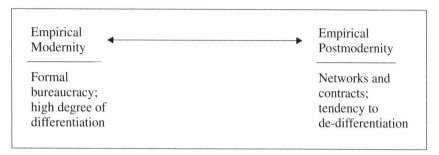

Figure 2:   A First Axis for the Analysis of Empirical Modernity/Postmodernity

The characteristic enterprise of modernity was a bureaucracy, involved in the mass production of a relatively undifferentiated product for a mass market. In the epoch of postmodernity size is no longer everything: small enterprises access large resources through the density of their networks and ties and can compete in small markets: de-differentiated production maps on to market differentiation. The flexibility of the former services the complexity of the latter. The matter may be thought of in terms of a number of contrasts (Table 1).

Table 1:   Thematic discontinuities in premodern, modern and postmodern eras

	Premodern era	Modern era	Postmodern era
Organization principle	Craft	Control	Commitment
Value source	Tradition	Exploitation	Knowledge
Social relations	Custom	Hierarchy	Networks
Management theory	Local and patriarchal	Contingently bureaucratic	Institutionally embedded
Key tendency	Task-continuity through mastery	Task-continuity through differentiation	De-differentiation within complex segmentation
Social mobility	Spatially restricted	Occupationally restricted	Organizationally restricted

To repeat: seen from the epochal, empirical perspective, there is more to the matter than style. There are now different phenomena to be analyzed, phenomena that are not simply a linear progression from the familiar past, but are discontinuous with it. The two aspects are related. Different phenomena require different analytical treatment to see them as such; otherwise, we could easily continue to recognize them for what they are not by applying a modernist frame to a postmodernist reality. For instance, organizations can be seen in terms of variations on a theme of Weberian bureaucracy, one that has sustained the "normal science" of organization analysis from its inception, through the Aston School, to the present day (Donaldson 1986). Of course, with the appropriate framework, we can see (and not see) anything we favor. Yet, in not seeing some things, because the framework we see through does not attend to data that would allow them to be seen, we marginalize some phenomena. For instance, in representing the empirical reality of a sample of 48 organizations in England, a backward corner of the modern world 30 years ago, the Aston School focused on just five of the fifteen characteristics of bureaucracy that its most famous theorist, Weber, had identified some fifty years earlier. When they researched and constructed their framework it was probably the case that factors such as "credentialization" and "disciplinization" were not significant organization processes. After all, British managers today are amongst the least credentialled and trained in the OECD. The situation was no better in the early 1960s. Because these dimensions were not registered then they do not figure now. Yet times change. A framework that represented some aspects of some organizations in England in the 1960s and has subsequently re-represented and replicated these features globally has done sterling service in seeing some things, repeatedly. Yet, the issue must be posed: has what it did not see and could not have seen become more important? Has what was marginalized become increasingly less marginal as times have changed? In answering these questions we must realize that something more is being argued for than that postmodern organization equals organic organization.

Postmodern Organization Does not Equal Organic Organization

It must be apparent that the focus on postmodern organization is not intended to be equivalent to the move from the mechanistic to the organic that has occurred within the major annals of organization theory and design (Daft 1992). While it embraces some of these aspects, the challenge goes much further. Of course, hardly anyone favors the mechanistic these days and we have developed myriad ways of writing and talking about its opposite. Yet a mirror image is always a reverse image. The constitutive basis of the original image remains unchanged. Nonetheless, the organic is a component of what has been termed one possible putative postmodern model. Yet, it is only part. Conventionally, it reflects changes in some aspects of the way in which an essentially modern management has mastered an uncertain environment. The general structure within which this refraction takes place does not change. While changes in contextual variables such as downsizing or the more uncertain nature of the environment might produce a shift from the modern to the postmodern, there are significant examples of putatively postmodern organizations, outside the focus of many modernist theories, which have never made that transition in the first place. Nor have their histories corresponded to other theorized transition paths, such as those prefigured in various economic theories of the firm (argued extensively elsewhere: Clegg 1990). They are different.

Changing times have brought changing locales of knowledge. Thirty years ago most of what we knew about management and organizations derived from North American models, even when application was elsewhere. Increasingly we know more about more places and this does not always fit easily into the old modernist models developed in the USA. To apply these models to phenomena embedded in culturally different institutional frameworks is seriously to risk misunderstanding the specificity of their difference. I have written about this elsewhere concerning the way that the French produce and consume their bread; how the Italian firm Benetton organizes its production and marketing and how, within the East Asian "model" of successfull NICs there is considerable diversity of organization forms (Clegg 1990). One of these, represented as "the Japanese model," has had a peculiar hold over the modernist imagination, particularly in the USA and Europe. It has seemed sufficiently different as to be "postmodern" in at least some of its characteristics, because it represents not only a further variation on a familiar theme but also some innovation. Specific forms of knowledge and practice, developed outside the modernist ascendancy, now challenge it.

The Modern and the Postmodern in Schematic Representation

Much of the descriptive difference between "postmodern" analysis and an analysis of "postmodernity" can be represented in tabular form. Yet, a further caveat must be advanced. Any such use of a four-fold table, of necessity, is crude and schematic. As Harvey (1989: 49) has said of another set of "schematic differences between modernism and postmodernism": it is "dangerous... to depict complex relations as simple polarizations, when most certainly the true state of sensibility, the real 'structure of feeling' in both the modern and the postmodern periods, lies in the manner in which these stylistic oppositions are synthesized." It is dangerous; but it is also necessary in a presentation of unfamiliar ideas with a short space for their dissemination[2].

It is with regard to such cautions and with due diffidence in the face of danger that I wish to make a brief theoretical digression, employing the terms of debate already prefigured in the introduction. Imagine two orthogonal axes defining a theoretically possible surface. Label the outer poles of the first, "modernism" and "postmodernism"; label the outer poles of the other "modernist" and "post-

modernist." Ascribe qualities to each pole. The modernism/postmodernism pole
specifies a realm of empirical practices, one that we have already met in Figure 1,
while the modernity/postmodernity pole specifies a realm of social theory. Social
theory constructs specialized interpretations of social practices, including theorizing. Its representation comprises Figure 3.

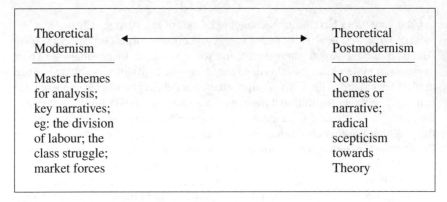

Theoretical   Theoretical
Modernism   ◄──────────────────────►   Postmodernism

Master themes   No master
for analysis;   themes or
key narratives;   narrative;
eg: the division   radical
of labour; the   scepticism
class struggle;   towards
market forces   Theory

Figure 3:   A Second Axis for the Analysis of Theoretical Modernity/Postmodernity

Sociologists of certain analytical persuasions are incorrigible four-fold table
constructionists. The present author is no exception. With two continua that most
customary thing to do is to rotate them orthogonally and create a fourfold table.
This is done in Figure 5.

Modernist theory, the upper left hand quadrant, typically is exemplified by the
construction of unitary, grand theory, characterized by master terms for analysis,
such as the "class struggle," the triumph of "market forces," or the necessity of
"system differentiation." These have been some predominant fictions of recent
times. Postmodernist theory, by contrast, in the space of the lower right hand quadrant, offers distinct, much more plural and contingent fictions, in which recurrent
themes grounded less in the story "intended" by the author and more in intertex-
tual practices of ironic reflexivity and self-referentiality, as the author seeks to
displace the possibilities of being over-written by the narrative codes and conventions that are at work. It celebrates possibilities excluded by modernism, the
sound of "other" voices, of marginalized or repressed phenomena. Difference is
the key concern: the familiar requires rapid de-construction and reinvention. All
belief in the truth value of those apparent realities sustained by conventional interpretation must be questioned. One should celebrate the ambiguities attendant
upon the constant reinvention of what apparently is into what may be.

The relationship between modernist theory and modern practice is straightforward and familiar within the field of management and organization theory.
Relationships between phenomena such as the particular adoption of a "formal

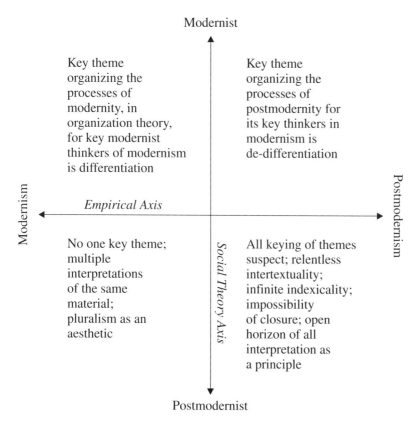

Figure 4:   Four Possibilities for Modern/Postmodern Analysis

organization structure" and the achievement of "economic efficiency" represent themselves in terms of a palpable reality secured and objectively bounded by assumptions that are both unutterably unrealistic and unreflexive. Perhaps this objectivism is both the cost and the benefit of the achievement?

The space of postmodern practice and the theory of postmodernity is different again. Some literary examples may help us find our way. One thinks of the kind of novel that constantly trips up the sense that the reader, using conventional, "natural" narrative devices, may be making of the text. An example might be Italo Calvino's (1981) *If on a Winter's Night a Traveller*. Here there is great doubt about representational practices; about capturing the reality of things in dominant categories of understanding, a suspicion of the essentialism of these categories. Moving from literature to social science one would anticipate that some most cherished and dominant of explanatory categories would be seen merely as the conventional reflexes of intellectual language games, with no authority other than the conventions, however established, of the disciplinary knowledges which produce them. For instance, one might think of some sociologists' "class struggle" and other economists "market forces." Incidentally, each of these explanatory devices, adversarial with each other as they might be, has more in common analytically than their self-understanding would allow. Each seeks to reduce the great diversity of culturally embedded social behavior to determination by an abstracted analytical prime mover owing more to ideology than to empirical realities. The critical task of postmodernity would be perceived as one in which the interpretations generated by these conventions would be interrogated, deconstructed and other, excluded, possibilities of interpretation playfully explored for the sake of difference.

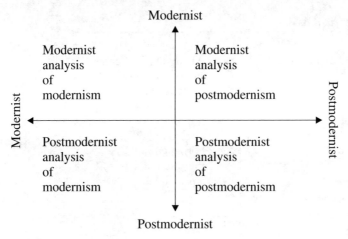

Figure 5:   Modern/Postmodern Analysis: Four Possibilities

It is possible, even in an area seemingly as pragmatic as management and organization theory, to adopt a playful exploration of the polymorphous possibilities afforded by the postmodern canvass, the bottom right hand quadrant. A postmodernist social theoretical understanding of putatively postmodern social phenomena thus would explore possibilities of interpretation for the pure pleasures of their text, in terms of irony, repetition and variation. Another option is that of the lower left hand quadrant, best represented in the work of Gareth Morgan (1986). A resolutely modern phenomena, formal organizations, in a postmodern theoretical gloss, are several things simultaneously, depending upon the metaphors in play. There is no discontinuity to the phenomena: it is just that different ways of seeing constitute it differently. (What the status "it" has in this formulation, other than as an occasion for metaphoricalizing, is unclear in this perspective.) I want to stress that these are not the choices I wish to pursue here. Instead, I wish to remain within the assumptions of modernist theory, locating myself in the upper right hand quadrant.

Within this quadrant, the task is to construct a pattern to postmodern phenomena as they effect management and organization, to construct through synthesis what the great German intellectual Max Weber called an "ideal type." It will be argued that today there are empirical tendencies which are working towards the dissolution of constituent aspects of the experience of modernity. I will seek to register some of these for the intellectual study of management. Thus, what I will present here will be a possible modernist understanding of the postmodern empirical condition, not an example of theoretical postmodernism.

I will propose as a hypothesis that in some significant respects some aspects of the organizational world are changing in such a way that one of the key narrative devices of the modernist imagination, the concept of "differentiation," is no longer an appropriate master-key for analysis. This is significant, for it has been such a master-key in the past. It was the increasing division of labor as the main theme of inquiry which in the past united seminal yet diverse thinkers such as Adam Smith, Karl Marx, Emile Durkheim, Herbert Spencer, Max Weber, Frederick Taylor and Alfred Chandler. All saw differentiation as the central process of modernization. If today, in some respects and contexts these tendencies to differentiation are being thrown into reverse, such that it is possible to conceive of a postmodern rationalization process which is premised on "de-differentiation" rather than differentiation, this does indeed signal a profound dissolution of scientific and cultural forms.

Where does one find this "profound dissolution"? Possible sites of this reversal of differentiation into "de-differentiation" are several and are found in various modalities, ranging from more social democratic tendencies in some European examples to more authoritarian democratic tendencies in Japan (Clegg et al. 1992). It is because Japan is currently the most mythologically potent symbol for this dissolution that I shall focus on it here.

Specter, Image and Model

A specter is haunting Europe. Indeed, were it not for a certain historical resonance used purely for dramatic irony one would want to make the haunting more global. It is not, however, the specter of communism to which one alludes. The specter haunting the future of European capitalism in its recent imagination is Japan, a specter which for some observers serves to make that present seem one whose time is already past. This specter has substantial implications for the construction of social theory as well as the construction of social reality. Nowhere are these implications more evident than in the analysis of organizations, the central mechanisms steering contemporary social evolution.

Once upon a time at least some of the claimants to steering capacity and direction would have navigated with a map of utopia. In those far away times, as

Oscar Wilde once put it, a map of the world which did not contain utopia was worthless. Almost all of these utopias were roadmaps to the soul of an organic, collective, communitarian conception constructed against the privatized world of markets, property and individualism. Today we live in a world whose maps have no need for past utopias imagined in any of the terms recently abolished with the discrediting of state socialism. Like it or not, that effectively means the abolition of utopia in the terms with which we have been most familiar in the western tradition. No matter that to most utopians these terms were distorted in their realization. The end of state socialism marks the ascendancy of a seemingly one-dimensional organizational world in which stark political and ideological contrasts have been over-ruled, in which there appears to be no critical alternative, other than a more extreme version of present realities, a hyper-reality promising more efficient, effective and productive designs of the present. In Eastern Europe at this time such imagining of our mundane reality is now utopia. Today there are few who are prepared to anticipate a utopia more radical than "the market." But of course, the whole rhetoric of the market is singularly and increasingly utopian. World trade increasingly takes place either within or between a relatively small number of very large global corporations, under conditions of central strategic planning. Such modern organizations are the focus of concern for organization researchers.

However spectral the future may be, for the last half-century understanding of these complex organizational structures has been dominated by an imagery of great power and a peculiar provenance. Again, some general examples of this imagery may prove helpful before proceeding to some more specifically organizational and managerial cases. The image has been captured in some of the centuries most significant artistic achievements in the centuries most innovative medium, the cinema, itself a product of modern organization. One thinks, for instance, of Chaplin's *Modern Times*, of Lang's *Metropolis*, or, more recently, of Gilliam's flawed masterpiece, *Brazil*. It is not only cinema, of course. In literature one might think of Kafka's *The Trial* or, more recently, Joseph Heller's *Catch-22*.

The image was captured most graphically for the study of management and organizations by Max Weber's "ideal type" of bureaucracy, the reference point for most significant research in the field. The peculiar provenance of this imagery resides, ultimately, in its roots in the religious vocation and disciplinary innovations designed to further it, stretching at least as far back as the third century after Christ when the Egyptian Pachonius designed not only one of the first monasteries but also a detailed set of monastic rules. These rules and their subsequent elaboration can be regarded as the religious roots of an emergent rationality which, in the West, from the late 18th and early 19th centuries onwards, was increasingly mediated through institutional forms of the state. When Weber sought to synthesize the ideal type of modern rational-legal bureaucracy he used organizational examples of the militaristic discipline of the Prussian state as it forged German unification under Chancellor Bismarck. Bureaucracy was originally an 18th century French

concept which Balzac had found quite natural to use in his novel *Les employées*
but which had, by the mid-19th century, come to appear as singularly German. By
the 20th century it was the German scholar, Max Weber, who was unanimously
regarded as its founding theorist. Interestingly, this example illustrates that until
quite recently the historical flow of organizational innovation was overwhelmingly from the public to the private sector. Times change.

Modern organization theory began life as a big picture, dealing with huge issues and employing a wide canvass in the work of Weber, whose comparative
sweep focused on most of the significant world religions and their civilizations.
In the path of giants those that follow will, perhaps inevitably, be pygmies. It is
noticeable that as organization and management theory became constituted as a
part of the "normal science" establishment in business schools, there was a considerable narrowing of scope from the foundational concerns of Weber's magiste-
rial project. By the 1960s the field had become overwhelmingly "Western," even
"Anglo-American," in its empirical data and correlatively cramped in the breadth
of its theoretical and intellectual vision.

Change was sudden and came with the discovery in the United States of the
"Japanese threat" at the end of the 1970s. Here there appeared to be "difference"
combined with strategic edge. Initially, this difference was seen primarily in cultural terms, giving rise to a whole literature of "excellence" back in the USA as
business academics capitalized on the idea that it was somehow the unique cultural attributes of Japanese organizations which gave them their competitive edge. It
was not a great step to seek out examples of excellence premised on aspects of
US culture, as Peters and Waterman (1982) did in their intellectually dubious but
commercially highly successful *In Search of Excellence*.

In the late 20th century the key organizational image and its spatial location
have shifted significantly from Europe and from bureaucracy. Again, one can use
cultural references to ease understanding. I am inclined to agree with David Harvey (1989), that in cultural terms the contemporary image is captured most evoca-
tively by Ridley Scott in the film *Blade Runner*. *Blade Runner* is set in Los Angeles in the year 2019. The key image lies in the contrast between an urban sphere
of glossy corporate dominance, where high-tech "Magic Mountains" tower over
a decayed social fabric colonized at street-level by seething small-scale production, predominantly Asiatic in cast and complexion. An organizational core is surrounded by a world of sub-contracting under conditions approximating limited
private affluence and extensive public squalor, in J.K. Galbraith's classic image.

It should not be surprising that in a later film Ridley Scott was to re-create this
street scene in contemporary, rather than futuristic terms, this time in Japan, in
his film *Black Rain*. It is not surprising because Japan is increasingly the icon of
postmodern times. In the last decade or so it is to this part of East Asia that images of hyper-reality have deferred, particularly those oriented towards the forms
of organization which are to be found behind the market-place. Often this has been
less a concern with the reality beneath the surface than a further refraction of im-

ages through myriad layers of illusion, illusion represented in terms of cultural difference, even uniqueness. Such analytical terms, which have been sponsored by the Japanese elite as an ideological construct, must be abandoned. Recourse to a unique cultural configuration as the key explanatory variable for understanding Japanese economic efficiency utilizes an "over-socialized" view of economic action as problematic as the opposite "under-socialized" view characteristic of the economics discipline. In their stead one requires a concern with the realities of Japanese organizational practice and its specific institutional formation rather than with myths of cultural uniqueness as an appropriate explanatory device (Clegg 1990).

As a hypothesis one may entertain the idea that Japan represents a form of organization which stands to earlier bureaucratic ideal types as "postmodernist" to "modernist." The ideal type, a one-sided accentuation and condensation of reality hypothesized as a model through which empirical phenomena might be viewed more sharply, with more clarity, has had a distinguished life of service in the fields of management and organizations. By contrast, I propose to construct the type of a postmodern organizational reality. In order to do so one may first retrieve some of the contours of modernist organizations before synthesizing the ideal type of postmodern organizations.

Modernist Organizations

Modernist organizations may be thought of in terms of Max Weber's (1978) typification of bureaucratized, mechanistic structures of control. Weber created a most potent metaphor with the famous "iron-cage" of bureaucracy. Its key processes were signified by a modernizing project composed of fifteen tendencies. Examples included an increase in specialization; hierarchization; stratification; formalization; standardization and centralization of organizational action. Empirically these were subsequently to be erected upon a base of mechanized, rationalized, divided and relatively de-skilled labor. Such labor was the product of innovations created by first-generation management theorists such as F.W. Taylor (1911), in his empirical study, design and de-skilling of manual work. Simultaneously, these innovations produced elements of more creative mental work as another part of the design, roles which were appropriated by the new organizational and social strata of "management" (see Clegg and Dunkerley 1980: chs. 3; 11). These foundations developed from the early 20th century onwards, particularly for mass consumer goods produced in large production runs in the United States.

Fordism added two complementary principles. First, the semi-automatic assembly line, organizing work into a straightforward linear flow of transformations applied to raw materials. Second, workers were fixed to jobs whose positions were rigorously determined by the configuration of the machine system. Individual workers lost control over their own work rhythm, and became fully adjuncts to the machine, repetitively repeating those few elementary movements designated for them as the rationalized sum of their formal organizational existence. The spread of variants of this form was rapid, the reach massive, even into the echelons of hitherto higher status managerial work. In the post-war era office bureaucracies were transformed into white collar factories.

By the 1970s this modernist model had began to run out of steam (Albertsen 1988: 348). A global slow-down in productivity growth in the established core of the world economy, fierce international competition and seemingly permanent inflationary pressures on wages combined to squeeze profits. At the same time, in the core countries the downward rigidity of wages prevented social demand from cumulative collapse. A prolonged "stagflationary" crisis was evident.

Within organizations productivity slowed down because there were fewer new areas left to rationalize. In addition, workers had become more resistant, especially during the prolonged period of post-war full employment. Efficiency gains were being outstripped by increasing costs of surveillance and control associated with the rigid separation of mental and managerial labor. In addition there was a wholesale "internationalization" and associated "de-industrialization" of areas and enterprises which had previously been strongholds of the model's application. Existing center-periphery relations "broke up as mature corporations began to decentralize units of standardized manual production to dispersed localities,... while concentrating managerial and financial functions within large metropolitan areas" (Albertsen 1988: 347).

Organizational responses to this changing state became evident in the 1980s with the appreciation of Japan as a possible source of new, postmodern models of organization. Where modernist organization was rigid postmodern organization is flexible. Where modernist organization was focused on the Strategic Business Unit (SBU) and specific end products' postmodern organization is centered on the management of the work-force "core competencies." Where modernist consumption was premised on mass forms of consumption postmodernist consumption is premised on niches. Where modernist organization was premised on technological determinism postmodernist organization is premised on technological choices made possible through "de-dedicated" microelectronic equipment. Where modernist organization and jobs were highly differentiated, demarcated and de-skilled, postmodernist organization and jobs will be highly de-differentiated, de-demarcated and multi-skilled. Employment relations assume more complex and fragmentary relational forms, such as sub-contracting and networking.

The implications of this for teaching in management are evident. Much of the curriculum may have to be confined to history because so much of it is irrelevant to the changed conditions of postmodern organizations. To the extent that we are prescriptive we will be prescribing yesterday's solutions for tomorrow's world. To that extent we strategically handicap those whom we educate and those who are their employees[3].

Tomorrow's managers and workers will still have to face some of the same problems as did yesterday's. Where they will differ will be in their responses. Their strategic choices are the key to the transition from modern to postmodern organizations. It is by contrasting modern with postmodern responses to perennial problems of organization that the nature of the changes required can be spelt out. Seven organizational imperatives will be used as dimensions to construct one possible ideal type of postmodern organization, using Japanese examples (see Table 2).

Table 2: Dimensions for analysis

1	2	3	4	5	6	7
Structuring strategic skills	Arranging functional alignments	Identifying mechanisms of coordination and control	Constituting accountability and role relationships	Institutionalizing planning and communication	Relating rewards and performance	Achieving effective leadership

Structuring Strategy

Typically, in the conglomerate form of large firms, strategic business units are the individual elements in a diversified business portfolio which often have disparate and unconnected end products. Typically, each unit has to meet centrally fixed "hurdle rates" in terms of their contribution towards profitability. If they do not, they are candidates for axing.

Japanese enterprise groups tend not to adopt the conglomerate model which is common to large firms in Britain. Very little emphasis is placed on merger as a mechanism of growth or diversification of business. In these putatively postmodern organizations boundaries between distinct business units are less important. Organization members are regarded as the repository of "collective learning" in the organization. This enables the coordination of diverse production skills and the integration of multiple streams of technologies that a policy of horizontal or vertical acquisitions hardly allows for, particularly where no substantive rationality other than an accounting logic guides the acquisitions (Prahalad and Hamel 1990: 82).

Postmodern organizations are more likely to share a common technology; harmonizing other flows with this are the "core competencies" of the corporation. If successful these will be difficult for competitors to imitate because they are the result not of accounting conventions applied to plant and product survival but of particular specific organizational cultures. Examples are the way in which competencies such as Sony's expertise in miniaturization or NEC's in digital technology can make a coherent strategy out of what might at first sight appear to be a diverse set of end-products. Complex inter-market relations among firms in an "enterprise group" are used to organize related and ancillary actions which would be subject to internal imperative co-ordination in more typical modern enterprises.

In modern organizations what will be co-ordinated are frequently a range of units with substantively dissimilar economic activities and cultures. Strategic costs of more orthodox modern organization can be identified. A tendency not only to under-investment but also under-utilization of human resources occurs. It is not the organization but the sub-unit within which accounting calculation occurs. This produces a tendency which can be likened to the "residents of an underdeveloped country hiding most of their cash under their mattresses. The benefits of competencies, like the benefits of the money supply, depend on the velocity of their circulation as well as the stock the company holds" (Pralad and Hamal 1990: 87). Human capital can be consciously audited in terms of the core competencies carried and the utilization made of these by senior managers (Prahalad and Hamal 1990: 89-90). The objective is to avoid destructive internal competition premised on skill-hoarding between specific sub-units. Instead, skills circulate, making productive organization-wide use of those people identified as carriers of core competencies. How strangely ironic it is that an executive will devote endless attention to capital budgeting processes but typically will have no comparable mechanisms for allocating human skills and the cultural capital of core competencies that they carry. Indeed, excessive concern with the former can lead to the squandering of the latter, even in organizations such as universities.

Excessive unit-bounded rationalism produces a concomitant inability to foster innovation. To breach this requires a lessening of the degree of specialization of functions and a diminution of unit-specific cultures, premised on factors such as occupational identity and community. Within Japanese enterprises, company socialization, in the guise of firm-specific training, enterprise unionism and tenure of employment for those in the internal labor market, is the norm. In the internal labor market, instead of a commitment to an occupation one finds that, because of permanent employment and seniority payment systems, workers tend to be more committed to their company than to their occupations (Cole and Tominaga 1976). At the center of this de-differentiated specialization of functions and the growth of organizational rather than occupational or business unit commitments are technical aspects of production. Applied technique includes the physical integration of a new piece of equipment into a production process. It also includes the human organization or system that sets equipment to work as well as its subsequent refinement and modification at the hands of the technically-skilled workforce. Integration of research and production through deliberately designed overlapping teams which work in production aids the rapid diffusion of technologies and helps to rejuvenate mature industrial sectors as well as the penetration of emerging areas either through invention, successful imitation or knowledge acquisition (Kenney and Florida 1988: 140).

Running counter to the classic findings of Tom Burns in the 1960s, which helped to found a modern orthodoxy in organization theory (see Burns and Stalker 1962), postmodern organizations are not separated by the mechanistic and the organic, the routine and the uncertain. Complex cross-cutting relations within enterprise groups which blur these boundaries are used to facilitate technological innovation. "Component companies in the corporate family are able to launch joint projects, transfer mutually useful information, and cross-fertilize one another" (Kenney and Florida 1988: 140) using networks which incorporate markets rather than vertical integration internal to one organizational reality. Pulling the various threads of this discussion together we can represent the contrast in tabular form (see Table 3).

Table 3: Structuring strategy in modernist versus postmodernist organizations

	Modern	Postmodern
Strategy	SBUs	Core competencies
Market	Mass	Niche
Technology	More deterministic	More choice
Work design	Highly differentiated, demarcated, de-skilled	Less differentiated, less demarcated, more multi-skilled
Employment relations	Employment contract	Sub-contracts, networking, joint ventures

Arranging Functional Alignments

In modern bureaucracies relationships typically have been settled by hierarchy. By contrast, many of these hierarchical relationships can be achieved through complex sub-contract arrangements and the extensive use of quasi-democratic work teams, using horizontal relationships to substitute for hierarchical functional arrangements. Vertical integration of component suppliers, in order to minimize transaction cost is replaced by a "just-in-time" (JIT) system where complex market relations with component sub-contractors are used to ensure that supplies arrive on the premises where they are needed. Large inventory stocks are dispensed with and the circulation of capital in "dead" buffer stock minimized. In Japan there

are large JIT production complexes spatially organized so that subsidiary companies, suppliers and sub-contractors are in contiguous relationships with each other,
extending through to tertiary sub-contracting relations.

A number of distinct advantages flow from the JIT system. One is that it displaces wage costs out of the more expensive core of workers to the cheaper periphery; another is that it leads to stable long-term relations with suppliers which
opens up multidirectional flows of information between the partners in the sub-
contracting network. Personnel as well as ideas are freely exchanged. Innovations
can be accelerated through the system (Kenney and Florida 1988: 137). This acceleration is facilitated by self-managing teams, within an overall structure of hierarchy, rather than by workers striving against each other under an individualistic and competitive payment and production system. The functional alignment
of activities is achieved by extensive use of the market principle through sub-
contracting. Within the self-managing teams work roles overlap and the task structure is continuous, rather than discontinuous. Workers allocate the tasks internally
(see Schonberger 1982). Production is not accelerated by redesigning work down-
wards in its skill content, by simplifying it further and separating the workers more
one from the other, as in the classical modernist organization. Tasks appear to be
designed to facilitate collective work. Japanese workers often move with the production line and work groups perform routine quality control, allowing quality
control departments to focus on non-routine aspects, such as advanced statistical
measurement or even work redesign.

Quality circles which include both operatives and staff specialists such as engineers not only reduce wastage but also serve to further technological and process improvements, substituting for quality surveillance as a separate management function. Hence, neither quality control nor maintenance are "externalized."
Much of the routine preventative maintenance is done by the operatives who use
the machines (Kenney and Florida 1988: 132). The greater flexibility of workers
extends to the technological design of work itself. Production lines in Japanese
enterprises are organized to be more flexible than a simple linear track. They can
be reconfigured easily between different product lines and do not conform necessarily to the linear layout. Multi-skilling is essential for this degree of flexibility.
Once more the discussion can be summarized in tabular form (see Table 4).

Mechanisms of Coordination and Control

About a third of Japanese organizations give their employees "spiritual training,"
akin to techniques of religious conversion, therapy and initiation rites. These emphasize social cooperation, responsibility, reality-acceptance and perseverance in
tasks. Such techniques apply particularly to members of the internal labor market, incorporated by the benefits they receive as well as the sanctions that quit-

Table 4:   Functional alignments in modernist versus postmodernist organizations

	Modern	Postmodern
Social relations	Hierarchy and imperative coordination	Contract and quasi-democracy
Social integration	Tendency to more vertical and authoritative controls	Tendency to more lateral and symbolic controls: e.g. JIT & Kanban
Quality control	Managerial surveillance	Self- & team-surveillance
Skill formation	De-skilling	Multi-skilling

ting would produce. Anyone who wanted to leave would be seen as untrustworthy by other employees and hence unemployable. It is a system which works well in securing loyal commitment by virtue of low turnover and dissent in the highly competitive core. Core labor market skill-formation is enhanced, compared to situations of much greater reliance on the external labor market as the source of recruitment.

The benefits of internal labor market skill-formation are not spread throughout the industrial system. Only about one third of the workforce in Japan is contained within the internal labor market. More than two thirds are not and these are workers who are domestic outworkers, peasants drawn from the politically and economically protected rural sector as seasonal workers, or who are involved in extended sub-contracting. This majority secure none of the benefits of the core workers yet it is upon their "flexibility" that the system rests. It is disproportionately women who are excluded. To the extent to which they are included they tend to be marginalized and their relative status and income decline markedly with age compared to men, at the steepest rate of disparity in the OECD.

In the core, empowerment on the shop floor appears to be relatively widespread, achieved through mechanisms like extensive firm-specific basic training, learning and involvement in work teams with more experienced workers. Job rotation also facilitates this learning. Such rotation takes place not only within the work teams but also more widely in the enterprise, a key component in the construction of the knowledge-base for core competencies.

The kanban system, used to coordinate work between different work teams, is used. Instead of top-down coordination of the work-flow in the form of superordinate commands and surveillance, the kanban system allows for communication flows which coordinate horizontally rather than vertically. Work units use work cards (kanbans) to order supplies, to deliver processed materials and to synchronize production activities. Communication is through the cards, laterally rather than vertically, reducing planning and supervision, creating empowerment as workers manage themselves. Increasingly, the process is becoming one of an "electric kanban," as giant video screens suspended above the shop-floor retail instantaneous information on the movement of jobs around the workshop. Nonetheless, although employees in this design are self-managers they are as visible and as likely to internalize the imperatives of control as any who were workers, prisoners, impoverished or patients trapped within the 19th century Benthamite Panopticon. Some things stay the same.

Empowerment through widespread use of communication of information has been seen to be a key feature of the ringi decision-making system, where printed documents circulate widely through the enterprise for comment and discussion. Consequently, when decisions are made after this exposure, then invariably snags and sources of opposition will have been "cooled-out," often in ways which are organizationally quite productive. Much the same can be said of the widespread use of "suggestion schemes," which although not compulsory, are so widespread that employees feel obliged to participate in them. At Toyota workers who chose not to were punished through criticism and smaller bonuses! (Kamata 1970: 82; his data is from the early 1970s however.)

Relative flexibility and empowerment extend throughout the organization structure. There is a wide use of management "generalists." Managers will not usually be specialists in accounting or finance, for instance. Management rotation creates a similar flexibility to that experienced on the shop-floor, blurring distinctions between departments, between line and staff managers, and between management and workers. Organizations will always leave some management slots vacant. Nominal subordinates may discharge managerial tasks. Job titles are thus denotive of seniority not function. Because of rotation and the fact that promotion of a subordinate is not threatening to the status of a superordinate, internal managerial competition is reduced. Managers tend to cross boundaries and share knowledge. They do so far more in the normal course of work where the quite rational anxieties induced by explicitly "face-threatening" systems are less present. De-differentiation, once more, is the key.

Power "around" modern organization concerns the way in which enterprises are inter-connected between their strategic apices. In the West this takes place primarily through the mechanisms of "interlocking directorships" and the share market. In these capital market based systems long term horizontal linkages, other than of cross-ownership or predatory behavior are rare. By contrast, Japanese enterprises operate under relatively stable capital market conditions compared to the highly volatile share-transactions of bundles of "ownership" which characterize British stock exchanges. Surprisingly, perhaps, to advocates of "free" markets this does not result in a lack of dynamism or a neglect of issues of coordination and control at the strategic apices of industry. In fact, it is the facility to achieve high degrees of such coordination and control in its complex inter-market organization and state facilitated integration which many commentators have seen as the strategic edge of Japanese capitalism.

The role of MITI, the Ministry of International Trade and Industry, has been
of particular importance in vertically coordinating enterprises in the achievement
of longer-term, macro-economic, industry-wide planning in Japan (Dore 1986).
Much of the market uncertainty which has to be organizationally buffered in the
West is displaced outside the organization. The system of financial ownership
does not generate as much risk in the first place while the state handles much
which does occur. Consequently there is no necessity for organizations to devise
strategies for unlikely occurrences: resources can be better invested in core activities.

Public policy enters into this general picture. The most urgent need will invariably be for sources of long-term credit to finance major new investments, to maintain debt-to-equity ratios consistent with minimal capital costs, and to cushion the
inevitable destruction of capital that flows from basic innovations in organizational practice. Financial assistance may be required to meet the "front end" costs of
marketing and establishing distribution and service networks, as well as policies
to protect the domestic market from other governments' predatory trade strategies. Industrial relations systems that do not put arbitrary limits on technological
innovation and the upgrading of work practices will also be required. Technical
inputs of equipment and components, as well as the maintenance of markets, will
depend upon insertion into a diversified manufacturing sector in which public policy plays a coherent role in establishing and maintaining linkages.

Despite frequent classically economic liberal claims that government should
not be in the business of picking winners, the institutional arrangements for
achieving this do seem to work smoothly enough in some countries. The issue
is whether or not there should be a strong framework and organizational commitment to instruments of public policy or whether or not there is a belief that such
interventions are illegitimate and best left to the movements of market forces. The
role that the state takes in developing industry policy with respect to new and declining branches of industry must operate to prevent the decline of national capitalism, with its employment and related quality of life issues, which might otherwise occur.

The discussion of this section is summarized in tabular form in Table 5.

Constituting Accountability and Role Relationships

Management involves accountability for role-related actions. The division of
labor of these may be more or less complex and individuated. In postmodern organizations both the level of complexity and the degree of individuation
of labor are less than is typically the case in a classical Weberian bureaucracy. De-differentiation appears to be operative. Skill formation is more intra-
organizationally than individually achieved. Further supporting this sense of

Table 5: Mechanisms of coordination and control in modernist versus postmodernist organizations

	Modern	Postmodern
Workforce commitment	Typically low, typically cash-nexus	Typically higher in internal labor market; typically symbolic
Labor market structure	Tendencies to dualism	Tendencies to more complex segmentation
Empowerment	Lower	Higher, through ringi system
Communication	Vertical, imperative	Horizontal, Kanban
Management	Specialist	Generalist, rotation
Role of the state	Low level of industry policy	High level of industry policy

group accountability and relationships is a reward system more oriented to team than individual work. All this is only possible where multi-and flexible-skilling is the norm, rather than restrictive, skill defensiveness. Where there is a high degree of skill division then more formalized and externalized coordination and control, in terms of the accountability of individuals, will be required (see Table 6).

Table 6: Accountability and role relationships in modernist versus postmodernist organizations

	Modern	Postmodern
Division of labor	Typically higher differentiation; tendency to further differentiation	Typically lower differentiation; tendency to de-differentiation
Countervailing powers	Independent and pluralistic; trade unions and professional associations	More dependent and less pluralistic; organizational rather than occupational communities
Domination of the individual's life-world	Lower; more plural life-worlds outside work	Higher; greater symbolic domination of work over civil society

Institutionalizing Planning and Communication

Where one is involved in imperatively coordinating only a fairly specific range
of business-related activity, leaving the broader picture to inter-market relations
and to state planning, one is involved in a more restricted and less audacious exercise than would be the case in trying to plan twenty or thirty unrelated units of the
typical conglomerate. Expensive mistakes, resulting from uncoordinated manufacturing strategies and managerial distraction, can occur even in the cases of integration and diversification motivated solely by manufacturing considerations.
They occur much more frequently in the case of mergers and takeovers that represent a second-best to internal expansion, and the situation is much worse in the
usual case where businesses are acquired with no manufacturing rationale at all,
as in most conglomerates.

In the case of Japan long term planning based on market research has been vital
in those areas where innovation, and not just importation, of technology have occurred, such as the consumer electronics industry. Government has played a major
role in supplying information and technological forecasts, through the importance
of MITI to national industrial policy. Japanese firms have an institutional freedom
to plan long-term as well as to emphasize quality-control in the actual production
process, related to the flexibility of the specialist core work force, which can easily
develop new activities from carefully nourished core competencies. While planning and communication can take place through abstract techniques of management control it is by no means clear that these techniques substitute adequately
for more substantively based judgments (see Table 7).

Table 7: Planning and communication in modernist versus postmodernist organizations

	Modern	Postmodern
Rationality	More formal, technical rationality	More substantive, grounded rationality
Planning	Shorter-term; finance based	Longer-term planning; substantively based

Relating Rewards and Performance

Performance and reward imperatives may be more or less related. Now, this can
be achieved in one or other of two contrasting ways. It may be achieved through
complex processes of individualization in effort-related bonus systems which of-

ten give rise to jealousy and rivalry. Alternatively, it may be done through linking rewards not to individual efforts but to organizational success and service. Of
course, this can only operate effectively where exit into an external labor market is
not an easy option. It is the latter strategy which has characterized Japanese management systems. The payment system has been oriented primarily to improving
overall organization performance, by tightly coupling length of service to frequent
promotion up a ladder of many small gradations. The seniority based nature of the
wages system in Japan, the nenko system, has been the major focus of much discussion of the relation between rewards and performance. Nenko seido, the combination of lifetime employment and seniority-based wages systems, applies only
to the core employees, who will be almost entirely males. The ease of dismissal,
low wage and fringe benefit costs, and the frequent part-time provision of female
labor are important in buffering and stabilizing the stable employment situation of
core workers. The basis of flexibility is disproportionately shouldered by female
patterns of labor force participation.

Wages in Japan are not simply based on age alone. Indeed, age through the
nenko system seems to be surviving in larger firms while it is being eroded in
the smaller ones. Performance elements enter into the wages equation. However,
they do so in a distinctive way. Bonuses are related to overall group or organizational performance. In practice there are two guide-lines or rules at work relating
rewards and performance in Japan. First, a single individual is never rewarded
alone, but the reward is distributed as equally as possible within the work group.
Secondly, the reward system has an expressive dimension, in addition to its instrumental qualities. Group rewards of a symbolic kind, like a group photograph or
company shield with the groups name on it, are important devices used to build up
the sense of practical and ideological community. How effective these are remains
open to question. Despite the popular image of Japanese employees as happy and
harmonious group workers the reality seems to be that they are not. Numerous international work attitude surveys indicate low levels of job satisfaction amongst
the Japanese, consistently below OECD averages. (The argument is summarized
in Table 8)

Table 8:   Rewards and performance in modernist versus postmodernist organizations

	Modern	Postmodern
Relation of rewards and performance	Individualization of effort-related bonus-system	Collectivization of organizational success and service
Types of reward	Primarily monetary and instrumental	Monetary made symbolic through extended seniority and job-ladder systems

Achieving Effective Leadership

Leadership is usually defined in terms which relate a "vision" of the future to some "strategies" for achieving it, which are capable of co-opting support, compliance and team work in its achievement, and which serves to motivate and sustain commitment to its purpose. In Japan, effective neutralization of countervailing sources of leadership from professional bodies and trades unions is an important component, as is the considerable attention paid to ensuring that leadership initiatives have broad-based support before they are adopted, through the mechanisms of the ringi decision-making structure, and the extensive use of generalist managerial job-rotation. These "organic" qualities are clearly important in allowing the adoption of systems of management which, in the absence of less effective leadership in gaining commitment, would hardly be viable, and allowing their extension into parts of the organization which would otherwise be more "mechanistic." Holding very little in the way of stocks and inventory and relying on components suppliers to supply these "just-in-time" for use in production cannot operate where supply is liable to frequent bottle-necks, disruption or downright "guileful" dispositions of key workers to milk positions of strategic contingency for what they are worth. The achievement of a situation where this is not the case, in leadership terms, is clearly related to the whole institutional fabric of the enterprise, in terms of phenomena such as the labor market structure and system of rewards. An even briefer summary than this text may be found in Table 9.

Table 9:   Effective leadership in modernist versus postmodernist organizations

	Modern	Postmodern
Leadership	Plural, competitive and top-down; mechanistically and imperatively coordinated from a center	Less plural, less competitive and more collective; organically coordinated through networks rather more than structures
Sources of countervailing tensions	Located in plural unions; and plural knowledge-commitments to strongly framed disciplinary professional knowledges	Located in complex systems of sub-contracting and outwork in the external labor-market

Organization Imperatives and their Representation

The imperatives of organization have been discussed in terms of a number of dimensions. These are represented in Table 9. Here, it may be seen, we have the ingredients for systematic empirical investigation, work that is still in its infancy (Orssatto 1994). What is worth remarking is the chief virtue of the Table proposed: it proposes a set of catories, empirically grounded, analytically coherent and empirically suggestive, with which the challenge of the new forms of organization and management may be analyzed in their own terms, not merely as the expression of an older, and timeless, essence. Think of these as a series of continua. Analytically, they make props for the imagination: the distinctions in the individual figures can generate items for the collection of data. The data collected would be organization data: using this data one should locate specific organizations comparatively in terms of more precise descriptors of their degree of postmodernness: postmodernness is thus a variable – organizations may have moved in this direction to a greater or lesser extent, on any of a number of dimensions.

For the future research needs to address the extent to which these dimensions of organization imperatives do form coherent patterns; the extent to which the coherent patterns form national clusters, and the extent to which they relate to more common criteria of organizational analysis. If the analysis is correct, then through asking these sorts of questions it ought to be possible to begin to address systematically some of the sources of organizational diversity which both modernity and postmodernity present to us.

If Japan represents one path towards postmodernity, it is clear that there have been winners and losers in this development. To recap, the winners have been men who were in internal labor markets in the big name companies and the enterprise group networks. The losers have been women and those more than two thirds of all workers who are outside the core labor market. With respect to women, the loss derives not from just a low level of labor force participation, but the nature of employment practices. Extended service is a key factor in remuneration. It is because there are very few women who have extended lengths of continuous employment with a single employer, that male-female wage differentials become so large in middle-age. It is the nature of the workforce participation which varies, with women's work being largely unskilled because they are not employed in the core enterprises and internal labor market, where continuous training and re-skilling is provided to permanent employees.

Overall, in comparative terms the labor market is relatively highly segmented, with comparatively less rights for labor and a more arduous regime of work than in many more social democratic OECD states. Longer hours and shorter recreation are the norm, with the annual average working hours of a Japanese worker amounting to more than 2,100 hours: by contrast, in Britain and the USA the average is 1,800-1,900, with about 1,650 the norm in Germany. Within the labor market core wages are relatively high, compared internationally – but so are the

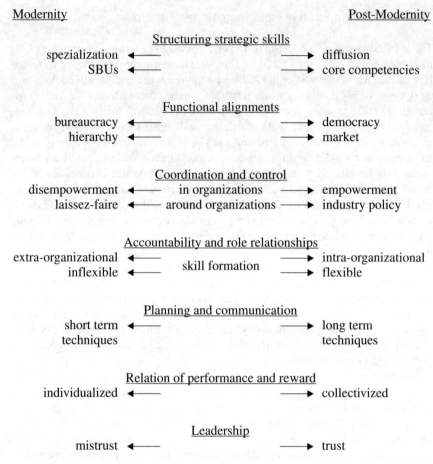

Figure 6: Dimensions of Modernity and Postmodernity

costs of basic consumer goods and services, with housing, in particular, being in-ordinately expensive per square meter, compared with OECD averages. Typical-ly, each person occupies far fewer square metres than would be the norm in most other OECD states. This is related to the political settlement of post-war Japan, premised on policies of agricultural protection which minimize land-use shifts from rural to urban utilization.

Of course, outside Japan, elsewhere in the world, there may also turn out to be losers on a wider scale, those trapped and organizationally outflanked in modernist organization forms as the leading edge turns ever more postmodern, and competi-tive advantage attaches to these new forms of design. The task for the future must be the minimization of this outflanking in order to maximize future possibilities for all citizens, for it is only through the development of world-class organizations that a country can and will flourish.

Conclusion

It might be thought that the argument of this chapter is in some respects a pan-egyric in praise of Japan as the postmodern future. I would not want to leave you with that impression. On the contrary, there are other possible, more social-democratic and inclusive choices in the construction of postmodern organization-al futures which would enhance rather than restrict organizational and economic citizenship (Clegg 1990; Clegg et al. 1992). For the future, if the Japanese mod-el remains influential, organizational postmodernity appears likely to be one in which an enclave of privileged workers will be formed on highly exclusivist prin-ciples of social identity, such as gender, ethnicity and age, characteristics which are tightly coupled to the processes of skill formation. Competitive edge is se-cured through the greater utilization of at least some of the most precious resource that any organization can ever have: its members. Not all member resources are tapped, however. There remain the excluded majority, disproportionately women, who are not in the core corporations, not in the core labor markets, do not have core competencies. Must they be left to the margins?

These postmodern conditions might easily become generalized, particularly in economies and societies already marked by wide disparities in wealth and high-ly stratified life-chances. One might anticipate that privileged individuals would easily be seduced by the organizational benefits on offer in this version of the post-modern package. It would not be too hard for such privileged individuals to be relatively indifferent to the majority. Indeed, they would be fortunate that they too were not condemned to the margins of postmodernity. On these margins ev-eryday life would be hard-pressed, compared to the enclave of privilege. Indeed, not only the returns from work but also the conditions of its pursuit would be an everyday struggle against the dark side of that dialectic which illuminates privi-lege as it blights indifference. Postmodernity would be a series of privileged en-claves stockaded within the bleak vistas of modernity – the *Blade Runner* sce-nario. Working within privileged and exclusive labor market segments, residing within a set of exclusive life-style options, briefly transgressing the boundaries which demarcate the sacred from the profane when commuting to the new citadels in the city within whose postmodern architectural style are cocooned these post-modern organizations: is that life in the postmodern age for the fortunate few whom "market forces" favor? Highly differentiated rights in work would be the basis of possibilities for participation in citizenship more generally, as one bought or was excluded from the options available, rather than being universalistically in-corporated in some way. It is unlikely that those within the arena of privilege will be obliged to listen to the excluded for as long as any dissenting voices remain organizationally outflanked, outside the stockade, occasionally rebellious perhaps, but containable and marginizable. The very existence of fierce competition for admittance to enclaves of privilege, together with appropriate policies of containment for those who neither resign nor compete but who seek to change the rules of the game, should suffice to secure this outflanking. Postmodern organizations may well function rather more to define, confine and confirm social limits cemented within the modernist project, rather than to transcend them.

For the future the applicability of the postmodern project remains an open question. The older, modernist type of organization model may be said to have sustained much of "normal" social science inquiry into management in the past. We have yet to chart the organizational correlates, environmental contingencies and institutional translatability attendant upon this postmodern way of re-making the world. For the future, one suggests, it is organizational postmodernism which will increasingly be on the agenda for teaching, research and practice.

Notes

[1] This chapter began life as an inaugural address to the University of St. Andrews.

[2] This dangerous technique will be used extensively in what follows, not in order to freeze or reify categories, but in order to aid understanding. Of course, if these insecure and equivocal categories are taken too literally, particularly for adherents of stylistic postmodernism, the bottom right hand quadrant in the four-fold tabular representations, they will seem nothing so much as a 'flattening out' and 'steam-rolling' of postmodern ideas. Yet, as I will argue subsequently, this is to decide, a priori, that only one version of the postmodern enterprise – that which has hitherto been termed the stylistic one – is the valid one.

[3] Incidentally, it is for this reason, if no other, that one is, and others should be, opposed to centralized initiatives that prescribe curriculum content. The risks are that the pattern prescribed will be inappropriate; in any case, to drive out the difference and serendipity which can attach to the plural production of knowledge by independent practitioners in a market-place of ideas in favor of a "charter" is to recall the management practices of pre-modernity, of Tudor times, rather than to look forward to postmodernity.

References

Albertsen, N. (1988), Postmodernism, Post-Fordism, and Critical Social Theory, *Environment and Planning D: Society and Space*, 6: 339-366.
Baumann, Z. (1987), *Legislators and Interpreters*. Cambridge: Polity Press.
Baumann, Z. (1988a), Viewpoint: Sociology and Postmodernity, *Sociological Review*, 36(4): 790-813.
Baumann, Z. (1988b), Is there a Postmodern Sociology?, *Theory, Culture and Society*, 5: 217-237.

Baumann, Z. (1989), Sociological Responses to Postmodernity, *Thesis Eleven,* 23: 35-63.

Baumann, Z. (1992), *Intimations of Postmodernity.* London: Routledge.

Boje, D. and R. Dennehey (1993), *Managing in the Postmodern World: America's Revolution Against Exploitation*, Dubuque, Iowa: Kendall Hunt Publishers.

Burns, T. and G.M. Stalker (1962), *The Management of Innovation.* London: Tavistock.

Calvino, I. (1981), *If on a Winter's Night a Traveller.* London: Picador.

Clegg, S.R. (1989), *Frameworks of Power.* London: Sage.

Clegg, S.R. (1990), *Modern Organizations: Organization Studies in the Postmodern World.* London: Sage.

Clegg, S.R. and D. Dunkerley (1980), *Organization, Class and Control.* London: Routledge and Kegan Paul.

Clegg, S.R. and S.G. Redding (eds.) (1992), *Capitalism in Contrasting Cultures.* Berlin, New York: de Gruyter.

Clegg S.R., W. Higgins and T. Spybey (1992), Post-Confucianism, Social Democracy and Economic Culture, in Clegg and Redding (1992), pp. 18-46

Cole, R.E. and K. Tominga (1976), Japan's Changing Occupational Structure and its Significance, in H. Patrick (ed.), *Japanese Industrialization and its Social Consequences.* Berkeley, Cal.: University of California Press, pp. 53-95.

Daft, R.L. (1992), *Organization Theory and Design.* St. Paul: West.

Dore, R. (1986), *Flexible Rigidities.* Stanford, Cal.: Stanford University Press.

Drucker, P. (1957), Introduction: This Post-Modern World, in P. Drucker, *Landmarks of Tomorrow.* New York: Harper.

Drucker, P. (1992), *Managing for the Future,* Oxford: Butterworth.

Giddens, A. (1992), Uprooted Signposts at Century's End, *The Times Higher Education Supplement*, January 17, pp. 21-22.

Granovetter, M. (1985), Economic Action and Social Structure: The Problem of Embeddedness, *American Journal of Sociology*, 91, pp. 481-510

Harvey, D. (1989), *The Condition of Postmodernity.* Oxford: Blackwell.

Kamata, S. (1982), *Japan in the Passing Lane.* New York: Pantheon.

Kenney, M. and R. Florida (1988), Beyond Mass Production: Production and the Labor Process in Japan, *Politics and Society,* 16(1), pp. 121-58.

Mintzberg, H. (1983), *Power in and Around Organizations.* Englewood Cliffs, NJ: Prentice-Hall.

Morgan, G. (1986), *Images of Organizations.* Beverly Hills: Sage.

Orssatto, R. (1994), A Influência dos Modos de Rascionalidadae na Estruturação das Inústrias Calçadistas de Novo Hamburgo/RS, paper presented at ANPAD, Curitiba, Brasil.

Peters T.J. and R.H. Waterman Jr. (1982), *In Search of Excellence.* New York: Harper and Row.

Pfeffer, J. (1993), Barriers to the Advance of Organizational Science: Paradigm Development as a Dependent Variable, *Academy of Management Review,* 18(4), pp. 599-620.

Prahalad, G. and G. Hamal (1990), The Core Competence of the Corporation, *Harvard Business Review,* (90), pp. 379-391.

Schonberger, R.J. (1982), *Japanese Manufacturing Techniques.* New York: Free Press.

Taylor F.W. (1911), *Principles of Scientific Management.* New York: Harper and Row.

Weber, M. (1978), *Economy and Society: An Outline of Interpretative Sociology* (2 vols.), Berkeley, Cal.: University of California Press.

Managing as if Tomorrow Matters: Embryonic Industries and Management in the Twenty First Century[1]

Stewart Clegg, Larry Dwyer, John Gray, Sharon Kemp, Jane Marceau

What is Embryonic Industry?

Embryonic industry is new and emerging. Its novelty lies in the application of distinctive practices to production, service or problem resolution in ways that are discontinuous with existing technologies, values and knowledge. The root metaphor is that of an "embryo." If there is not something that is new and discontinuous then there would be no new conception, nothing in embryo. At the core are innovation in products and processes. Innovation is not just technical; it is also organizational and managerial. Effective innovation harnesses technical innovation in products and processes to social systems that can manage, organize and deliver them to markets effectively (Eriksson 1990).

Examples of embryonic industry that are technology-driven would be, for instance, the development of laser devices, systems and techniques and their application in various fields. While this is a "new" technology its applications need not be novel for an industry to be embryonic. Existing technologies may be addressed to novel problems.

Embryonic industry is important for any country because it contributes to employment, has a multiplier effect, opens new markets, is a major source of "emerging exporters" and in general, creates wealth. AMRAD, a case that we will review briefly, is an exemplar of the wealth-creation and export opportunities that successful management of an embryonic industry can provide. Melbourne based AMRAD is an unusual company in that, as well as running a successful drug distribution business that turns over $45 million a year, it acts as a commercialization agency for ten medical research institutes spread around Australia. A contract basis frames most its research. External agencies conduct the research. AMRAD emerged out of public policy initiatives in Victoria in the late 1980s. AMRAD pays participating institutes to research new drugs to the commercialisation stage. Once it has a finished product on the market it also pays a royalty stream to the creator. Its product development lines at the present include an agent to speed up the production of blood clotting cells, a vaccine against the Rotavirus that causes life-threatening diarrhoea in babies, a new treatment for glaucoma and a drug to assist the treatment of bladder cancer.

Traditionally Australia had a fairly insubstantial pharmaceutical industry due to the tremendous investment requirement in capital and equipment and so much of the entrepreneurial and business skills needed for success in the world pharmaceutical market remained overseas. AMRAD, as a commercialization agency, accelerated the national "catch-up" process. The wealth creation opportunities are considerable. In 1995 AMRAD was involved in a $200 million listing in on the market. By this time it will have a core share register of serious long-term investors, including the Commonwealth Bank's fund management arm, the AMP Perpetual trustees, the NRMA Funds Management, the NAB Funds Management, QBE Insurance and Mercantile Mutual, as well as overseas institutional investors and a major Japanese drug company, Chugai Pharmaceuticals.

AMRAD demonstrates a number of key points. First, there is the important role that public policies played. Second, there is spectacular growth potential to be realized in a successful transition to an embryonic industry. Third, there is the example of Australia creating an embryonic industry where previously the niche had been colonized principally by overseas firms. Fourth, the management of embryonic industry will entail new forms of management strategy.

Innovation and Embryonic Industry

Embryonic industry is premised on innovation. The literature of innovation concentrates upon questions of technological innovation and emphasises radical transformations of product technology. While new technologies imply what is probably the greatest potential source of embryonic industry, they are not the only source. In practice, we found, the focus on embryonic industry requires a broader focus than on technology per se.

The crucial focus is on technological competence. Three aspects define this competence (Gattiker and Willoughby 1993). First, there are the cluster of "learning-related" aspects. The second aspect of technological competence concerns the cultural embeddedness of this competence in organizations and countries by individuals and groups. The priority given to cultural sources of innovation reflects this aspect. The third aspect of technological competence refers to the degree of scarcity of the allocation of the compatence in a particular locale. Much of our focus, particularly on how to cultivate embryonic industry through chains, clusters, networks and strategic alliances, address this issues of relative scarcity and how to overcome it.

For any organization to survive it must have some distinctive competence (Selznick 1957), those things that it does especially well when compared with its competitors in a similar environment. Within any organization two particular kinds of competence are particularly important: technological competence and cultural competence. Cultural competency refers to the ability to be able to harness and use culturally diverse myths, symbols, rituals, norms and ideational systems creatively to add value to an organizations activities. Technological competence may be defined, following Gattiker and Willoughby (1993: 463) as the ability "to receive and use information for solving terchnology and economic related problems and opportunities for making appropriate decisions."

Technological competence, and technology driven views of innovation, were at the core of the bulk of the research literature that we consulted, perhaps because the focus was on specific forms of innovation that were defined by their underlying technologies (e.g. Willoughby 1990; 1992). Yet, not all innovation is technology driven.

The relationship between market intelligence and innovation is central to the emergence of successful embryonic industry. Markets are as important as innovation. New markets open not only because of novel technologies; shifts in values and culture also are potent sources of innovation. Herein is a chief emphasis.

Embryonic Industry Can Be Culturally Driven

The diversity of cultures in a nation offers major sources of value for its enterprises. First, it does so by virtue of the introduction of cultural novelty. Food is the most evident case in point. Socially, innovation comes from cultural diversity just as it comes from a diverse gene pool biologically. The emergence of a "Mediterrasian" cuisine that is distinctively Australian as a source of culinary excellence has only been possible because of the culturally diverse ethnic traditions represented there. Innovative chefs can draw on the diverse traditions that the application of their skill and their biographies have exposed them to. From the cultural overlays come innovations. Shifts in values that derive from culture create new market opportunities. It is market intelligence that identifies these as opportunities. Innovators respond to these opportunities and, if successful, seed an embryonic industry.

A second major source of value for Australian industry comes from the diversity of the personnel who comprise it. In selling overseas, whatever the product, whether traditional or innovative, Australian enterprises have a remarkable opportunity to do good business through the serendipity of multiculturalism. Australians who are also competent speakers of a customer's language, because they already know the language as their community language, have a head start in doing good business in that culture. This is because they already have much of the tacit knowledge and implicit learning that those who are alien can acquire only slowly and painfully. In general, a great deal of learning occurs through making mistakes. In business this can be costly. Multiculturalism presents the possibility of much lower-cost learning. However, diversity requires good management for innovation. Australian enterprises have to learn what a valuable resource their multicultural habitat can be. They must use it and know how to manage it well. Specific recommendations that follow address the issue of diversity.

There is a third important attribute of culture in relation to embryonic industries. Recent studies assess and compare cultural attitudes towards technology. Such attitudes mediate the effective use to which technological innovation may be put (Gattiker and Willoughby 1993; Gattiker and Nelligan 1988; Early and Stubblebine 1989). Evidence suggests that some countries have a more positive governmental and public policy culture with regard to education for technology, such as Germany (Littek and Heisig 1991).

That Australia is now a country of great cultural diversity is axiomatic. Goldstone (1987) has suggested that situations characterized by cultural diversity and ferment are those that most readily foster innovation. Enforcement of a state of orthodoxy, the preservation of tradition as the yardstick of action, the veneration and conservation of the past, these promote nothing so much as intolerance, hostility and resistance to innovation. Pluralism encourages innovation organizationally (Perry and Sandholtz 1988).

In the appropriate conditions, Gattiker and Willoughby (1993: 474) observe,

If a firm or region can develop technological competence and manage the multicultural workforce successfully, and thereby improve its competitive advanrtage in global markets, it will ultimately succeed in securing more resources and wealth.

While this is correct, it underestimates the role that culture can play. While good management of the multicultural workforce is vital, there is more to culture than merely its proliferation across the diversity of employees. There is also the question of cultural identity in the marketplace, the identity of customers and consumers. While in all "postmodern" societies, by definition, these identities will be fragmented, disparate and heterodox, there are potentially profitable points of cultural convergence that can offer competitive advantage on a global scale. We will focus on what we believe to be one such unique opportunity for Australia.

Cutting across cultural diversity in Australia are some central, if contested, values. One of these may provide a major source of competitive advantage for embryonic industry in the development of a "green" profile for Australian enterprises and activities. Successful global examples exist, such as the Body Shop, and in the United States, Redken Cosmetics, which market products that claim to contain "natural" Australian ingredients. It is not only in the exploitation of green niches in existing product markets that opportunities present themselves. Additional openings derive from the application of new technologies to the problems of previous polluters or from powering existing applications through new green technologies.

The green movement may be many things. To some elements in the community it is a source of mischief, an irritation, an unnecessary constraint on economic and community activities. For others it is almost a sacred cause. For embryonic industry it can be an important source of competitive advantage. The values of green culture can be a major push for the adoption of processes that add value, as industries adapt to their demands. An unspoilt environment and ecologically sound produce from it will have a competitive edge in polluted and dense overseas markets. Accordingly, Australian quality should emphasize this advantage and become synonymous with green values. Green management, like green accounting, should become a central part of management education, development and training for the next century. The success of the bid by Sydney for the Year 2000 Olympics demonstrates this.

Australia does not yet have an international reputation for its application of "green values," although the well-publicized role of Greenpeace as consultants to the successful Sydney Olympic bid is a foundation that the country could build on. The knowledge that will be acquired from the guidelines that have been developed for this bid could become the basis for a "green" chain of "organization learning." The guidelines are simple but exhaustive. The Olympic village will:

- maximize the use of recyclable and recycled materials such as glass, paper and metals;
- use only recycled plastics;
- use CFC, HFC, and HCFC-free refrigerants and processes;
- use renewable sources of energy, including solar power;
- use building materials from sustainable sources;
- prepare pre-site audit of habitat and species;
- develop passive solar design of houses;
- maximize use of public transport and elimination of leaded fuels;
- utilize water conservation and recycling practices including dual flush toilet systems, roof-fed water tanks and water saving shower roses;
- recycle treated storm water and sewage effluent.

Companies that tender for contracts for the site will have to show how they are going to follow these guidelines. Components will be subjected to "life-style costings," an audit that takes into account the environmental impact of their manufacture, use and future disposal. All merchandizing contractors will be scrutinized as well. As a result of following these policies Greenpeace and the ecology group Ark will develop a data base on international best practice and products to cover every construction requirement. In addition, best practice definitions will also be specified for recycling processes, waste management, energy conservation, water re-use and recycling, toxic use reduction and renewable energy resources (Greenpeace Business 1993).

In the year 2000 more eyes simultaneously will be on Sydney and on Australia than ever before. At the same time, the "greenness" of the Olympics will be, we are confident, one of the major angles that will be represented to and by the International Press. What a competitive edge this allows for Australia to develop embryonic industry premised on green values in the interim, confident that the whole world will be watching. It could be an enormous world-wide and free commercial for the "green" values of Australian business. Perhaps a "green" business Olympics might be run in conjunction with the real Olympics to reward those participating firms that had most economically and effectively met the guidelines set? It would be an incredible spring-board for global business.

Within the management curriculum green issues ought not to be considered as a separate item, as a green ghetto of knowledge. On the contrary, green issues will impact on many areas of any management curriculum: upon manufacturing management; accounting; human resources management. Virtually all the substantive disciplines that contribute to management will feel the impact of "green values" in some way. At present, discussion, curriculum and textbook inspection suggest that the impact is slow and uneven.

Embryonic Industry Requires a New Paradigm of Management

Research confirms the emergence of a new paradigm of management, one that theoreticians see as having particular relevance for embryonic industry (Clegg et al. 1994). Not all practitioners will find the practice of this "new paradigm" easy, given past habits of power and the reluctance that often attaches to innovation in custom, even for those who make a point of innovation in technical practice.

What we might call a "female ethos" or a "feminization of management" clearly is becoming increasingly prominent. This does not mean that the ranks of management are becoming staffed with more women than in the past. The reference is, instead, to the substantive content of management activity, where "masculinism" characterizes older, military-derived models. To make the point clear, the adoption of such masculinist models could be the hallmark of "feminine" occupations as much as "masculine" ones. Nursing, historically, was a case in point (Chua and Clegg 1990). Here the employees were principally women, but the organizational model derived from the male world of the military, with its bureaucratized ranks, uniforms, distinctions and command structure. Certainly, the new paradigm is very different from older models of management derived from the military, through public sector bureaucracies (Weber 1978) and engineering practice (Taylor 1911), in the earlier years of this century.

The new paradigm emphasizes an increasing recognition of relational factors rather than competitive values; the need for firms to seek interdependence rather than dominance in the marketplace, and for business opportunities to be nurtured in an "emergent" manner through affiliation and co-operation. This is in opposition to previous emphases on rationality, separation and manipulation. One consequence may be to bring together firms who would previously have seen each other as competitive threats. These, taken together, have been felt by many authors to be more characteristic of "female" than of "male" behavior (see Barrett 1994).

In the past, while formal structures of imperative command crystallized as bureaucracy could aspire to control all that was within the reach of the organization, that control could never be total. The many "vicious circles" of attempts at control to repair a perceived power deficit by management leading to increased employee resistance are well recorded from Gouldner (1954) onwards (see Clegg and Dunkerley 1980). That control will be far less, and attempts to achieve it far more inappropriate, when the most important relations that the organization enters into are not within its grasp as a legally fictive individual, should be self-evident. As networks expand and as markets intrude into organizations, intra-organizational hierarchies, and control premised on them, recede in importance. As organizations seek value through the strength of their ties to and networks with other organizations attempts at imperative managerial control become intrusive and inappropriate. Control through networks, particularly where there is considerable complexity and short span of product life-cycles, means that emergent "windows of opportunity" requires rapid and widespread sharing of knowledge rather than its concealment from competitors. The old paradigm of management tradition and practice is increasingly obsolete for the managers of embryonic industries.

Table 1: "Old" and "New" Paradigms of Management

New Paradigm	Old paradigm
Organization paradigm	Organization discipline
Virtuous circles	Vicious circles
Flexible organizations	Inflexible organizations
Management leaders	Management administrators
Open communication	Distorted communication
Markets	Hierarchies
Core competencies drive product development	Strategic business units drive product development
Strategic learning capacities are widespread	Strategic learning occurs at the apex of the organization
Assumption that most organization members are trustworthy	Assumption that most organization members are untrustrworthy
Most organization members are empowered	Most organization members are disempowered

Exploring Tomorrow's Paradigm: Management and Organization Implications of Innovation Strategies

Organization Learning

Dodgson (1993a: 375) notes that organizations today need to learn quickly and continuously. Influential consultants urge that competitive edge attaches to those organizations that succeed in doing so (Peters and Waterman 1982; Kanter 1989; Senge 1989; Garrat 1987). Research suggests that it is the differential ability of smaller firms to learn quickly, particularly about technological opportunities, that has been responsible for a changing pattern of competitive relationships between large and small firms in favor of the latter (Rothwell 1992). For larger organizations, the rapidly accelerating pace of technological change demands learning because of the complexity of new product development processes (Rothwell 1992). Product life-cycles shorten and "lean production" emerges (Womack et al. 1990), based on alternative East Asian, particularly, Japanese, forms of organization using JIT, MRP, TQM, etc. (Clegg 1990; Clegg et al. 1992; Marceau 1992).

Learning may be "single-loop" or "double-loop" (Argyris and Schon 1978). Single-loop learning feeds back on to present competences and routines of knowledge and their application in order to remove obstacles to their functioning; double-loop learning, by contrast, is learning that transforms the existing stock of organizational know-how contained in these routines and competences. Organizations need both although the evidence suggests that learning which is "double-loop" is far more difficult to achieve (Argyris and Schon 1978).

Learning implies both outcomes and processes. The notion of virtuous learning circles suggests comparative improvement in efficiency, however one chooses to measure it, in whatever stakeholder terms: profits; quality of working; supply of jobs; consumer satisfaction; environmental impact or macroeconomic outcomes. Vicious learning, by contrast, implies diminished efficiency. Learning processes concern the achievement of these outcomes, the how and the why, rather than the what questions. Organization learning occurs by:

- Learning with clients, asking how, beyond market research, does the organization achieve a constant symbiosis and exchange with clients? (In some organizations employees are encouraged to attend meetings with customers and suppliers as part of the local organizational culture.)
- Learning from outsiders, asking how does the organization tap the knowledge of consultants, academics, subcontractors, the community? (Some of our research suggested that interpersonal networks of friendship seemed most important.)
- Learning from each other, asking how is knowledge passed on within the group, from group to group, from division to division, or even from sector to sector?

- Does the organization have a scheme for systematic knowledge capture and dissemination: is there a systematic scheme for capturing and disseminating knowledge at a strategic level (Peters 1992)?

According to McKinsey (1993: 57) managers in innovative firms have learned:

- that an appropriate top-manager's role is proactive, committed, hands-off detail, goal-setting and motivating;
- dream-driven goals should be the company aspirations;
- an ability to "zoom in" on customer needs, company strengths and the innovations required to ensure their match;
- project management that stresses cross functional teams, senior management sponsorship of projects and championing separate from the day to day organization politics;
- integrated innovation that deepens existing products and processes, as well as aiming to supersede them, where changes are pursued in close dialogue with the customers by all managers, including senior management.

Organizations and their managers need not only learn; Goldman and Nagel (1993) say that they must unlearn:

- that co-operation is less desirable than competition;
- that labor-management relations need be adversarial;
- that information is power and can be shared only to one's detriment;
- that trusting others makes one vulnerable;
- that complex problems admit of single technological solutions;
- that breakthroughs are the only targets to aim for;
- that markets will create themselves once better mousetraps are invented;
- that infrastructure requirements will take care of themselves once pioneers have thrown up superstructures,
- that standards are constraining and their formulation dull work;
- that only parts can be invented not whole systems.

Comparing companies that are winning with those that are losing market position, Hayes et al. (1988) conclude that the key difference is that winners "constantly strive to be better, placing great emphasis on experimentation, integration, training, and the building of critical organizational capabilities."

Conceptually, the notion of learning must be central. If management cannot learn then little justification exists for the practice of management development.

Strategic Learning

All members of an organization learn but some learning is more strategic than others. Strategic learning is interpretative. Traditionally, it is usually located at the organization apex, in top management. The leaders and managers of innovative firms in embryonic industries may find it difficult to renounce these traditional ways, particularly where business success seems premised on the special skills and knowledge that they can contribute as technologists to the company. Yet, they will have to do so if the embryo is to grow and develop to maturation. Highly successful new firms in embryonic industries maximize the circulation of learning throughout the "clever company." TCG is an example.

A flourishing Telecommunications complex has developed around the TCG Group, whose Chief Executive, Peter Fritz, participated as a respondent in the Embryonic project. This presents a most interesting case for our thesis, as examination of the work of John Mathews (1993a; 1993b), as well as Fritz's own account (Fritz and Ellercamp 1988), suggest. TCG is not a conventional organization but an example of what we refer to as a "network organization." In a number of significant overseas cases these network organizations have become identified with strategic advantage by firms and competitive edge by nations. Perhaps the most famous examples are those from Emilia Romagna in Northern Italy, particularly those centered on the Benetton complex (see Clegg 1990; Pyke and Sengenberger 1992, for example). Elsewhere, in Japan for instance, a similar identification has been made of the important role of small-firm networks in industry complexes; for instance, the Japanese car industry (see Kenney and Florida 1988). As Mathews (1993a) suggests, network organizations are coming to be seen as one of the principal organizational innovations for the 21st century. They are the result either of allowing market forces into what would have been large corporations or the clustering and networking of small firms with each other to form larger entities that behave like quasi-firms but retain the flexibility and responsibility of their smaller constituent parts. At their core are collaborative relations where conventional paradigms of firm behavior would lead one to expect competition.

TCG stands for Technical and Computer Graphics, a firm founded as a small computer services company in Sydney in 1971. Through a process of generating new start-ups it has grown to comprise nearly 30 firms, one of the largest privately-owned computer supplies groups in Australia. The firms specialize in different but related aspects of computing, telecommunications and information technology generally, that allows them to broker related aspects of design and fabrication amongst members of the corporate family, who bid in a competitive market for the work that is being tendered for. They are a model of "agile" firms within a common group. The TCG group is a genuine network whose internal relations are both market-mediated and embedded in a set of governance rules that aim to maximize co-operation within the competitive market form. Each firm is mutually independent but they give mutual preference to each other in contracting out. They do not compete directly nor do they seek to exploit other members of the group by making a profit out of intra-group transactions. Profits come from outsiders. Within the group there is total autonomy in venturing out, within the framework of accepted rules. This enables highly flexible opportunism with respect to niche opportunities. The group is not owned by a superordinate entity: mutual cross-holding within the group prevails. Rules within the group must be followed. Disobey the rules, and the firm has to quit the group. The group is organic: new members may enter easily, but not at the expense of other members of the group. Hence, start-up costs are usually obtained through firm's obtaining debt capital rather than the group acting as a venture capitalist, or approaching the formal venture capital market. Debt finance is easier to secure; the group provides credibility as well as collateral. Hence organic amoeba-like growth is relatively easy. So is cell-splitting. Group members may leave if they wish on terms negotiated on each occasion of splitting. Finally, the group has high permeability: each element within it transacts outside freely. TCG is, in Snow, Miles and Coleman's (1992) terms, a dynamic entity. It is one that has great economies of scale as well, through the provision of central services.

In many other respects it is a prime model for the kind of network relations that we believe will characterize embryonic organization and challenge existing models of more traditional organization and management. Innovation in TCG works through the network and its strategic alliances, that extend both within and outside the network. For the latter, the "chains" that add value through linkages come into play, linking the group to customers and users, and sometimes producers and suppliers, producing "fusion" in innovation as hitherto separate technologies "fuse" in new products and processes. TCG practices this method through what Mathews (1993a) refers to as "triangulation" or "triangular" collaboration, where they bring the customer for the innovation into the process as a partner with licensing and sell-on arrangements. Some of the products that TCG has brought to market in this way include the Rapid Aviation Refuelling Information System (RARIS), developed in tandem with ACME, an established aviation fuel metering supplier, and Mobil Oil, innovating a new application of the technology that TCG had developed initially as hand-held terminals in the grocery trade. Other product innovations include a Field Service Terminal, developed in conjunction with Toshiba, to specifications from the third partner, Telecom Australia. A third product is the Passive Transponder System for registering the whereabouts of whatever objects have been electronically tagged: the applications are endless; from checking on cattle in the bush to charging road users for road usage. In each case the strategy is similar: identify the market niche; find a partner to develop it; search for a major customer; extend the triangle further.

Daft and Weick's model of organizational interpretation modes (see Figure 1) demonstrates the distinctiveness of organizations in an embryonic industry. It presents four different strategic modes of rational behavior for innovation.

Strategic learning varies in terms of the breadth or narrowness of management search and interpretation mechanisms, and the degree of regularity or irregularity with which management actively scans and searches its environment. Narrow search and irregular scanning produce passive receptivity by management of novelty introduced from the organization's environment. Regular, broad and obtru-

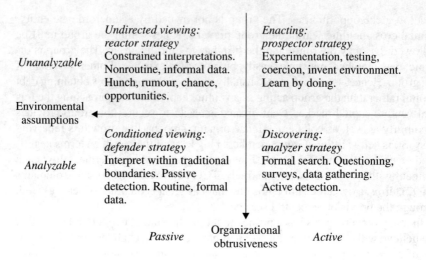

Figure 1:   Daft and Weick's Model of Organizational Interpretation: Model and Strategy

sive scanning through, for example, systematic monitoring of information, participation in training programs, networks and alliances, produces active creativity. The management of embryonic organizations engaged in innovation in an uncertain environment needs to devote resources to intelligence gathering as an aspect of learning. They need to scan their environments broadly, regularly and actively as "test-makers" (Daft and Weick 1982). Such management needs to enact interpretation, particularly where radical technological innovations creatively destroys or marginalizes existing competences.

Four critical axes define the radicalness of innovation. These are the degree of product innovation; the degree of process invariability and the degree to which the intellectual capital that the organization's technical core is premised upon is changing. It can be shifting in more or less dramatic and strategically different ways, as when an organization moves from one technological paradigm to another, or it may be more or less deepening, where the changes are far more incremental. Clearly, we are dealing with a continuum.

Where all of these axes score low we find a traditional organization. Where incremental product innovation combine with a moderate degree of process invariability, allied not so much with dramatic shifts in knowledge but the deepening of existing applications of intellectual capital, this defines an organization that is in an embryonic industry. Where product innovation is radical, the degree of process invariability high, and intellectual capital based on shifting paradigms is strategic, then we have an organization that is in an ultra embryonic industry. Figure 2 represents these distinctions.

The distinction between embryonic and ultra-embryonic industry has important implications, particularly for authority relations in firms. Redefinition of these occurs as the totality of knowledge within which they are organized changes:

More radical innovations require new organizational forms. It appears that new forms, initially, are better adapted to exploit new techno/market regimes, breaking out from existing regimes within which established corporations for historical, cultural and institutional reasons, might be rather strongly bound (Rothwell 1992: 234).

Extremely new firms in embryonic industries have little option other than to adopt a new form of organization:

These organizations construct their own environments. They gather information by trying new behaviours and seeing what happens. They experiment, test, and stimulate, and they ignore precedent, rules, and traditional expectations… An organization in this mode tends to construct markets rather than waiting for an assessment of demand to tell it what to produce (Daft and Weick 1982: 288-289).

The exception would be where they have an inspired founder who operates on undirected viewing. Any firm in an embryonic industry that tries to interpret innovation through conditioned viewing, one would predict, condemns itself to failure. None of the preconditions apply, especially where innovation is radical. Traditional rationality will not succeed in innovating. By definition, an organization innovating in an ultra-embryonic industry, cannot analyze its environment.

Network organization, such as that of TCG puts a different perspective on strategic learning. It improves immeasurably the probability that understanding is maximized through learning by doing it in the network and through its triangulation strategies. The network is a mechanism for fast-tracking organization learning about markets, applications, suppliers, in fact, everything that it would take the competitive stand-alone company far longer to learn. It provides, through organizational form, the solution to a problem. While new, small, firms may innovate, they lack the collective memory of past experience that efficiently bureaucratic large organizations have through their "files" of precedent (Weber 1978). Although large firms have the experience and the precedents they can fail to admit necessary innovation through the patina of tradition that they display as an excess of collective memory, often as a resource for resistance to change by well-entrenched organization members.

Virtuous Circles

Innovations introduce discontinuity into accepted ways of doing things. At their strongest these discontinuities are based on patents. Discontinuities are always challenging but they can be opportunities rather than threats. Virtuous learning makes opportunities while vicious learning confirms threats. It is not the presence

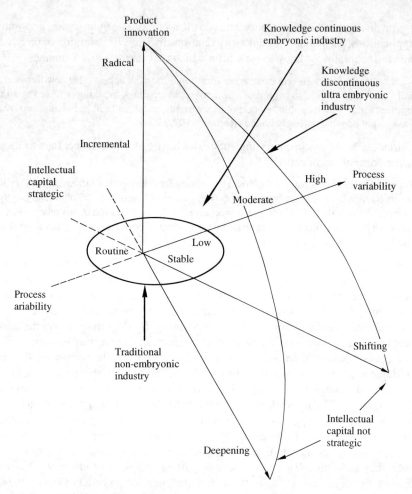

Figure 2: The Traditional Embryonic System of Organization

or absence of conflict that distinguishes the two types of learning. Conflict will be characteristic of any learning process that challenges deeply ingrained habits with the need to "unlearn" (Hedberg 1981). Novelty offers variation in industry designs and business recipes for success in that industry, sometimes by chance, sometimes by design. Virtuous learning will be system wide, not just specific to a particular organization's management.

Fairtlough (1993) picks up on many of these learning themes in his discussion and description of Celltech as a successful firm in an embryonic industry. Virtuous circles, he insists, build openness, trust, empowerment and commitment. (Also see Dodgson's 1993b account of the central role that both inter-and intra-organizational trust play at Celltech.) Once in motion, virtuous circles have a multiplier effect within the organization. Accordingly, collaborative and open forms of decision-making eliminate the inefficiency of traditional hierarchical styles of secrecy, sycophancy and sabotage. Instead, decisions are based upon expertise, openly elicited and listened to in the organization. Moreover, Fairtlough (1993) argues that innovative firms seek allies to which they can bond for periods of mutual benefit. These may be either mature or similarly firms in embryonic industry. Hence, following Fairtlough's (1993) findings, collaborative network arrangements will be crucial to the success of embryonic industries.

Organic Structures

Much management literature recommends organic styles of management. They seem particularly apt for new firms in embryonic industries. There is a freedom from rigid rules; they are participative and informal, horizontal and project based. A multiplicity of views characterize the organization. Communication is face-to-face; there is little explicit bureaucracy. Small wins are celebrated and improvement sought in everything on a continuous daily basis. Recognition and reward of failure should occur if learning is to take place, a point that research in Focus Groups underscored. (Also, for a consultancy perspective, see Peters 1992: 12-13.) Organic structures encourage interdisciplinarity and boundary spanning. Flexibility about changing needs, threats and opportunities goes together with a non-hierarchical structure and a free flow of information up as well down the organization (Rothwell 1992).

Leadership

There is a distinction of increasingly dubious worth but it is one used often enough. It is the distinction between "management" and "leadership." All managers may need some leadership skills in flattened organization structures and vision, rather than being the prerequisite of a charismatic leader, may well be something that is best nurtured by group processes. The managers and leaders of tomorrow's firms will be the same; leadership, in the terms that Bennis (1993: 10) recommends and that other writers have tagged the "new leadership studies" (Bryman 1992) is stressed again and again: the importance of a compelling vision; a "climate of trust" based on competence, congruity and constancy; the creation of meaning and the ability to learn from mistake; the importance of a healthy and empowering environment; the strategic importance of flatter, flexible, adaptive, decentralized and learning systems and organizations (Bennis 1993).

Management increasingly has more affinity with activities of listening, learning and launching conversations rather than commanding, controlling and communicating imperatives. In management and business, metaphors of military discipline, drill and docility are in decay. However, the embryonic firm is not a seminar series. Clear leadership is vital. The style must be participative but it must be there when the technology is being developed internally. The three major leadership roles identified are those of communicator, integrator and planner (Brown and Karagozullu 1993) which combine with the symbol-laden aspects of the management of meaning and organization *realpolitik* (Clegg 1989; Bolman and Deal 1991).

Communications

Management communications are vital also, as Fairtlough (1994) identifies. They must be frequent, informal as well as formal, integrative across functional lines rather than down functional hierarchies (Brown and Kargozoglu 1993). Fairtlough's Celltech experience recommends the minimization of hierarchy and the maximization of integrative "compartments," an analogy that Fairtlough takes from molecular biology. If two kinds of molecule co-operate they can improve their accuracy of replication at least tenfold. If they stay closely associated, they can evolve together and the scientist can aid this joint evolution by putting the two kinds of molecule in a compartment that keeps the compatible variants together and apart from other similar molecules. Once established, compartments start to compete with each other in a Darwinian fashion. Create compartments similarly, within organizations, he recommends. In these compartments all barriers to discourse, functional, technical and hierarchical, should be minimized (Fairtlough 1994). Something approximating an "ideal speech situation" (Habermas 1984) becomes the norm where excellent communication is possible within the small compartment where multi-order feedback leads to great creativity. Mutual understanding is high, shared values predominate. There is a common language for communication, there are common criteria for judgment. Strong ties of affection and trust develop between the small number of people involved. They get to know each other well, and share the experience of working together to achieve shared goals (Fairtlough 1993: 5).

Compartments need order in the creative flux and to achieve this the manager of the embryonic industry needs to be something akin to the creative genius of a Duke Ellington (without the famous temperament), able to work not only to their own charts but also those of collaborators (like Billy Strayhorn), comprehending the whole and seeing interrelationships, involving people in the ensemble and improvising in harmony with others to maintain the dynamic from the focal point outwards: from the CEO (McGrath and MacMillan 1993) through a technically sophisticated and involved membership (Senker and Senker 1992).

Organizational Life Cycles

If all organizations in embryonic industries must strive to be organic they must do so even more at the initial stages of the life-cycle. In management terms new firms seem to have a relative advantage to established firms the greater the undercutting of existing competences posed by the technology that they use. Abernathy and Clark (1985) have coined the term transilience to describe such innovations. Where both technology and market links are novel there is a process of "radical innovation" at work. The whole "architecture" of the firm and the knowledge embedded in it as a coherent set of components requires innovation. In new organizations in embryonic industries the comparative advantage of a clean slate enables them to manage transilience better.

At the outset, when dealing with new technologies, new firms can have a competitive edge. This fits the pattern in biotechnology. Start-ups like Celltech and Genentech pioneered the application of novel recombinant-DNA technologies. Bringing such innovation to market is often achieved through "dynamic complementarity," the pairing of organizationally separately located resources and skills. Sometimes, as Genentech's case, it fails and the innovative firm becomes incorporated within a larger corporate entity like Roche. Technology breakthroughs, once achieved, accommodate within the established market linkages and subsequent product development of pre-existing large firms.

Below a certain threshold of transilience in innovation it is more probable that its organization and management will shift from new organizations in ultra-embryonic industries to more established, knowledge continuous organization in embryonic industries. Knowledge that undercuts existing competences in both technology and market terms overcomes the threshold. Radical innovation opens up new markets and applications that create great difficulties for established firms (Cooper and Kleinschmidt 1986; Anderson and Tushman 1990; Daft 1982) and opportunities for new firms, particularly the ultra-embryonics.

In the initial phase of a firm in an embryonic industry great hunches and research serendipity may be enough to get started but evidence shows that these cannot sustain the firm in the long term. Reaction has a short shelf life as a strategy for managing sustained innovation. Embryonic maturation requires more intrusive and active interpretation. In contrast, "prospector" and "analyzer" strategies are the path to managerial excellence for firms in embryonic industries. The more incremental trial and error strategy of the prospector best suits exploratory learning that undercuts existing competences, while competence enhancement and exploitation presuppose an analyzer strategy of systems analysis, computation and extensive scanning by the discovering enterprise.

"Radical" innovation always involves an overthrow of existing competences: that is its definition. Less dramatic but as important is "architectural" innovation, which, while less totally challenging, is difficult to manage. TCG is a case in point. It works well because it has given explicit consideration to the design of the "architecture," the organization forms, within which its evolution has occurred. Organizations that want to develop embryonic activities through the management of this form should routinize search for the unexpected, through constant market questioning, surveys and data gathering, as well as through constant organization learning. The Focus Group data underscored the strategic importance of this "market intelligence" for new firms in embryonic industry.

Organizational life cycles have a distinct market related curve. Typically, technology based firms start out from a strong consulting and Research and Development contracting base, and over a few years become more product oriented firms, with an increased emphasis on sales and marketing, and a diminished technology fixation. The suggestion is that the life-cycle of these firms significantly shifts to a more sales and marketing oriented focus, the more so that the firm has not a single but a multi-founder situation. Roberts (1990) and Shanklin and Ryans (1984) note that as the competitive environment becomes more stable, typically a function of maturity, the marketing function becomes more important for high-technology companies. Roberts' (1990) research, carried out in 114 technology-based firms within the Greater Boston area of the USA, resonates with the insight that single founders of an embryonic firm, fired by their technological vision, find it difficult to let go – sometimes to the commercial detriment of the firm. Van de Ven (1993: 212) notes that "entrepreneurs who run in packs will be more successful than those that go it alone to develop their innovations." The development of an appropriate infrastructure for entrepreneurship is essential. Successful entrepreneurs are not heroic individualists so much as partners in a collective achievement. Once more, network ideas of governance seem to recommend themselves.

Markets

Markets don't have to be mass or even big. Peters (1990: 15) is a fan of "nanomarketing." He notes that "all markets are microtizing." Successful companies of any size will learn to respect tiny markets, or else he warns. Closely linked to this he warns that successful innovation is a numbers game: "Lots of tries, lots of lead users, lots of tiny markets – and maybe a hit or two from time to time" (Peters 1990: 17). Perhaps it is because Peters is widely read, but this message came through strongly from Focus Groups in Wollongong, Sydney and Brisbane.

One aspect of technology cases was very striking. Product quality and customer-responsiveness were the omni-present goals for the small firms that have started-up new. Customer needs were known intimately. Users of the products were constantly being visited by both market and technical personnel. All marketing personnel were technically trained engineers and scientists, not "marketers." Products only get to market with strong senior management sponsorship.

Core Competences

Innovation in organizations comes from the nurturing and application of "core competences." In an influential *Harvard Business Review* article, Prahalad and Hamel (1990: 82-85) define core competence in the following way:

The diversified corporation is a large tree. The trunk and major limbs are core products, the smaller branches are business units; the leaves, flowers, and fruit are end products. The root system that provides nourishment, sustenance and stability is the core competence... Core competences are the collective learning in the organization, especially how to co-ordinate diverse production skills and integrate multiple streams of technologies... Core competence is communication, involvement, and a deep commitment to working across organization boundaries... The tangible link between identified core competences and end products is what we call the core products – the physical embodiments of one or more core competences. Honda's engines for example, are core products, linchpins between design and development skills that ultimately lead to a proliferation of end products.

Goldman and Nagel (1993) suggest that routine "organizational unlearning" characterizes firms seeking to build on their core competences, particularly those of a strong human resource team.

Armed with the wisdom gained through unlearning, whilst preserving their core competences, established firms will be ripe for embryonic industry status, perhaps in temporally specific partnerships with firms in ultra-embryonic industry, in a portfolio of opportunities that is risk-spreading.

The key thing is to know what the core competences are and to nurture them, not to be deflected through their application in whatever business one may be in at the moment. Products do not make a business: competences do.

Paradoxically, new firms in an embryonic industry are advantaged by their lack of collective memory. Thus they have little to unlearn. However, they lack the collective learning of core competences that Prahalad and Hamel (1990) stress. They need a specific strategy to resolve the paradox: the resolution is recourse to prospector strategies and network intelligence.

How to Cultivate Embryonic Industry

Embryonic industries are not immaculate conceptions. Relations tend to produce them. Relationships are rarely random occurences. There is a context to all relationships. Embryonic industries flourish in an industry complex. Organizations other than innovative firms populate this complex and require analysis. Embryonic industries flourish in and through relationships with other agencies, including mature firms, suppliers and producers, customers and users, government bodies and instruments of public policy, research and development laboratories, markets and occupational interest groups. If this industry complex is not recognized then much of what is important and relevant about embryonic industry can be overlooked.

No enterprise is an island. Interlinked communities of practitioners in and around organizations develop a complex system of interdependence. This links firms, government, and key stakeholders in an industry complex (see Figure 3). The firm is at the center of the embryonic industry complex. In order to innovate firms must manage several processes successfully, as indicated. In addition, firms have various kinds of relationships with other elements in the complex. The industry complex involves more than a collection of autonomous organizations, and, within these, inter-firm relations involve more than price competition. The functioning of the complex has an impact upon the organization of individual firms, their strategies, and their collective competitiveness relative to sectors located elsewhere.

Building on work done by Rob van Tulder with Ben Dankbaar (1992), we can conceptualize the context within which firms exist in terms of four distinct nexi. These delineate the producers and suppliers of human and other resources; the consumers and users of the products, processes and services of firms in embryonic industry; research and development and relevant public policies. Figure 1 represents the "embryonic industry complex framework." Each of these elements in the complex represents an important part of the environment in which any firm in an embryonic industry will operate. If it cannot attract human and other resources it will not survive. Once attracted they require appropriate and effective management. If it cannot recruit consumers and users to its products they will not survive in the market place, and, to the extent that the firm is dependent upon these, neither will it. If it cannot access appropriate or secure research and development that enable it to innovate new products and services then it faces the prospect of a declining market as others that manage these matters more effectively outflank them. Finally, any government that does not develop appropriate public policies to facilitate these developments will risk erosion and decline of wealth and employment creation opportunities and of its tax-base. Hence, public policies for industry development are essential and responsible as supporting conditions that would promote and encourage important leadership and management skills for enterprise productivity, innovation and international competitiveness.

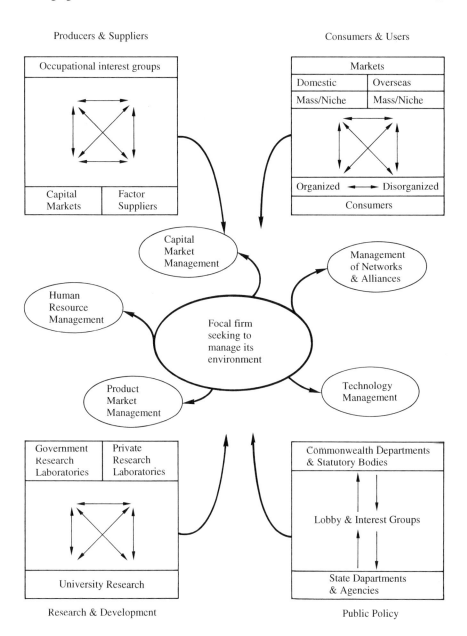

Figure 3:   Embryonic Industry Complex and a Focal Firm

What frames the embryonic industry complex? An industry consists of firms as organizations. Organizations typically seek to cope with the uncertainties of their existencc in various ways: they strive for a unifying culture, for standard procedures, for adequate resources and so on. Each of the areas that the organization has to deal with represents a potential zone of uncertainty that may only partially be within its power to control. In striving to exercize this control it will require management of those resources that impinge on its arena of operations. The producers and suppliers of human and other resources; the consumers and users of the products, processes and services of firms in embryonic industry; research and development and relevant public policies, all frame the context. The requirements and reality of each organization will differ but, at the minimum, they will need to develop strategies that manage human resources; product and material markets, for both inputs and outputs, capital, technologies, and enter into relationships, often of networks and alliances, with other organizations. Some of these other organizations locate within the frame of the complex, as unions, employers' associations, government departments, lobby groups, research laboratories, financial institutions, customers, suppliers. Others will be firms with an interest in their arena: competitors and established firms that might be seeking opportunities for their capital, human resources and product markets or who might want to tap into that of a firm in an embryonic industry because of perceived symbiotic, competitive or complementary opportunities. Hence, substantively the frame fills rapidly with firms and other organizations in embryonic industries. For reasons of analytical simplicity, we display only one such firm, the focal firm, in Figure 1 the "Embryonic Industry Complex and a Focal Firm."

Of particular importance in this model is the corner occupied by public policy, because it is from this corner, under conditions of conflict, resistance, lobbying and negotiation, that the "rules of the game" emerge that frame the understandings of the participants in the complex.

All industry develops in a framework of public policy, whether perceived as benign or hostile, whether intentionally or not, on the part of government.

Public policy need not entail "meddling" by bureaucrats who are risk-averse nor need it load entrepreneurs with burdensome obligations to government that they can ill-afford. For instance, following a suggestion that Professor Urs Gattiker made to us, government might fund an independent not-for-profit agency which invests in embryonic industries, and, if the firm succeeds, changes its equity into an investment that can eventually be re-sold at a profit that can then be re-invested into new projects. Such a scheme would centralize resources, avoid duplication, and lessen the search proceedures that entrepreneurs would have to engage in.

Firms are "embedded" in a socially organized context and involved in a series of relationships with other organizations within the arena, in patterns that repeat throughout the intricacies of the connections thus constituted. These patterns will have several "normal" forms: these are those of "chains," "clusters," "networks" and "strategic alliances." Rather than represent these graphically, we will describe them discursively.

Chains

The industry context, conceived of as a set of linkages that connect disparate organizations, may form a linear chain. Critical linkages can put virtuous pressure on management to improve innovation. The McKinsey Report (1993: 42) into 'Emerging Exporters' recognizes the importance of these chain linkages when it urges the construction of supply chains, for which it argues the government should provide "adequate support and resources." Public policy would thus seek to increase pressure and thus enhance value in the chain of linkages through competition combined with co-operation, an idea with far reaching implications. Creative use and shaping of the market through production linkages might focus, for instance, on consultative buyer/vendor relations, inter-firm associations and extra-firm agencies that facilitate continuous improvement in production (Best 1990: 19-21). Value enhancement comes through the pressures in the chain. Demands by organizations that suppliers meet quality standards that it, or an industry standard, mandates, are a common instance of this type of chain functioning as a "virtuous circle." Government can have a role to play in the achievement of this, through defining a public policy framework that is standard setting.

Clusters

The original idea of firms that can cluster together came from the model of an "industrial district," where there are many small and medium sized enterprises that integrate at a local level and specialize in phases that are all part of the same production cycle (Bianchi 1993: 18). Typically, well established with industrial and artisanal traditions, in some cases the districts may have developed in part as a consequence of local state interventions, such as the Northern Italian industrial districts that Weiss (1988) has studied. In other cases they may be the result of federal government leading the way through a decision to site a key industry in a particular area. It was such a decision that transformed Huntsville, Alabama, from a sleepy cotton town to a dynamo of the space race and the spin-off industries that it developed, a case we studied elsewhere (Clegg et al 1994).

In the absence of a leading role for government procurement revolving around an industry complex such as that of the defence industry, other strategies must present themselves. One of those that has seen widespread adoption is the idea of the "incubator" as a conscious device for encouraging localized high-technology clustering. Incubators are catalysts for small-business generated developments in a tightly focused geographical area and have a valuable role to play in regional programs. They play an important role in facilitating the transfer of technology and ideas from large organizations such as universities, government research bodies and large corporations to the marketplace through aiding the development of new business ventures.

The clustering of research excellence, both public and private, and the creation of a deliberately "hot-house" atmosphere in which small organizations can grow in proximity to each other and to established potential commercial partners is a deliberate strategy of clustering (discussed in some more detail in Part 3.2 of the Full Report in Clegg et al. 1994).

Networks

The concept of networks has been introduced earlier in the chapter. Networking programs as an instrument of public policy usally encourage networks between medium and small business, a feature of the AusIndustry business network programs. It is an important strategy to enhance management skill development. In Australia the Bureau Of Industry Economics recognizes the network concept as a distinct organization and management form, one that has a number of advantages, that include:

- risk-spreading and resource sharing, avoiding costly duplication of independent effort;
- enhanced flexibility compared to other forms of integration, such as a take-over or merger, particularly where product life-cycles are short;
- increased access to know-how and information through collaborative relations at the pre-formal knowledge stage.

One example of an innovative and embryonic network organization that we came across in our research was Ozsoft (Nicholson 1993), a network organization proposed to service many small software companies within the Melbourne region. Ozsoft proposes itself as a network that offers services. It will identify markets, future trends, do competitive analysis, advise on pricing, product ideas, recommend joint venture partners, facilitate product presentation, technical advice, identify overseas markets, manage network relationships, aid with development and marketing funding, cash flow management, legal expertise, taxation and accounting support among others. What is significant is that Ozsoft is a "practice" generated proposal which in many of its particulars seems to tap many of the most recent themes in the literature. The concerns articulated are representative of real transformations occurring in the organizational world, not just a fashionable theoretical concern with networks.

Networks link in a loosely coupled cellular structure a chain of value-adding activities that constantly bring new material and elements into the network. In addition, the velocity and circulation of novelty through the cells adds value by virtue of the permeable and linked relations that comprise it. They represent compartments as described by (Fairtlough 1994) and accordingly enhance innovation opportunities.

Strategic Alliances

Strategic alliances characterize, in particular, those fast growing knowledge intensive product sectors that now account for around 42% of the exports from OECD countries. In recent years, given the substantial financial resources necessary for the development of new technology, more firms are entering strategic alliances, often with competitors, while others are turning to their government to secure support for their technological strategies. Strategic alliances can result in the emergence of networks linking multiple partners, often on an international basis. The importance of networks, between scientists and industrialists, scientists and venture capitalists, venture capitalists and industrialists, is considerable. Venture capital may come from traditional investment companies such as Advent or it may come from an industrial enterprise that "ventures." The brokerage role that a successful venturer supplies is crucial. Embryonic firms frequently emerge from brokerage of well-managed networks. Universities can be a locus for this brokerage as well as an opportunity for much organization learning.

Strategic alliances are often a significant mechanism for accessing external assets in the commercialization process. The assets include capital, product design and marketing resources. For other partners establishing alliances with emerging firms offers access to leading edge technical developments in the new field. For emergent firms, those that are ultra-embryonic in particular, strategic alliances may be crucial for bringing an innovation to the marketplace where "large organizations also play an important role since size and financial muscle are critical for the long pull in an increasingly global economy" (Amara 1990: 145). Other important benefits of such collaborative relationships include shared risks and accelerated technical progress and market entry. A particular form of alliance is "corporate parenting" or "mentoring." Rather than being an opportunistic project-related alliance, this is more permanent, where larger and more established firms play a role in embryonic firm growth through equity participation, providing access to technology, markets, finance, assistance, management skills and credibility (McKinsey 1993: 60). For example, Invetech, an Australian firm, manufactures laboratory instruments through its subsidiary Australian Biomedical Corporation. To do so it has relied on an alliance with the Swiss multinational, Leica. The alliance has provided not only established distributional and marketing channels but also a brand-name recognition that would otherwise be impossible to achieve.

Strategy complementarity refers to the degree to which the strategies of partners are complementary. It reflects the potential offered by an alliance to support the partners' respective strategic initiatives. Established firms often have difficulty in understanding technologies that are different to those they use. Hence, firms in ultra-embryonic industries (where almost everything is uncertain and novel in terms of products, processes, technologies and markets) that most require the complementary services of established firms may be precisely those to whom they are least likely to be available. Complementary curricular knowledge may also be scarce.

Reform of the management curriculum to encompass the interests of firms in embryonic industries furthers the interests of established ones as well. It provides managers on both sides of potential alliances who are more knowledgeable about the other parties' needs. The BHP guide to successful parenting is an invaluable tool for managing parenting alliances (McKinsey 1993: 61). It could become a key resource for the twenty first century management curriculum as it develops a focus on issues of "partnering" rather than on "competition." With the centrality of networks "partnering" takes on a heightened salience.

Established firms, as well as venture capitalists, that might have asset complementarity with an embryonic firm, through marketing or technology applications, need to broker linkages. Cantley (1986) suggests that:

- well thought out technological forecasting;
- frequently updated forecasts in the light of current developments;
- and active search for shared management experience across different projects and for new project opportunities

are the analyzer strategies required by established firms or market intelligence with respect to embryonic industry.

As any student of Machiavelli would attest, alliances are risky, however desirable or necessary they may be. What can firms do to minimize the risks associated with strategic alliances? One thing that they can do is to learn from one area of organization life with considerable experience in managing alliances: the management of strategic high-tech co-operative projects in the military (Farr and Fischer 1992). Distilling the wisdom of their research and translating it into a broader set of applications, suggests that "careful attention to the structure and organization of the managerial role is of paramount importance in assuring eventual project success" (Farr and Fischer 1992: 67). Some of what they say resonates with the more impressionistic contribution of Peters (1992) as well as the practical experiences of practitioners from whom we learned in the Focus Groups.

Managers of successful strategic alliances ensure that alliances are project-focused, that project teams have real decision authority and 100% project assignment; that clear goals and deadlines exist; that there are policies for their implementation and a religious adherence to time-frames for technical, market and other tests. Project teams will include key functional representation with authority to act and project leaders chosen by the team with functional representatives reporting to them. Organization careers will become strings of projects where each project team is self-sufficient and includes "outsiders" like user-representatives. Teams will have a social and celebratory dimension that acknowledges team accomplishments and disappointments (Peters 1992: 22-3; Farr and Fischer 1992).

Goals need harmonizing in alliances as Farr and Fischer (1992: 61) found from their study of successful and failed alliances in European military projects. The success of a project relates closely to keeping the benefits of a project partnership in direct proportion to the relative contribution of each participant. Where project participants had prior experience with relevant technology or previous cooperative programs it increased the probability of success in any given project. Project loyalty overrides enterprise loyalty in successful projects. There are important implications of this for any enterprise entering alliances on a project basis. The team commitment has to be greater than for the enterprise interest. Such commitments help successful projects better to handle uncertainties introduced by the politics of the alliance by ensuring fuller goal commitment, irrespective of change.

Farr and Fischer (1992) also have significant comments concerning coping with international differences that are particularly useful for Australian firms for whom many alliances are likely to be international, because of the size and structure of the domestic economy. They note that in the military cases that they studied, "geographical, cultural, and language barriers appear to be far less of a problem than are differing technical and managerial practices" (Farr and Fischer 1992: 66). One can abstract from Farr and Fischer (1992: 66) some simple, pragmatic but important points that have management implications for alliances that are international:

- successful strategic alliance managers cope with geographical differences by extensive use of confidential e-mail, faxes and couriers and factor jet-lag into travel plans and meetings;
- grasp and factor in cultural differences;
- create schedules that allow for different work standards and holidays;
- co-locate project teams in a single office;
- engage "culture" consultants;
- overcome language differences by specifying an official language in advance and arrange interpreters and translators;
- use multi-lingual teams wherever possible and develop courtesy-level proficiency in the other language(s);
- minimize managerial differences by defining and understanding different contracting policies, procedures, terms and key management processes in advance.

Management Education as if Tomorrow Matters

Recent criticism of management education has concentrated on a curriculum that stresses financial calculation over the management of substantive processes (also see Higgins and Clegg 1988). The core of the criticisms focus on management that is too centered on short-term financial and accounting criteria.

Management education, at every level of provision, if it is to counter these criticisms, should emphasize:

- the centrality of cooperative rather than just competitive behavior both within and between organizations;
- that managing the politics of knowledge is central to successful management;
- that complex problems rarely are amenable to single technological solutions;
- that "market intelligence" should be the central focus of all management education (Goldman and Nagel 1993).

In terms of the organization of management education a free and competitive market in management ideas and institutions seem to be the best historical model for innovation, rather than one founded on the chartering of élite privileges to a small, select number of institutions. After all, it was with these arguments that Adam Smith (1961), in *An Inquiry into the Nature and Causes of Wealth of Nations*, first mounted his moral case for the supremacy of capitalism as an allocative system over that of absolutism or mercantilism. Competitive markets allow diversity to flourish by affording multiple niches within which innovations might take seed and grow.

An additional point is that the emphasis on networks and alliances as organizational forms, and on collaboration as a management practice, is something that should extend into management education, development and training. Accordingly, universities, technical education providors, professional associations, private training providers and firms must link in a system that celebrates diversity, accentuates quality and which formal bodies accredit where appropriate. Management education institutions will have to develop skills in order to educate managers appropriately for the twenty first century.

These point, particularly at graduate level, to more varied modes of education delivery and assessment than presently exist. The new styles will involve problem based learning that is project centered, involving multi-functional teams with cross-cultural work placements in business overseas. Providers will design their curriculum in collaboration with overseas partners to maximize exchange of skills, in both faculty and students. Degrees will require work at more than one institution, cross nationally. However, without some incentives that encourage a focused view on strategic objectives for market place realities it is unlikely that such initiatives will flourish.

Europe is in the vanguard in these initiatives in terms of institutional collaboration. It occurs both through firms and tertiary institutions. In Germany, conscious internationalization programs are conducted by banks and large companies as staff move globally to gain comparative experience. Students in Management in one European institution, like De Montfort University in Leicester, UK, spend one semester of work in Leicester, and a semester, respectively, at a French and Spanish partner institution. There is no reason why many more universities cannot offer their students the same experience of an international marketplace. Institutional partnering needs careful choice. It is best if the focus of the institutions is complementary rather than overlapping. Doing the same thing twice in different contexts will achieve little.

Internationalizing the Management Curriculum

One key point emerged from our research. The majority of the texts, cases and ideas used in current teaching derive from the highly idiosyncratic and individualistically focused Anglo-American culture. Gattiker and Willoughby (1993: 460) observe, writing from Canada and Australia, respectively, students often write papers dealing with technological and cross-national issues based primarily on US-grounded models and studies. Thus, North American ethnocentrism (i.e. the tendency by scholars to overlook the applicability of their concepts and theories beyond their own country and/or culture) will extend into the training of future managers by those learning about technology and cross-national issues through North American "tinted glasses."

Management education needs to focus on analysis of comparative management and technical practices, rather than assume that a particular approach that is endemic to a national context is universal. Being English speakers in a distinctive but small country, dominated as we are by the intellectual and cultural productions of North America and the United Kingdom, compounds this problem. What is available to us in English may not even be useful in our national context. More attaches to a successful curriculum than retooling American texts with Australian cases. Indeed, all of our research points to the need for cultural relativism and cultural listening rather than unitary models of national or organizational culture.

The curriculum requires stretching to focus much more on a global curriculum and to enable students to learn more of the business recipes used in other countries. Japan is the obvious example but students should learn about both other societies in our region and from the experience of other small but highly developed countries, such as the Netherlands and the nations of the Scandinavian region. One feature that has been said to characterize firms in these countries is that they are predisposed to "organization learning" (Clegg 1990; Marceau 1992), a theme that we explore briefly in the next section.

Teaching Organization Learning Skills

Firms that are not "agile," that cannot develop new products or services, that do not attend to their customer needs will not survive long where they are in increasingly competitive business environments, unsheltered and unprotected. Since the object of innovation is to commercialize products valued by customers, acceleration of the process should not jeopardise the quality of the firm's offerings. It requires continuous, open and timely communication sensitive to the need to nurture effective teamwork among all members of the firm and its alliance partners to achieve this acceleration. Personnel training and the allocation of sufficient resources to make technologies effective and efficient should accompany the implementation of innovation.

Successful new product performance suggests that product innovation is an activity that can be learnt (Cooper and Kleinschmidt 1986; Dwyer and Mellor 1991). The learning cited by the above authors applies predominantly to production issues. Whether it works equally for product innovation is unclear. Incremental product innovation involves modification to existing products in the context of given levels of technology. Discontinuous innovation often transforms these, as it radically alters technologies, occupational definitions and the authority relations that existing knowledge relations constitute. There is usually a considerable time lag as the sociocultural impact of changes flows through. (The locus of these changes is not necessarily technological. One may think of examples such as the shift to greater diversity in organizations that have been typically monocultural or single gender: the armed forces are a case in point. Innovations in traditional organizations will require that more exploratory and far reaching learning skills develop. Often new sociocultural management skills will need importation, as the Australian Navy is slowly learning.)

It is not just that firms need to learn from their learning; the experience of learning requires institutional expression if it is to be efficient. Focus groups, particularly in Brisbane, affirmed the success of learning networks in which entrepreneurs from one industry share experiences. The case in point involved CEOs, collaborating on the basis of openness and trust, sharing experience and commercial information to gain collaborative advantage. This form of cluster learning has much to recommend it as unobtrusive, inexpensive and consistent.

The Role of the CEO

Given that innovation is likely to become increasingly important to firm survival over time, learning will assume greater significance the faster discontinuous futures approach. Top management, in particular, has an important role to play in the acquisition of the learning skills that institutionalize innovation. This role includes linking the organization to key outside contacts that serve as "learning agents"; cultivation of particular technical skills within the organization; encouraging an innovative mindset among personnel; locating, defining and linking skills within the organization and matching skills with the organization's strategic plan. Top management is best able to establish innovation as a central value (McKee 1992). Communication and political skills should lie at the heart of the training that is appropriate for management for the twenty first century.

The CEOs of twenty first century firms should not be afraid to be their own venture capitalists: they should back employee's hunches and fund them. Benetton have done this to great advantage, creating the most global and successful of popular fashion houses. Many of the firms they subcontract to in Emilia Romagna are of their own creation. CEOs need teaching to abandon vertical integration and instead to force market relations into the firm, to subcontract extensively, and to create numerous joint ventures and alliances, especially with new firms, where they are in more established industries.

Highly responsive and agile enterprises can sometimes broker roles as "virtual companies" that exploit transient or niche markets as they emerge, where management achieves a speed and flexibility that matches that of the technologies involved (Goldman and Nagel 1993). Such agile management, characterized by strategic focus on long term financial performance, seeks opportunities for growth and profit in constant change that flexible management can exploit. Authority diffuses in the agile enterprise rather than being concentrated in a chain of command. Instead of a static corporate structure based on fixed, specialized departments, agile corporations have a dynamic structure, keyed to the evolving needs of cross-functional project teams. They are totally integrated organizations. Work goes on concurrently rather than sequentially and is not necessarily contained within the envelope of the legally distinct corporate entity. Subcontractors, partners, customers and endusers interrelate in the concurrent design and production network. Management becomes less and less functionally oriented and more and more the management of diverse project teams, creating new alliances with embryonic industry firms. There are implications of this to apply to corporate governance in management education (but see Mathews 1993b). Diversity, in all its characteristics, whether premised on diverse knowledge, whether occupational or particularly, other social identities, is a central issue of heightened salience in contemporary Australia as a multicultural country.

The Management of Diversity

There is no Australian culture. Not in the singular. Australia is in this respect a thoroughly postmodern society, a society of pluraslism. Australian cultures exist. The scene is one of diversity. It is for this reason that in discussion of "culture" we wish to break ranks with the predominant wisdom. When management theorists and practitioners have emphasized the importance of culture, they have done so, since at least Peters and Waterman (1982), in terms that eulogise the importance of a "strong" culture. It has become almost axiomatic to discuss the necessity of having a unitary culture for organizations that are to achieve excellence. Rather than contribute further to a discussion of culture that mistakes the existence of strong symbols and rituals for a sign of unitary culture, rather than as a mechanism designed to try and create one where it is usually absent, we think that such discussion in the context of a culturally diverse society may better orient towards consideration of cultural diversity as a strength rather than a weakness.

Multiculturalism, the widespread use of community languages and the vitality offered by ethnic communities that are not being forced into a melting pot are major advantages. Australian management education can build upon these to gain competitive advantage in the markets that our community languages and cultures represent. If multicultural management is to become a reality in the fastest possible time then skills adequate to the management of diversity must become a central component of management education, development and training.

It is not only the need to integrate cultural and language elements with the curriculum of management that is important. One of the fastest growing areas in the United States Academy of Management is "the management of diversity" and we need to develop the same skills here in Australia. A great deal of management is culturally implicit behavior, as feminist evaluation of the masculinist bias of management has identified. Yet it is not only gender cultures that are at work in organizations. There are also cultures of ethnicity that require surfacing and managing in their assumptions. The development of the management of diversity is a necessity for the management curriculum, particularly for embryonic industry. This is because, as we have identified, there is a central role for cultural entreprencurialism to play in developing innovation. Yet, if it is not only to be in the area of ethnic businesses that these innovations occur, then other organizations in Australia will have to develop capabilities that allow them to add the value that cultural diversity makes implicitly available, rather than to resist it in the name of a strong culture – one that would frequently be Anglo-Celtic, whatever else it might be.

Recruitment to Networks

Firms that network internationally have access to:

- intelligence on competitors;
- new technologies;
- product sources;
- new product applications and new manufacturing processes.

As McKinsey (1993: 34) noted, it is decreasingly production costs and increasingly factors such as "product design, technology application, marketing and branding" that drive competitive success.

In scanning the business environment, an initiative, modeled in part on a scheme reported by McKinsey (1993: 56), may be useful. Linking technology and innovation in California is the University of California Access Model, an information platform that includes information on technology available for licensing in universities and federally sponsored research programs in progress and the product lines and capabilities of over 39,000 high-tech corporations.

For firms in embryonic industries the greatest creativity in scanning the business environment often has to be exercised in ensuring that there is a steady supply of an appropriate amount of venture capital. The relation between venture capital and embryonic industry management is two way. Venturers have to acquire a sound grasp of the management needs of embryonic organizations striving to innovate in the marketplace. The finance specialism is not a stand-alone set of techniques. Management education needs techniques that allow both venturers and managers of firms in embryonic industries to communicate more effectively.

Beyond simply putting scientists and technologists together in the same faculties as management academics, the further development of a new paradigm of management requires a shift towards a problem oriented and project team curriculum that integrates management with other applications, such as science and technology, or design. The specific needs of the successful management of embryonic industries require explicit attention. Firms involved in innovation in embryonic industries look nothing like the corporate bureaucracies that are still the model for much management education, with its stress on functional knowledge and location within a predominantly Anglo-American field of practice.

Conventional business knowledge organized in a traditional graduate management mode of delivery is of little relevance to the manager of a firm in an embryonic industry, trying to manage networks and alliances rather more than functional areas or disciplinary problems. Many entrepreneurs in new fields are creative artists, technological innovators or scientists. They do not have time to take on a post first degree management qualification. Where they do, they find much of the curriculum irrelevant for their needs.

There is an additional issue. Management knowledge is required at an earlier stage of their organizational lifecycle; before, rather than after, having had to struggle to run their embryonic firm. Management education at the post first degree level (in honors and above) needs to shift from the education of individuals into the training of project teams. It should move from a disciplinary to a problem focus. The teams should work on projects that require using a range of skills from the team to co-operate with the teachers' design and delivery of the program and instruct students in cooperating in the practical resolution of the problems faced. New project centered and inter-disciplinary technology and science degrees focused on the management of projects may be part of an answer. Such an approach should include industry alliance and permits modular training and education by either ally. The research project noted that the University of Western Sydney-Macarthur was conducting with ANSTO, ICI, and Caltex a technology management program that had many of these features. Importantly, industry and the University developed the program as a strategic opportunity. For reasons of economy of effort and targeting of critical consumers, within tertiary education, efforts may focus most effectively on honors and graduate students, rather than the general undergraduate student body.

More use of the skill bases of under employed and retired strategic managers in contributing to teaching teams are possible. The Canadian Federal Business Development Bank, provides training and counselling services at local and regional levels that use such retirees. In Huntsville demonstrated the important role that senior military retirees played in building embryonic enterprise. Technology changes and restructuring have produced in Australia a pool of retired, unemployed or under employed strategic managers. Educators, firms in embryonic industries, and these managers, would gain by network association.

Conclusion

Embryonic industries pose considerable challenge to management and leadership in the 21st century, as this chapter has suggested. If the provision of these needs is met there will be ample opportunity for industry to flourish in the high value, elaborately transformed manufacturing area. Getting it right will mean considerable institutional change. As the chapter has highlighted, one cannot view embryonic industries in isolation. They pose particular challenges that transcend consideration of organizational life-cycles, industry complexes and initial and mature businesses. The process that we have conducted in translating views, opinions and arguments for the research is such as to suggest that in many areas of the present institutional, curriculum and conceptual delivery of management education, there is more that could be done not only better but also differently.

To reiterate our main conclusions. A new paradigm of management is emerging, one that is representative of a more "feminized" and less "masculinist" practice than in the past. Some of its characteristics are the centrality of organization learning in order to try and achieve "virtuous circles" that involve more flexible organizations. These organizations will be less marked by a separation between management and leadership than in older organization forms, communications will tend to be open and constituted as discursively free between equals, on a contingent basis. In particular, this openness will characterize early stages of the life-cycle for firms in embryonic industries. Such firms will tend to have markets that are intrusive and extensive, success in which will be a major source of motivation and reward. Core competences will be nurtured in these organizations and strategic learning capacities will be widespread rather than restricted to the apex of the organization. A corollary of this is that organization members will be trusted and empowered because the knowledge that they can contribute is the most important factor for the success of the organization.

Enterprises can benefit not only from world class science as a source of innovation but also gain a competitive advantage in the markets from cultural innovation.

Embryonic industries cannot be analyzed in isolation but need to be seen in a model of the "embryonic industry complex" that focuses on linkages of chains, clusters, networks and strategic alliances. Within the embryonic industries complex public policies need to address issues of training, perhaps through schemes that exchange individual education credits for trade-offs in the institutional organization of the workplace. In addition, they need to address how best to cluster in nodal points firms that can grow endogenously. Within the embryonic industries complex producers and suppliers can be sources of networks for innovation and customers and users can be sources for the exchange and flow of information about needs, techniques and technologies among buyers, suppliers and related industries.

There is a need to integrate management with the teaching of technologies, cultures, and other subjects in an integrated delivery, based on problem-centered project work. The management of ambiguity, equivocality and uncertainty are the central underlying communication competences for curriculum development in management. CEOs need to be taught to abandon vertical integration and to force market relations into the firm and to subcontract extensively, creating numerous joint ventures and alliances, especially with new firms if they are in more established industries. Firms need to be oriented towards the constant benchmarking of educational best practice in an open, competitively ranked environment. Innovations that develop within management education that meet market approval will thus more quickly flow through the whole system. Innovation is the lifeblood of the embryonic firm and organizational *glasnost* furthers its development. Management needs to value intangible as well as tangible contributions.

There are no guarantees that if one adopts the advice tendered here that one will manage as if tomorrow matters. However, without some attempt at learning, we are confident that tomorrow's managers will merely reiterate the errors of today's. Tomorrow does matter: both managerially, for the future of the assets that one is stewarding; culturally, for the preservation and enrichment of life-chances for the society in which one dwells, and ecologically, for the future of the planet and the species. This chapter seeks to reflect these conjoint emphases.

Note

[1] This chapter reports research done in Australia, for the Australian Federal Government, hence the frequent reference to Australia in the text.

References

Abernathy, W. and Clark, K. (1985), Innovation: Mapping the Winds of Creative Destruction, *Research Policy,* 14, pp. 3-22.
Amara, R. (1990), New Directions for Innovation, *Futures,* 22(2), pp. 142-152.
Anderson, P. and Tushman, N.L. (1990), Technological Discontinuities and Dominant Designs: A Cyclical Model of Technological Change, *Administrative Science Quarterly,* 35, pp. 604-633.
Argyris, C. and Schon, D.A. (1978), *Organizational Learning: A Theory of Action Perspective,* Reading, MA, Wesley Publishing.
Barrett, M.A. (1994), The "Feminization" of Management: Implications for Management Education, in Clegg et al. (1994).
Bennis, W. (1993), Creative Leadership, *Management,* November, 10, pp. 10-15.
Best, M. (1990), *The New Competition,* Cambridge, Polity Press.
Bianchi, P. (1993), The Promotion Of Small Firm Clusters and Industrial Districts: European Policy Perspectives, *Journal of Industry Studies.,* 1(1), pp. 16-29.
Bolman, L.G. and Deal, T.E. (1991), *Reframing Organizations: Artistry, Choice and Leadership,* San Francisco, Jossey-Bass.
Brown, W. B. and Karagozoglu, N. (1993), Leading the Way to Faster New Product Development, *Academy of Management Executive,* 7(1), pp. 36-47.
Bryman, A. (1992), *Charisma and Leadership in Organizations,* London, Sage.
Cantley, M.F. (1986), Long-term Prospects and Implications of Biotechnology for Europe: Strategic Challenge and Response, *International Journal of Technology Management,* 1(2), pp. 209-229.
Chua, W.F. and Clegg, S. R. (1990), Professional Closure: The Case of British Nursing, *Theory and Society,* 19, pp. 135-172.
Clegg, S.R. (1989), *Frameworks of Power,* London, Sage.
Clegg, S.R. (1990), *Modern Organizations: Organization Studies in the Postmodern World,* London, Sage.
Clegg, S.R. and Dunkerley, D. (1980), *Organization, Class and Control.* London, Routledge and Kegan Paul.
Clegg, S.R., Dwyer, L., Gray, J., Kemp, S., Marceau, J. and O'Mara, E. (eds.) (1992), *Leadership and Management Needs of Embryonic Industries: A Research Report for Midgley & Company on behalf of the Industry Task Force on Leadership and Management Skills,* Canberra: Department of Employment, Education and Training.
Clegg, S.R., Higgins, W. and Spybey, T. (1992), Post-Confucianism, Social Democracy and Economic Culture, in Clegg, S.R., Redding, S.G. and Cartner, M. (eds.), *Capitalism in Contrasting Cultures,* Berlin, New York, de Gruyter, pp. 31-78

Cooper, R. and Kleinschmidt, E. (1986), An Investigation into the New Product Process: Steps, Deficiencies and Impact, *Journal of Product Innovation Management,* 3, pp. 71-85.

Daft, R.L. (1982), Diffusion of Modern Software Practices: Influence of Centralization and Formalization, *Management Science,* 28, pp. 1421-1431.

Daft, R.L. and Weick, K.E. (1982), Towards a Model of Organizations as Interpretation Systems, *Academy of Management Review,* 9(2), pp. 284-295.

Dodgson, M. (1993a), Organizational Learning: A Review of Some Literatures, *Organization Studies,* 14(3), pp. 375-394.

Dodgson, M. (1993b), Learning, Trust, and Technological Collaboration, *Human Relations,* 46(1), pp. 77-95

Dwyer, L. and Mellor, R. (1991), Organizational Environment, New Product Process Activities and Project Outcomes, *Journal of Product Innovation Management,* 8, pp. 39-48.

Early, P.C. and P. Stubblebine (1989), Intercultural Assessment of Performance Feedback, *Group and Organization Studies,* 14, pp. 161-181.

Eriksson, I.V. (1990), Educating End-Users to Make More Effective Use of Information Systems, in U. Gattiker and L. Larwood (eds.), *End-User Training,* Berlin, New York, ode Gruyter, pp. 59-102.

Fairtlough, G. (1993), Innovation and Biotechnology, a talk presented to the *Science Policy Research Unit,* Sussex University England,19 February.

Fairtlough, G. (1994), *Creative Compartments: A Design for Future Organisations,* London, Adamantine Press.

Farr, M.C. and Fischer, W.A. (1992), Managing International High Technology Co-operative Projects, *R&D Management,* 22(1), pp. 60-67.

Fritz, P. and Ellercamp, P. (1988), *The Possible Dream: TCG, An Australian Business Success Story,* Melbourne, Penguin.

Garrat, R. (1987), *The Learning Organization,* London, Fontana-Collins.

Gattiker, U. and T. Nelligan (1988), Computerized Offices in Canada and the United States: Investigating Dispositional Similarities and Differences, *Journal of Organizational Behaviour,* 9, pp. 77-96.

Gattiker, U. and K. Willoughby (1993), Technological Competence, Ethics, and the Global Village: Cross-National Comparisons for Organization Research, in R.T. Golembiewski (ed.), *Handbook of Organizational Behavior,* New York, Marcel Dekker, pp. 457-85.

Goldman, S.L. and Nagel, R.N. (1993), Management, Technology and Agility: The Emergence of a New Era in Manufacturing, *International Journal of Technology Management,* 8(1), pp. 18-38.

Goldstone, J.A. (1987), Cultural Orthodoxy, Risk, and Innovations: The Divergence of East and West in the Early Modern World, *Sociological Theory,* 5, pp. 119-35.

Gouldner, A. (1954), *Patterns of Industrial Bureaucracy,* New York, Free Press.

Greenpeace Business (1993), Greenpeace Plan Helps Win Sydney Olympics Bid, *Greenpeace Business,* 16, p. 5.

Habermas, J. (1984) *Reason and the Rationalisation of Society,* London, Heinemann.

Hayes, R.H., Wheelwright, S.C. and Clark, K.B. (1988), *Dynamic Manufacturing: Creating the Learning Organization,* New York, Free Press.

Hedberg, B. (1981), How Organizations Learn and Unlearn, in P.P. Nystrom and W. Starbuck (eds.), *Handbook of Organizational Design,* Oxford, Oxford University Press.

Higgins, W. and Clegg, S.R. (1988), Enterprise Calculation and Manufacturing Decline. *Organization Studies,* 9(1), pp. 69-89.

Kanter, R.M. (1989), The New Managerial Work, *Harvard Business Review,* November-December, pp. 85-92.

Kenney, M. and Florida, R. (1988), Beyond Mass Production: Production and the Labour Process in Japan, *Politics and Society,* 16(1), pp. 121-58.

Littek, W. and U. Heissig (1991), Competence, Control and Work Redesign: *Die Angstellten* in the Federal Republic of Germany, *Work and Occupations,* 18, pp. 4-28.

Marceau, J. (ed.) (1992), *Reworking the World: Organizations, Technologies and Cultures in Comparative Perspective,* Berlin, New York, de Gruyter.

Mathews, J. (1993a), Gulliver's Travails. Breaking the Bonds that Constrain Productivity: Teamwork and Organizational Innovation, *Industrial Relations Research Centre,* University of NSW. Kensington.

Mathews, J. (1993b), TCG. R&D Networks. The Triangular Strategy, *Journal of Industry Studies,* 1(1), pp. 65-74.

McGrath, R.G. and MacMillan, I.C. (1993), Technology and the CEO: Seeking Tomorrow's Edge, *Chief Executive,* 82, January-February, pp. 64-67.

McKee, D. (1992), An Organizational Learning Approach to Product Innovations, *Journal of Product Innovation Management,* 9, pp. 232-245.

McKinsey and Co. Inc. (1993), Emerging Exporters: Australia's High Value-Added Manufacturing Exporters, Final Report of the Study by McKinsey and Co. for the Australian Manufacturing Council, Melbourne.

Nicholson, M. (1993), On a Possible Structure to Help the Small Australian Software Developers, Discussion Paper, La Trobe University, Bundoora.

Perry, L.T. and K.W. Sandholtz (1988), A "Liberating Form" for Radical Product Innovation, in U. Gattiker and L. Larwood (eds.), *Studies in Technological Innovation and Human Resources, Vol. 1 – Managing Technological Development,* Berlin, New York, de Gruyter.

Peters, T. (1990), Get Innovative or Get Dead, *California Management Review,* Part 1: 33(1), pp. 9-26, Part 2: 33(2), pp. 9-23.

Peters, T. (1992), *Liberation Management,* MacMillan, New York.

Peters, T. and Waterman, R. (1982), *In Search of Excellence: Lessons from America's Best Run Companies,* New York, Harper and Row.

Prahalad, C.K. and Hamel, G. (1990), The Core Competence of the Corporation, *Harvard Business Review,* May-June, 3, pp. 79-91.

Pyke, F. and Sengenberger, W. (eds.) (1992), *Industrial Districts and Inter-firm Cooperation in Italy,* Geneva, International Institute of Labour Studies.

Roberts, E.B. (1990), Evolving Toward Product and Market-Orientation: The Early Years of Technology-Based Firms, *Journal of Product Innovation Management,* 7, pp. 274-287.

Rothwell, R. (1992), Successful Industrial Innovation: Critical Factors for the 1990s, *R&D Management,* 22(3), pp. 221-239.

Selznick, P. (1957), *Leadership in Administration,* New York, Harper and Row.

Senge, P.M. (1989), *The Fifth Discipline: The Art and Practice of the Learning Organization,* New York, Doubleday.

Senker, J. and Senker, P. (1992), Gaining Competitive Advantage from Information Technology, *Journal of General Management,* 17(3), pp. 31-45.

Shanklin, W.L. and Ryans, Jr., J.K. (1984), Organizing for High-Tech Marketing, *Harvard Business Review*, November-December, pp. 164-171.

Smith, A. (1961), *An Inquiry into the Nature and Causes of Wealth of Nations,* Indianapolis, Bobbs-Merrill.

Snow, C., Miles, R. and Coleman, H. (1992), Managing 21st Century Network Organizations, *Organizational Dynamics,* Winter, pp. 5-20.

Taylor, F.W. (1911), *Principles of Scientific Management,* New York, Harper.

Van de Ven, A. (1993), The Development of an Infrastructure for Entrepreneurship, *Journal of Business Venturing*, 8, pp. 211-230.

Van Tulder, R. and Dankbaar, B. (1992), The Illusion of a Common Supranational Interest: Democratising the Standardisation Process in Factory Automation, in J. Marceau (ed.), *Reworking the World:Organizations,Technologies and Cultures in Comparative Perspective,* Berlin, New York, de Gruyter.

Weber, M. (1978), *Economy and Society*, Berkeley, San Francisco, University of California Press.

Weiss, L. (1988), *Creating Capitalism: The State and Small Business Since 1945,* Oxford, Blackwell.

Willoughby, K.E. (1992), *Biotechnology in New York: A Global Industry in a Global Community*, State University of New York. Stony Brook, N.Y., Center for Biotechnology.

Willoughby, K.W. (1990), *Technology Choice,* Boulder, Col., Westeview Press.

Womack, J.P., Jones, D.T. and Ross, D. (1990), *The Machine That Changed the World,* New York.MacMillan.

Organization Studies and Transformations in Modern Society

Paul Jeffcutt

Introduction

This chapter examines the conditions of emergence and contemporary development of the theory and practice of organization (i.e. Organization Studies) as a
constituent of modern society. The concern is with Organization Studies as a realm
of knowledge which addresses human progress and understanding, as well as
with Organization Studies as an empirical practice in which complex organizations have become both vehicles of and harbingers of progress in modern society.
Through this frame we shall concentrate on both the workplace or the firm (i.e.
the organization) as a significant constituent of the moral and economic order of
modern society, and the professional territory of management as both the authority for and a set of techniques for intervening in (i.e. organizing) this moral and
economic order.

The Human Sciences and Order

Articulating the emergence of modern society, as (Foucault 1974: 344) has argued,
is the formation of what he describes as "a body of discourse that takes as its object man as an empirical entity." This body of discourse, he argues, constitutes
around three fundamental and interconnected spheres, the sciences of life, labor
and language, which together describe the "Human Sciences."

The human sciences are not, then, an analysis of what man is by nature; but rather an analysis that extends from what man is in his positivity (a living, speaking, laboring being) to
what enables this same being to know (or seek to know) what life is, in what the essence of
labor and its laws consist, and in what way he is able to speak. The human sciences thus occupy the distance that separates (though not without connecting them) biology, economics,
and philology from that which gives them possibility in the very being of man (Foucault
1974: 353).

Foucault argues that it is through the transition to modern society, when the "inextricable link" between human beings and their "world" became ruptured and fragmented, that the space that the Human Sciences occupy (i.e. between human beings and their "world") is formed. Accordingly, the Human Sciences and modern society interact through their common concern with the fundamentals of living, speaking and laboring (as empirical positivities) as well as with life, language and labor (as realms of knowledge).

The development of this interconnection, between empirical positivities and realms of knowledge, articulates transformations experienced in different forms and in different phases over the past 200 years on a truly worldwide scale. These interconnections, on the one hand, can be traced through emerging modern understandings of social progress articulated from moral philosophy and political economy to the developing disciplines of sociology and anthropology (see Jeffcutt 1995). On the other hand, these interconnections are also evident in the formation of a moral and economic order in the "advanced" societies of Western Europe through which the transitional mass of the rapidly expanding population were managed, both as a "body" and in terms of their individual bodies (see Stallybrass and White 1986). Accordingly, by the late 19th century:

European man had changed his outlook. He still craved perfection – certainly progress – but he now saw the Industrial Revolution as its harbinger. Moreover, he had assumed administrative responsibility for innumerable 'savage' groups in his various imperial domains. Even if familiarity had not bred contempt, it had disabused him of most of the artless idealism of the Enlightenment. He regarded the 'savage' as an example no longer of human excellence but of an early stage of sociocultural development: a living ancestor from whom he had progressively distanced himself, whom with proper tuition he could persuade to follow in his wake, and who, carefully studied, would reveal the secrets of his own remote past (Lawrence 1987: 20).

The role of the Human Sciences in modern society was thus to fulfill this task; to study humanity, to reveal the secrets of their past, and to empower their future development. Indeed, the 19th century "grand theories" of society all encompassed this project, and proposed evolutionary analyses of stages of sociocultural development (i.e. Marx and Engels, Spencer, Tylor; see Austin-Broos 1987)[1]. Interlinking these "grand theories" was the articulation of not only particular moral and economic hierarchies (i.e. stages of cultivation and civilization) but also the uncovering of the underlying laws or principles by which social and cultural change had taken (and would continue to take) place[2]. Indeed, through such "grand theories," the Human Sciences became constituted not only as agencies of the articulation of, but also as agencies of intervention in, the moral and economic order of modern society. Consequently, the emergence of the Human Sciences can be understood as inseparable from the emergence of the need to manage humanity (and vice versa). Or as Achebe (1975) put it, in the context of the colonial approach to cultural "others"; understanding was a precondition for control, whilst control constituted adequate proof of understanding.

Accordingly, we may rewrite the project of the Human Sciences as they emerged in modern society, into such a facilitation of social progress through control. This project is clearly encapsulated in the progressive social theory of both Tylor (Social Anthropology) and Spencer (Sociology). Tylor described his work as "a reformers science" which would develop a "positive morality." On the one hand, this would provide a "doctrine of development" to enable the continuation of the progress that had been made by particular cultures (i.e. races) in former times; on the other hand, this would expose the remains of crude superstitions of earlier stages and "mark them out for destruction." The focus of this work he summarized as "aiding progress and removing hindrance" (Tylor in 1871, cited in Stocking 1987: 194). Spencer's work was centrally concerned with the functional evolution of societies from simple to complex; in his "Principles of Sociology" he saw this work as providing "a relative and an absolute standard" by which to "estimate social progress" (see Thompson et al. 1990).

In terms of the focal issues of control and change, the social evolutionism of Tylor and Spencer can be seen in contrast to the historical materialism of Marx and Engels. On the one hand, social evolutionism suggests that increasing difference, complexity and heterogeneity are functional to progress and can be managed to stabilize at more "advanced" levels of order in civilization. Whilst, on the other hand, historical materialism suggests that conflict and contradiction in the social relations of production are tensions which build to an inevitable transformation of these relations in the formation of a more "advanced" society. Although the pattern of change is held in common; in the former, the complexity of progress can be managed to recreate order; whilst in the latter, the contradictions of progress cannot be managed but a new order does follow struggle and transformation.

These evolutionary social hierarchies positioned a self conscious cultural elite at the head of a moral and economic order, with responsibility for the management and ordering of cultural "others." This was in essence a self-important cultural mission of investment in and patronage of the spirit of progress, as realized in both edifices and activities of modernization. Such a mission was both reforming and regulatory, with a broad focus, from the topography of the mass (e.g. Haussman's "regularization" of Paris) to individual "failings" (e.g. Contamination Acts, Temperance). Important amongst this regulation and reformation were the institutions and the new professionals of the Human Sciences. Accordingly, during the 19th century we have the proliferation of a wide range of learned societies and publications concerned with the science of progress and sociocultural evolution (see Stocking 1987), the founding of new "civic" universities concerned with developing and applying the technologies of progress (see Sanderson 1988), and the endowment of new posts, often by industrialists, in the Human Sciences (e.g. Chairs of Anthropology, Economics and Sociology, see Gordon 1991). As a founder of the London School of Economics observed,

Social reconstructions require as much specialized training and sustained study as the building of bridges and railways, the interpretation of the law, or technical improvements in machinery and mechanical processes (Webb in 1899, cited in Searle 1970: 85).

Such considerable investments by a cultural elite in fields of activity that held the promise of the management of progress resonated with learned debate on the issue of civilization and progress. Here, both Coleridge and Arnold (see Williams 1958) argued for an endowed elite who would be responsible for both maintaining and developing the levels of cultivation in society. Indeed, this was a role that both Tylor and Spencer claimed for their work. Although perhaps the most potent symbol of the link between modern society, cultivation and progress is that of the Nobel Prize; founded by the inventor of dynamite who invested his substantial wealth in order that annual prizes could be awarded, after his own death, to those "who have conferred the greatest benefit on mankind."

The pre-eminence of this cultural elite in modern society entailed the responsibility of managing both continuity (e.g. the maintenance and enhancement of standards of cultivation in society, whereby individuals are ranked and separated on a scale of sociocultural evolution through their possession of particular abilities, qualities and deficiencies); and change (e.g. the harnessing and utilization of productive forces, whereby civilization is developed through progress to more advanced stages of order than backward and unsophisticated societies). In both forms of managerial duty, the central issue was that of control and the privileged medium through which this control was articulated was that of the Human Sciences.

As we have been arguing, the practice of the Human Sciences has thus been to order the fragmented space they inhabit between human beings and their "world" (through which they also emerged) as well as to order the subjects and objects of this discourse (e.g. articulated through sociocultural understandings of the interrelationship of human beings and their "world"). Accordingly, the Human Sciences can be characterized by their concern for praxis, the management of the border between theorization and practice. Hence, the order of the Human Sciences is to intervene, and the interventions of the Human Sciences are to order, both their space and the surface between human beings and their "world."

Organization Studies as a Human Science

We have considered the interconnections between modern society and the Human Sciences as establishing both the authority for and a set of techniques for intervening in the moral and economic order of society. Consequently, modern society emerged in symbiosis with the Human Sciences, to be characterized, as we have observed, by the regulation of individual bodies as well as the body of the population as an organic, progressive but differentiated whole. We may thus understand the workplace or the firm (i.e. the organization) as a constituent of that moral and economic order, as well as an important site of intervention in that order. Indeed, it was the great institutions of modern society, from the arenas of government to those of the market, which emerged as both agencies of and harbingers of progress (i.e. following Tylor and Spencer). Complex organizations by their very rationality and sophistication, thus embodied both progress over backwardness and the promise of the attainment of further heights of civilization. As we have considered, such sociocultural hierarchies were echoed in practices of intervention (i.e. management), where self-control and social regulation enabled the cultivation of the progressive qualities of abstinence and foresight over the regressive qualities of instinct and impulse.

We shall go on to consider the modern field of Organization Studies to be distinguished by a dual focus; on the theorization of organizational analysis, as well as on the practice of organizing (commonly described as management). Iconographic as the starting point for the emergence of these twin activities is the work of the North American mechanical engineer and management consultant F. W. Taylor. In the light of our earlier discussion, "scientific management" can be understood as a reforming and regulatory "grand theory" through which an organization would become a "mini-society" that was archetypally modern. The modern "scientifically managed" organization would thus comprise a utopian moral and economic order in which management and workers would be functionally divided and specialized, whilst their interactions would be scientifically regulated and harmonized around efficiency, progress and reward. Scientific management thus offered a model of organizational progress through which the disorder of change could be managed and controlled to provide both mutual benefit, meaning productivity and profitability, and the harmonious recapturing of a more advanced order. However, the equity and reciprocal benefits of this "great mental revolution" were not immediately apparent to the managements and workforces of the industrialized countries of the world in the early 20th century. Accordingly, the "one best way" of organizing propounded by Taylor soon become modified, through the popularization of "efficiency systems," into variations that were contingent on the resistance of particular managements and, to a lesser extent, workforces.

We shall consider the significance of "scientific management" not as a point of origin for the theory and practice of organization, but rather as a prime channel of convergence which integrated pre-existing discourses and practices from the Human Sciences[3]. "Scientific management" should thus be seen both as a conduit and an important platform of departure from which Organization Studies, formed through over a century of antecedent struggle in the modern interrelationship of human beings and their "world," began to take on the shape and qualities that have been subsequently canonized as identifying its field, its discourse and its discipline (as both a mode and an object of understanding).

As we have been considering, this territory of Organization Studies between human beings and their "world" becomes visibly delineated and described through the articulation of "efficiency systems" that sought to improve labor productivity without compromising managerial structures of authority. These efficiency practices and discourses are properly connected under the rubric "Taylorism"; since, on the one hand, such "efficiency systems" can be considered as consolidations that are both distinct and derived from Taylor's work on "scientific management," whilst on the other hand, such efficiency practices and discourses need to be considered as being inextricably interconnected with disciplinary discourses from the Human Sciences, focused on the progress of organized activity. As we shall observe, it is this loose and contingent collection of discourses and practices of control and discipline that develop to become connected under the rubric "Taylorism" and form the explicit "field" of Organization Studies.

The practices and discourses of "Taylorism" thus represent a rationalization and a consolidation of "scientific management." An overarching philosophy of organizational progress was retained, in which the disorder of change could be scientifically managed and controlled to provide the stabilizing benefits of increased productivity and profitability. Yet, we also find that, on the one hand, managements have restored their rationality and regained control over disorder through technologies of work intensification, product standardization and accountability. Whilst, on the other hand workforces have likewise retained their demarcations and hierarchies through the consolidation of skilled worker's participation in the supervisory process (e.g. rate-setting) to the disadvantage of the unskilled (i.e. female, migrant and black labor, see Lash and Urry 1987).

Evolving beyond its technical and national origins, Taylorism became an important component of the philosophical outlook of modern industrial civilization, defining virtue as efficiency, establishing a new role for experts in production, and setting parameters for new patterns of social distribution... A mental revolution that had been so deeply embedded in the structure of industrial society that it was a social philosophy that no longer could be casually abandoned (Merkle 1980: 62)

Accordingly, it is appropriate to understand the Taylorizing process of organizational change as indeed part of a great "mental revolution." Although these organizational changes should be perceived as a symptom of wider and more far-reaching revolution in both thought and practice, than had been advocated in Taylor's utopian proposals, which had begun to emerge over a hundred years earlier in the transition to modern society. As part of the process of the modern organization of capital (i.e. intensification, see Lash and Urry 1987) great institutions were developed in the industrialized countries of the world. These complex, formal organizations became the very vehicles of progress, both embodying superiorities that distanced them from their past and also promising further benefits from the harnessing of human beings and scientific potential into productive and profit making capacities. Through such institutions, many controlled by dynastic families, the socio-economic and the socio-cultural orders of modern society became joined in the pursuit of progress (see Marcus and Hall 1992). As a consequence, organizations need to be understood as both sites and embodiments of the modern struggle for progress, as well as formations which comprise the dynamic moral and economic order of modern society. By the late 19th century the sociocultural evolution, that is, both the cultivation and the civilization of the industrializing countries of the modern world, because expressed through their complex organizations.

Each institution has brought with its development demands, expectations, rules, standards. These are not mere embellishments of the forces which produced them, idle decorations of the scene. They are additional forces. They reconstruct. They open new avenues of endeavor and impose new labors. In short, they are civilization, culture, morality... if one is going to live one must live a life of which these things form the substance. The only question having sense which can be asked is how we are going to use and be used by these things, not whether we are going to use them (Dewey in 1927, cited in Person 1929: 112).

Organization Studies as an explicit articulation of the Human Sciences becomes formed approximately a century after the emergence of modern society, yet, during these 100 years, Organization Studies is already there in the disciplinary discourses and control practices of modern society, articulated through human sciences predominantly concerned with sociocultural evolution. These partly visible and overlapping components converge and continue their development more collectively through the conduit of "Taylorism." With this visible integration of a loose collection of organizational discourses and practices, the territory of Organization Studies, as a Human Science of modern society, between human beings and their "world," becomes visible, formatively delineated and described. Accordingly, pre-existing disciplinary discourses and control practices continued their part in the symbiotic process of evolving with, as well as managing and intervening in, the moral and economic order of modern society.

These twin processes, interconnecting the Human Sciences and Modern Society, articulate the formation of Organization Studies as both an arena of organizational theory and practice. Unsurprisingly, in Organization Studies we encounter a very similar process to that which we observed in the formation of Sociology and Social Anthropology as arenas of theory and practice. In both cases, "grand theories," for example, the sociocultural evolution of society or a great mental revolution in organizations, became articulated through a mix of paternal and authoritarian management strategies in the modernization of a moral and economic order. The idea (formed in the early 20th century) of organization as a rational, technical bureaucracy characterized by accountability and efficiency that operates in a mass market, is thus an embodiment of the idea of progress in society as well as being inseparable from practices of intervention (i.e. modernization) that are seeking to modify the moral and economic order towards these ends; both in terms of specific sites, such as organizations, and in society in general.

Consequently, Organization Studies from the early 20th century becomes consolidated as a Human Science that is concerned with organizational progress in the advance of industrial society. Moreover, this is a progress that is defined in terms that are common to the Human Sciences (as the regaining of the stability of an improved order from the dislocation and disorder of change) but articulated in respect of the specificities of productivity, accountability, consumption and profitability. Accordingly, organizations are conceptualized as rational-technical entities within an industrial society, and Organization Studies undertakes a pragmatic, interventionist and consultancy oriented approach to its sites of interest. Enabling this formation of a "fresh" arena of the Human Sciences is, as we have observed, on the one hand the growing significance of organized activity as both sites and embodiments of progress. Whilst, on the other hand, is the convergence of pre-existing discourses and practices which regulated social organization to become visibly interconnected around the integrative conduit of the "sciences of organization."

Organization Studies thus becomes an archetypal Human Science seeking to intervene in and to order the space and the surface between "organizational man/woman" and his/her "organizational world." As a consequence of this formation, Organization Studies becomes canonized as the Human Science concerned with the colonial process of regulation and control of social order both in- and outside of organization (i.e. both producers and consumers). As we have observed, this orientation is first explicitly articulated by the disciplinary discourses and practices of control we considered under the rubric "Taylorism," and supported by a wide range of professionalization processes around the "sciences of organization."

Organization Studies and Transformation

It is entirely appropriate that Organization Studies should explicitly emerge at the "height" of modern society (see Hassan 1985), in the early 20th century. Suffused by an intensity and diversity of experimentation, artists (e.g. Futurists, Vorticists), musicians (e.g. Stravinsky, Bartok) and writers (e.g. Joyce, Lawrence) sought to represent the dynamism of modern life, at the same time as innovation in transportation and communication (e.g. aircraft, motor vehicles, radio) intensified the transformation of human beings and their "world" through simultaneity, movement and plurality. Not only was there an enormous and rapid increase in the volume of commodities, but a mature "colonial" trading system also enabled the distribution and marketing of these raw materials, services and finished products on a worldwide basis.Characterized by processes of ordering and control based on rational calculation, Organization Studies became the "visible hand" of intervention in the institutions of modern society through which progress could be both effectively pursued and reliably achieved. This "visible hand" was effected and empowered by new professionals in their interventions (i.e. management) in complex organizations which sought to harness and integrate forces for change at the leading edge of the transformation of society.

The young factories!
They live heartily.
They smoke higher than the peal of the bells.
They are not afraid to hide the sun,
Because they create sun with their own machines.
Like a dog shaking itself on leaving the sea,
The foaming factory scatters around itself
Drops of energy which wake the city (Jules Romains, "L'Eglise," 1908; cited in Tate Gallery 1991: 4).

The form in and through which Organization Studies became canonized was that of rational-technical organization or "bureaucracy." As we have been observing, this was the archetypal modern efficiency system of both theory and practice (see Clegg 1990). On the one hand, this form was understood as exhibiting both technical and sociocultural superiority over less capable forebears (i.e. as a more advanced form of organizational order, see Lash and Urry 1987). Whilst, on the other hand, this form promised a means of both consolidating gains that had been made and achieving continuing improvement in the moral and economic order of society (i.e. the process of modernization, see Harvey 1989). As we shall consider, "bureaucracy" was understood as the organizational vehicle of progress for both liberal capitalist society, that is, a non-discriminatory impartiality in the exercise of individual freedoms and responsibilities (see Perrow 1972) and communist society, meaning a productive system as the foundation of a workers' state, which would eliminate shortage, provide and distribute resources for all (see Lenin 1968). However, these particular promises of progress were only partially realized and at considerable human cost (see Bauman 1989, 1992).

To further develop our consideration of the "management" of progress in modern society we now need to focus on tensions between construction and destruction that are inherent to this idea and experience of change. We have considered progress as the dynamic through which modern society would be transformed for the better, through an amalgam of constructive and destructive forces. On the one hand, progress would effect the destabilization of former continuities through the functional energy of division. On the other hand, progress would also effect the adaptive "invisible hand" of reformation through which an improved order would be reconstructed. As we also considered, the transition to modern society was characterized by a strong sense of loss (as articulated in the nostalgia of Cobbett) and disputes over the direction of development (the romanticism of Coleridge). However, the maturation of modern society became increasingly characterized by a self-confidence that the tensions of change could be effectively managed to ensure the developmental continuities of socio-cultural evolution. The Human Sciences thus exercised both regulation and reassurance in modern society through the articulation of progress over regress and optimism over nostalgia.

Although in the exercise of these disciplinary discourses and practices of control, the fear of the future is powerfully there in the disorder that needs to be both contained and censored (i.e. managed). As we have considered, this fear is largely articulated in terms of the mass of society, focusing on both their individual bodies and the body of the population.The contamination of the mass both individually and collectively was sought to be contained as these cultural "others" were harnessed, through paternal and authoritarian strategies, in the pursuit of progress. However, as Marx and Engels observed so presciently, construction and destruction are each brought into tension through progress:

Constant revolutionizing of production, uninterrupted disturbance of all social conditions, everlasting uncertainty and agitation distinguish the bourgeois epoch from all earlier ones. All fixed, fast-frozen relations, with their train of ancient and venerable prejudices and opinions, are swept away, all new-formed ones become antiquated before they can ossify. All that is solid melts into air, all that is holy is profaned, and man is at last compelled to face with sober senses, his real conditions of life, and his relations with his kind (Marx and Engels 1888: 45-46)

These tensions are further revealed through 19th century reinterpretation of the myth of Prometheus, classically articulated in the story of Frankenstein (Shelley 1969). Science in its search for progress and the creation of a perfect order, creates instead a fallible and perverted order (a monster) which destroys its creators. In the Human Sciences, the pre-eminent interveners in the development of modern society, these tensions are necessarily articulated through an ambivalence towards the project of progress. On the one hand, facilitating sociocultural evolution as the agency of modernization; whilst, on the other hand, criticizing the transformations of sociocultural change.

From this foul drain the greatest stream of human industry flows out to fertilize the whole world. From this filthy sewer pure gold flows. Here humanity attains its most complete development and its most brutish; here civilization works its miracles, and civilized man is turned back almost into a savage (de Tocqueville in 1835, on Manchester, cited in Kumar 1978: 64.)

Such ambivalence in the early phase of transition to modern society was articulated by oppositions in the Human Sciences. On the one hand, we can consider social theory which optimized the opportunities of the process of transition (e.g. Saint-Simon, Comte, Tylor, Spencer); whilst, on the other hand, we can consider romantic and nostalgic reactions to such change (e.g. Cobbett, Carlyle, Coleridge). Of particular interest was social theory which sought to incorporate the tensions of this ambivalence to social change.For example, we can observe the reforming work of Marx and Engels which offered a far-sighted critique of the process of modernization (i.e. the bourgeois revolution) allied to an alternative conception of social progress (i.e. towards advanced Communism). At the same time, we can consider the more paternal work of Arnold who sought to manage the threat of the mass through the educational (i.e. civilizing) activity of the state.

In the phase of "high modernism" (i.e. the early 20th century, see Hassan 1985), with Organization Studies formed as an explicit and expert facilitator of progress (e.g. the theory and practice of "Taylorism"), the critical voices of sociocultural change emerged from older arenas of the Human Sciences like Anthropology and Sociology. In this phase, the organization of the mass continues its preeminence as the representation of progress in modern society. The bureaucratic ordering of complexity, as practiced in business enterprises and other institutions, thus becomes a persuasive model for the organization of the greater collectivities of modern society (e.g. the city). This interconnection, through communication technologies, of the complexity of social organization with the rationalization of systems of administration, is a site of both romantic regret (Tönnies 1887) and pessimistic observation (Simmel 1903).

They were nearing Chicago. Signs were everywhere numerous. Trains flashed by them. Across wide stretches of flat open prairie they could see lines of telegraph poles stalking across the fields toward the great city (Drieser in 1900; cited in Tallack 1991: 4)

The relationships and affairs of the typical metropolitan usually are so varied and complex that without the strictest punctuality in promises and services the whole structure would break down into an inextricable chaos. Above all, this necessity is brought about by the aggregation of so many people with such differentiated interests, who must integrate their relations and activities into a highly complex organism (Simmel 1903, cited in Kumar 1978: 71).

It is in the work of Weber and Durkheim, emerging in this period of "high modernism," that the critique of the theory and practice of organization as the archetype for progress became most explicit. For Durkheim, the complex organizations of modern society became sites for the reconstruction of solidarity in a society that was being transformed through the process of modernization. Organizations were thus understood as articulating a collective moral and economic order that was formed through tensions between integration and regulation (see Thompson et al. 1990). Organizations needed to be approached as representations of a "conscience collective" (i.e. a shared moral code, see Gordon 1991); in other words, as symbolic forms which articulate culture.

In a series of profound and probing discussions of education, politics, professional organization, morality and the law, Durkheim demonstrated that these modern spheres must be studied in terms of symbolic classifications. They are structured by tensions between the fields of the sacred and profane; their central social processes are ritualistic; their most significant structural dynamics concern the construction and destruction of social solidarities (Alexander 1988: 3).

For Weber, the complex organizations of modern society were sites of rationalization whereby the uncertainty and disenchantment of modernization was managed
and controlled. Bureaucracy was thus both a response to and a reflection of the
modern condition. On the one hand, the uncertainties and disenchantment of the
modern world were made manageable through rational action; whilst on the other
hand, the freedom to act was constrained by this imposition of an ethic of rational
calculation. Under these circumstances, the modern world becomes manageable
through the proliferation of bureaucratic organizations, but at the price of modernization. This was a bargain which empowered the construction of ever-expanding
organizational "iron cages" where individuals worked to meet the functional requirements of a system determined by objective, calculable rules for optimal performance.

The iron cage is not only a prison but also a principle. As a principle it 'makes us free' to be
modern. It makes us free because it is only through the purposefulness and goal directed-
ness of organization that the uncertainties of disenchanted modernity could be coped with.
In Weber's view it would be only false prophets who would insist otherwise. Rational calculation would limit uncertainty to a world which was, in principle, manageable. The freedom of modernity, experienced in the loss of entrapment within received meaning, is not
something which is merely one-dimensional, something wholly positive. It is also something simultaneously experienced negatively – as a loss of freedom to organizational and
rational constraint (Clegg 1990: 33).

For both Durkheim and Weber, organizations articulate the modern condition, in-
scribing an order (i.e. "solidarity" or "rationality") through which the disorder (i.e.
"uncertainty," "disenchantment," or "anomie") that was implicit to this condition
was made manageable. However, this was a manageability that was only achieved
through loss, essentially the loss of individuality to the "coercion" of community
(Durkheim) or the "iron cage" of bureaucracy (Weber). Indeed, it is clearly significant that these understandings emerged at a transitional stage in modern society
when the "invisible hand" of the market was becoming explicitly superseded by
the "visible hand" of management in the formation of social order. Consequently,
it is the combination of these two forms of order ("solidarity" and "rationality")
that characterizes the later 20th century development of Organization Studies (see
Clegg 1990) as well as the management of the centrally planned societies of both
capitalist and communist nation-states (see Bauman 1989; 1992).

Conclusion

Organization Studies can thus be understood as a thoroughly modern constituent
of the Human Sciences; being characterized by the heterogeneity, division and
disorder of the modern condition as well as being predicated upon the ordering
and management of this very condition through its theory and practice. This fun-

damental tension is articulated in two complementary and contradictory foci of activity which together constitute the "field" of Organization Studies.

On the one hand, we can observe an area of knowledge that is inevitably cross- and multi-disciplinary. Where a theoretical field concerned with the analysis of organization has become relatively recently established (i.e. with the majority of its work having been conducted over the past 60 years), formed from theoretical foundations that were largely dominated by other Human Science disciplines (e.g. Anthropology, Economics, Politics, Psychology, Sociology) which developed earlier in the 19th century, this is hardly surprising. Whilst, on the other hand, we can observe an area of practice that is inevitably cross-institutional and multicultural (in terms of place, size, sector, scale, scope, etc.). Where a field of professional practice has become established, again largely over the past 60 years, which has sought to manage difference in the pursuit of progress, both across and within the diverse settings of organized activity. Such practices of organizational ordering were again formed on foundations of practice which emerged earlier in the regulation of modern society.

Consequently, Organization Studies, from its explicit "high modern" formation at the turn of the century develops a plural structure that is both "multidisciplinary" and "multi-cultural." On the one hand, this plurality reflects the functional areas of business enterprise, such as marketing, production and accounting, the distinctive concerns of which have been sought to be integrated through the functional practice of management. As we have observed, it was the rise of such complex organizations as "high modern" sites of societal progress, to which the rise of Organization Studies has been symbolically interconnected. On the other hand, this plurality reflects the Human Sciences, as Organization Studies becomes an arena of contestation and collaboration between already established disciplines which sought to pursue the broader issues of order/disorder and progress in modern society through organization (i.e. representing both a specific site of interest and an archetypal expression of the modern condition).

However, Organization Studies, in its canonization as an explicit arena of Human Science concerned with the organization of progress, became at the same time shadowed by an ambivalence to modern society. On the one hand, facilitating the modernization of efficiency systems and the extension of bureaucracy into organized life (e.g. Taylorism); whilst, on the other hand, both recognizing and exposing the coercion, repression and provisionality that accompanies this search to extend progress through manageability (e.g. Weber, Durkheim). This ambivalence becomes articulated through both the forming and crossing of significant boundaries:

- Organization as a site of tension between order and disorder in social change.
- Organization Studies as both a practical science of management and a theoretical science of manageability.

- Organization Studies as a multi-disciplinary Human Science that is concerned with the development of functional arenas of organizations, as well as with organization as an embodiment and expression of change in modern society.

These interconnections are vital and sustaining, distinguishing Organization Studies as an activity that is both concerned with and constituted by modern boundaries and tensions. Accordingly, whilst Organization Studies is necessarily the theory and practice of organization both in and of modern society, these are difficult interconnections that have frequently been oversimplified in a search to reduce their ambivalence and ambiguity. The development of Organization Studies in the 20th century can thus be characterized by moves which aim to separate and reduce the tensions that are constitutive of the theory and practice of organization (see Locke 1989; Hassard and Pym 1990, Reed and Hughes 1992). As we shall consider (see also Cooper 1986, 1989), this selective focusing on "order" (e.g. strategy and structure) is linked to a corresponding censorship of "disorder" (e.g. provisionality and ambiguity). Furthermore, such tensions are endemic to modernity.

There is mode of vital experience – experience of space and time, of the self and others, of life's possibilities and perils – that is shared by men and women all over the world today. I will call this body of experience 'modernity.' To be modern is to find ourselves in an environment that promises adventure, power, joy, growth, transformation of ourselves and the world – and, at the same time, that threatens to destroy everything we have, everything we know, everything we are (Berman 1983: 15).

This desire to create order from disorder permeates the modern world, and can be observed from late 19th century "depth-models" of the person (e.g. conscious/subconscious, Freud) and society (e.g. superstructure/base, Marx), to late 20th century syntheses of apparently incommensurable theoretical perspectives (e.g. images of organization, Morgan 1986). Whether exposing the dark underside of society for reform or expressing a liberating vision of the future, the aspiration of the cultural practices of modernism is to seek to attain a fresh and renewing order through the resolution of tensions that are vital to modernity (articulated so graphically by Baudelaire and Berman, see above). As we shall observe, these archetypally modern tensions between transformation and destruction have the promise of being resolved or overcome through strategies of innovation and experimentation.

   With the essential truth of the world being understood as underlying and hidden, the essential focus of modernism becomes the revelation of that truth through rational processes of uncovering (Boyne and Rattansi 1990). Here a complex surface that appears incoherent, contradictory and unstable (e.g. the symbolic world) is able to be understood, ordered and coordinated (i.e. rationalized) at theoretically submerged levels of unity (i.e. "reality"). This characteristically modern belief in a harmonious and unified deep-structure of reality privileges the processes by which that reality is knowable (i.e. intellectually and culturally penetrable), particularly privileging the authors of such penetrations. Modernism is thus focused on the process of interpretation and its problematics (see Ryan 1988), a process which entails a restless searching for new strategies that are more original or authentic in their revelation and expression of underlying structure. Correspondingly, modernity has been characterized by the institutionalization of such creative searching, both scientific and artistic, exemplified by the widespread establishment of institutional bases for such intellectual effort (i.e. municipal universities, galleries, theaters etc.), and the patronage of an associated avant-garde. Through the intellectual heroism of such a modernist "vanguard," the tensions of disorder, ambiguity and disunity that were recognized as endemic to the condition of modernity, seemed to be able to be progressively resolved or overcome in the project of achieving order, meaning and unity. As we considered earlier, complex organizations and their associated professionals represented important vehicles of progress for modern society.

Over the past hundred years Organization Studies has thus exhibited the character of an archetypally "high-modern" field of activity (see Reed 1985, Clegg 1990), where innovations and experimentations in the theory and practice of organization have been restlessly pursued, consumed and discarded (as "fads") in an apparently insatiable will to progress. This process is exemplified, over the past decade, by the concerns of the Organization Studies avant-garde becoming redefined from "systems" and "structures" to "culture" and "symbolism" (see also Jeffcutt 1993; 1994a; 1994b). As part of this process of redefinition, the practice of organizational analysis became redescribed as a skill that was more "artistic" and "authorial" than "technical" (e.g. "connoisseurship," see Turner 1988) in its revelation of the qualities of organized activity. In this way, a newly empowered field of theory and practice (i.e. organizational interpretation) became able to offer a more persuasive means (i.e. micro/qualitative rather than macro/quantitative) of revealing the order that was understood as lying beneath the apparent disorder of complex organization. Consequently, the major focus of researchers and practitioners in organizational interpretation has been a search to manage disorder through the rationalization of the organizational irrational and the harmonization of the organizational dysfunctional (see Jeffcutt 1993, 1994a, 1994b). The major features of this "turn" have been the articulation of visions of progress that are both nostalgic and utopian (e.g. heroic and romantic organizational narratives); the dispensation of persuasive strategies for remedying current deficiencies or obstacles to the achievement of such visions (e.g. charismatic turnaround, cultural regeneration), alongside the elevation of a particular avant-garde (i.e. the interpreters of organizational culture and symbolism) in Organization Studies. The quest of this reforming vanguard thus became the "management" of uncertainty, a search to re-establish order from the disorder (i.e. fragmentation and incoherence in the theoretical and empirical base of Organization Studies) that earlier prophets and prophecies had been incapable of solving.

However, organizational interpretation has been but one of a series of recent "fads" (Pascale 1991), representing an intensified quest for order through which the modernizing momentum of organization studies has developed into a "late-modern" phase. Characterized by restless searching for meta-narratives that will effect ever more novel forms of closure, "late-modern" Organization Studies presents a succession of "last-words" which promise to achieve the impossible (i.e. resolving the ambiguities of undecidability) through strategies which can only accomplish the mundane; the plausible redescription of hierarchies that inscribe particular relations of privilege and authority (i.e. power/knowledge). In this way aspiring meta-narratives provide the leverage whereby existing elite forms may be superseded, but importantly also maintain the pre-conditions for their own subsequent supersession. For example, the persuasive supplanting of a formerly privileged modernist genre in Organization Studies (i.e. narratives of open systems/contingency) enabled the rise of a new avant-garde form (i.e. organizational interpretation), however, this did not necessarily coincide with the supersession of the former elite (see Weick 1985). Even so, the eminence of organizational interpretation remained short-lived as it became rapidly challenged by aspiring meta-narratives (e.g. re-engineering). Accordingly, it is important to go on to consider this avant-garde process of "reforming modernism" from a postmodern perspective.

The periodization "postmodern" was first employed by the historian (Toynbee 1954) to characterize the increasing instabilities of rapid social change during the 20th century. Toynbee's analysis of the problems of social change, akin to the "future shock" of Toffler (1971), is a clear precursor of Bell's (1974) prognosis of "post-industrial" society. Such visions, and fears, about the nature and character of the functions and dysfunctions of intensive scientific and socioeconomic change, presaged a proliferation of accounts that have articulated a fundamental shift in both the organization of society and the ways in which that organization is understood (see Harvey 1989; Lyotard 1984). However, whilst such accounts are joined by their assertion of a breach between the modern and the postmodern, they also express widely differing articulations of this transition; in respect of both the nature of the threshold with modernity and the characteristics that symptomize the postmodern condition. Two broad positions can be identified here; firstly, accounts which can be designated "late modern," where the postmodern condition becomes an extrapolation or extension of modernity (e.g. Bell 1974, 1976; Harvey 1989) secondly, accounts which can be designated "postmodern," where the postmodernity becomes a condition that is both beyond, and a rejection of, modernity (e.g. Lyotard 1984; Baudrillard 1988).

Having already examined the former position in Organization Studies, we shall now concentrate on the latter. Here, modern order is understood as a pursuit of privilege through the maintenance of hierarchies that seek authority through the censorship, suppression and proscription of other equally viable alternatives. With the postmodern being both beyond and against the modern, postmodernism becomes characterized by the interrogation, disruption and overturning of such meta-narratives. These are positions which can be clearly differentiated in terms of their management of the interrelationships between organization/text and author/representation (see also Jeffcutt 1993, 1994a, 1994b, 1995).

Modernism with its conception of a unity and order that underlies complexity is, as we have considered, primarily concerned with the problematics of interpretation; here the focus becomes the diversity of means by which an underlying reality is uncovered and made meaningful (i.e. ordered, coherent, rational). In contrast, postmodernism is concerned with the problematics of representation; here the focus becomes the textuality by and through which a complex surface of difference is articulated (i.e. the strategies and tactics of ordering). Hence for postmodernism, in Derrida's famous dictum, "il n'y a pas hors-texte," there is nothing beyond or outside of the text (see Norris 1982: 41). This challenging statement is typically postmodern, being crafted to evoke multiple and ambiguous interpretation. We may deduce that, on the one hand, all we have is textuality (i.e. there is no deeper level of reality that text like a conduit is able to reveal); whilst, on the other hand, everything is textual (i.e. all forms of ordering, whether discursive, spatial or temporal, can only be understood as textual). In postmodernism, textuality is thus both a metaphor for the human condition (see Lyotard's "language games" and "micro-narratives," 1984) and the only means through which the condition of humanity can be articulated (i.e. as inscriptions upon different surfaces, e.g. the body, see Foucault 1979; Lash 1990); landforms and space, see Jencks 1984, in a process of production and consumption of artifacts).

The textuality of postmodernism is clearly both challenging and controversial, particularly to modernism's confined and privileged understanding of text as a purely documentary product (exemplified by the numerous commentaries that seek to limit postmodern textuality to an artistic superstructure determined by a material substructure, e.g. Jameson 1984; Harvey 1989; Featherstone 1991). The hierarchies formed by modernism's articulation of the material-textual interrelationship become overturned and imploded by postmodern textuality, in which there is nothing beyond or outside of the text (in a number of senses, see above). Postmodernism is here subverting modernist fundamentals (i.e. notions of authority, uncovering and truth) by asserting that any text cannot exist as a self-sufficient whole, and cannot function as a closed system (see Worton and Still 1990). Thus meaning is as much a product of acts of consumption as it could be of acts of production; hence authorship becomes a "voice" that is seeking to achieve particular forms of privilege and censorship, but is incapable of maintaining authority, in an ultimately undecidable process of multivocal intertextuality. As a consequence, meaning becomes provisional rather than universal, plural rather than singular; articulating difference rather than unity (see Collins 1989).

Accordingly, modernist order is understood as logocentric, privileging a heroic and rational voice that aspires to originality, purity and authenticity whilst censoring and suppressing the undecidable. It is this melée of contradictions, "unity of disunity" (Berman 1983), that manages order from incoherence through the suppression of difference, which postmodernism overturns and implodes. The strat-

egy which postmodernism adopts in this process is that of recognizing and articulating difference, a tactic of destabilization from the margin which is initially
comparable to that of a late-modern avant-garde seeking to reform a modern order.
However, the significant difference here, between late-modern reform and postmodern overturning, concerns the issue of undecidability. Postmodernism (like
reforming modernism), in attempting to overturn a disciplinary and prejudicial
order through the articulation of ambiguity and contradiction from the margin,
is (unlike reforming modernism), not seeking to coordinate this difference into a
fresh hierarchy through the articulation of a superior vision of progress. Postmodernism hence articulates a postmodern condition of undecidability and perpetual
redefinition, rather than the nascence of the prioritizations of a fresh elite.

In the final analysis we may draw three significant conclusions which refer to
important contemporary debates in both the theory and practice of organization
(e.g. Hassard and Parker 1993; ESRC 1994). In these respects it is to be hoped
that a process of postmodern overturning in Organization Studies will be able to
instill some life into the aridity of petrified texts, equally as well as some text into
the witlessness of instrumental life.

Firstly, that Organization Studies can be understood as a Human Science that
is centrally concerned with the tension between order and disorder in society. It is
both distinguished from and connected to other Human Sciences (e.g. Sociology,
Social Anthropology) by its focal site of interest (i.e. the complex organizations
of modern society) and its master concept (i.e. manageability) through which its
interventions, in both theory and practice, are framed.

Secondly, we have considered the development of Organization Studies over
the past century to be a field of activity canonized in the pursuit of progress and
characterized by the restless search for new styles or forms that could be consumed as ultimate answers to perennial quests for manageability (see Pascale
1991; Huczynski 1992). Although, as we observed through our discussion of organizational interpretation, such "last words" would, by their very nature, always
be incomplete and unable to provide closure. Their destiny was inevitably to be
discredited, discarded as inadequate "fads" and superseded in Organization Studies apparently insatiable will to progress.

Thirdly, despite the inevitability of the failure of the "fads" of Organization
Studies to deliver ultimate answers to perennial questions of order and disorder,
such partial challenges to established boundaries and prioritizations can be understood as reorientations that open the potential for more significant change in our
modern world. Indeed, such challenges emerge as a "carnivalesque" force to challenge the "canons" of Organization Studies; for example, over the past decade the
eccentricities of the former backwater of organizational interpretation became re-
discovered as the "leading-edge" of the theory and practice of organization. However, as I have also argued (see Jeffcutt 1993, 1994a, 1994b), the development of
organizational interpretation in the Organization Studies mainstream has partially

challenged, redescribed and extended the whole plethora of modern boundaries of which the theory and practice of organization is composed.

Consequently, we need to recognize that such openings can also enable the pursuit of the long-overdue task of redescribing Organization Studies from a modern to a postmodern science of human practice. However, since symbolic inversion effects a redistribution as well as a retention of hierarchy, such overturning needs to be understood not as ultimate and complete (i.e. as an avant-garde process) but as a first step in a process of transformation that is both continuous and infinite, where boundaries implode and hierarchies "metaphorize" (see Cooper 1989).

A postmodern Organization Studies would become both a multi-disciplinary Human Science and a multi-cultural human practice across a diversity of sites and settings of organized activity, interconnected through a focus on the tensions that constitute the threshold and boundary between articulations of order/disorder. Such work can be understood as connecting a Derridaian philosophical praxis (i.e. deconstruction-overturning-metaphorization), with a Foucauldian critical historical practice (i.e. the interdependence of formations of knowledge and relations of power). Postmodern Organization Studies is thus not only concerned with the overturning of the theory and practice of organization (e.g. as tightly-bounded male managerial/academic domains in search of progress and/or truth), but also with the unbounding (implosion) of the logics and parameters of decidability that make such modernizing projects possible (e.g. as totalizing grand narratives that are incapable of achieving such closure).

Organization Studies, in such an articulation, would be both beyond modernity and a rejection of modernization, as both visions and tactics of progress; whilst its work would be characterized by the "serious play" of marginality and double coding. For example, with the adoption of "ex-centric" voices (e.g. of organizers rather than managers) and tactics of critique (e.g. irony, parody) towards a modernist dominant, alongside the interrogation of these very formations of leverage (i.e. self-reflexivity). Although, in exposing the contradictions of modern Organization Studies (e.g. as commodifying elite heroics in both academic and managerial work) the objective would not be the reimposition of a newly purified order. Instead, postmodern Organization Studies would articulate a self-reflexive process that would seek to redescribe its composition and constituency as a human practice of organizing that is itself transient and transitional. In short, a position where the understanding of organization is inseparable from the organization of understanding.

Notes

[1] Marx and Engels proposed an evolutionary analysis that understood societal development as a process of conflict in which social relations were constituted and transformed through a series of stages (i.e. from primitive Communism, through slavery,

feudalism and capitalism to advanced Communism). Tylor proposed an evolutionary analysis that understood cultural development as a process of cultivation and civilization through a series of stages (i.e. savagery, barbarism and civilized man). Spencer proposed an evolutionary analysis that understood societal development as a process of functional specialization and adaptation through both stages and cycles (i.e. from militant society to industrial society).

[2] For Marx and Engels the laws of history were to be found in the economic substructure of society, constituted in the social relations of production. For Tylor and Spencer the laws of civilization and social progress were to be found in the interaction between the capacities and deficiencies of individuals and the environmental conditions of different societies.

[3] The four arenas of organizational theory and practice which became explicit and interconnected through "scientific management" have significant pre-histories through the 19th century: "management" (see Chandler 1977; Joyce 1987), "accounting" (see Miller and O'Leary 1987), "occupational psychology" (see Sanderson 1987; Hoskin and Macve 1988), "marketing" (see Goodall 1986). Accordingly, these discourses and practices focusing on ordering and organizing can be understood as experiencing about a hundred years of dispersed and fragmented development prior to their consolidation and professionalized incorporation into the theory and practice of organization (see Jeffcutt 1994c).

References

Achebe, C. (1975), *Morning Yet on Creation Day*, London, Faber.
Alexander, J. (ed.) (1988), *Durkheimian Sociology: Cultural Studies*, Cambridge, Cambridge University Press
Austin-Broos, D. (ed.) (1987), *Creating Culture,* Sydney, Allen and Unwin.
Baudrillard, J. (1987), *America*, London:Verso.
Baudrillard, J. (ed.) (1988), *Selected Writings*, Cambridge, Polity.
Bauman, Z. (1989), *Modernity and the Holocaust,* Oxford, Polity.
Bauman, Z. (1992), *Intimations of Postmodernity,* London, Routledge.
Bell, D. (1974), *The Coming of Post-Industrial Society*, London, Heinemann.
Bell, D. (1976), *The Cultural Contradictions of Capitalism*, London, Heinemann.
Berman, M. (1983), *All that is Solid Melts into Air*, London, Verso.
Boyne, R. and Rattansi, A. (eds.) (1990), *Postmodernism and Society,* London, Macmillan.
Bryman, A. (ed.) (1988), *Doing Research in Organisations*, London, Routledge.
Burrell, G. (1984), Sex and Organizational Analysis, *Organization Studies*, 5(2), pp. 97-118.
Chandler, A. (1977), *The Visible Hand*, Cambridge, Harvard University Press.
Clegg, S. (1990), *Modern Organizations: Organization Studies in the Postmodern World*, London, Sage.
Collins, J. (1989), *Uncommon Cultures*, London, Routledge.
Cooper, R. (1986), Organisation-Disorganisation, *Social Science Information*, 25(2), pp. 299-335
Cooper, R. (1989), Modernism, Post Modernism and Organizational Analysis 3, *Organization Studies*, 10(4), pp. 479-502

ESRC (1994), Report of the Commission on Management Research, London, ESCR Secretariat.

Featherstone, M. (ed.) (1988), *Postmodernism*, London, Sage.

Featherstone, M. (1991), *Consumer Culture and Postmodernism*, London, Sage.

Foucault, M. (1974), *The Order of Things*, London, Tavistock.

Foucault, M. (1979), *The History of Sexuality, Volume 1*, Harmondsworth, Penguin.

Goodall, F. (1986), Marketing Consumer Products before 1914, in J. Davenport-Hines (ed.), *Markets and Bagmen,* Aldershot, Gower.

Gordon, S. (1991), *The History and Philosophy of Social Science*, London, Routledge.

Harvey, D. (1989), *The Condition of Postmodernity*, Oxford, Blackwell.

Hassan, I. (1985), The Culture of Postmodernism, *Theory, Culture and Society* 2(3).

Hassard, J. and Parker, M. (eds.) (1993), *Postmodernism and Organizations*, London, Sage.

Hassard, J. and Pym, D. (eds.) (1990), *The Theory and Philosophy of Organisations*, London, Routledge.

Hoskin, K and Macve, R. (1988), The Genesis of Accountability, *Accounting, Organisations and Society*, 13(1), pp. 37-73

Huczynski, A. (1992), *Management Gurus*, London, Routledge.

Jameson, F. (1984), Postmodernism or the Cultural Logic of late-Capitalism, *New Left Review* 146, pp. 53-93.

Jeffcutt, P.S. (1993), The Transition from Interpretation to Representation in Organization Studies, in Hassard, J. and Parker, M. (eds.), *Postmodernism and Organisations,* London, Sage.

Jeffcutt, P.S. (1994a), The Interpretation of Organization. A Contemporary Analysis and Critique, *The Journal of Management Studies*, 31(4), pp. 225-250.

Jeffcutt, P.S. (1994b), From Interpretation to Representation in Organizational Analysis; Postmodernism, Ethnography and Organizational Symbolism, *Organization Studies*, 15(2), pp. 245-278.

Jeffcutt, P.S. (1995), *The Management of Transition; Culture and Complex Organization in Modern Society*, London, Sage.

Jencks, C. (1984), *The Language of Postmodern Architecture*, London, Academy.

Joyce, P. (cd.) (1987), *The Historical Meanings of Work*, Cambridge, Cambridge University Press.

Kumar, K. (1978), *Prophecy and Progress*, Harmondsworth, Penguin.

Lash, S. (1990), *Sociology of Postmodernism*, London, Routledge.

Lash, S. and Urry, J. (1987), *The End of Organised Capitalism*, Oxford, Polity.

Lawrence, P. (1987), Tylor and Frazer, in D. Austin-Broos (ed.), *Creating Culture*, Sydney, Allen and Unwin.

Locke, R. (1989), *Management and Higher Education Since 1940*, Cambridge, Cambridge University Press.

Lyotard, J. (1984), *The Postmodern Condition,* Manchester, Manchester University Press.

Marcus, G. and Hall, P. (1992), *Lives in Trust*, Boulder, Westview.

Marx, K. and Engels, F. (1888), *The Manifesto of the Communist Party*, reproduced 1952, Moscow, Progress Publishers.

Merkle, J. (1980), *Management and Ideology*, Berkeley, University of California Press.

Miller, P. and O'Leary, T. (1987), Accounting and the Construction of the Governable Person, *Accounting, Organisations and Society*, 12(3), pp. 235-265

Morgan, G. (1986), *Images of Organisation*, London, Sage.

Norris, C. (1982), *Deconstruction*, London, Methuen.

Pascale, R. (1991), *Managing on the Edge*, New York, Simon and Schuster.

Perrow, C. (1972), *Complex Organizations*, Evanston, Illi, Scott Foresman.

Person, H. (ed.) (1929), *Scientific Management in American Industry*, New York, Harper.

Reed, M. (1985), *Redirections in Organisational Analysis*, London, Tavistock,

Reed, M. and Hughes, M. (eds.) (1992), *Rethinking Organisation*, London, Sage.

Sanderson, M. (1987), *Educational Opportunity*, London, Faber.

Sanderson, M. (1988), The English Civic Universities and Industrial Spirit 1870-1914, *Historical Research*, 61, pp. 90-104.

Searle, G. (1970), *The Quest for National Efficiency*, Oxford, Blackwell.

Shelley, M. (1969), *Frankenstein*, London, Oxford University Press.

Simmel, G. (1903), The Metropolis and Mental Life, in K. Wolff (ed.), *The Sociology of Georg Simmel*, New York, Free Press

Stallybrass, P. and White, A. (1986), *The Politics and Poetics of Transgression*, London, Methuen.

Stocking, G. (1987), *Victorian Anthroplogy*, New York, Free Press.

Tallack, D. (1991), *Twentieth Century America*, London, Longman.

Tate Gallery (1991), *Dynamism*, Exhibition Catalogue, Liverpool, Tate Gallery.

Thompson, M., Ellis, R., Wildavsky, A. (1990), *Cultural Theory*, Boulder, Westview Press.

Toffler, A. (1971), *Future Shock*, London, Pan.

Tönnies, F. (1887), *Community and Society,* translated 1963, New York, Harper and Row.

Toynbee, A. (1954), *A Study of History*, London, Oxford University Press.

Turner, B. (1988), Connoisseurship in the Study of Organisational Cultures, in A. Bryman (ed.), *Doing Research in Organisations*, London, Routledge.

Tylor, E.B. (1958), *Primitive Culture,* New York, Harper and Row.

Weick, K. (1985), The Significance of Corporate Culture, in P. Frost et al. (1985).

Williams, R. (1958), *Culture and Society*, London, Chatto and Windus.

Williams, R. (1976), *Keywords,* London, Croom Helm.

Worton, M. and Still, J. (eds.) (1990), *Intertextuality*, Manchester, Manchester University Press.

Lessons from Premodern and Modern for Postmodern Management

David Boje

Introduction

My thesis is that individuals with a will to power hide behind various masks[1]. We each, I believe, wear "pre," "mod," and "post" masks (abbreviations hereafter for pre-modernism, modernism, and postmodernism). I have a mask for my pre voice with its traditions, nostalgia, and folklore. I have a mask for my mod voice with its rules, laws, data, bureau-speak, rationality. I have a post voice for my pre-occupation with rebellion, my opposition to oppression, my curiosity about marginality, my search of history, my affirmation of feminism, my intolerance for racism, and my efforts to de-hierchize formal organizations. Each mask is politically correct to its reality, but I live between these multiple realities. The game for me is to be the chameleon. I can pretend to use my post mask, but be doing the most bureaucratic work. Or, I can invoke a traditional mask and unleash post changes. I make choices that I believe many people in the post world working in mod bureaucracies, inside pre liberal arts universities make everyday.

This chapter will discuss trends in organization theory that are pre, mod, and post. I do not subscribe to linear time or linear progress, but instead see a layering, crisscrossed inconsistency, and even outright contest among the three discourses (Jeffcutt 1993; Knights and Morgan 1993; Hassard 1993; Reed 1993). Like Clegg (1989; 1990) I look at this as a power arena in which the discourses, even within the individual, are in contest. I am anti-Kuhnian, in that I do not subscribe to the evolutionary or even revolutionary paradigm-shift model, one whereby we are, as Vaclav Havel (1992) has argued, like so many others, witnessing the death of the mod era:

It has brought an end... to the modern age as a whole. The modern era has been dominated by the culminating belief, expressed in different forms, that the world – and Being as such – is a wholly knowable system governed by a finite number of universal laws that man can grasp and rationally direct for his own benefit. This era, beginning in the Renaissance and developing from the Enlightenment to socialism, from positivism to scientism, from the Industrial Revolution to the information revolution, was characterized by rapid advances in rational, cognitive thinking.

The problem I see with Havel's epitaph is that, like Warren Bennis's epitaph for bureaucracy in the 1960s, it is premature. Neither "modernism" nor its Franken-stein creation, "bureaucracy" is dead. Rather, the global, technical recipe for hu-man control and environmental, as well as human, domination is methodically and systematically repackaging arms, legs and eyeballs into yet another mask. This mask has a post face, but is composed of many pre and mod body parts.

Making this point in organization theory is difficult because of the wholesale denial of history. Kuhnian-paradigms, in contrast to Latour's (1987; 1988) multi-faceted and more politicized history of science, tempt us into theorizing that is a historical, but editorially-correct explanation of purposive, regular, capitalist competitive progress. Organization theory, if historical at all, has swallowed the progress myth (Lyotard 1984) and the technical fix myth so deeply, that we must, in my opinion, do a Foucault-style genealogy in order to add to mod a more pre as well as post story of history. The full scope of this genealogy goes beyond what we can do in this chapter. Here our task is to look at some of the historical turning points that are left out of most organization theory texts (at least American texts).

One contribution of this chapter is to assert that postmodern theorists have not been very explicit about levels of analysis. Much of the pre, mod, post totalism mixes levels of analysis in ways that are problematic for organization theory. The levels are world, organization, and individual. If we are in a post world, then are the organizations and individuals struggling to adapt to this nexus of cultural, po-litical, social, aesthetic, economic, and environmental world order change? If we accept for a moment the world order change thesis, brought on by the bankrupt-cy of communism, the death of Renaissance Humanism and Enlightenment, the end of the Industrial Revolution, and the collapse of the ecosystem, then does this mean that the pre and mod individual and organization are fish out of water? If we are in post times, then to be pre or mod is to be out of step with the global, planetary, information civilization. Another contribution of this chapter is to look at what is hidden within the pre, mod, and post and within the levels of analysis problem. For example, if a mod organization hires a post individual, will this be a good for either party? If the mod organization, is not completely mod, but contains enclaves and pockets of post project groups, can the mod framework continue to channel, contain, and discipline the post enclave?

In this chapter, I would like to play with several theories positing alternative formulations of pre, mod, and post eras, focus upon the differences between taking an era by era, paradigm by paradigm, fad by fad approach on the one hand, and looking at a post-Kuhnian-perspective, allowing for multiplicity and contest, on the other. In short, what if instead of leaving pre, and mod behind, as post makes its impact upon our present, we allowed for all these discourses to be in contest (Boje and Dennehy 1993)?

One problem with postmodernity is that there are as many postmoderns as there are moderns. Jürgen Habermas, for example, "pokes fun at the loose way in which some writers throw the phrase 'postmodern' around, and laughs at them as "posties" (Toulmin 1990: 8). Each "postie" has their own postmod agenda. Peter Drucker uses the category "postmodern" to capture the transnational boundaries of 20th century organizations. Modernity ends when organizations transcended national sovereignty in the 16th and 17th centuries. Globalism is not the invention of the late 20th century.

Skeptical of the Era Approach

Did mod replace pre and is post now replacing mod? With AIDS, the sexual revolution, regional wars, the information revolution, the death of communism, and world-wide recession, some feel that we face significant historical transitions and discontinuities reshaping the intellectual posture of the 21st century. But, is this coeval with witness to the death of mod? Given the entrenched rational character of organization studies, organization theory is the very last knowledge discipline to grapple with the transition (Steingard et al. 1993). Entrenched rationality, quite specific interests masquerading as disinterest, means that much organization theory in the past de-selected topics like torture, child labor, slavery, colonialism, imperialism, and even a good critique of capitalism, from their story of the origins of organization theory. A little Taylor, a paragraph on Max Weber, and an obligatory footnote to Mary Parker Follett is all you find in most organization theory text (notable exceptions are Clegg and Dunkerley 1980; Clegg 1990; Boje 1993b). Discourses of Taylorism do not obviate the progress through science and efficiency grand theory (Jeffcutt 1993: 7-8). Post organization theory needs to drop the worship of abstract theory and include stories of domination, marginalization, and exploitation. Organization theory is too de-vilified, too sanitized, too white, too male, too objective, too pseudo a science (Chio 1993; Holvino 1993; Calás 1993).

When did mod start? Was it with Renaissance Humanism, the Industrial Revolution or with Descartes' philosophy and the dawn of Cartesian logic and positivism? If it was the Industrial Revolution, when did that start? Did the Industrial Revolution begin with the replacement of hand tools by steam power tools and the development of large-scale industrial production in England from about 1760 or did it begin much earlier with Gutenberg's invention of moveable type and the printing press in the 1450s? Did the spread of Cartesian and positivistic logic underpinning modernism, take a different historical course in different countries? When did the rational philosophy which valued systems over people and environments start? These questions must be addressed if we are to write a postmodern organization history. Table 1 presents a crude catalog of alternative formulations of pre, mod, and post.

Table 1: Alternative Formulations of Pre-Modern, Modern, and Postmodern Eras

	Pre-modern	Early Modernism	Mid-modernism	Late Modernism	Neo-modernism	Postmodernism
	Feudal	Gutenberg and Renaissance Humanists	Descartes' Philosophy Newton Science Hobbes Politics	Late Industrial Revolution	Computer Revolution	
Dates	??? to 1300	1450-???	1630s-??	1750/1920s-??	1960S to ???	1970s to ???
Class	Noble class; Knights carry swords	Apprentice to journeyman to master; Knights decline	Restrictive Church and state repression	Managerial class restrictive of everything	Information workers and core control	Individual control
Labor	Farm vassalage for basic survival; Craft production	Child, slave and serf labor; Fraternal guilds	Child, slave and serf labor in city slums	Factory employs child labor; Worker is cog in machine; Deskilling of labor specialties	Worker as digitized input; 3rd World cheap labor; Seek low eco-restrictions	Worker as skilled: Ecologically responsible; Social audits
Leisure	Not much	Festivals for days off	Time off for nobility and clergy	High stress work cultures	Computer work everywhere you go	Time off for leisure and family
Rationality	Work slaves to death; All "others" are beast labor	Tolerance of rationality and humanism	Descartes' philosophy; Rational inquiry of Galileo, Kepler, Newton; Political theories by Hobbes.	Hire slaves, children, and third world at sub-wages; 1750s steam engine; Taylorism and Fordism	Re-intro of "lean" Taylorism internalized time and motion TQM, JIT, Kaizen idea control	Raise wages of skilled workers; Fall of TQM; Cult of performativity and stress
Humanism	Humanism for nobility	Renaissance humanists: Desiderius Erasmus, Francois Rabelias, William Shakespeare, Michel de Montaigne, Francis Bacon	Decline of Renaissance humanism; Rise of nation states	Technological fix to human condition; Humanism reserved for nobility and managerial class	System is more important than person; Myth of information society	Re-assertion of individualistic humanism of Montaigne and Bacon

Pre-Modernism: Is Pre Inferior to the Ways of Mod and Post Organization?

Pre is not a periodizing concept to mark the emergence of mod organizations, it is its own economic, political, social, and artistic style of discourse (Boje 1993c). For example, the way of some native American was more socially and environmentally responsible than both mod and post forms. They were self-managing, self-reproducing, humanitarian, aesthetic, and democratic. Like other posts I see no privilege for the new (Graff 1979; Karnoouh 1986; Bauman 1987; Vattimo 1988). Despite their humanism, native people in America were moved to reservations for "their own good." For their own good natives of Mexico, South America, and parts of South West America were depopulated, tortured, and treated worse than animals in the search for gold and the cultivation of cotton and tobacco crops.

Pre Feudal

Pre forms of organization include the military, Church, university, guilds, and the Crown. Workers were artisans, serfs and slaves. There were no days off and Kings, clergy and masters held rank, privilege, and status over those at the bottom. Tyrants and other nobles ruled the social order, as peasants farmed and crafted for their needs. Religion exorcised people of their uncertain ways (Hirschman 1976: 53). In pre times feudal lords ruled with a hybrid of reason and passion (Hirschman 1976: 43-4). Knights and nobles ruled in a network of small kingdoms balanced by a network of church officials and parishes. There was also premod torture so that the spectacle it presented enabled the sovereign to leave the story of authority in the markings left on the human body. Racism and sexism were acceptable. Many of these forms have survived the mod detour into "supposed" postmod times. The post approach to humanist sex and race relations, while without iron brands, has not improved the quality of working life, nor has it changed power relations (Henriques et al. 1984: 13).

Modernism

Mod was introduced in order to liberate society from oppressive, repressive, and subjugated forms of social, religious, and business organization (Touraine 1990). Mod bureaucracy, law, economics, and politics was a rationality to overcome the domination, oppression, and inequality of a premod world. Dating the start of modernity is problematic because there are many modernisms. In Table 1, for illustration, we list Descartes and the early and late industrial revolution. We are therefore ignoring shifts in architecture, national revolutions such as the French Revolution. Thus, for instance, taking political revolution as the defining moment, 1776 or 1789 is the preferred start time for Habermas.

Early Mod

Early modernism begins with the dawn of Renaissance humanism and the innovation of printing. For Haval, mod began with the Renaissance, but for Toulman (1990), the Renaissance falls at the boundary of pre and mod. The Renaissance posed few changes in the organizations of "medieval" Europe, but "the seeds of Modernity germinated and grew, without reaching the point at which they were a threat" (p. 23).

Before Gutenberg's printing press, organizations owed loyalty to a feudal kingdom more than to a national loyalty. The Crown and the Church lost their monopoly over the book, and people could now decide for themselves what to believe. Gutenberg lost his printing business in civil courts to his scheming partner Faust, whose brother-in-law happened to be the judge. Gutenberg, the father of moveable type and the printing press, and author of an invention whose quality could not be surpassed for four centuries, died penniless. Enterprise, innovation and meeting the market were no guarantee of business success where the framework of law was less than rationalized and more than capricious.

Renaissance players include humanists such as Leonardo (1452-1519) and Shakespeare (1564-1616). It also included Michel de Montaigne's writings of the 1570s and 1580s that present a powerful humanist philosophy of skepticism as a way to escape dogmatism (Toulman 1990: 36). He and Francis Bacon wrote about human experience from a non-doctrinal perspective. The Renaissance Humanist view are a sharp contrast to the usual starting point for modernity, which is well after 1600 with Galileo's mod science and Descartes' mod philosophy. "Montaigne is scornful about attempts to separate mental activities from bodily changes" (Toulman 1990: 37).

Philosophy is very childish, to my mind, when she gets up on her hind legs and preaches to us that it is a barbarous alliance to marry the divine with the earthly, the reasonable with the unreasonable, the severe with the indulgent, the honorable with the dishonorable; that sensual pleasure is a brutish thing unworthy of being enjoyed by the wise man (Montaigne as cited in Toulman 1990: 38).

Enlightenment would eclipse humanism and de-emphasize the individual by focusing upon the needs of larger structures, formal laws, and religious values. The individual became subjugated to institutional structures.

"Subjects get lost in the flood of structures that overpower the individual" (Rosenau 1993: 46). By the 1630s the Holy Roman Empire was an empty shell and sovereign nation states had the power. The 30 years War in Europe (1618-1648) and a series of plagues in France and England were organizational catastrophes. The Church was rejecting Protestant reformation by direct confrontation and was unsympathetic to scholars who questioned doctrine. Mod-advocates stress the enlightenment project (Habermas 1981). All these changes had profound organizational implications.

Philosophical Shifts

Most postmod theorists challenge the notion of modernity being progress, or a set of eras in which humanity is better off with each paradigm revolution. Rather, modernity with its celebration of positivism and its performativity systems, is a discourse that has marginalized the philosopher's pre-modern concerns with humanism. But, I think, we need to ask, "who had humanism and who did not in the pre-modern era?" Philosophers were privileged enough to think about humanism, in a time when getting enough food to survive was the pre-occupation of non-nobility.

Instead of a progression from pre-modern, modern, and then postmodern – the "Omega theory" of Toulmin (1990: 167) posits that modernity looped back to its starting point, for three centuries. We are returning to the skepticism of Montaigne. Could it be that postmodernism is a retrogress to 16th century Renaissance humanism after the dead-end of modernity?[2]

The 1960s and 1970s were times of cultural change that shredded our philosophical, political, ecological, scientific, and industrial traditions. Traditions that were deeply rooted in Descartes' method of systematic doubt, the non-emotionality of Freud, gave way to postmodern. In fact Toulmin contends that the Renaissance was actually a reversal of Renaissance values.

Thus, from 1630 on, the focus of philosophical inquiries has ignored the particular, concrete, timely and local details of everyday human affairs: instead, it has shifted to a higher, stratospheric plane, on which nature and ethics conform to abstract, timeless, general, and universal theories (Toulmin 1990: 35).

Counter-Renaissance

The rationalists retreated from the humanists as theory in the abstract separated itself from more practical considerations. This split can be seen in the universities of the 15th and 16th century, where science and humanities were separated into separate fields. Science was split from story. Who tells this story to whom, in what forum, and using what characterizations is the stuff of rhetoric and politics and no longer relevant to science. There you have it: the pre-modern intellectual respected the differing circumstances of specific kinds of contexts. Case analysis was favored over grand theory. Science increasingly determined story research to be dishonest since the focus was on particular, localized cases in specific contexts. 16th century humanists in the humanities favored ethnographic methods and "local knowledge." The mod detour of logical positivism and technical rationality would take philosophy away from its focus on grounded stories for a few centuries.

Traces Survive in Post Times

Enlightenment Humanists advocated a technical fix to social problems which pioneered in industrial organization theory the elevation of efficient systems of managing people and machine productivity at the expense of the environment, leisure, aesthetics, and subjects, as well as advocating the employment of slaves to advance the wealth and position of their masters. The Renaissance humanists were advocates of freedom, liberty, and the quest for human potential. But the Renaissance Humanism would be carefully guarded for those at the top of social and economic pyramids, while the "others" became part of the dispassionate and rational, technical machine. In seeking social justice and equality, humanism sometimes naively, and sometimes rationally, led to and legitimated injustice and inequality, including Fascism, Marxism, National Socialism, and Stalinism (Foucault 1987: 168-169; Laffey 1987; Touraine 1988; Rosenau 1993: 48). Liberal humanism was a privilege of the noble class.

Late Mod, Industrial Revolution Shifts

Peter Drucker (1957) pegs the rise of modern times at the shift to Cartesian thought. Peter Drucker, wrote as early as 1957 in his book *Landmarks of Tomorrow* about the collapse of "modernity" with its emphasis on the nation-state as a self-sustaining political unit in the 17th and 18th century, giving way to organizational institutions that transcend national boundaries.

Late Mod, Industrial Revolution

Rational planning, organizing, and control were personified in Frederick Taylor and Henry Ford. The rationalization of production was combined with the rationalization of administration with Max Weber and Henri Fayol. Organizational science adopted rational ways of testing rational concepts with rational methodologies. At this point bureaucracy and factory become wed. Even where most might think that it begins to unravel with the garbage-can model (Cohen et al. 1972), mod organization rationality contains the limits of individuality in search of problems and solutions. Kreiner (1992: 44) and Hassard (1993: 2-3) showed us that the technological core is buffered by boundary spanning managers from the turbulence and uncertainty surrounding the formal garbage can. Behind their mod mask, the MBA students assign their human resources. On occasion, they peek from behind their mask, we hope, in order to look at privilege, marginalization, and environmental collapse.

Neo-Mod Times in Organization Theory

There appear to be many different "schools" of organization theory since the post World War era, but their common element is the celebration, even by denial, of the technically, scientifically, logically rational organizational machine. These grand narratives, obsessively recount efficiency, control, conformity, certainty, and prediction (Kreiner 1992: 38; Hassard 1993: 7-8). Postwar theorists wane sarcastic about the over-structured, over-specialized, over-governed, over-mechanized, over-coupled, over-gazed mod organizations (March and Simon 1957; Weick 1976; Pondy et al. 1983; Benton 1990). Yet, as Kilduff (1993), in his deconstruction of March and Simon's *Organization* has shown, the attack is another celebration of the machine image (Morgan 1986).

Is TQM, Just Reincarnated, Neo-Mod Taylorism?

Much of the hype about TQM, CPI, Kaizen, flexible manufacturing, and lean production from the gurus of Japanese industrial organization is re-labeled, re-discovered, and re-packaged in search of Taylorism (Boje 1993a, Winsor 1993; Winsor and Boje 1993; Steingard et. al 1993; Bailey and Heon 1993). The machine has been dismantled into computer sub-routines, networked by teams, and re-coupled, although loosely, into an ideological system that would make Adam Smith, Frederick Taylor, and other capitalist theorists proud. Despite the disputes of organization theory with performativity and bureaucracy, they drew their administrative philosophy from the mother's milk of modernism. Instead of the "technically rational machine" we now celebrate the "technically rational computer network." Organization theory reproduces the disciplinary machinery to conform the human resources of society toward performative ends (Burrell 1988; Lyotard 1984; Foucault 1979). Disciplines makes individuals into a specific technique of a power that regards individuals as objects of its exercise (Clegg 1989). Instead of the premod power of visible spectacle, it is now the power of calculated economy derived from the use of hierarchical observation, normalizing judgments, examination, panoptic gaze, etc. Chain of command is hierarchical observation in which each level observes the one below it.

In treating the body as a machine, discipline uses it more productively than did torture and punishment as formations of power. According to Cooper and Burrell (1988: 110), "Postmodernism reveals formal organizations to be the ever-present expression of an autonomous power that masquerades as the supposedly rational constructions of modern institutions." As we have scientifically researched mod organization, we have erected an objective, rational, and certain image of formal corporate order normalized into multiple choices on scantrons.

Since we teach formal organization as decidedly rational, we teach students to ignore their exploitative, dominating, and resource-wasting practices (Boje 1993c). Even our reformulations of mod organization, such as the rhetoric of being "In Search of Excellence in Customer Service, Quality, and Speed of Delivery" hides from our students the burnout, politics, privilege, inequality, and capriciousness of corporate domination. We teach students to identify and prefer the "mod mask" (Kreiner 1992).

Much of human resource management, as split off from organization behavior and theory is instruction in how to invoke higher order needs in more diverse ways to get more bottom line output with less resistance to evaluation and salary rewards and punishments (Collinson 1993). Even teamwork is an ideology of tyranny (Sinclair 1992). When did this masquerade begin?

There is a known link between the military-industrial-big government and social and ecological dysfunctions in capitalist countries (Knights and Morgan 1993). Will the earth survive mass production and mass consumption? The world has 202 billionaires, three million millionaires, and 100 million homeless people living in cars, cardboard boxes, and under bridges. The world's average income is $5,000, well below the US poverty line. This divide between the fortunate and unfortunate is a grand canyon. The haves are exploiting the resources of the have nots to perpetuate the gap. People in the 1990s are 4.5 times richer than their great grand parents, but not 4.5 times happier.

Mods seeks a better world that is knowable, governable, subject to rational systems and rational mechanisms. Mod is a mix of Renaissance Humanism, Enlightenment Humanism and a scientific philosophy extending from positivism to scientism. It also owes heritage to the Industrial Revolution and extends into the information revolution.

Before 1600, abstract theory and grounded, concrete practicality were in balance, but since that time, universal theory and skeptical tolerance went to sleep. It would be reawakened in the 1960s with the marches of Martin Luther King, the Vietnam protests, the women's movement, and lesbian and gay movement, the gray movement, the environmental movement, the handicapped movement, and the appearance of the Japanese manufacturing system on the shores of Europe and America.

Postmodernism

The first step to recovery is reclaim our sense of person from the modernist machine of hegemony (Hetrick and Boje 1992; Sinclair 1992). We live with a mechanistic world-view that casts us as mindless and heartless cogs in the modernist machine. Can we work fewer hours, consume fewer resources, take more time for family and friends? Or, will we bury ourselves in garbage, unemployment, and survival manuals against the horrors unleased on civility, the ecology, selves?

Post organization theory is a search for new forms of workplace organization that get us beyond mod domination and exploitation. Postmods seek to free themselves from mod obsession with efficiency, order, certainty, hierarchy, technology, authority, social engineering, administration, and commerce that resulted in the Holocaust, world wars, Vietnam, Stalin's Gulag, computer digitization of humans, homelessness, and the oppression of Blacks, women and other groups (Rosenau 1992: 129). Oppression has been justified for the good of the victims or the unintended consequences of the pursuit of the mod project of rationality, science, technological progress, and enlightenment.

Postmods, according to Rosenau (1992: 46-50) have killed the mod subject for three reasons: (1) the subject is an invention of modernity; (2) the subject is caught in humanist philosophy; (3) the subject is caught in a subject-object duality. Killing the mod subject to set free the postmod subject is no less severe than killing the premod native in order to free rational man for rational control.

For a variety of reasons, numerous theorists started to become post-mod in the early 1970s. This was when the environmental consciousness movement began with Rachel Carson's *Silent Spring*. In the United States, we protested bombings in Cambodia and Vietnam. Others did elsewhere as well. Many point to the world wide oil embargo and deep recession of the early 1970s. Others point to the age of the computer and its revolution in information networking across our planet. Richard Rorty takes what Toulmin (1990: 12) terms a "frankly ethnocentric" position in which each culture can judge rationality by its own logic. Whose rationality are we looking at when each individual, according to post psychology, has multiple selves and therefore multiple rationalities?

Implications of Mod Subject, Pre Humanism, and Subject-Object Duality

After killing the mod subject, postmod reintroduces the passion and individuality of premod humanity into organization theory (Kreiner 1992: 46). With the erasure of the mod subject, hierarchy has yet to be abolished. The computer, more than the iron cage machine, is used to keep people classified, normed, and specialized into functions: they become, literally, objectified. The problem with this logic is that with the flattening of hierarchy, the objectification process, is accelerating as humans are now being digitized by check out stands, phone bill computers, IRS computers and the panoply of everyday life. Humans have been scanned into the machine. The most extreme case is in Singapore, where every individual and every building in Singapore has been scanned into the computer in the biggest computer social engineering project of our time. The result is a self-gaze and a self-subjectification resulting from people defining themselves as computer codes. Rather than mod being dead, it is in contest with post philosophy. And I believe that just as Renaissance Humanism fell asleep with the birth of rationalism and positivism, a similar scenario is overtaking us today.

How is Post being Manipulated and Controlled by Mod Discourse?

Formal mod bureaucratic organization are being decoupled in order to make space for innovation and self direction. In Japan, there is pending legislation to force more leisure time into the economic machine. Formal organization is moving away from central planning but not central control through computer networking and other means of electronic surveillance. Whereas mod organization theory attributed innovation to the hierarchy of objective reasons and the construction of ideas from functional positions, post organization theory attributes entrepreneurship to autonomy of the working team and even to the autonomy and freedom of the individual from the formality of the bureaucratic corporation. Under TQM, even efficiency rises with the self-surveillance of the individual as she/he fills out Kaizen reports and statistical charts on the time and motion study of themselves.

Killing the child of Enlightenment and rationalism is supposed to emancipate the individual from mod organization categories and variables such as group, team member, position holder, level, causal antecedent, agency, efficacy, intervention site, human resource designer, and rational decision-maker (Rosenau 1992). The question is are we throwing the child out with this mod bath water? Affirmative postmods are optimistic about the ability of the individual to craft a world free of domination and exploitation, one that will improve the human condition around the world, and save our planet.

Conclusions

The premise of this chapter is that rather than some paradigm shift from pre to mod to post, all three discourses are in struggle. We can no more kill the mod subject than we can rid ourselves of the IRS or Motor Vehicle departments. In true mod form, autonomy and freedom is being systematically and methodically exploited to attain higher levels of performativity. This is being accomplished as mod organization gurus introduce Kaizen, TQM and other Japanese innovations while ignoring the roots of Taylorism and machine, not "lean" production. Enthusiasm and team spirit is being similarly exploited to build corporate loyalty and identity (Sinclair 1992). On the other side of this contest, teams do allow people to work in temporary association until they must return to mod organization life. A bit of post space is being cultivated within the mod space in order to coopt the individualism and entrepreneurial sentiments towards corporate purposes. Post organization theory holds many options for domination of the many factions of a complex organization by a core of more privileged and more intrusive elites. Mod rationality seeks to re-harness passion that it exorcised in its denunciation of the evils of pre organization.

Post is being coopted. It is too easy to overlook the dysfunctional aspects of post.

- There is an oppressive gaze in all three discourses. If mod is a "machine cage," then pre is an "iron cage," and post is a "computer cage."
- Give up our attempt to develop a post science. It is enough to tell pre, mod, and post stories. Trying to scientize post gets us back to mod. I agree with Lyotard (1984) that science and story are equal. In fact, science is just a story pretending not to be a story.
- Are all truths equal? Nazi, racist, sexist truth merits exposé. These exploitative truths compete with positivism for world domination.
- Progress is a myth. The myth is that through scientific and technological progress, the world is a better and better place. Organization theory is the step child of this dream (Burrell 1988). Organization theory reproduce disciplinary modes of domination in society.
- Freedom is a myth. The world may be post, but the organizations that populate the world are decidedly mod and premod. Worldwide, despite the collapse of communism and the Berlin wall, there are fewer democratic governments and more people experiencing torture and other severe human rights violations, than there were ten years ago.
- Is post falling into the same trap as Marxism? It was predicted that the ruling class would be overthrown as workers organized, but instead they became part of the middle class. In this postmod world, the networking is happening, the flattening of pyramids is a fact, and people are in teams, but individual freedom is elusive.

- Is the post individual a rebel? The rebel causes ripples in a modernist organization. If the rebel makes too many waves, then his or her ripples will get noticed
  in the pond. If the ripples become waves, then there will be counter currents set
  in motion to drown the rebel.

The Post Rebel

If pre focused on the persona of the king and the peasant, while mod invented the
rational persona, what is the post individual? Nietzsche (1979) provides a glimpse
of the death of the unified, logical, rational, transcendent, do-good, subject born
of enlightenment and science. What if we kill the mod subject only to reveal a
Nietzscheian subject that is nihilistic, self-deceptive, lacking in consciousness,
willful, vengeful, and power-seeking (Nietzsche 1979: 79-97)? What difference
is this from the mod subject who is dominating, controlling, and deciding (Vattimo 1988)?

- The post-rebel will avoid humanism because of its track record of oppression.
- The post-rebel will avoid causes and politics because privacy is preserved by
  anonymity.
- The post-rebel avoids academic science because the organization theories en-
  trap their followers.
- The post-rebel remains flexible in order to step in, out, and between the many
  masks advocated in a pluralistic world.
- The post-rebel is able to set aside organizational masks to be him or her self.
- The post-rebel pursues a singular, not a community identity.
- The post-rebel prefers temporary over permanent employment and social causes.
- The post-rebel has a "live and let live" philosophy. She/he intervenes to protect
  privacy and individual privilege.
- The post-rebel prefers spontaneity over planned, rehearsed, and highly organized events.
- The post-rebel leaves only scattered traces. She/he joins the excluded, hangs
  with the marginals, and retains distance from the forces of dominance and privilege.
- The post-rebel is not anti-hierarchy, anti-centralization, anti-state, anti-intel-
  lectual, and anti-social, She/he just moves between them like boulders along
  the open highway. It is a celebration of life at the margin, going beyond "rational limits" (Ryan 1982: 158).
- The post-rebel avoids pre, mod, and post.

Notes

[1] As a postmodern rebel, I invoke my privilege as a postmodern author to come out from behind my "we, our, one says, theorists say" modernist masks and use my "I" voice(s) (Boje and Dennehy 1993). I also invoke my privilege to use story data (Boje 1991a 1991b), even personal narratives (Boje 1992), instead of non-storied empirical data. Since there is a growing postmodern audience, I do not feel the need to hide behind pretensions. I would like to thank Paul Jeffcutt, Michael Reed, Stewart Clegg, Bob Dennehy, and numerous others who provided helpful comments on earlier drafts of this paper. Stewart Clegg also assisted with the final drafting.

[2] I think this dead-end was reached just about when Nixon lied about Cambodia, when we in the USA had to get into long gas lines in the early 1970s and when the United States lost the war with Vietnam (Reed 1993).

References

Bailey, D. and F. Heon (1993), Organizational Science and International Development: Wait! Whose "Development" Are we Talking About?, paper presented at the New Orleans Meetings of the International Academy of Business Disciplines (April 8-11).

Bauman, Z. (1987), *Legislators and Interpreters: Modernity, Post-modernity and Intellectuals*. Ithaca, NY: Cornell University Press.

Benton, P. (1990), *Riding the Whirlwind: Benton on Managing Turbulence*. Oxford: Basil Blackwell.

Boje, D. (1991), The Storytelling Organization: A Study of Story Performance in an Office-Supply Firm. *Administrative Science Quarterly*, 36, pp. 106-126.

Boje, D. (1992), The University is a Panoptic Cage, Disciplining the Student and Faculty Bodies, paper presented to August National Academy Meetings Show Case Symposium on Postmodern Management: Diversity and Change, Las Vegas.

Boje, D. (1993a), Toyotaism: Deconstructing our 21st Century Organizations, paper presented at the New Orleans meetings of the International Academy of Business Disciplines (April 8-11).

Boje, D. (1993b), On being Postmodern in the Academy: An Interview with Stewart Clegg. *Journal of Management Inquiry*, 2(2), pp. 191-200.

Boje, D. (1993c), Back to the Guilds: Lessons for Postmodern Learning Organizatons. To appear in *Management Learning*, 1(1).

Boje, D. and R. Dennehy (1993), *Managing in the Postmodern World: America's Revolution against Exploitation*. Dubuque, Iowa: Kendall Hunt Publishers.

Burrell, G. (1988), Modernism, Postmodernism and Organizational Analysis 2: The Contribution of Michel Foucault. *Organization Studies*, 9(2), 221-235.

Calás, M.B. (1993), Testimonios de Mis Hermanas: Research Approaches from the Third World, paper presented at the 1993 Academy of Management Meeting, Atalanta, GA (August 10).

Chio, V.C.M. (1993), In Search of a Bridge to a Bare Wooden-Floored Stilthouse in Penampang, paper presented at the 1993 Academy of Management Meeting, Atalanta, GA (August 10).

Clegg, S.R. (1989), *Frameworks of Power*. London: Sage.

Clegg, S.R. (1990), *Modern Organizations: Organizations Studies in the Postmodern World.* London: Sage.

Cohen, M.D., J.G. March, and J.P. Olsen (1972), A Garbage Can Model of Organizational Choice. *Administrative Science Quarterly*, 17(1), 1-25.

Collinson, D. (1993), Resistance, Knowledge and Power in the Workplace, paper presented at the 11th EGOS Colloquium, Paris, July 6-8.

Cooper, R. and G. Burrell (1988), Modernism, Postmodernism and Organizational Analysis: An introduction.' *Organization Studies*, 9(1), 91-112.

Drucker, P. (1957), *Landmarks of Tomorrow*. New York: Harper.

Freire, P. (1970), *Pedagogy of the Oppressed*. New York: Seabury Press.

Foucault, M. (1979), *Discipline and Punish*. New York: Pantheon.

Foucault, M. (1987), What is Enlightenment?, in *Interpretive Social Science, A Second Look,* eds. Paul Rabinow and William M. Sullivan. Berkeley: University of California Press.

Graff, G. (1979), *Literature Against Itself*. Chicago: University of Chicago Press.

Habermas, J. (1981), Modernity versus Postmodernity. *New German Critique*, 22, 3-14.

Hassard, J. (1993), Postmodern Epistemology and Organizational Knowledge: Toward a Conceptual Framework, paper presented at the 11th EGOS Colloquium, Paris, July 6-8.

Haval, V. (1992), The End of the Modern Era. *New York Times* (March 1).

Henriques J., W. Holoway, C. Urwin, C. Venn, and V. Walkerdine (1984), *Changing the Subject: Psychology, Social Regulation, and Subjectivity.* New York: Methuen.

Hetrick, W. and D. Boje (1992), Organization and the Body: Post-Fordist Dimensions. *Journal of Organizational Change Management*, 5(1), 48-57.

Hirschman, A.O. (1976), The Passions and the Interests: Political Arguments for Capitalism before its Triumph. Princeton, NJ: Princeton University Press.

Holvino, E. (1993), The Chicana Worker Meets OD: A Deconstructive Reading of Productive Workplaces, paper presented at the 1993 Academy of Management Meeting, Atalanta, GA (August 10).

Jeffcutt, P. (1993), Organization Studies and Transformations in Modern Society, paper presented at the 11th EGOS Colloquium, Paris, July 6-8.

Karnoouh, C. (1986), The Lost Paradise of Regionalism: The Crisis of Post-Modernity in France. *Telos,* 67(Spring), 11-26.

Kilduff, M. (1993), Deconstructing Organizations. *Academy of Management Review*, 18(1), 13-31.

Knights, D. and G. Morgan (1993), Organization Theory snd Consumption in a Post-Modern Era. *Organization Studies,* 14(2), 211-234.

Kreiner, K. (1992), The Postmodern Epoch of Organization Theory. *International Studies of Management and Organization,* 22(2), 37-52.

Laffey, J. (1987), The Politics at Modernism's Funeral. *Canadian Journal of Political and Social Theory*, 11(3), 89-98.

Latour, B. (1987), *Science in Action: How to Follow Scientists and Engineers through Society.* Cambridge: Harvard University Press.

Latour, B. (1988), *The Pasteurization of France*. Cambridge: Harvard University Press.

Lyotard, J.-F. (1984), *The Postmodern Condition: A Report on Knowledge*. Minneapolis: University of Minnesota Press.

March, J. and H. Simon (1957), *Organizations*. New York: Wiley.

Morgan, G. (1986), *Images of Organization*. Beverly Hills, CA: Sage.

Nietzsche, F. (1964), *The Will to Power: An Attempted Transvaluation of All Values*. Vol. II, Books III and IV. New York: Russell and Russell.

Nietzsche, F. (1979), On Truth and Lies in a Nonmoral Sense. *Philosophy and Truth, Selections from Nietzsche's Notebooks in the Early 1870s*. Atlantic City, NJ: Humanities Press.

Pondy, L.R., P.G. Frost, G. Morgan and T.C. Dandridge (eds.) (1983), *Organizational Symbolism*. Monographs in Organizational Behaviour and Industrial Relations, Volume 1. Greenwich, CT: JAI Press.

Reed, M.I. (1993), Rediscovering Hegel: The New Historicism, Organization and Management Studies, paper presented at the 11th EGOS Colloquium, Paris, July 6-8.

Rosenau, P.M. (1992), *Post-Modernism and the Social Sciences: Insights, Inroads, and Intrusions*. Princeton, NJ: Princeton University Press.

Ryan, M. (1982), *Marxism and Deconstruction: A Critical Articulation*. Baltimore, MD: John Hopkins University Press.

Sinclair, A. (1992), The Tyranny of a Team Ideology. *Organization Studies,* 13(4), 611-626.

Steingard, D.; S. Dale; E. Fitzgibbons and D. Boje (1993), The Emergence of Postmodern Administrative Science, Toward an Ecology of Collective Human Studies, paper presented at the New Orleans meetings of the International Academy of Business Disciplines (April 8-11).

Toulmin, S. (1990), *Cosmopolis: The Hidden Agenda of Modernity*. New York: The Free Press.

Touraine, A. (1988), *Return of the Actor: A Social Theory of Postindustrial Society*. Minneapolis: University of Minnesota Press.

Touraine, A. (1990), Modernity and the Subject, paper presented to the International Sociological Association Congress, Madrid, July 10.

Vattimo, G. (1988), *The End of Modernity: Nihilism and Hermeneutics in Post-modern Culture*. London: Polity.

Weick, K.E. (1976), Educational Organizations as Loosely Coupled Systems. *Administrative Science Quarterly,* 21(1), 1-19.

Winsor, R. (1993), The Human Costs of Total Quality, paper presented at the International Academy of Business Disciplines in New Orleans, Organizational Theory Track, April 8-11.

Winsor, R. and D. Boje (1993), The Resurrection of Taylorism: Total Quality Management's Hidden Agenda. *Journal of Organizational Change Management,* 6(4).

Notes on Contributors

David Boje is located at the College of Business, Loyola Marymount University, Loyola Bvd. at W. 80th St. Los Angeles, CA 90045-2699 in the USA. He is well-known for his research on "organization storytelling" and on "postmodernism," both concerns that he has promoted actively in various professional fora, such as the American Academy of Management.

Michael Brocklehurst works at The Management School, Imperial College, 53 Prince's Gate, Exhibition Road, London SW7 2PG in the UK.

Thomas Clarke and *Richard Bostock* are both at Leeds Business School, Leeds Metropolitan University, Calverley Street Leeds LS1 3HE, in the UK. Thomas is the DBM Chair in Corporate Governance and Richard is completing a PhD in the same area.

Stewart Clegg is Foundation Professor of Management at the University of Western Sydney, Macarthur, PO Box 555, Campbelltown NSW 2560, in Australia. He is a well known researcher in the fields of sociology, particularly on "power," and in organization studies.

François Dupuy is Professor of Sociology of Organisations (CEDEP-INSEAD, Fontainebleau) and Senior consultant (BOSSARD, Paris). He co-authored with Jean-Claude Thoenig several books on Public Bureaucracies and Markets.

Larry Dwyer is Associate Professor at the University of Western Sydney, Macarthur, PO Box 555, Campbelltown NSW 2560, in Australia. Presently, his research and teaching is developing the field of tourism management.

John Gray is a lecturer at the University of Western Sydney, Macarthur, PO Box 555, Campbelltown NSW 2560, in Australia. He is presently researching "innovation," with particular emphasis on the legal profession.

Paul Jeffcutt is located in the Division of Business Studies, University of Stirling, Stirling FK9 4LA, Scotland, in the UK. He has published widely on issues of "postmodernism" in journals such as *Organization Studies*.

Sharon Kemp works at the University of Western Sydney, Macarthur, PO Box 555, Campbelltown NSW 2560, in Australia. She is presently researching the management of science policy.

Clóvis L. Machado da Silva and *Valéria Silva Da Fonseca* are both at the Universidade Federal de Santa Catarina, Curso De Pós-Graduação em Administração Caixa Postal 476 88 049, Florianóplis, SC, in Brasil. Clóvis is one of Brasil's most eminent organization theorists, and is presently President of ANPAD, the main professional association in Brasil. Valéria is a Doctoral student in the university.

Jane Marceau works at the ANU, in the Urban Research Programme of the Research School of Social Sciences, in Canberra. Previously, Jane has been a researcher for the OECD and is known widely for her work on graduate management education in elite business schools, as well as more recent work on technology and on public policy.

Albert Mills is a member of the Faculty of Management, University of St. Mary's, Halifax, Nova Scotia, in Canada. He has authored a number of research papers and books in organization theory, focusing, in particular, on the intersection of "gender" and "organization rules."

Michael Muetzelfeldt works in the Department of Administration and Professional Studies, Deakin University, Geelong Vic 3217 in Australia where he directs research on "citizenship," working in an interdisciplinary social science environment.

Gill Palmer is Dean of the Faculty of Commerce, University of Wollongong, PO Box 1144 Wollongong, NSW 2500, in Australia and has been a major contributor to the Industrial Relations literature in Britain and Australia.

Suzana Braga Rodrigues works in the Fundação de Amparo a Pesquisa-Fapemig, Rua Raul Pompéia n. 101-São Pedro, 30 330 080 30170 Belo Horizonte, Minais Gerais, in Brasil. She is internationally distinguished as one of Brasil's foremost organization scholars and is a past president of ANPAD, the national professional association.

Andrew Sturdy ist Lecturer in Organizational Behaviour at the the School of Management, Bath University, Bath. *David Knights* works at The University of Manchester Institute of Science and Technology. Both have been very active in the development of the labor process perspective, researching in the financial services industry, in particular.

Jean-Claude Thoenig, Centre national de la recherche scientifique, Groupe d'analyse des politiques publiques, Université de Paris 1 Département de science politique, 13 Rue du four F-75006 Paris, France, is one of France's premier social scientists in the organizations field, and a founder member of EGOS.

Ioanna Tsivacou works in the University of the Aegean, 30 Vougaroktonou str. 114 72, Athens in Greece. She has been an active proponent of "soft systems theory" for a number of years, working at the interface of systems and critical theory.

Index

Booth, C., 87
Bostock, R., 6
Bourdieu, P., 57, 74, 93, 116, 117, 118, 119, 120
Bowles, T., 77
Bowman, J. R., 227
Boyne, R., 320
Bradley, H., 99, 100
Bray, W., 197
Brenner, O., 184
Brittan, A., 187
Brocklehurst, M., 5, 105, 106
Brown, J. S., 226
Bryman, A., 281
Burawoy, M., 221
Burchell, G., 74, 85
Burke, P., 121
Burnham, J., 156
Burns, T., 34
Burrell, G., 191, 192-3, 337, 338, 341
Burris, B. H., 123
Burton, C., 187
Byrne, J., 159

Cadbury, A., 156, 162
Cahier, M., 78
Calás, M., 191, 331
Calvino, I., 227, 243
Cantley, M. F., 292
Carlyle, T., 316, 317
Carney, S., 19
Carson, R., 339
Cathelat, B., 78, 79, 92
Chambers, J. D., 98
Chandler, A. D., 245, 326
Chaplin, C., 246
Charkham, J., 160, 161, 163
Checkland, P., 213
Child, J., 120, 122, 131
Chio, V. C. M., 331
Chua, W. F., 272
Clark, K., 283
Clark, L. H., 88
Clarke, T. F., 6
Clegg, S. R., 7, 20, 26, 115, 126, 127, 132, 151, 215, 219, 220, 229, 241, 248, 263,

272, 273, 274, 276, 282, 289, 294, 295, 315, 318, 329, 331, 338, 343
Clutterbuck, D., 103-4
Cobbett, W., 315, 316
Cockburn, C., 221
Cohen, M. D., 337
Cohen, S., 119
Cole, A., 75, 92, 93
Cole, R. E., 251
Colebatch, T., 25
Coleman, H., 277
Coleridge, S. T., 310, 315, 316
Collier, J., 116
Collins, R., 323
Collinson, D., 116, 117, 118, 119, 120, 122, 123, 124, 126, 127, 128, 185, 186, 187, 338
Collor de Mellor, F., 141, 149
Comte, A., 316
Considine, M., 21, 26
Cooper, C., 187, 296
Cooper, R., 283, 320, 325, 337
Cotta, A., 35, 38, 447
Cox, M. G., 191
Crozier, M., 44, 45
Curtis, T., 83, 84, 91, 93

Da Vinci, L., 333
Daft, R. L., 240, 277-8, 279
Dahl, R. A., 35
Dandridge, T., 227
Daniel, J. P., 96
Dankbar, B., 286
Davidson, M., 187
Dawson, P., 182
de-Toqueville, A., 316
Deal, T. E., 116, 144, 282
Deetz, S., 116-17
Defert, D., 86
Demaziere, D., 131
Denmark, F., 180, 184, 186
Dennehey, R., 238, 330, 343
Derrida, J., 323, 325
Descartes, R., 331, 333, 334, 335, 336
Dessuant, P., 224, 225
Dewey, J., 313
Dicken, P., 156

This igloo book belongs to:

••

Published in 2016
by Igloo Books Ltd
Cottage Farm
Sywell
NN6 0BJ
www.igloobooks.com

HON002 0816
2 4 6 8 10 9 7 5 3 1
ISBN 978-1-78670-148-0

Illustrated by:
Alice Bonacina, Boaz Gabai, Caroline Romanet, Diane Le Feyer, Gerald Kelly,
Mays Dabs, Mike Love, Stefano Tambellini

Printed and manufactured in China

My Treasury of
Brothers Grimm Fairytales

igloobooks

Contents

Contents

Sleeping Beauty

Once, long ago, there was a king and queen who wanted a child more than anything. They waited for many years, then finally, their wish came true. On a fine summer day, their beautiful baby daughter was born. The king and queen were overjoyed.

"We shall have a fantastic feast!" cried the king. Everyone at the palace was busy making preparations for a magnificent party to celebrate the arrival of the new princess.

Friends and family were invited to the celebration. The king also asked the fairies who lived in his kingdom, all except one, who was very grumpy.

On the day of the party, there was music and dancing and a splendid feast. Guests brought lovely presents for the baby. The gifts from the fairies were the most wonderful of all.

The first fairy gave the princess the gift of beauty and the second granted her the gift of kindness. The third fairy approached the princess's crib, but before she could speak, the sky turned dark and a crack of thunder boomed through the palace.

Another fairy suddenly appeared. She was furious that she had not been invited to the party.

"My gift to the princess is a curse," she shrieked. "On her sixteenth birthday she will prick her finger on a spinning wheel and die!" With a swirl of smoke and a crackle of magic she was gone.

The guests were shocked into silence, but the third fairy thought fast.

"I can't undo her curse, but I can lessen it," she said. "The princess will not die, instead she will fall asleep for one hundred years."

The king ordered every spinning wheel in the land to be burned. No one told the princess about the curse and she grew up happy and carefree.

On her sixteenth birthday, the princess was so excited she got up early and went to search for her presents. The princess was sure her parents had bought her something special, they had been acting strangely for the last few days.

The princess searched everywhere, but found nothing new until she came across a small door. She turned the rusty key and stepped inside.

In the middle of the room sat an old woman at a spinning wheel. It was the grumpy fairy. She had come to make sure her curse came true.

The princess had never seen a spinning wheel before and watched in wonder as it turned wool into thread.

"Would you like to try?" asked the old woman.

"Yes, please," said the princess, who had been given the gift of good manners. The princess sat down and began to spin.

"Ouch!" the princess cried as she pricked her finger. Suddenly, she felt very tired and spotted a bed in the corner of the room. The princess stumbled onto the bed and fell asleep.

At the very same moment, everyone in the palace fell into a deep slumber. The cook lay her head on the birthday cake she had been icing and started to snore.

The king and queen, who were still in bed, turned over and fell back asleep. Even the royal cat and dog curled up in their baskets to snooze.

Everything was silent and still. As the days and weeks went by, thick brambles grew up outside and the palace was almost hidden from view.

The story of the sleeping princess spread across the land. Many brave men came to rescue her, but they could not cut through the thick, thorny branches.

Then one day, a prince came riding through the woods. He too had heard the tale of the beautiful princess who slept in an enchanted palace. When he saw the royal flag fluttering above a tangle of wild bushes, he knew he had found the right place.

Determined to rescue her from the evil curse, the prince swung his sword through the brambles.

Ignoring the scratches from the spiky thorns, the prince carried on until he had cut a path to the palace door. He stepped over the sleeping guards and went inside.

The prince rushed from room to room, past sleeping servants, and dozing pets. At last he reached the room where the princess lay.

As soon as the prince saw the beautiful girl, he fell in love. The prince gave the princess a kiss and with the lightest touch of his lips, the curse was broken. "You are my sleeping beauty," he said.

The princess awoke and her heart filled with love when she saw the handsome prince. He took her hand and together they walked through the palace, where everyone was stretching and yawning as they woke up from their long slumber.

The king and queen were delighted that the curse had been broken. They arranged a magnificent wedding for the prince and princess with music, dancing, and a splendid feast. Everyone had a wonderful time and they all lived happily ever after, except for the grumpy fairy, who was never seen ever again.

Twelve Dancing Princesses

Once upon a time, there was a king who had twelve daughters. The princesses slept in twelve beds in one room. Every night they would go to bed, but in the morning their shoes were worn-out, as if they had been dancing all night.

The king locked their bedroom door and even stationed guards outside, but it was no use. Every morning, the princesses' dancing shoes were worn-out.

The king became more and more troubled about his daughters. They hardly spoke to him and they always seemed dreamy. Whenever the king asked why, they just laughed.

Eventually, the king decided that something had to be done.

"Whoever finds out the secret of my daughters' worn-out shoes can have half my fortune," proclaimed the king. "He can also marry whichever princess he likes, too!"

Many brave princes and knights arrived at the castle. They all swore they would find out the princesses' secret, but as each one stood guard, the princesses gave him a goblet of wine. The wine was enchanted and made the princes and knights fall into a deep sleep.

When they woke in the morning, the princesses' shoes were as worn-out as ever and the men went home empty-handed.

One day, a soldier arrived at the castle. "I have a magic cloak that makes the wearer invisible," he told the king. "Maybe it will help me solve this mystery."

The king agreed and the soldier went to guard the princesses. When they were about to go to bed, the eldest princess handed the soldier a glass of wine. When the princesses weren't looking, the soldier quickly poured the wine away.

Then the soldier lay down and pretended to go to sleep. After a while, he heard the princesses getting up from their beds. They all giggled as they put on their finest clothes.

"Our enchanted wine has sent that silly soldier to sleep," said the eldest princess.

"Are you sure he's really sleeping?" said the youngest princess.

The soldier pretended to snore very loudly.

"Of course he is," said the eldest princess. She clapped her hands three times and a little trapdoor flew open.

All the princesses rushed through the trapdoor. Quickly, the soldier put on his cloak and became invisible. He ran past the princesses, down the secret stairway.

"What was that?" said the youngest princess. "Someone went past!"

"It was just a cold breeze," said the eldest princess.

The soldier followed the princesses down a long, dark tunnel that led far underground. The tunnel led to a forest full of silver trees. The princesses ran on through a forest of gold and then another forest where all the trees were made of diamonds.

Soon, the princesses reached the shores of a great underground lake. In twelve little boats, twelve handsome princes were waiting.

The princesses each boarded a boat and the soldier followed. Invisible in his cloak, he climbed into the boat with the eldest princess and her handsome prince. The boats headed for a faraway island.

"How strange," said the prince to the eldest princess. "I must be tired today. My arms ache and I'm rowing much slower than usual."

The soldier stayed as quiet as he could until they reached the island. The princesses climbed out of the boats and went to a dazzling palace.

The princes and the princesses danced all night long. None of them could see the soldier, so he had to keep jumping out of their way in case they bumped into him and revealed his secret.

After many hours, the princesses had danced so much that their dancing shoes were worn and tattered.

The princes rowed the princesses back across the lake and this time the soldier sat in the boat with the youngest princess.

"The king will never believe this!" thought the soldier. "I must bring him proof."

So, as they went back through the forests of diamond, gold, and silver, the soldier broke a twig from each of the trees. With each loud snap, the youngest princess jumped.

"Someone's following us!" she said. But the eldest princess always ignored her warnings.

As the princesses reached the trapdoor, the soldier crept past them and ran up the stairs. He took the cloak off, lay down, and started snoring loudly. The princesses thought he had been asleep all the time and got into bed just before dawn.

The next morning, the soldier took the twigs of silver, gold, and diamond straight to the king.

"I have solved the mystery, Your Majesty!" he said.

The king called the princesses to him and the soldier told his story.

When he'd finished, something magical happened. The twelve princesses rubbed their eyes, blinked and looked around them, as if they had just woken up.

"We were enchanted!" they said. "Those twelve magical princes had cast a spell on us and made us dance every night!"

"Thank you for freeing us from the spell!" said the youngest princess.

The king gave the soldier half of his fortune. He fell in love and married the youngest princess and they danced every night.

The Elves and the Shoemaker

Long ago, there lived a shoemaker and his wife who were very poor. They only had enough money to buy leather for one last pair of shoes.

"I must make and sell these shoes tomorrow," said the shoemaker. "Otherwise there will be no money for food." Wearily, he put the leather in his workshop and went to bed.

The next morning, when the shoemaker came downstairs, he found that the leather had been made into a pair of beautiful shoes.

"Who could have done such amazing work?" asked the shoemaker. He put the shoes in the window and soon sold them. With the money, the shoemaker was able to buy leather for two pairs of shoes.

That night, the shoemaker left the leather out on his old workbench.

The next morning, when he came downstairs, he saw two pairs of shoes. They were so finely made, they sold instantly.

"Now I have enough money to buy leather for four pairs of shoes," said the happy shoemaker. That night, as before, he left the leather in his workshop.

Sure enough, the next morning, there were four pairs of beautiful shoes waiting on the workbench. The delighted shoemaker was able to buy more and more leather and each day he found more and more perfectly made shoes.

Soon, the shoemaker's little shoe shop became famous throughout the land. The shoemaker and his wife became rich, but they still had no idea who was making the shoes.

"We must find out," said the shoemaker's wife.

So, that night, they hid behind a curtain in the workshop and waited. The sun went down and soon it grew dark. The shoemaker and his wife watched and waited, but nothing happened.

Then, at midnight, the shoemaker and his wife heard scampering and chattering. They peeped around the curtain and saw two tiny elves dressed in rags. The elves climbed up onto the workbench and picked up the leather. Astonished, the shoemaker and his wife watched in wonder as the elves set to work.

Very carefully, one elf cut the leather with scissors. The other elf picked up a needle and a spool of silk thread and began to sew. The two elves worked so fast, their hands hardly seemed to move. They snipped and sewed and hammered, until suddenly there was a beautiful pair of shoes on the workbench.

The elves worked on into the night and, after many hours, they had turned all the leather into shoes. When they had finished, just before the sun rose, they dashed out of the door.

No matter how much leather the old shoemaker bought, the elves would arrive each night and make even more shoes.

The shoemaker continued to make lots of money, but there was something troubling him.

"Even though we have grown rich from the work of the elves, I still miss making shoes myself," he said to his wife. "The elves have brought us so much happiness. I wish we could do something to repay them."

Then the shoemaker had an idea.

"Their clothes are so ragged and worn. I think it's time we did something for them."

With the money they had made, the shoemaker and his wife bought the finest material they could find.

His wife cut and sewed until she had made two tiny suits of the richest crimson and gold, as well as two tiny hats to go with them.

The shoemaker made two tiny pairs of shoes in the softest leather. When they were finished, the clothes and shoes were laid out on the workbench.

"We must see if they like their presents!" said the shoemaker's wife. So, she and the shoemaker hid behind the curtain again. They waited until they heard the door creaking open and the elves scampered in.

When the elves saw the tiny suits, they jumped for joy. They threw off their ragged old clothes and tried on their new ones. They looked very sharp indeed! When they saw the tiny shoes, they leapt up and down in excitement.

"Nobody has ever made us shoes before!" they cried.

When they were all dressed up, the elves admired each other.

"Now we're too good-looking to make shoes any more!" they said.

With that, the two little elves jumped off the workbench and ran out of the door.

The shoemaker and his wife were sorry to see the elves go, but then the shoemaker looked at all the leather they had left behind.

"At last," he said, "I can make my own shoes again!"

The shoemaker set to work straight away. He spent all day hammering and sewing, making shoes that were even more beautiful than before.

The shoemaker and his wife were very happy. People came from miles away to buy his wonderful shoes and they were never poor again. The elves never returned to the little shop, but the shoemaker and his wife never forgot them. They were always grateful to the tiny shoemakers, who had helped change their lives.

Snow White

Once upon a time, a king had a lovely baby daughter. She had hair as black as ebony, skin as white as snow, and lips as red as cherries. Her name was Snow White.

Snow White's mother had died and the king wanted a new wife. He married a very beautiful, but jealous, queen who had a magic mirror. Every day, the queen asked, "Mirror, mirror, on the wall, who is the fairest of us all?"

The mirror always answered, "Oh, beautiful queen, you are the fairest one of all."

Time passed and Snow White grew to be a beautiful young woman. One morning, the queen looked into the mirror and asked, "Mirror, mirror, on the wall, who is the fairest of us all?"

The mirror answered, "Snow White is the fairest one of all!"

The queen was furious. "I will not allow it!" she screamed. "I will get rid of Snow White." So, the wicked queen summoned her huntsman.

"Take Snow White to the deepest part of the forest and kill her," she ordered.

The huntsman was a kind man. He didn't want to harm Snow White, so he took her into the forest and left her there.

It was getting dark and Snow White felt very frightened. She looked around for a way out and saw a path running through the trees. It led to a little house.

Snow White tapped on the door. It swung open, so she slowly stepped inside. In the middle of the room was a little table set with seven little plates, seven little spoons, and seven little cups.

Snow White called out, but there was no one home.

Tired and hungry, Snow White ate some food from one of the plates and drank from one of the cups, then she went upstairs and lay down. She was fast asleep when the owners of the house came home.

They were seven little dwarfs who had been working all day in the hills.

"Someone has been in our house," they said and all began talking at once. Their voices woke Snow White. She sat up in bed and rubbed her eyes.

When the dwarfs heard Snow White's story, they felt sorry for her.

"You can stay here as long as you like," they told her.

Snow White loved living with the dwarfs. They took good care of her and in return she cleaned the house and cooked their meals.

"You will be safe here, but never let anyone into the house while we are away," they told her.

Back in the palace, the wicked queen thought that Snow White was dead. She asked the mirror if she was now the most beautiful in the land.

The mirror answered. "Oh, queen, your beauty is so rare. Yet, Snow White living in the woods is a thousand times more fair!"

This made the queen angrier than ever.

"I will get rid of Snow White myself," she vowed.

The queen disguised herself as an old woman. Then she filled a basket with the shiniest, rosiest apples she could find. The wicked queen went to the house in the forest and knocked on the door.

"Buy my lovely apples," she said to Snow White.

Snow White forgot what the dwarfs had told her.

"I would love to buy an apple," she said.

The queen picked out the reddest, juiciest apple.

"Taste it, my dear," she said, smiling wickedly, for the apple was poisoned. Snow White took a bite of the apple and she fell to the ground.

"That is the end of you," cackled the queen as she left.

When the dwarfs came home and saw Snow White lying so still, they began to cry. They thought she was dead.

"It must be the work of the wicked queen," they sobbed.

The dwarfs dressed Snow White in her prettiest dress, put flowers in her hair, and laid her in a glass case.

"Now everyone can admire her beauty," they said.

The dwarfs took turns watching over Snow White.

Later that day, a handsome prince rode past. When he saw Snow White, he immediately fell in love with her.

"I have never seen anyone more beautiful," he said. "Allow me to gaze on her beauty."

The dwarfs lifted the glass case and the prince held Snow White in his arms and kissed her gently on the lips. As if by magic, Snow White opened her eyes.

"Where am I?" she asked.

The prince took her hand in his.

"You are safe with me," he told her.

At the palace, the queen couldn't wait to ask her magic mirror, "Mirror, mirror, on the wall, who is the fairest of them all?"

The mirror answered, "Oh, queen, your beauty is so rare, but Snow White is the one that is more fair."

The queen's face darkened with anger and, in a terrible rage, she picked up the magic mirror and threw it across the room. It hit the wall and smashed into a thousand jagged pieces.

Then the wicked, jealous queen stormed out of the palace forever.

The prince asked Snow White to marry him. He took her back
to his palace. The seven dwarfs were overjoyed that their friend had
found happiness.

"You must come and live at the palace, too," Snow White told them.
"You will never have to work again."

Snow White and her handsome prince made a lovely couple and the
seven dwarfs were their guests of honor at their wonderful wedding.
No one saw or heard of the jealous queen again and Snow White and
the prince lived happily ever after.

The Frog Prince

Once upon a time, there was a beautiful, but spoiled, princess. Her father, the king, bought her anything she wanted. The princess had a wardrobe full of beautiful dresses and a bedroom full of expensive toys. Her favorite was a shiny golden ball and every day, she played with it in the palace gardens.

One day, the princess dropped the golden ball into the royal pond. "I want my golden ball back!" she cried as she stomped her feet.

"I'll fetch your ball, Princess," said a small voice. It belonged to a little, green frog who was sitting on a lily pad.

"I'll fetch your ball if you'll let me eat from your plate, drink from your cup, sleep in your bed, and give me a kiss," said the frog.

The spoiled princess didn't think it mattered if she made a promise and didn't keep it.

"I promise I'll eat with you, let you drink from my cup, let you sleep in my bed, and I'll give you a kiss," she said. "Just get my ball!"

The frog dived into the royal pond. Moments later, he reappeared with the golden ball in his mouth. The princess took the ball and ran off without even saying thank you.

The next day, the princess and her father sat down to a huge banquet. There was every kind of food imaginable, piles of pies, mountains of candy treats, and hundreds of delicious cakes.

As the princess was about to eat her second cupcake, there was a faint knocking on the door of the banquet hall. It was the little, green frog.

"You promised I could eat from your plate and drink from your cup, princess," he croaked.

"Ugh!" said the princess. "I don't want to eat with you. You're a slimy, warty frog!"

The king looked sternly at his daughter.

"That frog helped you when you were in need," he said. "If you make a promise, you should keep it."

The frog hopped up onto the table and ate from the princess's special gold plate and drank from her gold cup. He gobbled up all the ice cream and he even took the last ham sandwich and the last cupcake.

When the king threw raisins in the air, the frog caught them in mid-air with his long, sticky tongue. The king roared with laughter, but the princess didn't find it funny at all.

At the end of the meal, the frog gave a big burp. He hopped over to the princess and croaked, "Now you must take me up to your room, so we can have a slumber party."

"Ugh, Daddy, do I have to?" the princess asked the king.

"You gave your word," replied the king. "Princesses do not break their promises."

So, the princess picked up the cold and slippery frog and took him to her bedroom in the highest tower. She put the frog down in the corner of the room, but he leapt onto one of her nice, clean royal pillows. He stretched out, yawned, and fell asleep.

The princess climbed into the big golden bed beside the frog and tried to sleep. Just as she was nodding off, the frog began to snore. It was a big, croaky, rattling kind of snore. The princess clamped a pillow around her head, but she couldn't block out the horrible sound!

All night, the princess lay awake, unable to sleep. When morning came, she felt so tired. She could hardly keep her eyes open, but the frog had slept for hours and was wide awake.

"It is time I left," said the frog and the princess felt very glad. "First, you must fulfill the last part of your promise," croaked the frog. "You must give me a kiss."

The princess could think of nothing worse than kissing the warty, slimy frog, but she remembered what the king had said.

"A promise is a promise."

So, she pursed her lips, leaned over, and gave the frog a big kiss.

As the princess kissed the frog, he suddenly began to glow. The princess stepped back and watched as the frog shimmered, glimmered, and slowly began to change.

Suddenly, there was a shower of bright stars and in the frog's place stood a handsome young man.

"I am a prince who was enchanted by an evil witch," he said.
"I was doomed to stay a frog until I found a princess who would kiss me.
You have freed me from the spell!"

The princess thought the prince was very handsome.

"I've learned my lesson and will never need anything to make me
happy, other than you," she said.

The prince and princess kissed and decided to spend the rest of their
lives living happily together.

Tom Thumb

Once, there lived a man and a woman who longed for a child. Every day, they would listen to the little children who ran around outside their garden.

"I wish we had children to fill our lives with fun," said the woman. "Just one child would be enough to make me happy. Even a really small one, no bigger than my thumb."

A few months later, the woman's strange wish came true. She had a baby boy who was perfect in every way, but was as tiny as a mouse.

The man and his wife gave the boy as much food as they could afford. Yet, no matter how much he ate, he grew no bigger than his mother's thumb. So, the man and the wife named their son Tom Thumb.

Although he was small, Tom was clever and he loved to help his parents around the house. He could squeeze into small spaces and sweep out the dust or sew up the holes in their clothes with tiny stitches.

Each day, Tom helped in the garden. He pulled up weeds and planted seeds, but when it was time to go to the forest to cut wood, Tom's father told him to stay behind.

"I don't want to stay behind," thought Tom. When his father wasn't looking, Tom crept into his father's pocket to hide. As soon as they got into the woods, Tom gave his father a fright by shouting up to him.

"Hello Dad, I'm here in your pocket."

Tom's father was upset, but he didn't stay angry for long. He fished Tom out of his pocket and sat him on a twig while he chopped wood.

As they laughed and chatted together, two strangers came walking through the woods. Hearing the talking, they wandered into the clearing and saw Tom with his father.

"We could make a fortune if we put that tiny boy in a show," whispered one of the men.

"People would come from all over the world to see him," agreed his friend. The strangers offered Tom's father a bag of gold in exchange for Tom because they wanted to take him away.

"My son is more precious than all the gold in the world," said Tom's father proudly. Tom climbed on to his father's shoulder and whispered in his ear.

"You are very poor, Father. Take the gold and let me go. I'll be back before bedtime."

After much persuasion, Tom's father agreed and one of the strangers gave him a bulging bag of gold coins.

The man sat Tom Thumb on the brim of his hat so he could see the countryside as they traveled. They walked for several miles before they stopped to rest.

"Please put me down so I can take a nap," said Tom. "All this traveling has made me tired."

Placing Tom on a large leaf, the man and his friend lay back in the warm grass and were soon snoring loudly. Tom jumped up and ran away. When he heard the men searching for him, he hid down a rabbit hole.

As it got dark, the two men gave up and went away. Tom had escaped, but he was far from home.

Tom walked and walked, but his steps were so tiny that he didn't get very far. Exhausted, he settled down in an empty snail shell to sleep. Just as he was dozing off, he heard loud voices. Two thieves were arguing about the best way to break into a house.

"Pick the lock and creep in quietly," suggested one thief.

"No," said the other, "let's smash a window, grab what we can and run."

"I can help," shouted Tom as loudly as he could. One of the thieves picked up the shell and they stared in amazement at the tiny boy.

The thieves took Tom to the house and watched him squeeze through a small gap under the door. "Climb up to the window and undo the lock," they whispered.

Instead, Tom started banging pots and pans and shouting as loudly as he could. "Sssh!" said the thieves. "Be quiet or we'll get caught."

"You mustn't rob this house!" cried Tom, banging the pans even louder.

There was the sound of footsteps upstairs and a light turned on.

"Who's there!" shouted an angry voice. The thieves were so frightened they ran away into the woods.

The man who owned the house was surprised to find a tiny boy sitting in his kitchen. Tom Thumb introduced himself and explained that he had scared the thieves off.

The man was so grateful that he offered Tom a reward, but all Tom wanted was to go home. The man was happy to help and they set off at once on his horse and cart.

When they reached a little cottage near the woods, Tom called out, "I'm home!"

Tom's parents cried with joy and Tom hugged them tight and promised never to leave home again.

Hansel and Gretel

Long ago, by a dark wood, lived a poor woodcutter who had two children named Hansel and Gretel. Even though they were poor, the children were happy. Every day they played in the woods and fed their bird friends in the forest.

One day, the woodcutter said, "I am bringing a stepmother home to live with us. I want you to love her as much as you love me."

Hansel and Gretel hugged him.

"We will try, Father," they said.

However, the stepmother was cruel. She wanted the woodcutter to get rid of Hansel and Gretel.

"We are so very poor and there isn't enough food to go round," she said to him one day. "The next time you go into the woods, you must take Hansel and Gretel and leave them there."

"What will become of them?" asked the woodcutter, sadly.

"Don't worry," replied the sly stepmother. "They're old enough to look after themselves. They'll be just fine."

Hansel overheard his stepmother and decided to make a plan. He filled his pockets with bread and when they went into the woods, he dropped a trail of breadcrumbs on the ground.

When their father had finished cutting wood, he turned to Hansel and Gretel with tears in his eyes.

"Wait here," he said sadly. "I will be back shortly."

Then he kissed them and left.

Hansel and Gretel waited and waited, but their father didn't come back. Hansel hoped the trail of breadcrumbs would lead them back home.

When Hansel looked, the breadcrumbs had vanished.

"The birds must have eaten them," he said, and Gretel began to cry.

Then, Hansel noticed a little house behind the trees. Its roof was made of gingerbread and its walls were made of cake. The window frames were striped sugar candy and the door was made of chocolate.

The children were very hungry, so they broke off some of the cake from the walls.

Suddenly, the door swung open and a sweet, old lady appeared.

"Come in, children," said the old lady. Hansel and Gretel stepped inside, but the door slammed behind them. "You are my prisoners now," said the woman, who was really a witch.

The witch cackled as she locked Hansel in a large cage and made Gretel do all the housework. She fed the children lots of candy. At first they tasted nice, but soon Hansel and Gretel got tired of eating so much sugary food. They wondered why the witch was feeding them so much.

That night, Gretel overheard the witch talking in her sleep.

"I will have plump children for my supper soon," she mumbled.

Gretel told Hansel what the witch had said. So, the next day, when she came to test how plump Hansel's finger was, he held out a bony twig. The witch had bad eyesight so she didn't notice.

"I won't eat you today," she said.

Soon, however, the witch grew tired of waiting.

"Maybe I'll have both of you for supper tomorrow," she hissed. "Stack the firewood under the oven, Gretel, I want it to be good and hot when it is lit tomorrow," she said and went to bed.

"We must do something," whispered Hansel to Gretel.

The next day, the witch was about to light a fire under the oven.

"I want you to check if it's big enough to fit both of you," said the witch, opening the oven door.

"How do I do that?" asked Gretel.

"Get inside, of course," said the sly witch.

Gretel looked at the oven. "Will you show me how?" she asked.

The witch couldn't resist showing off. She hiked up her skirts and leaned in. Quick as a flash, Gretel pushed her inside and slammed the door.

"Let me out," screamed the witch, but Gretel ignored her. Instead, she rushed across the kitchen and freed Hansel.

They ran outside and their little bird friends flew down from the trees. They led the children along the winding forest paths, back home to the woodcutter's cottage.

When their father saw them he was overjoyed, "I realized that your stepmother was wicked and I sent her away," he said.

Hansel and Gretel hugged their father. They went back to their happy, simple life and were never troubled by the wicked witch again.

Four Skilled Brothers

Long ago, four brothers set off to seek their fortunes along four different roads. On the first road, the eldest brother met a hunter.

"I will teach you how to be quick and cunning, so you can sneak around quietly without being seen," said the hunter. So, the eldest brother went with the hunter and learned how to be quick and cunning.

The second brother met an astronomer.

"I will show you the secrets of the stars and you shall have this fine magic telescope," said the astronomer. So, the second brother went with the astronomer and learned how to use the telescope.

The third brother met a magician. He promised that he would show him how to make a person vanish into thin air. So, the third brother agreed to go with the magician and learn all about magic.

The youngest brother met a tailor who was looking for an apprentice. He promised to teach the brother everything he knew. So, the youngest brother went with the tailor. He taught him how to make fine clothes and gave him a magic needle that could sew any two things together.

When the four brothers had learned their skills, they returned home. Each one wondered how he might put his skills to good use.

One morning, a messenger arrived. The king's daughter had been snatched by a fierce dragon.

"The king is offering a large reward to whoever can free the princess," said the messenger. The four brothers agreed at once that they must rescue the king's daughter.

The brother who had become an astronomer looked through his magic telescope. He searched all over the world. Finally, he spotted the princess and the dragon on a rocky island far out at sea.

The four brothers took a ship and set sail for the island. When they drew near, the astronomer looked through his telescope again.

"The dragon is asleep with his claw on the princess," he said.

"Don't worry," said the brother who had learned to be quick and cunning. "I know what to do."

He climbed out of the ship and crept close to the sleeping dragon. He lifted its claw and silently freed the princess. He took her back to the ship, but just as it was setting off, the dragon awoke.

Roaring with anger, the dragon stretched out its powerful wings and flew after them. No matter how fast they sailed, the dragon flew faster, breathing fire and smoke.

The brother who'd learned to be a magician waved his wand and made the dragon disappear.

Just then, there was a huge crash as the ship hit some rocks. The magic wand fell into the sea and the ship began to sink below the blue waves. The four brothers and the princess grabbed the splintered planks to keep afloat in the rough waves.

"We're going to drown!" cried the frightened princess.

At last, the sea became calmer.

"Who will save us?" asked the princess.

"I haven't used my skills yet," said the youngest brother, who had trained to be a tailor.

He gathered all the bits of ragged sail and pieces of wood. Then he began to sew them with his magic needle. Before long, there was enough to cover all the floating planks and make a little boat. Everyone began to paddle and soon, they reached land.

News spread quickly that the four brothers had rescued the princess. A golden royal carriage came to pick them up and they rode through the streets to shouts and cheers.

The king was so delighted to have his daughter safely home. He commanded that there would be a special celebration throughout the kingdom. For the first time in ages, the palace was filled with laughter. Everyone danced and feasted.

The king was so impressed by the skills that the brothers had used to save his daughter, he gave each of them a place in the royal household. The first brother became the royal hunter, the second became the royal astronomer, the brother who had become a magician entertained everyone at royal parties. As for the fourth brother, he made a beautiful wedding dress for the princess and they were married soon after.

The brothers had used their skills for good and they all lived long and happy lives.

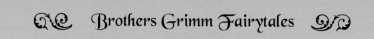

Little Red Riding Hood

Once there was a little girl who lived on the edge of a dark wood. Her grandmother had given her a red cloak with a hood. The girl liked the cloak so much and wore it so often that everyone called her Little Red Riding Hood.

One day, Little Red Riding Hood's mother was baking some cupcakes in the kitchen.

"Can you take a basket of these cakes to Grandma's house?" she said. "Grandma is sick and I'm sure they will cheer her up. It's a long way, so make sure you stay on the path and don't talk to strangers."

Little Red Riding Hood put on her red cloak and her mother filled the basket with the freshly baked cakes. She kissed her mother goodbye and set off, but before she reached the forest path, her mother called out.

"Remember what I said, always stay on the path and never talk to strangers." Then she waved and went back inside.

Little Red Riding Hood nodded and waved back as she set off into the deep, dark woods.

Grandma lived in a pretty cottage in the middle of the woods. Little Red Riding Hood had visited her lots of times, so she knew which path to take through the tall trees.

As she walked along, she heard someone calling her.

"Little girl," growled a gruff voice. "Where are you going today?"

"I'm going to visit my grandma," replied Little Red Riding Hood.

The voice belonged to a wolf, who stepped out on to the path in front of her.

"Where does your grandma live?" he asked.

"She lives in the clearing in the middle of these woods," said Little Red Riding Hood. "I'm taking her some cakes to help her feel better."

The wolf licked his lips. He'd much rather eat a little girl than a cake. So, he thought carefully and came up with a cunning plan.

"If your grandma is sick, you should take her some flowers," he suggested. "There are lots of pretty ones growing here that are sure to make her smile."

Little Red Riding Hood thought this was a great idea and immediately started picking a bunch of the most beautiful blooms. While she was busy, the wolf ran all the way to Grandma's house.

When he got there, the wolf locked poor Grandma in a closet. Grabbing one of her nightgowns and a nightcap, he quickly closed the curtains and jumped into bed.

Just then, Little Red Riding Hood knocked on the door.

"Come in, dear," said the wolf, trying to sound like Grandma.

"You must have a very sore throat," said Little Red Riding Hood. She put down the basket of cakes and walked toward the bed to give her grandma a kiss. As she got closer, she noticed something strange.

"Grandma, what big ears you have," said Little Red Riding Hood.

"All the better to hear you with," replied the wolf in a squeaky voice. Little Red Riding Hood took a step closer.

"Grandma, what big eyes you have," she said.

"All the better to see you with," said the wolf. She moved closer still and peered into her grandma's face.

"Grandma, what big, sharp teeth you have!"

"All the better to EAT you with," said the wolf, leaping out of bed. There was a terrible commotion as he chased poor Little Red Riding Hood all over Grandma's cottage.

Luckily, a kind woodcutter was passing by. He heard the terrible banging and crashing.

"I bet that wolf is up to no good again," he said. He raised his sharp axe and burst in. "I fancy a nice bit of wolf for my supper!" he cried.

When the wolf heard this, he ran off yelping into the forest, never to be seen again.

Just then, Little Red Riding Hood heard a knocking sound coming from the closet. She opened the door and found Grandma inside.

"I'm glad that nasty wolf is gone," she said. "He was very rude."

Grandma hugged Little Red Riding Hood and thanked the brave woodcutter. They all sat down and had drinks and some of the delicious cakes that Little Red Riding Hood had brought.

After that, Little Red Riding Hood never wandered off the forest path and she never talked to strangers ever again.

Rapunzel

Once upon a time, there was a wicked witch who had a beautiful garden full of fruit trees. Next door lived a man whose wife longed to taste the fruit from the witch's garden.

"Please get one for me," she begged. "If I don't eat that fruit I will waste away."

Her husband knew that the garden belonged to a witch, but his wife asked him so many times that at last he gave in.

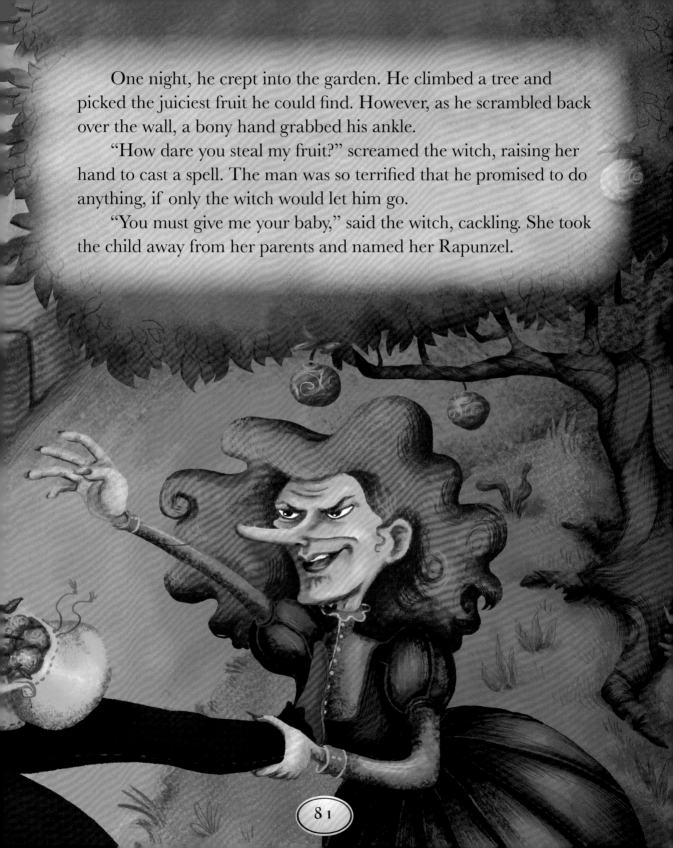

One night, he crept into the garden. He climbed a tree and picked the juiciest fruit he could find. However, as he scrambled back over the wall, a bony hand grabbed his ankle.

"How dare you steal my fruit?" screamed the witch, raising her hand to cast a spell. The man was so terrified that he promised to do anything, if only the witch would let him go.

"You must give me your baby," said the witch, cackling. She took the child away from her parents and named her Rapunzel.

The witch locked Rapunzel in a tall tower with no doors and only one window. Over time, she grew into a beautiful young woman with long, golden hair.

When the witch wanted to visit Rapunzel, she stood at the bottom of the tower and called out, "Rapunzel, Rapunzel, let down your hair."

Then, the young woman would hang her hair out of the window for the witch to climb up.

One day, when Rapunzel was all alone, a prince rode by on his horse. He heard her singing and was so enchanted that he stayed to listen. When the witch came to visit, the prince hid behind a bush.

The prince watched in wonder as the witch called out, "Rapunzel, Rapunzel, let down your hair."

He saw Rapunzel drop her hair out of the window and instantly fell in love. The prince waited until the witch had gone and then stood at the bottom of the tower.

"Rapunzel, Rapunzel, let down your hair," he shouted, trying to make his voice sound like the witch's.

Rapunzel hung her hair out of the window. She was shocked when a handsome prince climbed up instead of the witch, but he was so charming and kind that she soon fell in love with him.

The prince visited every day. Each time he brought a ball of silk thread with him and Rapunzel set to work weaving it into a ladder. When it was almost long enough for her to escape, she heard the witch approaching and quickly hid it away.

As the witch climbed up her hair, Rapunzel couldn't help complaining that she was much heavier than the handsome prince.

The witch flew into a rage. She grabbed a pair of scissors and chopped off Rapunzel's long hair. Then, she took her out into the wilderness and left her there all alone.

The witch returned to the tower and waited for the prince. It wasn't long before he arrived and called out to his true love, "Rapunzel, Rapunzel, let down your hair."

The witch threw down the hair she had cut from Rapunzel and the prince climbed up. When he saw the witch at the window he yelled out in fright.

"She's gone," the witch screamed, "and you will never find her."

The prince was so frightened, he let go of the hair and fell into a tangle of brambles. The sharp thorns tore at his clothes and scratched him. He staggered away, sure that he would never see Rapunzel again. The sad prince was heartbroken.

For days the prince searched for his lost love. He called her name, but all he heard was the wind in the trees and the birds singing. Their sweet voices reminded him of Rapunzel and he felt sad and alone.

At last, he stumbled into a wild place where no trees grew and no birds sang. He sank to the ground to rest, but suddenly a beautiful sound made him jump to his feet.

A lovely clear voice was singing the saddest song he had ever heard. It was Rapunzel. When she saw her prince she cried with joy.

The prince took Rapunzel home to his palace and they were
married the following day. Everyone in the kingdom celebrated the
royal wedding. The streets were decorated with flags and streamers and
everyone danced, sang, and had fabulous feasts. No one was as joyful as
the prince and his new bride, Rapunzel. They lived happily ever after.

The Brave Little Tailor

There once was a tailor who worked hard to make fine clothes. He was very small, so everyone thought he must be timid and weak. "He couldn't harm a fly," they said, laughing. The little tailor didn't think it was fair that the villagers called him timid.

One sunny day, the little tailor opened his window while he ate his lunch. A cloud of flies buzzed into the room. They swarmed around his plate and crawled all over the bread and jam. The tailor swatted them away and knocked seven of the flies to the floor.

Impressed by what he had done, the tailor set to work making himself a belt with the words, "Seven in one blow," sewn on to it. He wore it as he walked around the village and rumors of his bravery soon began to spread.

"I heard he trapped seven rats," said one of his neighbors.

"No, it was wild boars," replied another.

Within a week, word had got around that the little tailor had beaten seven dragons with one hand. When the local giant heard this tale he was very angry.

"I am stronger than anyone in the land," he roared. "We'll soon find out if this tailor is as strong as me."

One day, the giant strode through the village to the tailor's house and challenged him to a contest. The giant picked up a boulder that was lying nearby and squeezed it in his fist. The tailor watched in dismay as water ran out of the boulder.

"Your turn," bellowed the giant. "If you're so strong, let's see you squeeze water from a rock."

"The rocks out here aren't hard enough," said the tailor. "I have the perfect one inside."

He dashed into his house, grabbed an old sponge and held it under the tap. He carried the soaked sponge outside and squeezed it hard.

The giant gasped as water ran out of the tailor's tiny hand.

"Well, you won't be able to beat me in a throwing competition!" the giant boomed.

He picked up a stone and tossed it into the air with a swing of his massive arm. It soared through the clouds and out of sight. Eventually they heard the stone land with a thud.

When the tailor went to pick it up, he spotted a gray bird sitting on the ground.

Without the giant seeing, he gently picked up the bird.

"My rock will go so far that it will never come down," he boasted. He lifted his arm and threw the bird. It flew off into the sky and disappeared.

"I'm impressed, but not impressed enough to believe that you can beat me," said the giant. "Let's see who can push this cart the farthest."

"I'll go first," said the tailor. Then, leaning down to take off the brake, he placed his shoulder against the cart and pushed with all his might. The road from the tailor's house was on a slight slope, so the cart rolled easily downhill.

When he got to the bottom, the tailor secretly put the brake back on. The giant leaned his enormous shoulder against the cart and gave it a shove. It didn't budge. He pushed with all his strength, but could not make the cart move.

"Now it's my turn to come up with a challenge," said the tailor. "Can you jump over this tree?"

The giant bent his big knees and tried to spring up in the air, but he was so heavy his feet barely lifted off the ground.

When it was the tailor's turn, he asked the giant to reach up and bend one of the branches down for him. The giant was keen to see the tiny tailor leap over the tree, so he did as he was asked. The tailor held on tight to the end of the branch. When the giant let go, it sprang back up flinging him over the top of the tree to land on the other side.

Roaring with frustration, the giant pulled the tree out of the ground.

"I may not be able to jump over a tree, but I can carry one," he said growling.

"So can I," said the tailor. "You hold the trunk and I'll lift the branches up."

The giant lifted the big tree, while the tailor skipped round behind him and climbed up into the branches.

"This is easy," he called out.

"It's heavier than I thought," said the giant, grunting. He tried to glance behind, but he couldn't see anything through the leafy branches.

Soon, the giant was too tired to hold the tree up any longer and he dropped it on the ground. By the time he had turned around, the tailor had jumped down from the branches and was lifting up a twig with one hand.

"What shall we do next?" the tailor asked with a smile.

The weary giant shook his huge head. "I give up, you are the strongest in the land," he admitted. "I'm going to lie down."

The ground shook as the giant plodded off, yawning and grumbling to himself.

The tailor went back home, whistling happily. After that, the villagers never made fun of him again.

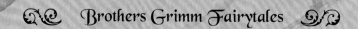

Rumpelstiltskin

Long ago, there was a poor man who visited a wicked king. The man was so nervous and wanted to impress the king so much, he told him that his daughter could spin straw into golden thread.

The king was very greedy. He made the man bring his daughter to the palace. Then, the king took her to a room full of straw.

"You must spin this straw into gold by morning, or you will die," he said.

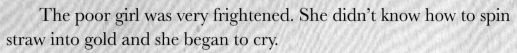

The poor girl was very frightened. She didn't know how to spin straw into gold and she began to cry.

Suddenly, a strange little man appeared. He was dressed in green from head to toe and had a long red beard.

"Why are you crying?" he asked.

The girl told the man all about the wicked king's request. The little man just smiled and laughed.

"I can help you," he said.

The little man jumped up and down with excitement. "What will you give me if I do it for you?" he asked.

The girl offered him her necklace and he skipped over to the spinning wheel. Overnight, he spun every stalk of straw into long golden thread. When he had finished, he snatched the necklace and then disappeared.

The girl was still staring in amazement at the thread when the king arrived. That night, the delighted king wanted the girl to spin even more straw.

"You know what will happen if you don't," he said.

Once again, the girl was left alone.

"I cannot spin straw into gold," she said and she began to cry.

Just as the tears began to trickle down her face, the little man appeared.

"What will you give me if I spin this straw into gold?" he asked.

The girl took a ring off her finger and held it out to him.

Grabbing it quickly, the man hopped over to the spinning wheel.

He spun all night and transformed the yellow straw into shining gold.

At daybreak, he vanished, just as he had done the morning before.

The king was amazed when he saw the heaps of glistening gold thread. He took the girl into a room filled with even more straw.

"Turn all of this into gold and I will make you my wife," he said.

For a third time, the strange little man appeared in the room. This time, when he asked the girl what she would give him for turning the straw into gold, she had nothing left to offer him.

"Then you must promise to give me your first child," he said and swiftly started spinning. Before daybreak, all the straw had been spun into gold.

The king kept his promise. He married the girl and made her his queen.

The following year, a beautiful baby was born. The queen could not have been happier. Then, one evening as she laid the baby in its crib, the little man appeared.

"Give me what you promised," he demanded.

The queen cried and begged him not to take her child. She offered him all the treasure in the kingdom, but the little man did not want gold.

"If you can guess my name, you can keep your baby," he laughed. "You have three days to try."

On the first day, the queen wrote a list of every name she knew. The little man laughed as she read each one out.

"You'll never guess my name!" he cried as he disappeared in a puff of smoke.

The next day, the queen sent a messenger to gather every name in the kingdom. Once again, she read the list to the strange little man.

"Is it Birdbrain, Beetlebug, or Crumchucker?" she asked.

The little man howled with laughter and jumped up and down.

"No, no, NO!" he replied.

Then, on the third and final day, a messenger returned with a strange story to tell.

"High up in the hills, I saw a funny little man dancing round a fire and singing a strange song."

"Tonight I dance and magic I make. Tomorrow the boy child will I take. No one knows my clever game, that Rumpelstiltskin is my name!"

The queen waited for the little man to appear. As before, she read out all sorts of names. The man laughed at each one until the queen read out the last name on her list.

"Then your name must be RUMPELSTILTSKIN!"

The little man was furious. He stamped his foot and screamed. Suddenly, he disappeared in a puff of smoke.

After that, Rumpelstiltskin was never seen again and everyone lived happily ever after.

The Golden Goose

nce upon a time, there was a woodcutter who had three sons.
The two older sons were very clever and proud. They thought
their younger brother, Hans, wasn't nearly as clever as
they were.

One day, the eldest brother went into the forest to chop wood, taking
with him some bread and ham from his mother. A little old man saw him
and asked if he could spare something to eat.

"Go away," said the eldest brother. "If I give you my food, I won't have any for myself."

The eldest brother went to chop down a tree, but a branch fell on his arm and he had to return home.

The next day, the middle brother went out to chop wood, taking some bread and cheese that his mother had given him. He, too, met the little old man.

"Can you spare some food?" the man asked.

"Leave me alone," said the middle brother. "Why should I give you any food?"

When the middle brother tried to cut down a tree, a branch fell on his foot and he had to return home with no wood.

On the third day, Hans traveled far into the forest to chop wood. He also met the little old man who asked him for a bite to eat.

"You are welcome to share all that I have," said Hans.

The old man ate the food and thanked Hans.

"For your reward, chop down that big oak tree over there," he said.

Hans chopped down the tree and, to his amazement, inside was a goose with golden feathers.

"Carry the goose and journey through the forest," said the old man, before he suddenly disappeared.

Hans carried the goose through the forest. Before long, he came to an inn. It was nearly dark so Hans decided to stay for the night.

That night, the innkeeper's eldest daughter saw the golden goose.

"Nobody will notice if I take just one of its golden feathers," she thought. When the girl tried to pluck a golden feather, she found she couldn't let go of the goose.

The goose was magic and her hand was stuck for good!

She called for her sister.

"Grab me and pull me off this goose," she said, "and we will have a golden feather!" But when her sister grabbed her, she found she was stuck, too.

The innkeeper's third daughter came down to see what all the fuss was about. Before she knew it, she was stuck to the second sister.

The next morning, Hans came down to find the three sisters stuck together. He pretended not to notice them, picked up the goose and left the inn. The sisters had no choice but to follow him. As Hans walked away, the innkeeper saw him.

"Hey!" he cried "Where are you all going!"

He grabbed the youngest sister and found that he, too, was stuck.

Hans thought it was very funny. He walked all day, with the innkeeper and his daughters stuck behind him, puffing and panting.

Along the way, they met a rich merchant.

"If you sell me that goose," the merchant said, "I will give you fifty pieces of gold."

But as soon as the merchant touched the innkeeper, he, too, was stuck to the line!

Hans walked happily along with the goose, not caring at all about the people that were following him. As they reached a field, the merchant called to two farm workers.

"Come save me from this magic goose!"

The two ploughmen rushed up to help the merchant. As soon as they touched him, they joined the chain.

Hans didn't care. He just strolled on, whistling happily, until he reached a great city.

In this city there was an enormous gray castle, where a king lived with his only daughter. The king's daughter was the saddest person alive.

The king had tried everything to make her happy.

"I will give half my kingdom to anyone who can make my daughter laugh," he said. Many clowns and jesters performed in front of the princess, but she never laughed at any of them.

That day, outside the palace, the princess saw Hans marching past, happily along carrying the golden goose. Behind him were the three sisters, the innkeeper, the merchant, and the two ploughmen puffing and panting behind him!

The princess couldn't believe her eyes.

"That's the silliest thing I've ever seen!" she said. Her smile turned into a snort, then a giggle, and finally she laughed!

When the princess and Hans met, they fell in love. The goose was so happy that she fluttered her feathers and everyone was released. They fell over in a big heap and everyone laughed even more.

Hans and the princess were soon married and lived together, happily ever after.

Cinderella

There was once a girl named Cinderella who lived with her cruel stepmother and two nasty stepsisters. Poor Cinderella was treated like a servant. She did all the washing, cooking, and cleaning while her stepsisters lazed around or went out to shop for the latest fashions.

Cinderella wore a ragged old dress and her stepsisters loved making fun of how tattered and shabby she looked. Even with the finest clothes and hours spent combing and curling their hair, the stepsisters could never look as beautiful as Cinderella.

One day, an invitation arrived from the palace. The prince was throwing a grand ball and he had invited Cinderella and her stepsisters.

"Of course you won't be able to go, Cinderella," her stepmother told her nastily. "You'll be much too busy helping your sisters get ready."

"The prince wouldn't want someone as scruffy as you at his royal party," sneered one of the stepsisters.

"Now polish my purple shoes and make sure my jewelry is super sparkly," ordered the other stepsister, stuffing a chocolate in her mouth.

Cinderella was heartbroken. On the day of the ball, she spent hours helping her stepsisters get ready and when they had left, she sat down and cried.

With a fizzle and a flash, a kind old woman appeared in front of her.

"I am your fairy godmother," she said. "Why are you crying?"

"I wish I could go to the ball," said Cinderella, sobbing.

The fairy godmother asked her to fetch a pumpkin. Cinderella was puzzled but she did as she was told and returned with the biggest pumpkin she could find. With a wave of her wand, the fairy godmother turned the pumpkin into a golden carriage.

Cinderella watched in amazement as her fairy godmother changed six little mice into horses to pull the golden carriage. Then she turned a rat into a coachman and two lizards into sharply-dressed footmen.

"You shall go to the ball," she cried.

Cinderella looked down at her ragged dress and sighed.

"Thank you, but I can't go looking like this."

"Of course not," agreed her fairy godmother and she waved her wand again. Cinderella gasped as her dress became a splendid ballgown made from pink silk and covered in jewels. Magical, dainty glass slippers appeared on her feet.

"Have a wonderful time," her godmother said. "But you must be home by midnight, that's when the spell wears off."

When Cinderella arrived at the ball, all the guests turned to stare. She looked so beautiful, no one recognized her, not even her own, mean stepsisters.

"She must be a princess," they whispered. "Look at her dazzling dress and stylish shoes."

The prince was enchanted by Cinderella's beauty and asked her to dance. They whirled round the room and danced all night.

The evening flew by and Cinderella was so happy dancing and laughing with the prince that she forgot to keep an eye on the time.

When the palace clock began to strike midnight, she gasped in horror. The prince must not see her beautiful ball gown turn back into the ragged old dress.

Cinderella said goodbye and dashed down the palace steps towards her golden carriage. She was in such a hurry that one of her glass slippers fell off and was left behind.

The next day, the prince declared that he was in love with the mystery guest and wished to marry her. He had found Cinderella's glass slipper and planned to have every lady in the land try it on until he found her.

The prince rode from house to house, searching for his true love. When he arrived at the stepmother's door, she quickly shoved Cinderella into the garden.

The stepsisters took turns trying to squeeze a foot into the tiny glass slipper, but their toes were too big and would not fit inside.

The prince was about to give up and move on to the next house when he spotted Cinderella in the garden.

"Who is that?" he asked at once.

"Oh, she's just a servant," lied the stepmother.

But the prince demanded that Cinderella be brought inside to try on the slipper. She smiled at him shyly and slid her foot perfectly into the slipper.

Laughing with joy, the prince swept Cinderella into his arms. She gladly agreed to marry him and they lived happily ever after.

Snow White and Rose Red

Once upon a time, there were two girls who lived with their mother in a little cottage. One of the girls had pale golden hair and she was named Snow White. The other had dark hair and rosy cheeks and she was named Rose Red.

The cottage was in the middle of a forest and every day Snow White and Rose Red would go out to pick flowers for their mother. They knew the forest very well and no matter how far they wandered, they never got lost.

One cold winter's night, Snow White and Rose Red were cuddled up with their mother by the fire. When suddenly, there was a loud knock at the door.

Snow White and Rose Red ran to open the door and saw a big brown bear outside. They screamed and tried to slam the door, but the bear said softly to them, "Please let me in. I am so very cold and hungry."

"Let the poor creature in," said their mother.

Snow White and Rose Red were very scared, but they let the bear come inside.

"Thank you," said the bear in its deep, growly voice.

They soon realized that the bear was very friendly and meant them no harm. After that, the bear returned to the cottage every day and became friends with Snow White and Rose Red.

They would play hide-and-go-seek in the forest and run around in the sunshine having fun. The two girls came to love their new friend. Then, just as spring was beginning, the bear told them that he had to go away.

"I must find my treasure," he said. "It was stolen by an evil dwarf and if I don't get it back by the next full moon, I will stay like this forever!"

The two sisters were puzzled. They wondered what the bear meant, but before they could ask, he had disappeared into the forest.

Some time later, Snow White and Rose Red were out picking flowers when they heard shouting. They followed the noise and found a funny little old man. He was a dwarf whose long beard had got trapped by a falling tree.

"Don't just stand there, help me!" shouted the dwarf rudely.

The girls tried to pull him free, but it was no use. Rose Red had an idea. She freed him by cutting the tip of the dwarf's beard off.

Instead of being grateful, the dwarf was furious.

"How dare you cut my beard!" he screamed. He grabbed a sack tied with string and ran away without even saying thank you.

That afternoon, Snow White and Rose Red were walking by a stream when they heard shouting again. Looking down the bank of the stream, they saw that the dwarf had gotten his beard caught in his fishing rod and a big fish was pulling him into the water.

The sisters grabbed him and pulled hard, but the fish was too big. Again, Rose Red got out her scissors and snipped off more of his beard.

The dwarf was even angrier than before.

"There's hardly any of it left!" he shouted, angrily.

With that, the dwarf grabbed a second sack tied with string and ran off into the forest.

In the evening, Snow White and Rose Red went to pick some flowers from a pretty meadow. Above them, an enormous eagle was circling. It saw something in the field and swooped down.

Snow White and Rose Red saw that the eagle had grabbed the little dwarf. It was pecking at him and trying to fly off with him.

"Help me!" screamed the dwarf, who was now holding three sacks.

Snow White and Rose Red grabbed the dwarf and pulled him away from the eagle's claws. The eagle flew away, leaving the dwarf's clothes in tatters.

This time, the dwarf was even angrier than before.

"How dare you destroy my clothes, you good-for-nothing fools!" he shouted. "I'm going to teach you a lesson. I'm going to put a horrible curse on both of you and turn you into mice!"

The dwarf raised his arms, but before he could cast his spell, the bear burst out of the forest and bared its teeth. The dwarf ran off into the hills, leaving his three sacks behind.

Snow White and Rose Red opened the sacks. They were full of rubies, emeralds, and pearls.

"It's my treasure!" cried the bear.

There was a flash of blinding light and suddenly the bear was gone. In his place, stood a handsome prince.

"I was cursed by that dwarf to roam the forest as a bear, until I could get my treasure back," the prince said. "You have freed me from my curse! We must go to my brother's castle. He thinks I have been dead for many years."

Together, they journeyed to the castle, where the prince's brother was overjoyed to see him. It wasn't long before Snow White and Rose Red married the two brothers and became princesses. They didn't see the wicked dwarf again and both couples lived long, happy lives.

The White Snake

Once upon a time, there was a king who had the knowledge of all things. No one knew how the king knew so much, but every day after dinner, his most trusted servant brought him a secret dish covered with a cloth. Nobody except the king knew what was in the dish.

One day, the servant was so curious that he took the cover off the plate. There, molded in the shape of a white snake, was a delicious sweet-smelling dish. He couldn't resist eating a tiny piece.

Suddenly, the servant found he could understand the birds outside the window. Eating the magic snake food had given the servant the power to understand what animals were saying!

Later that day, the queen's ring went missing and the servant was accused of stealing it. He ran outside to hide and heard two magpies talking to one another.

"Look what I found," said one magpie. It jumped up and down in excitement but accidentally swallowed the queen's ring!

Quickly, the servant grabbed the magpie and took it to the queen. He gave the magpie a squeeze and it coughed up the missing ring and everyone knew the servant wasn't a thief.

The king rewarded the servant with a gold coin and the servant decided to use it to travel across the land and seek his fortune. As the servant was riding away from the kingdom, he heard some strange voices.

"Help, help!" they said. "We're trapped!"

The servant got off his horse and found three fish in the river. They were trapped in the reeds and couldn't get out. The servant parted the reeds and let the fish go free.

"Thank you!" said the fish. "We won't forget it."

The servant was about to continue his journey through the forest when he heard some more voices.

"We're so hungry!" they cried. He looked around, until he saw three baby doves on the ground. They had fallen out of their nest and couldn't get any food.

The servant took pity on the baby birds and shared his lunch with them.

Soon, they were strong enough to fly away.

"Thank you!" cried the little doves. "We won't forget it."

After many days of riding, the servant suddenly heard the sound of many tiny voices.

"Please don't destroy our home," they said.

The servant looked down to see hundreds of tiny ants. "This pile of dirt is our house," they said.

The servant carefully rode his horse around their house.

"Thank you," said the little ants. "We won't forget your kindness!"

Soon, the servant reached the gates of a great castle by the sea. Men from the castle were blowing loud horns and calling out: "Whoever completes an impossible task will win the king's daughter's hand in marriage!"

When the servant saw the king's daughter, he fell in love. "I must win her hand in marriage," he said. "No matter how hard the task is!"

So, the servant came to the castle and told the king he would complete the impossible task. The king took him down to the sea and threw a golden ring far into the water.

"Fetch the ring by tomorrow morning," the king said sternly. "If you do not, my soldiers will throw you into the sea!"

All day, the servant swam in the sea, looking for the ring. It sank far too deep for him to reach.

"I have failed," he said sadly. "The king's soldiers will throw me in the sea and I will drown!"

Then, at dawn, he heard a splashing sound. It was the three fish he had saved from the reeds. One had the gold ring in its mouth.

The servant thanked the fish, and took the ring to the king, but the princess was too proud to marry a servant.

"He must complete another task," she said.

This time, the king's soldiers poured ten huge bags of grain all over the palace gardens.

"Pick up every single grain by morning," said the king. "Or you will never see the princess again!"

The servant tried to pick up the grains, but there were far too many for him, so he fell asleep in despair.

When he woke, he found that the ten sacks were full of grain. Not a single one was missing! His ant friends had visited him in the night. They had worked hard to put all the grain back in the sacks.

When the princess saw this, she was secretly pleased. But she was too proud to say so.

"Bring me an apple from the Tree of Life at the world's end," she said. "Then I will marry you."

The servant wandered far and wide, but couldn't reach the world's end. As he lay down, ready to give up, he saw three birds flying towards him. It was the baby doves he had fed. They were fully grown and one carried the apple from the Tree of Life in its beak.

Overjoyed, the servant returned to the castle with the apple. This time, even the princess was impressed. There was a celebration and the servant and the princess were married at once.

The Fisherman and His Wife

Once upon a time, a poor fisherman lived with his wife in a tiny shack by the sea. The shack had only one room and its roof was full of holes. Every day, the fisherman rowed out to sea in his tiny, old fishing boat.

"I hope I catch some fish today," he would think to himself. But he never caught enough. The fisherman and his wife often went hungry and cold, until one sunny day when he finally felt a big tug on his line.

"This fish must be huge," he thought, as he reeled it in excitedly. "My wife and I will share such a wonderful meal tonight."

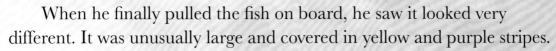

When he finally pulled the fish on board, he saw it looked very different. It was unusually large and covered in yellow and purple stripes.

"I wonder if it's good to eat," said the fisherman.

"Don't eat me!" said the fish. "I'm not very tasty."

"Wow! You can talk?" The fisherman's eyes widened in shock.

"I'm an enchanted fish. I can grant wishes," the fish replied.

"I don't want to eat such a special fish!" said the fisherman. "Don't worry. I'll put you back in the sea."

"Thank you!" said the fish, as the fisherman let him go. "In return, I will grant you a wish."

The fisherman thought about it. "No, no," he said. "I don't want a reward."

When the fisherman got home that night, he told his wife about the strange fish.

"You silly man!" said his wife. "Why didn't you take the wish? Tomorrow you will find the fish and ask it for a cottage."

The next day the fisherman rowed back out to sea.

"Little fish! Little fish! Come to me and grant my wish!" the fisherman called. The fish popped out of the water.

"I've changed my mind," said the fisherman. "I wish for a cottage to live in."

"Go home," said the fish. "Your wife is waiting for you in your new cottage!"

Sure enough, when the fisherman got home, he found his tiny shack had been transformed into a pretty little cottage.

"Isn't this wonderful!" said the fisherman to his wife.

For the first few days they were very happy in their cottage but then, the fisherman's wife started to complain.

"Our cottage is too small compared to our neighbors'," she said. "Go back and ask the magical fish for a mansion."

"My dear, the fish has been very kind," he replied. "We shouldn't ask for more."

"Just do it!" ordered his wife.

The next day, the fisherman rowed out to sea again.

"Little fish! Little fish! Come to me and grant my wish!" the fisherman called out.

When the fish appeared, the fisherman said that he had changed his mind. "We want a mansion instead."

"Go home," said the fish. "Your wife is waiting for you in your new mansion."

When the fisherman got home, he found the little cottage had turned into a grand house, complete with servants and lots of fine furniture. But the fisherman's wife still wasn't happy.

"The servants are too slow," she said, "and these plates don't go with the wallpaper. Go back to that fish and tell him to change this mansion to a palace. I want to be queen!"

The fisherman was horrified, but he wanted his wife to be happy. He went back out to sea the very next day. This time, the sea was stormy and dark. His little, old boat rocked and bobbed in the waves.

"Little fish! Little fish! Come to me and grant my wish!"

He called out above the howling wind.

"What is it now?" the fish asked.

"My wife wants a palace and she wants to be queen," replied the fisherman, sheepishly.

"Go home," said the fish, "Your wife, the queen, is already waiting for you!"

When he got home, the fisherman found his house transformed into a huge palace made of gold.

Soon, the fisherman's wife started to complain again. She was tired of sitting on her golden throne.

"I don't like being a queen. Nobody does what I tell them. The other kings and queens probably hate us! What if they invade our country? I would much rather be empress of the whole wide world. Go find that fish and tell him to make me empress."

"But my dear," said the fisherman, "the enchanted fish has already given us so much. What if we make him angry?"

"Who cares?" said his wife. "I want to be empress of the whole world and I want it now!"

The next day, the fisherman set out in a horrible storm. Thunder rumbled and lightning flashed around him. In a scared voice, the fisherman called out, "Little fish! Little fish! Come to me and grant my wish!"

The fish popped its head out of the water. "What do you want?" he sighed.

The fisherman summoned up all his courage and said, "My wife wants to be empress of the whole world."

"Go home," said the fish, "and see what's waiting for you."

The fisherman rowed back to shore.

When he got home, he found his wife waiting for him, in their tiny old shack!

Queen Bee

Long ago, two brothers set out to find a magic castle. Their younger brother wanted to go, too.

"You can come with us," said the older brothers. "But you must do what we say."

On the way, they came to an anthill. The older brothers, who were mean and cruel, wanted to push it over.

"No!" cried the kind younger brother.

At a pond, the older brothers wanted to capture the ducks.

"No!" said the younger brother. "Leave them alone."

Next the older brothers came to a beehive with a queen bee.

"Let's smoke out the bees and steal their honey," said the older brothers, but again, the younger brother refused to let them.

Soon, the brothers arrived at the castle. Everything was still and quiet. In the stables, the horses had been turned to stone. A stone cat sat on a windowsill and a stone dog slept beneath it.

"It is as if a spell has been cast on it," said the youngest of the brothers.

Just then, the brothers noticed an old man. He was sitting at a stone table in a little room. They called to him and the old man beckoned them to come inside.

"I have three tasks for you," he said. "Whoever completes the tasks will release the castle from the evil spell and marry a beautiful princess."

"Give me a task," said the older brother. "For nothing is too difficult for me."

"Very well," said the old man. "Hidden beneath the moss in the forest are a thousand pearls. Find them and bring them to me before nightfall or you will be turned into stone."

The older brother left immediately. He searched the forest inch by inch, but he only found one pearl and by nightfall he had turned into stone.

"What is my task?" asked the second brother.

"You must find the key in the lake that unlocks the door to the princesses' bed chamber," the old man told him.

The second brother left immediately. The water in the lake was cold and deep. He dived into the lake a hundred times, but couldn't find the key and by nightfall, he, too, turned into stone.

The youngest brother wondered how he would succeed where his brothers had failed. The old man appeared and asked the youngest brother to bring him the thousand hidden pearls.

As he set off, the youngest brother met the ants he had saved earlier. They had found all the pearls for him.

The old man then set the youngest brother the task of finding the key in the cold, deep lake.

The youngest brother went to the lake.

"We will help you," quacked the ducks who he had saved earlier. In no time at all they had dived into the lake and found the key.

"What shall I do now?" said the youngest brother. Just then the old man appeared.

"You will find three princesses in the castle," he said. "If you can kiss the right one, then the spell will be broken."

The youngest brother set off to the castle to find the princesses.

In the castle, the three princesses were asleep.

"Which one must I kiss?" asked the youngest brother.

"The one who has eaten honey," said a little voice.

It was the queen bee from the hive he had saved.

The queen bee flew to the middle princess and buzzed loudly.

"This is the one," she said.

The youngest brother kissed the princess and the spell was broken and everything came back to life.

The youngest brother fell in love with the princess and they married soon after. His brothers were never cruel or mean again and every time they saw a queen bee, they smiled.

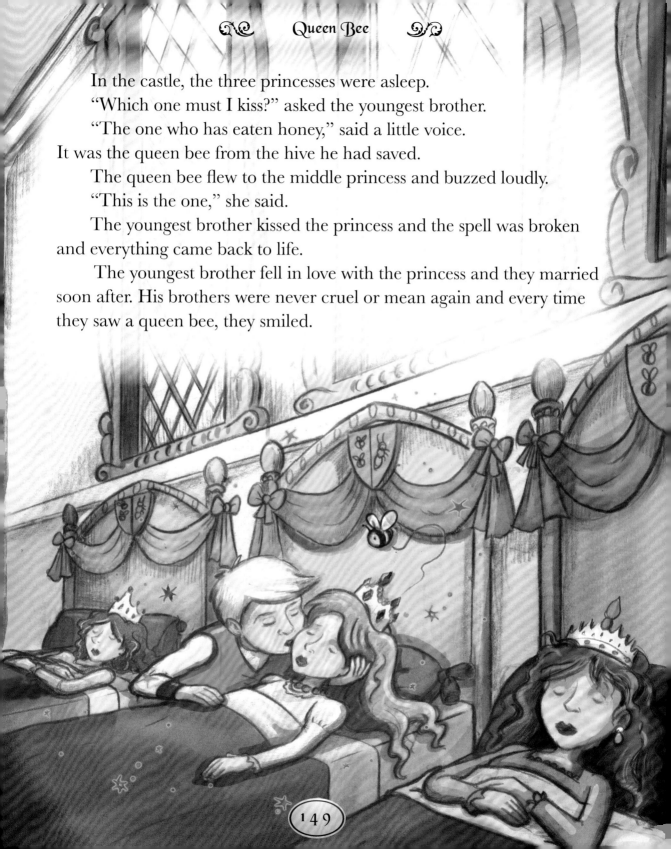

Jorinda and Joringel

O nce, there was a wicked witch who could disguise herself as an owl. The witch did not like pretty girls and if any came near her castle, she would change them into songbirds and put them in cages.

As it happened, a beautiful young girl named Jorinda lived close to the witch and one day, she went for a picnic there with her sweetheart, Joringel. The pair were so happy to be together, they took no notice of where they were going.

Soon, they found themselves at the witch's castle. High on a ledge, a large owl hooted.

"Hoo-hoo!"

The owl flew down and circled round Jorinda and Joringel three times. Suddenly, they couldn't move or speak.

As quick as a flash, the owl changed into the cruel witch.

"Now I have you," she cried, pointing a bony finger at Jorinda.

In a flash of light, Jorinda was turned into a nightingale. The witch grabbed the bird, shut it in a cage, and ran into the castle.

Joringel was heartbroken. He was powerless against the witch. There was nothing he could do to rescue Jorinda, so he made his way sadly back home.

That night, Joringel dreamed about a beautiful red flower that could free everything from the witch's spell. It grew in a strange and barren land that was far away.

"I must find the flower," said Joringel, waking up, and he set off without delay.

Joringel walked through valleys and over mountains, until his legs ached and his shoes were torn. He searched day and night without rest.

After many days, he found what he was looking for. Hidden in a crack in a rock was the bright, red flower and in its center was a dew drop as big as a pearl.

Joringel made his way back to the castle. As he approached, he took out the red flower and held it in front of him. The castle gates sprung open and he heard the sound of birdsong. Joringel followed the sound to the room with all the bird cages.

"Which one is Jorinda?" he said, looking round at all the bird cages.

Just then he caught sight of the witch. She was sneaking away, carrying one of the cages.

"Stop!" cried Joringel.

The witch turned to face him.

"Stay away," she hissed and fired a spell.

Joringel held the red flower in front of him and the spell exploded in a thousand sparkles that flashed and disappeared.

Joringel was unharmed and the witch shrieked with rage.

"You will never have her," screamed the witch, holding up the cage with Jorinda inside. "She will die first."

As quick as a flash, Joringel leaned forward and touched the witch with the bright red flower. She let out a terrible wailing scream, dropped the cage, and crumpled to the ground in a heap of ash.

Joringel caught the cage as it fell. The door opened and the little nightingale flew out. Joringel touched it with the flower and the spell was broken. In front of him was his sweetheart, Jorinda. Jorigel knelt in front of her.

"Will you marry me?" he asked.

"Yes, I will," said Jorinda, kissing him. "But first we must remove the spell from the other birds."

One by one, the birds were turned back into pretty girls. They thanked Jorinda and Joringel with tears of joy.

Hand in hand Jorinda and Joringel returned to their village where they lived a long and happy life.

Sweet Porridge

Once upon a time, a little girl lived alone with her mother. They were very poor and quite often didn't have enough to eat. One day the little girl said to her mother. "I am so hungry. Is there some bread we could eat for breakfast?"

The mother put her arms around the little girl, for she loved her very much.

"Dear child," she said. "We have nothing to eat today. The cupboard is bare. Go into the woods and look for some nuts and berries."

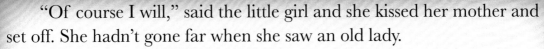

"Of course I will," said the little girl and she kissed her mother and set off. She hadn't gone far when she saw an old lady.

"What are you looking for, child?" asked the old lady.

"Some nuts and berries," said the little girl. "My mother and I have nothing to eat."

The old lady felt sorry for the little girl.

"This will help you," she said and she gave her a very special pot. "Cook, little pot, cook," ordered the old lady and the little pot cooked some good sweet porridge.

Then the old lady said, "Stop, little pot, stop," and the little pot stopped cooking. "You will never be hungry again," she told the girl.

The little girl thanked the old lady and ran home.

The girl showed the pot to her mother.

"What is that?' her mother asked.

"It's a magic pot," the little girl told her, putting the pot on the table.

"Cook, little pot, cook," she said to the pot, and the pot cooked enough sweet porridge for them both.

"Stop, little pot, stop," said the girl, and the pot stopped cooking.

The mother was amazed.

"That is wonderful," she said to her daughter. "You have done well." She put her arms around the little girl and hugged her.

That night the mother and the little girl ate a good meal and went to bed feeling full and happy.

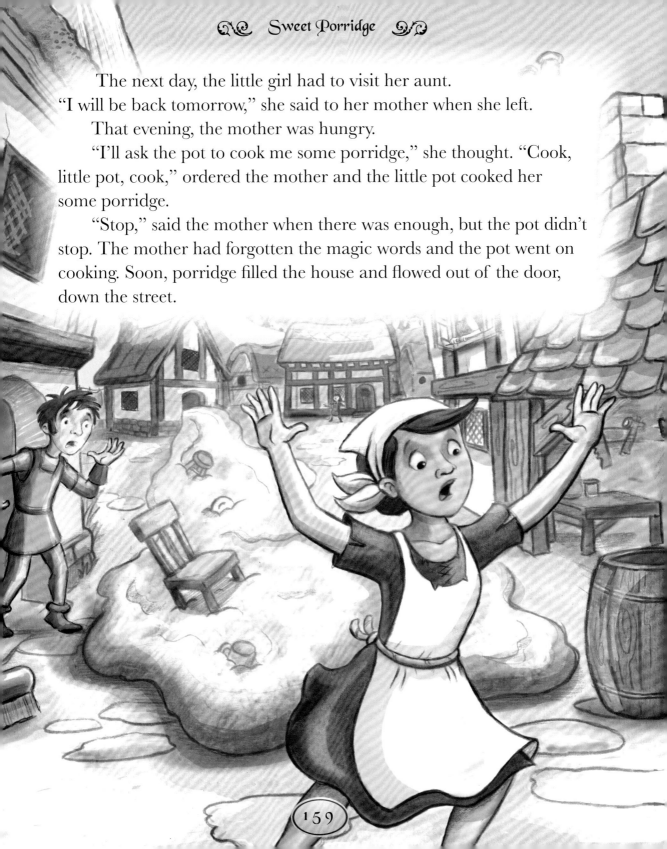

The next day, the little girl had to visit her aunt. "I will be back tomorrow," she said to her mother when she left.

That evening, the mother was hungry.

"I'll ask the pot to cook me some porridge," she thought. "Cook, little pot, cook," ordered the mother and the little pot cooked her some porridge.

"Stop," said the mother when there was enough, but the pot didn't stop. The mother had forgotten the magic words and the pot went on cooking. Soon, porridge filled the house and flowed out of the door, down the street.

It wasn't long before nearly the whole town was full of porridge. "What will we do?" asked the townspeople.

Just then, the little girl came back. "Stop, little pot, stop!" she cried and suddenly the pot stopped.

"There's only one thing you can do," replied the girl. "You must eat your way back into your houses."

So, everyone got bowls and pots of honey and start to eat. They all had a wonderful time gobbling up the sweet porridge and after that, no one ever went hungry again.